Lawyers in a
postmodern world

Open University Press
New Directions in Criminology series

Series Editor: Colin Sumner, Lecturer in Sociology,
Institute of Criminology, and Fellow of
Wolfson College, University of Cambridge

Current titles:

Imperial Policing
Philip Ahire

Lawyers in a Postmodern World
Maureen Cain and Christine B. Harrington (eds)

Feminist Perspectives in Criminology
Loraine Gelsthorpe and Allison Morris (eds)

The Enemy Without: Policing and Class Consciousness in the Miners' Strike
Penny Green

Television and the Drama of Crime
Richard Sparks

Censure, Politics and Criminal Justice
Colin Sumner (ed.)

Corruption and Politics in Hong Kong and China
T. Wing Lo

Reading the Riot Act
Richard Vogler

Lawyers in a postmodern world

translation and transgression

EDITED BY

Maureen Cain and Christine B. Harrington

Open University Press
Buckingham

Open University Press
Celtic Court
22 Ballmoor
Buckingham
MK18 1XW

First Published 1994

A catalogue record of this book is available from the British Library

ISBN 0 335 09694 8 (pb)   0 335 09695 6 (hb)

Typeset by Inforum, Rowlands Castle, Hants
Printed in Great Britain by St Edmundsbury Press Limited,
Bury St Edmunds, Suffolk

Contents

List of contributors

Maureen Cain is Professor of Sociology at the University of the West Indies, Trinidad. She has written extensively in the fields of sociology of law, criminology and feminist method. Her books include *Society and the Policeman's Role* (Routledge, 1973) and *Growing Up Good* (Sage, 1989). She is currently writing a book on feminism and realist methodology.

Yves Dezalay is a 'charge de recherches au CNRS' (Centre National de la Recherche Scientifique, France), and works for the Centre de Recherches Interdisciplinaires de Vaucresson, where he is in charge of a unit working on the sociology of the professions. He has published many articles and is currently editing two books, *Professional Competition and Professional Power* (with David Sugarman, Routledge, 1994) and *Batailles territoriales ou rivalités de cousinage* (LGDJ, Paris, 1993).

Martha L.A. Fineman is the Maurice T. Moore Professor of Law at Columbia University in the City of New York. In addition to numerous articles and book chapters on feminism, family law, the regulation of intimacy and sexuality, Professor Fineman is the author of *The Neutered Mother, The Sexual Family and Other Twentieth-century Tragedies* (forthcoming) and *The Illusion of Equality* (Chicago, 1991). She is a contributor and co-editor of a number of collections of papers from the Feminism and Legal Theory Project that she developed at the University of Wisconsin Law School in 1984, and now located at Columbia Law School. These include *The Public*

Nature of Private Violence (forthcoming) and *At the Boundaries of Law* (Routledge, 1991).

Christine B. Harrington is an Associate Professor of Politics at New York University. She is the author of articles and books on legal ideology, interpretive sociolegal research, dispute process, alternative dispute resolution and informalism, and the relationship between law and state. Her books include *Shadow Justice* (Greenwood Press, 1985). She also edits a series of books on law and society (with John Brigham) for Routledge, New York. She is currently writing a book on the role of the American legal profession in forming the twentieth-century administrative state.

Sue Lees is Professor at the Women's Studies Unit at the University of North London where she set up one of the first Women's Studies degree programmes in Britain. She has had a long-standing interest in the law and in mechanisms of social control; has undertaken research into female adolescence and is at present studying multi-agency approaches to sexual assault. She has published widely and is the author of *Losing Out* (Unwin, 1986) and *Sugar and Spice* (Penguin, 1993).

Doreen McBarnet is Senior Research Fellow at the Centre for Socio-Legal Studies and a Fellow of Wolfson College, Oxford. Her past research has included work on criminal justice, published as *Conviction: Law, the State and the Construction of Justice* (Macmillan, 1981). More recently she has been working in the areas of business law, tax avoidance, corporate finance, law and accounting, the Single European Market, and the role of the legal and accounting professions in all of these. She has published a range of articles on these themes and two books are in preparation.

Frank Munger is a Professor of Law at the State University of New York at Buffalo. His research has examined the role of law in social change in a variety of contexts, including eighteenth- and nineteenth-century English working class movements, American court reform, patterns of litigation, and the evolution of three southern West Virginia communities from 1870 to 1940. In his current research he is studying the implementation of the Americans With Disabilities Act, and the effects of poverty on family structure. He is currently general editor of the *Law and Society Review*.

Wilfried Schärf is an Associate Professor at the Institute of Criminology, University of Cape Town, South Africa, where he was Director in 1990 and 1991. Over the course of his career Schärf has developed a brand of academic activism in which interventionist research is aimed at prefiguring a post-apartheid political and academic discourse. His current work is on transforming policing for a future South Africa. He is an adviser to the African National Congress on policing matters.

Stuart Scheingold is Professor of Political Science at the University of Washington. His recent research has focused on cause lawyering and on the politics of criminal justice systems. In the past he has worked extensively on the European Community. His books include *The Politics of Street Crime* (Temple University Press, 1991), *The Politics of Law and Order* (Longman, 1984), *The Politics of Rights* (Yale University Press, 1974), *Europe's Would-be Polity* (Prentice Hall, 1970) and *The Rule of Law in European Integration* (Yale University Press, 1965).

David Sugarman is Professor of Law in the Department of Law at Lancaster University. He has published widely on legal history, company law, sociology of law and the legal profession including, *Legality, Ideology and the State* (Academic Press, 1983), *Law, Economy and Society* (co-edited with G. Rubin, Professional Books, 1984), *Regulating Corporate Groups in Europe* (co-edited with Gunther Teubner, Nomos, 1990), *Law and Social Change in England 1780–1914* (Fukosha, Tokyo, 1993), *Professional Competition and Professional Power* (co-edited with Yves Dezalay, Routledge, 1994) and *Law and History* (Dartmouth, 1994).

Sally Wheeler is a Lecturer in Law at Nottingham University. In 1992–3 she was a Simon Research Fellow at Manchester University. She has published a number of articles and a book, *Reservation of Title Clauses* (Oxford University Press, 1991) on insolvency law and practice. Her current work is on nineteenth-century insolvency law and its representation in Victorian culture and literature.

Series editor's introduction

This series is founded upon the socialist and feminist research carried out over the last decade in the Institute of Criminology, Cambridge. It is also concerned to publish any work which renews theoretical development, or opens up new and important areas, in criminology. Particular attention will be paid to the politics and ideology of criminal justice, gender and crime, crimes of state officials, crime and justice in underdeveloped societies, European criminal justice, environmental crime, and the general sociology of censure and regulation.

Behind the series is a belief that criminology must resist being limited to policy-oriented studies and must retain its integrity as an area of independent, critical enquiry of interest to scholars from a variety of disciplinary backgrounds. A criminology that wants to remain dynamic and worthy of its complex subject matter must therefore constantly renew theoretical debate, explore current issues and develop new methods of research. To allow itself to be dominated by the narrow focus of government departments, or a short-run philosophy of current political relevance, is to promote its own destruction as an intellectual enterprise. A criminology which is not intellectually alive is useless to everybody. We live in increasingly international societies, and a new age, which require a broad, non-parochial vision to ensure their viability and health. Administrative criminology may be necessary for wise government, but, unless it works closely with independent, critical and intellectually rigorous thought, all it can offer governments is pseudo-scientific verbiage. Both, we believe, must be committed to a general drive towards increased democratization and justice, if they want to avoid a drift into the twin culs-de-sac of police science and political propaganda.

Some might argue that criminology is an outdated term in that few people today believe that a causal science of criminal behaviour is possible. Indeed, the books in this series will all look more like studies in the sociology of law or political sociology, since their focus is upon the political character of the state sanction of crime. We have decided to retain the term criminology, however, because we intend this series to contribute to the contemporary redefinition of its meaning, so that the term will in future clearly include work on crime matters from within the sociology of law, political sociology, social history, political economy, discourse analysis, anthropology, development studies and so on. Criminology will thus merely refer to any kind of study concerned with crime and criminal justice; an umbrella term covering a multitude of topics and approaches. The task for all of us is to give it a meaningful substance to meet the emerging challenges of the 1990s. The cold war is over. Now we enter a phase which will demand, from all of us, a new clarity on fundamental social values, and a stronger vision of the kinds of social censure and social regulation necessary to promote peace, health, growth, equity and cooperation on an international scale.

The present volume is a welcome addition to the series, not only because Maureen Cain has long been associated with the Cambridge Institute, but because criminology has not devoted enough time to the work lawyers do in translating and constructing law and thus to their role in the creation of what we call criminal justice. The volume examines both the lawyer's role as a trader in words and as a wordsmith whose work rarely limits the traders in capital. It points up the gendered character of legal discourse and the impact that has upon women. It discusses some of the links between the forms of legal process and the substantive role of the branch of law concerned. Lawyers and law work are deeply imbricated within the web of class, gender and ethnic relations which structure the social world and its legal rules. This fact, of course, greatly affects the possibilities for legal work to transform oppressive social relations and the last section of this book looks at the problems faced by radical legal practice.

What is especially important for criminology here is that Cain and Harrington's book pulls together essays which demonstrate what a socially constructed phenomenon law is. While criminology often plods on with the sublime assumption that law comes purely from the legislature or the judges, this book expresses the view, so well developed now in the sociology of law, that law is very much a conglomeration of partly connected social practices and rhetorics carried out by very specific professionals – lawyers – working within a very socially structured world. Law is not some arcane mystery that floats down from the heavens but a concrete, social product of the labour of lawyers. That legal profession warrants close attention therefore. It, too, is a social product at the mercy of many societal winds and currents.

Since the 1970s, we have become more down-to-earth about what can and what cannot be achieved through legal work, and the debates will continue. But what is significant now is that these debates are not only informed by sophisticated social and political theory, as the present volume testifies, but also by an acute awareness of the practicalities involved in taking legal action. There is less of a tendency to talk in black-and-white terms. Law is not simply law, and legal process is not simply legal process. There are many variations on a theme, and several deviations. Inevitably, this increasingly sophisticated work must filter into criminological theorizing about the 'reality' of crime.

Socialist and feminist jurisprudence on crime and the criminal law is now coming to recognize not only the diversity and complexity of the social character of law, but also the difficulty of establishing precisely the nature of the 'social' structuration of law, and this can only be achieved through concrete studies of legal practice informed by contemporary social theory. The social or 'social reality' is not a fixed or given fact open to simple observation, but a dynamic set of processes which must be carefully examined in each specific instance and in each specific setting. Consequently, no socialist or feminist criminology can rest content with comfortable, old, axioms about class, men and women, and 'the law' and must constantly re-work its understanding of the changing role of lawyers' work in modern societies. The present volume takes us further forward on this whole path.

Colin Sumner

Introduction

Maureen Cain and Christine B. Harrington

What lawyers do, the constitutive role their work plays in shaping power relationships in society, is the focus of this collection. Recently, much attention has been paid to studying the power structure of the legal profession (Heinz and Laumann 1982; Halliday 1987; Abbott 1988; Abel 1988b, 1989; Nelson 1988; Powell 1988). We now know significantly more about the social structure of the legal profession. Yet, for the most part, the theoretical aspects of this body of work say more about professions in general than about lawyers' work in particular. There is a tendency to focus on the character of lawyering as an occupation, emphasizing the power of professions (see Freidson 1986) and the nature of professionalism (see Nelson *et al.* 1992a). This occupationist orientation leaves undertheorized problems about the specific place of lawyers in society. In this collection of essays, we contribute to redressing this imbalance by focusing on legal practices across a range of fields and in several countries. We are concerned with lawyers' power, and while their occupational organization is an important aspect of this, for a more complete understanding of what lawyers do with and to generate their power, many other configurations of relationships must also be examined.

In coming to grips with lawyers' power, it is important to examine both the ways in which lawyers mediate the relationship between state and capital, and the ways in which lawyers represent working-class and underprivileged clients. Beyond these traditional concerns, lawyers' work can now be seen to impact on the way gender is constituted, as well as on the meanings of race and ethnicity. By focusing on lawyers' work in and on the social structure, and by focusing on legal practice, we hope to advance that emergent body of work on lawyers and lawyering which sees the law as more than law talk (discourse) while recognizing the constitutive potency of the law talk itself (Cain 1979; Gordon 1984b; see Harrington, this volume). This means understanding lawyers' work not only in terms of its place in a stratified professional culture, but more broadly locating lawyers' work in relation to other social relations, historical transformations and diverse cultural settings.

The collective work of this volume argues that lawyers are best understood as involved in creative institution building on behalf of capital. Paradoxically, this theoretical formulation enables us to explore and theorize not only relations with the state, but also alternative forms of law work that are carried out on behalf of those typically excluded from the control of capital and from influence in the central state, and the limits which legal relations and discourses pose for these alternative practices. In particular, we problematize the liberal Weberian view, which is the only 'classical' position to take lawyers seriously, and seek instead to build on the insights of Gramsci and Foucault. This involves a discussion of the connections between ideas and the institutional forms which they constitute and in which they are embedded. It also poses the problem of the class, gender and racial specificity of law in a new way. Having posed the problems in this way, the issue of the 'powerless', of class–gender–race dichotomies, becomes clearer. New institutional forms are required to express and resolve their emergent needs. The struggle for rules (discourse) and the struggles for institutions are shown to be interconnected, and intimately connected with what have been shown to be the limits of the law.

We put forward a theory about the creative capacities of lawyers in constituting both the forms of capital and state power, which argues that lawyers' work shapes as well as reinforces the power relations in society. Because of the historical integrity of these relationships, law work for powerless groups necessarily must have a different form which at times transgresses established legal relations themselves. Any contemporary social theory on lawyering must address the question of how far lawyers and the legal process can be used to assist the underprivileged. This question can only be addressed by an approach which integrates studies of lawyers operating within the central state and on behalf of capital and studies of lawyers operating on behalf of those typically excluded from sites of power. We must move beyond separate analyses for separate clienteles. This volume is a small movement in that direction.

The book is divided into three parts. Part 1, 'Understanding lawyering', sets out a more fully developed introduction to our theoretical perspective. Part 2, 'Constituting capital and the state', discusses the constitutive powers of lawyers' work in relation to capital and state power and the inventive and creative works of *translation* and institution-building that these lawyers perform. Part 3, 'Towards prefigurative legal practices', explores whether or not legal practice can be equally effective in bringing about relational and institutional changes to meet the needs of those sections in society typically regarded as powerless. These lawyers perform *transgressive* work, breaking the discursive and relational boundaries which inhibit effective action on behalf of those on the losing end of social relationships. Such new forms are discursively and relationally vulnerable; the discussions in this volume reveal both their potential and their vulnerability. We have explained both the vulnerability and the potential by showing theoretically the connections between these transgressive approaches to lawyers' work and the more conventional and prestigious modes of legal practice. Our purpose in creating these three sections, therefore, is not to reproduce the existing divisions in our understanding of what lawyers do. Rather, we join together in one volume different kinds of practices by articulating sets of structural constraints that operate upon them.

Part 1. This enterprise begins with discussions of the ever-changing relationship between law and capital. These discussions traverse Britain, France and the USA, at periods from the nineteenth century to the present day. What is presented could not, for these empirical reasons alone, be a continuous discourse. There are also theoretical differences between the authors. As editors, we have not tried to iron out these differences. We believe that no one formulation can make an authoritative claim to truth, and that the reader will be more enlightened by the diversity and choice.

The unity of the chapters lies in the common subjects and objects of their discourse: the law, legal discourse, the legal field, and legal practitioners. Power, too, is immanent in each of these pages, as variously subsisting in relational structures, ideologies, discourses. Part 2 is about deploying the powers of capital in alliance with and through the medium of legal practice.

The first two chapters reveal both the diversity and the unity of direction and concern. In her chapter, 'The symbol traders', Cain takes the reader on an intellectual journey, which has also been her own intellectual journey. In the process, she demonstrates weaknesses in earlier approaches to the study of lawyers that block or inhibit a full understanding of the relationship in which they stand to capital. She also shows how insights about this relationship generated by earlier studies can be accumulated and re-situated in a theoretical context that offers more opportunities for keeping theoretical pace with the ever-changing nature of these relationships. Her critique of the grand old men of the sociology of law – Marx, Weber, Gramsci and Foucault – explores, once again, the limitations of these positions in the same spirit of garnership, seeking an after-harvest of ideas to feed the new approach.

As an alternative, Cain argues that post-modern insights about the positive power of discourse must be accepted. However, since discourse and discursive practices are fundamentally social, she argues too that not only is discourse constitutive of relationships and institutions, but that relationships are constitutive of discourse, as well as conditions of existence for its emergence and persistence. The notion that one or the other must be given primacy is jettisoned. In the closing pages, she portends Part 3 of the book, arguing that this notion makes it possible to envisage ways in which legal practice in its discourses and relationships could be transformed into something qualitatively different, albeit still called law.

Harrington's chapter, 'Outlining a theory of legal practice', starts with a critique of both functionalist and structuralist approaches to the study of lawyers and their work. In seeking an approach that leaves space both for structure and for lawyers' autonomy, she elaborates what she characterizes as the ideology approach. Lawyers' ideology is seen as constitutive of relationships and of institutions. These connections can only be explored in historical analyses that also explore the specific political conditions which shape and make possible the development and negotiation of legal practice.

While Cain's chapter focuses specifically on relations with capital, Harrington adds two dimensions to the complexity of these developments. First, she is interested in developments in legal language that are deployed to constitute and support new institutional arrangements. The forum and the discourse are integrally, not extrinsically, connected. It is a general theoretical point: Harrington explores it in connection with the development of federal agencies and the administrative state. Secondly, inter- and intra-professional struggles play a crucial role in Harrington's account. Here she is able to connect a market-oriented theory of professionalism (Larson 1977; Abel 1988a) with changes in both the central state and the developing needs of client groups.

Part 2. Doreen McBarnet's argument in 'Legal creativity: law, capital and legal avoidance', is about a different but integrally related aspect of creativity. In finding ways for their clients to avoid the law – and in particular the tax laws – lawyers create quasi-institutionalized evasion practices, which persist until new legislation (usually) forces their amendment and a new set of practices is invented. Thus she demonstrates in a series of detailed analyses that regulation does not lag behind corporate practice, but is rather a dynamo of its change. In this scenario, legislation does no harm to anyone, even those whose activities it is intended to curb, and its primary effect is to benefit corporate lawyers.

But McBarnet also points out a dark side to this happy picture. First, not every client gets to be creative. Professional organization, techniques, rules, forms, institutions and ideology all militate against the underprivileged client. Moreover, rule of law ideology inhibits the development of alternative forms which might keep judicial decisions closer to the intentions of the legislators. Thus McBarnet's chapter, too, while not dealing explicitly with these issues, demonstrates that law is more than law talk, that discursive practices are not only institutionalized by discourse, that changing the talk alone will not change the world. Relationships as well as discourse shape who will be effective as an agent of discursive change.

In her ethnographic account of 'Capital fractionalized: the role of insolvency practitioners in asset distribution', Sally Wheeler demonstrates how suppliers lose out to finance capital in bankruptcy proceedings, even when they are ostensibly protected by a Reservation of Title clause. In the practices which subvert the law here, relational factors – who has control of the goods and the knowledges, suppliers' orientation to the next sale rather than to careful records of sales already completed – undermine discursive ones. Thorough and original ethnographic work of this kind is rare in those fields of law which affect capital, and this one goes to the heart of the matter, in that it discusses not the use of law to keep down the downsiders, but rather law as it operates between the two fractions of productive capital and finance capital. Hitherto we had believed that legal mechanisms truly functioned within capital in an even-handed way, as dispute settlement devices. Not so, it seems. As global capital changes its form to conglomerates of several hundred companies functioning worldwide (Hadden 1983, 1984), so finance capital predominates increasingly over productive capital. Within the state, this involves a shift in power from the legislature to the executive, where lawyers with experience of international conglomerates are in demand as advisers and employees (see Cain, this volume). Representation in the legislature is designed, quite purposively, to be local, and has no space or place for the representation of international concerns. At the level of law, the building of international institutions and alliances is important, but also, as Wheeler's chapter shows, at home as well as abroad the complex relations of law operate to benefit financial rather than productive capital. Wheeler's chapter, then, rich in specific detail and firmly grounding the complex avoidance argument in research, sets loose a train of thought which needs exploring further.

In his discussion of 'Blurred boundaries: the overlapping worlds of law, business and politics' in the UK context, Sugarman again addresses the complexity and range of the activities which lawyers have undertaken, and largely still perform, as both members of and servants to an emergent and aspirant middle class. For their employers their unique value appears to have lain in their flexibility, as the utility of the law itself lies in its malleability, or perhaps, more accurately, in its elasticity disguised and justified as fixity. What lawyers sell to their clients is a technique of language, of translation and transformation, coupled with the right to refuse to do either. They also, as regular users, understand and in part constitute the limits of discourse – they can locate (and constitute) the spaces where legal discourse cannot yet follow, the parts that legal discourse cannot yet reach.

Sugarman adds to the antecedent discussions in two important ways. His chapter makes clear that there are multiple choices affecting the ways personal and professional purposes articulate *with*, and in part constitute, wider environing structures. Secondly, he discusses at length the public and political roles of lawyers in the UK during the two hundred years from 1750 to 1950. He shows how professionalization leads to moral and cultural authority for lawyers. This authority can be used to express their own views *qua* occupation, and here his argument connects with that of Harrington, as also to express foundation principles (the rule of law) which legitimate their practices on behalf of clients. It also created space for lawyers on local authorities, on committees, and gave them centrality in middle-class networks. How these spaces were used we can, as yet, only guess, but Sugarman offers important clues. Not surprisingly, they were used to the benefit of their economically prosperous clients. But lawyers also generated a body of 'rights talk' which has been of far wider (if double-edged) social benefit. Professionalism as a practice and an ideal overcame some of the conflicts of interest between groups of lawyers and the sectors of clients whom they served. But this book reveals that professionalism itself is not a neutral mode of organization. Sugarman's wide-ranging discussion shows with historical precision how the law–state–capital relation has been forged in discontinuity and how intraprofessional struggles and strategies have in their turn shaped these developments.

Sue Lees' discussion of 'Lawyers' work as constitutive of gender relations' involves a gear change, for she explores how the categories of law, and the practice of Old Bailey judges, constitute the sexuality and the gender of women. Based on observations of thirty cases, analyses of press reports and judicial interpretations, Lees reveals that the law is gendered: the defence of provocation means something quite different for a male defendant than for a female defendant. Even here, at the heart of British justice, the interpretive spaces which the rules create allow the golden lady on the roof to slip one eye out of her blindfold, to tilt her scales, and to create two justices, one for male murderers (and male victims) and another for female murderers (and female victims). This is because the spaces in the law are filled by common sense, and the co-man sense deployed is male. Here, then, criminal defence lawyers appeal to a common and gendered knowledge which they share. Their reading of the law is in its terms. And by representing this gendered reading to the judge, whose dicta are likewise in its terms, criminal law itself is en-gendered.

Is this the same as the constitution of the law by capital? Well, yes and no. The process is a recognizable one, the deployment of legal skills on behalf of a group with external power progressively, slowly and silently generates a body of case law which is inimical to women. What is different is that (1) lawyers defending women are as equally well paid as lawyers defending men, yet they do not seem able to reverse the process, and (2) neither men nor women, in this context, are repeat players.

These differences in the processes of capitalizing and en-gendering law suggest that the politics surrounding the use of law by women may be different from the politics surrounding the use of law by poor people, racial minorities, working-class people and other subordinated groups. Doubtless there is a specificity in the relation of law and lawyers to each of these groups, as well as a sufficiently common experience to provide the basis for alliance. Feminists have begun to explore these issues (e.g. Snyder 1985; Smart 1986, 1990). What must be avoided is a generalizing from one set of experiences to the relationships of all downsiders with law as such. Lees makes no such grandiose claims, but once again her study points a direction for future research.

Another gear change concludes Part 2 of this collection. Yves Dezalay brings us up to date in time and takes us forward in theory, by considering what may be a flight of capital from the formal courts to informal or private adjudicative sites (see also Sarat and Silbey 1992). His argument in 'The forum should fit the fuss: the economics and politics of negotiated justice' is that informal and formal, low and high, justice are part of a single professional field, united in contradiction and symbolic conflict. The argument is made both historically and comparatively. As capitalism displaced judgment by aristocratic notables in France, to be replaced by experts in separate courts, so in the USA the emergent system of low justice was hierarchized, with high justice, true professionals, presiding over a low justice distributed by para-professionals. In the UK, notables – a magistracy of middle-class wives – have remained.

For the more powerful clients of the legal system, the recent movements of 'escape' from formal courts have been different, as well as internationally varied. Crucially, what has occurred is a separation of the legitimation function from the norm enunciation function. It is the latter which is being informalized. This process, we could add, will allow a more direct control by capital. But Dezalay, while noticing these points of articulation, is in this chapter more concerned to document the play of relational and symbolic forces in the internal field, the inter-professional and intra-professional struggles which map and define the field of legality as a unity. Thus if reform can be displaced to the informal sphere, change can occur while the immobility of law can also be presented and defended. The intra-legal informal sphere offers another mechanism for closure of the discursive rift between change and stasis with which Cain opens the discussions in Part 1 of this book.

Dezalay leaves us with a new exposure of the dilemma which Part 3 of this volume addresses. If law is and has been progressively constituted by powerful forces, can weaker and less privileged citizens use it too? And can their lawyers help them to do it? Is legal creativity for sale on an open or a closed market? These are the issues that preoccupy the authors of Part 3.

Part 3. 'Towards prefigurative legal practices' explores whether or not legal practice can be equally effective in reforming relationships within the state on behalf of those sections in society typically regarded as 'powerless' (see also Abel 1985c). If law historically developed a form appropriate for the facilitation of capitalist expansion, how can this form be used in the short run, and should it, or how should it, be changed in the long run? What is the direction? An exploration of lawyers' work on behalf of workers, women, minorities, dispossessed black people and depressed communities gives some prefigurative indications. The four chapters in this section speak to this issue. What clearly emerges from these studies is that legal practice itself has to be transformed in order to be an effective prefigurative enterprise. However, the sites occupied by powerless people are diverse. They have no particular unity as the 'powerless', 'underprivileged' or the 'poor'. This means that to be effective, legal practice itself has to take different forms depending on the structural location of those for whom lawyers are working. Politically, the development of this specificity is a strength; it means that the solutions are being tailored to the experience of problems. It is also a weakness in that diverse Others confront the One of professionalized law.

Prefigurative legal practices – practices that envision alternative power relations and articulate new meanings sometimes woven into conventional legal practice – also present challenges to the interpreter. In this section of the book, we present four accounts of efforts to transgress professionalized law and legal practice. Not only will you experience the diversity between class, race and gender struggles brought to and shaped by law, but we hope you will engage in the interpretive challenge of assessing how and what these people and their legal representatives contribute towards prefigurative legal practices. The scope and character of what is being transgressed in law by prefigurative practices is perhaps easier to pin down than are the boundaries of the new social relations they forge. For the very notion of 'prefigurative' is unsettling about the future, while offering more clarity on what should be changed in the present order of things.

Part 3 opens with the traditional problem of how labour lawyers organize their work in relation to the working class, capital and the legal profession. However, Frank Munger's analysis of the transformation of legal practice from 1870 to 1920 in a rural coal mining town, 'Miners and lawyers: law practice and class conflict in Appalachia, 1872–1920', is anything but traditional. His study challenges established wisdom on the close relationship between the American class structure and the delivery of legal services following industrialization (e.g. see Auerbach 1976). Through a careful and original historical study, Munger documents the formulation of a small network of lawyers in southern Appalachia whose practice encompasses both coal operators and miners. Munger argues that access to legal representation for miners was probably more responsible for the increase in accident cases than union activity or favourable state court precedent. He sets out to explain why lawyers who represented miners and who were friends with coal operators brought as many actions against the companies as cases defending them. However, Munger finds that these lawyers did not respond similarly to miners when it came to representing them in strikes. Here only a small and more prominent group of attorneys provided representation. This pattern coincides with the intensification of class differences in the community around 1910 and the fact that miners were more politically selective in their choice of legal representation in strikes.

Munger's study cautions us against an orthodox class analysis of legal representation on the one hand, and a romantic vision of victorious class struggle through law on the other. Instead, he offers a pragmatic interpretation of his data, arguing that the impact of industrialization on the organization of legal practice and representation of workers was shaped in part by the cultural forces and social relationships in this community. This study locates economic transformations in the broader context of a rural community and the nature of lawyers' work which develops within that community.

While this discussion of access to legal representation for miners explores a set of relations between labour, capital and lawyers in Munger's account, in Martha Fineman's chapter, 'Feminist legal scholarship and women's gendered lives', gender comes into the analysis and produces a different cut on the prefigurative possibilities of lawyers' work. Clearly, women's access to the legal profession is not in and of itself a transforming condition. Indeed, the push women experience to assimilate into the hierarchy of the legal profession is at the core of what Fineman challenges as she advances a feminist methodology based on difference. Fineman turns to the area of family law practice to ground her analysis of women's different experiences with law and legal institutions. In this sense, she unites legal practice with feminist theory, demonstrating the need for feminist practitioners to work out the relationship between women's different experiences in their practice. This argument also speaks to those feminists whose work has focused too exclusively on theoretical debates; the message is to locate feminist legal theory in practice.

Just as Fineman articulates the challenge of grounding women's gendered existence in a constitutive analysis of law and legal institutions, so too does she articulate the difficulties of seeing multiple dimensions to 'difference'. How does/should feminist legal practice address overlapping class and race differences without silencing the shared gendered aspects of our lives? Fineman's chapter addresses this question and in so doing clarifies how a feminist methodology of difference is 'radically non-assimilationist'.

In Wilfried Schärf's chapter, 'Para-legals and prefiguration: working in black townships towards a post-apartheid South Africa', the problem of how to mobilize prefigurative legal practices is dealt with directly, and perhaps most dramatically, as he traces part of the revolt against South Africa's system of apartheid. He describes the consciousness-raising role of para-legals who help formulate an alternative notion of legality in their relentless attack against abuses of power and authority by the police – abuses which render police actions illegal. Schärf highlights the dimension of struggle over legal form as well as legal outcome in his study of para-legals who work within the popular township courts of South Africa, but who have independent ties to the Legal Education Action Project (LEAP). Their legal practice involves negotiations with the local state, which in some ways are analogous to the negotiations with the central state conducted by lawyers working on behalf of capital. However, the outcomes are markedly different. Schärf reveals the difficulties, failures and tiny successes of attempts to create popular courts in South Africa, the most positive aspect of which is the role of para-legals in a power vacuum all too often filled by brutally warring forces.

Schärf makes clear that these para-legals are not only engaged in struggle against apartheid South Africa, but they too have the daunting task of prefiguring a post-apartheid legal consciousness and legal profession. Schärf identifies structural and cultural factors that help to forge this challenge. In particular, he notes the significance of ties between anti-apartheid lawyers (LEAP) and the United Democratic Front (UDF), an extra-parliamentary alliance of several hundred organizations including civic associations, women's organizations, labour unions, professionals and others which had its main role in the years when the ANC was banned. For LEAP, building democratic working styles within their legal practice was influenced by their work with the UDF. Schärf discusses the radicalizing effect of democratic values on working towards a prefigurative legal practice.

Radicalizing the legal profession is again taken up in the final chapter by Stuart Scheingold, 'The contradictions of radical law practice'. Turning to the British, on whose system South Africa's is modelled, Scheingold describes the constraints socialist lawyers face as they work in a conventional legal culture. Scheingold's study, based on interviews with radical lawyers in London in the late 1980s, probes what he calls a 'paradox at the positivist core of English professional ideology' – an awareness that the socially constructed character of law enables lawyers to make arguments on behalf of client interests, alongside a 'lawyer's credo' which represents these constructions as 'facts'. How do radical lawyers, themselves ambivalent about their relationship to the organized bar, live with this paradox while advancing a prefigurative enterprise? Scheingold focuses on this problem as a way of understanding the relationship between conventional professional ideology and radical practice.

After describing 'decommodification' as an important organizational aspiration for radical practice, Scheingold offers a critical, but unusually careful, assessment of whether the shortcomings of radical practices are soluble or are inherent contradictions. This chapter rounds off a volume that started with considerations of state forms as themselves an object and result of struggle – but leaves the reader in a markedly different theoretical and political place.

Three themes run throughout the chapters in this volume. One emphasizes the need to combine an analysis of lawyers as having established an integral relation between law and capital (Parts 1 and 2) with an exploration of the extent to which these creative discursive skills can be used on behalf of a range of powerless people (Part 3). A second major theme, and perhaps a second contradiction which we try to raise, is how post-modern insights about legal discourse can be connected with an institutional analysis. Here the question is whether the limits of what lawyers do can be anticipated or theoretically examined from a post-modern perspective on legal discourse. The chapters in Part 1 address this problem at a more general theoretical level, while subsequent chapters speak to this issue in the light of the specific and concrete circumstances which each chapter analyses. It is our view that post-modern analysis does not allow for an anticipatory or theoretical exploration of limits, and so can offer little guidance for practice. It is this third concern, that the volume, particularly Part 3, should offer guidance for progressive lawyers and sociolegal scholars.

PART 1

Understanding lawyering

1 The symbol traders

Maureen Cain

The lawyers' trade is a trade built entirely upon words [p. 11] . . . As though it were possible for the human mind to pull a specific result out of an abstract concept, like a rabbit out of a hat, without first, knowingly or unknowingly, putting the result into the concept, so it can later be found there.

(Rodell 1939: 43)

Introduction: On the sociology of lawyering

This introduction addresses two questions: why study lawyers and why study other people's studies of lawyers? I shall answer both in a personal, anecdotal way, because I believe that these anecdotes are necessary and useful in moving towards an understanding of the place of lawyers in capitalist relations.

Why, then, should a sociologist bother to study lawyers? I put this question to myself in 1970, when I first taught sociology of law, and when I first taught non-lawyers about lawyers. In teaching law students, the 'why bother' question did not arise. They had their own existential self-confidence: for them it was self-evident that the study of lawyers was of interest. I felt, however, that sociology students had a right to know why their time should be spent on lawyers rather than on bus drivers, students, farm workers or radio therapists. It was necessary then, as now, to justify theoretically and politically this massive expenditure of energy and resources.

Sociologists have typically answered the 'why bother' question by looking at the power of lawyers: how it is exercised (their relationships with, often, poorer clients) and what it consists in (their relationships with capital and the state). Most recently, lawyers' role as generators of their own discursively based power has come into focus, in the systems perspectives of Teubner (1984) and Luhmann (1985), as well as in the deconstructionist attempts of the 'critical legal theorists' and the post-modernists (see, e.g. Goodrich 1986; Fitzpatrick and Hunt 1987; Douzinas *et al.* 1992). The argument behind most of these approaches is that lawyers play a significant part in the ordering of society; in order to theorize and evaluate this, their place in and contribution to the class, sex/gender and race/ethnic structures must be understood. It is therefore very important that we take time out to study lawyers.

It is also very important that we attempt to study lawyers from the standpoint[1]* of one or another underprivileged segment of the popu-lation rather than from their own standpoint or that of capital. Certain aspects of their relations with capital will only come into view if we look from the downside up. Indeed, workers for capital probably 'know' what their relations with lawyers are in a way which is perfectly ade-quate for their everyday functioning. It is downsiders[2] struggling prac-tically and theoretically with their need to use law while not wanting to be contained by it (e.g. Medcalf 1978; Mathiesen 1983; Snyder 1985; Smart 1986, 1990) who will benefit from a sociological analysis of that relation. So we have two interconnected issues, the power of lawyers and the political need to understand that power in order to deploy or eschew it as the case may be.

Lawyers' power has been understood in many different ways, and constantly rediscovered and re-understood from the mid-nineteenth cen-tury to our own day. Since the 1970s, I myself have been struggling towards a formulation of lawyers' relations with capital which will also help to answer the question 'can law help the poor?' I formulated the notion – to be amended later in this chapter – that lawyers are best conceived as conceptive ideologists of capital (Cain 1979) and began to explore the contradictions of the profession's self-image (Cain 1976). In the 1980s, I hawked an earlier version of this chapter around Australia and New Zealand. Now, in the 1990s, I re-address the issues with an even firmer commitment to a standpoint epistemology. This constant return and departure is neither a search for truth nor mere self-indulgence. It results from a recognition that ways of understanding these relationships are politically potent (they indicate what we should do) and almost inev-itably revealing. It is in this spirit, too, that this chapter is constituted as a dialectical critique of ways in which the relationships between lawyers, capital and the state have been formulated in the past. There is little to be gained from a mere trashing of earlier approaches. What I hope to do

* Superscript numerals refer to numbered notes at the end of each chapter.

instead, by this chapter's long discussion of never quite out-moded positions, is to enhance my own and the reader's understanding of where we are now by retracing the intellectual journey that has been made. It is my hope that by shaking the kaleidoscope of earlier approaches,[3] I will add depths to the point of temporary arrival which concludes this chapter, for other people as well as myself.

It is also necessary to explore the limitations of these earlier approaches. How did they manage both to inform and to prevent more fundamental questions from being raised? As we shall see, people have been writing about the relations between lawyers and capital throughout this century; they have even been writing about the creative skills of lawyers; but the issues have been formulated in a way that now seems to have limited rather than enhanced our understanding.

This chapter, therefore, engages in a theoretical reading of a wide range of studies and materials, focusing in particular on relatively early attempts to formulate the law–state–capital relation. The classical arguments of Weber, Marx, Gramsci and Foucault appear in section 2 of the chapter, for most of the earlier approaches discussed do not acknowledge the existence of these works either explicitly or in their formulations. Christine Harrington, in the next chapter, picks up the story of this dialectical movement of change and understanding and brings it up to date.

One additional spin-off from this reflexive journey of dialectical critique may be to assist readers new to the field to impose some order on the miscellany of materials 'on' lawyers, for they do not simply 'add up'; nor is there a continuous progression to where we are now. More specifically, in Section 1 the chapter deals first with those texts by lawyers that produced an occupational self-image. I call these *legal eulogies*, and use them to demonstrate the fundamental tension in legal ideology which the idea of creative lawyering involves. The next body of literature is concerned with *lawyers as professionals*. A number of insights into the law–capital relation are generated by these texts, but the problematic in which they are couched sets limits to their utility for understanding that relation more fully.

Closely related to these are a small collection of studies of *legal deviance*, in which capital is cast in the role of villain. Studies of *careers of lawyers* set somewhat different limits to our understanding, although these too offer data and insights about law and capital which are of sufficient importance to warrant a separate discussion. All these themes have emerged and re-emerged over a period of fifty years. Their very persistence demands that they be explored and evaluated for their yield from a downsider standpoint.

At this point, the argument changes gear, and focuses first on powerful but underestimated studies of *lawyers and politics*, or the lawyer–state relation, and of *lawyers and capital*. Section 2 starts with a reconsideration of the classics, with a view to seeing how the many descriptions emerging

her problematics can best be articulated with a theory of society
explain *both* law's relation to capital *and* its relation to those
ˌ.ιders whose standpoint I share. The formulation should also explain why women have a more ambiguous relation to law than do working-class people or, perhaps, black people. A theory is advanced in which neither relationships nor discourse may be accorded primacy. When the integrity *and* the separate potency of both discourse and relationships are considered, a new understanding of the possibilities for downsider justice can emerge.

Readers are invited to view the chapter as a constantly interrupted journey, one in which despite the many cul-de-sacs a few insights are found at each stage. These, eventually, are relocated and reconceived to create an understanding of lawyering which connects with my vision of the future (Carr 1961).[4] My image is one of a society where the system of justice no longer supports the major imbalances of power and resources in society, but rather works to minimize the effects of these.

SECTION 1 TRADING SYMBOLS FOR CAPITAL: CREATIVITY, AUTONOMY, PROFESSIONALISM AND DEPENDENCE

Legal eulogies: The production of an occupational self-image

Legal eulogies are produced, usually, by successful lawyers and judges or their biographers in the form of biographies and autobiographies (Cain 1976). They also appear in obituaries (Treiber 1987). Typically, they are hymns to law, which is regarded as the foundation of social order and therefore self-evidently both necessary and legitimate. The progressive English judge Norman Birkett captures this view:

> In my view, the contribution the law makes in all its branches, the Judiciary, the two branches of the legal profession is, in a word, they are creating order, and without the law creating that necessary order none of the other professions could survive or flourish at all.
>
> (Birkett 1964, cited in Cain 1976: 231)

Or, as one law school dean puts it:

> From the standpoint of an educator, the more people who are trained in legal methodology, the better it is for our society.
>
> (cited in Miller 1992: 18)

The biographical materials lend support to teleological histories which 'explain' how British or American law came to be so good (e.g. Maitland 1901/1957; Cohen 1929; Mathew 1937; Daniel 1976).

Not only is the law an object of praise, of course; so too are its bearers, the lawyers. Bresler's (1961) comment that English judges are 'largely . . .

gifted and talented members of the upper class' (p. 197) stands as one example; another is Megarry's (1962: 72) 'I want to emphasise . . . not so much the intellectual skill but the selflessness and integrity of English lawyers'; even legal 'how to do it' books emphasize how praiseworthy the practitioners are of this craft (Cecil 1958; Due Cann 1964; Napley 1970; Wickenden 1975). But therein, of course, lies the rub. For once it is acknowledged that law is a craft, then the *creative* skill of the craftsperson has to be acknowledged.

Lawyers, of course, know that they are making law, whether or not judges accept or deny this aspect of their work (Jaffe 1969). In Common Law countries, it is the lawyer's argument which is accepted or rejected by a judge. Making a new argument, so that a new distinction or analogy – a new rule – enters the law is a prestigious activity. Having a case reported – an indication that a new distinction or analogy has been made or attempted – is a public acknowledgment of their skill which excites and pleases lawyers. In the mainland European system, academic lawyers and judges as well as elite lawyers engage in this activity. Weyraugh's (1964) judges frequently said that they 'found' their conclusion first and worked backwards to the legal reason – precisely what a private lawyer does whose starting point is her client's chosen outcome, arguments for the achievement of which must be found.

There is therefore a paradox within legal ideology, which in this respect appears to be the same in all the advanced industrial societies of the west. While lawyers know that changing the law is not just their job but the most prestigious part of their job, 'The Law' is none the less regarded as having existed from the beginnings of civilization, if not for all time. This way of thinking is described by Bourdieu (1987: 242) as 'ontological glorification' (see also Fitzpatrick 1992).

A discursive contradiction of this magnitude in its foundational ideology leaves the occupation as a whole perpetually vulnerable. For example jurisprudence itself can be seen as one massive attempt to achieve closure, by emphasizing that legitimacy lies in procedural rather than substantive rules (e.g. Hart 1961). However, while the jurisprudential attempts to achieve closure in thought continue, the legal professions by their mode of organization have long achieved closure in practice. In Britain at least, there have been few unseemly struggles for 'control of the text' (Bourdieu 1987: 214). In the USA, too, the eulogistic images serve as both descriptions of and, to some extent, norms for occupational life as in the case of Sam Erwin, who despite his conduct of the Watergate hearings claimed to be 'just a country lawyer' (Clancy 1974). Judging from the literature,[5] the norms are almost unanimously subscribed to. Eulogies even achieve the ultimate incorporation of left lawyers, who in these pages became eccentric stars (the fate of Sir Patrick Hastings and Clarence Darrow) or conservative 'really', the fate of

,erald Gardiner according to his approving biographer wife (Hastings 948; Darrow 1957; Box 1983).

Outside of the books, the structural mechanisms for securing ideological unity, for ensuring that the boundaries of legal creativity are effectively policed, are extraordinarily complex. In Britain, there remains an elaborate system of patronage and sponsored mobility for barristers and judges (Cain 1976; Abel 1988a, b); the Norwegian system depends on the social production of legal academic stars whose analytic interpretations therefore carry authority (Mathiesen 1980). And to supplement the formal devices in the Italian and German systems of legal control (Dahrendorf 1962; Rueschemeyer 1973; Di Federico 1976; Treiber 1987), there are strong informal processes of 'recognition' and prestige. Weyraugh (1964) cites one leading German lawyer: 'I am acquainted with most of the leading lawyers in the German cities and industrial centres. We are a small and select group' (p. 137). In the USA, one may hazard that where distance and size make such intimate knowledge difficult, the local bar associations more than adequately effect both local informal policing of the ways the rules are changed and a pan-national networking which guarantees the necessary intra-professional unanimity.

There are three main points to carry forward from these reflections: (1) lawyers know they create law, and are organized to police effectively the discursive mode of this creativity; (2) the unanimity achieved by this policing enables them to see the law 'itself' as unchanging, while in all its particulars it is infinitely malleable; and (3) those wishing to understand lawyers should read what they say about themselves, no matter how pompous, tedious or self-adulatory the text may be. Lawyers are not wrong about themselves. The problem is rather that they do not understand the implications of their being so right.

The professional 'man': Lawyers as archetypes

In 1857, Byerley Thomson was already writing about the lawyer as the archetype of the professional man. And very largely lawyers have remained among that small number of occupations which have been *presumed* by sociologists to 'be' professional. The social organization of lawyers, rather than being questioned, has been used as a model of what a profession really is. In this way, entry requirements, ethics, collegiality, etc., were identified as signs or indicators of true professionalism by the empiricist or trait-seeking studies (Carr Saunders and Wilson 1933/1964). This approach has now been discredited, specifically by Johnson (1972), and generally by the critiques of empiricism which emerged with Popper (1965, 1968) during the heyday of empiricist sociology, and which have since burgeoned. But the same concerns about what the professionalism of lawyers consists in persist up to the present day. To these may be added more recent questions about the political weight of lawyers when organized *qua* professionals. Despite the fact that the concern with lawyers as professionals originally had questionable philosophical roots,[6] a great deal about the relationship between lawyers and capital can be gleaned from these studies, and re-conceived in the emergent theory developed here.

The three points that I wish to carry forward from these studies concern the developmental work that lawyers do for large companies, the self-increasing character of the autonomy lawyers have successfully claimed, and the relationship between capital and the organized profession. However, I start this section with the standard sociological concern of the positivist era which was with 'professionals' working in large organizations.

Given that autonomous decision making by the occupational group was one of the empirically identified characteristics of the archetypal professional, how did they manage to remain professional when subjected to bureaucratic direction? How did they deal with this situation of 'being' a professional in a non-professional setting (e.g. Kornhauser 1963; Billingsley 1964) or when other professional 'traits', such as primary loyalty to the client, were suddenly removed? For some occupations, especially female ones such as social work or nursing, the absence of items from the 'known' checklist of traits was used to demonstrate that these workers hadn't quite made it, but were only 'semi-professionals' (Etzioni 1969). In the case of high-status men such as lawyers, the lack of fit caused a great deal of anxiety among sociologists. It would be unthinkable to describe members of an archetypal profession as only semi-professional. Thus Kornhauser (1963), for example, argued that the people working in these anomalous conditions (in his case scientists) must experience considerable stress as a result of their endemic role conflict. The more recent discussions of the lack of autonomy of lawyers employed in large law firms (Heinz and Laumann 1982) demonstrate a continuing concern with this issue.

The central methodological flaw in these works is the confusion of an attempt to conceptualize the characteristics of a particular cluster of occupations (trait theory) with the capturing of a fixed essence of what professionals really are: a confusion of a way of thinking with the reality purportedly described. The highly paid men (mainly) who work as in-house counsel for the multinationals seem not to let their lack of fit with sociological theory worry them too much. By their office practice they are constituting what it is to be a lawyer, by their political practice they are constituting what it is to be professional, regardless of whose categories they fit. These jobs remain both sought after and prestigious – or, at least, in the USA, the preserve of men and women from prosperous families who have received an elite law school training.

The traditional sociological concern about whether or not lawyers working directly for capital are true professionals was therefore misplaced. But a wealth of significant descriptive information, which has most certainly influenced my own formulations of the relationship between law and capital, was generated by empiricist accounts which lawyers produced. Let Smith speak for the genre:[7]

> The wise business executive seeks the advice of company counsel during the formulative considerations of policy and practice of his [*sic*] company.
>
> (Smith 1958: 224)

In other words, it becomes very clear from these accounts that lawyers working for large corporations are not only doing prophylactic work as far as company policy goes – that is, avoiding negative legal problems – they are also willy-nilly *influencing the direction of company development*. Papers such as these, often written for an audience of lawyers, are among the earliest intimations of legal creativity in relation to capital.

Studies of professionalism focus on occupational autonomy or freedom from external regulation because occupational groups themselves have put this question on the political agenda. The paradox is that while, as Heinz and Laumann (1982) have argued, a lawyer's autonomy in dealing with a case may be least when working for capital in the form of a large corporate client, these very autonomy claims can be used on occasion in ways that are of particular value to corporate capital. The following discussion of the relation between lawyers and capital, therefore, takes issue with the question of autonomy as it has emerged in those accounts which focus on the profession.

By the mid-nineteenth century in England, there was an increasing self-awareness among 'professionals' which, internally, encouraged organization and, externally, was used to legitimate the claims to autonomy which that same organization made possible (Reader 1966; Duman 1982; Lewis 1982).

> By 1860 or thereabouts the elements of professional standing were tolerably clear. You needed a professional association to focus opinion, work up a body of knowledge, and insist upon a decent standard of conduct.
>
> (Reader 1966: 71)

A Royal Charter making possible centralized and exclusive training and examination also helped.

In the USA, a similar process was hampered by greater localization and worse communications. An expressly anti-professional ideology also hindered a rapid expansion of the powers of the organized bar in the USA. Such was the insistence on the democratic election of such important political personages as judges that until the mid-twentieth century 'elite lawyers confronted a bench that mostly failed to meet their professional norms' (Botein 1983: 50). None the less, in the early years of this century the elite (big business) lawyers in the Chicago Bar Association successfully welded that organization's left and right wings in a campaign for judicial independence from the full rigours of the democratic process (Cappell 1982; Halliday 1987). At the level of the Supreme Court, the American Bar Association (ABA) also waged a long and ultimately successful campaign to achieve what effectively amounts to professional vetting of Supreme Court judges (Grossman 1965).

In Britain, the bar directly but informally controls the appointment of judges via the 'soundings' made by the Lord Chancellor's Department. According to Cecil, the Lord Chancellor consults with his [*sic*] permanent secretary who:

> . . . has his ear to the ground and has a pretty good idea of the standard of most barristers who might be considered in the running for a judgeship.
>
> (Cecil 1970: 47)

There has been, then, in both societies, an expanded recognition of the entitlement of the profession to both independence from external control and exclusive control over decision making in relation to their field.

The trait approach, by demonstrating that to be a professional it was necessary to be autonomous, has also been used with great effect by the lawyers who have managed to turn the archetypal professional's 'right' to autonomy into a demonstration of their own virtuous ability to be more independent than others, and in this way to expand their power. Both Abel-Smith and Stevens (1967) and Morrison (1973) have demonstrated that it is this claim to be more independent than others, by now interpreted as a specific skill in neutrality, that makes judges and sometimes senior lawyers the 'obvious' choices to chair commissions of enquiry and a wide range of government committees. The successfully claimed autonomy of lawyers justifies its own self-expansion.

Lawyers' occupational self-image also involves subscription to a code of conduct (Bellow and Moulton 1981). On the face of it this, too, like the claim to autonomy, might be thought to inhibit the relationship between lawyers and capital. However, it appears that the correspondence between personnel working for capital, whether as in-house counsel or in major law firms, and those holding influence as a member of the professional association, turns that potential limitation also to advantage. Lieberman (1978), Abel (1981b) and Nelson (1985) have argued that in practice the ethical code sets few limits to the activities of the lawyer for the large company, serving rather to enhance his or her status by making possible the denigration of the non-elite lawyers and leaving the practical dependence of elite lawyers on their corporate clients untouched. As Lieberman says, 'the association pinned the stigma of immorality on the "lower" class of lawyer' (p. 50). The canons of ethics, however, 'had no bearing on the way the elite practiced' (p. 61). So the relationship with capital in the form of the corporate client is not touched or challenged by ethical concerns.

The committee structure is also a mechanism for linking lawyers, via their professional associations, directly with capital. Green (1976) has mapped the close ties between ABA offices and big business via the chairpeople of committees. He cites H.L. Russell, a counsel with Eastern Airlines, who chaired the Association's Committee on Aviation at the time of his study. E. Brasfield, counsel for Humble Oil and General Motors, chaired the Committee on Environmental Controls. The Association's neutral and professional advice on these matters would thus be shaped by its articulation with capital.

Cappell, in relation to the Chicago Bar Association, effectively captures this complex relation:

> The organisational structure guarantees that those board members with specific substantive interests, usually derived from practice and client characteristics, will generally be in a position to control the deliberative outcome of the issues.
>
> (Cappell 1982: 336)

The autonomy of lawyers in their practice and in their organized occupational forms is real. I am describing articulation – a set of mechanisms for producing alignments of discourse and policy – rather than determination. Certainly it would be simplistic to equate ABA influence directly with the influence of corporate capital. In the first place, the professional associations need their independence to be seen to be real, and this means that their advice must be expressed in legal discourse. While malleable, like all discourses, this mode does set limits to what may be said. Finally, and more telling than these arguments, is the fact that the ABA (and also professional organizations outside the USA) has an important internal audience for its activities, its own membership. As both Cappell (1982) and Halliday (1987) have revealed in the limited case of Chicago, a bar association needs to retain its own sophisticated and divided membership, and this sets limits to its activities.

Studies that take the notion of the profession as their starting point span a long period in time, use diverse methodologies – some of which are seriously flawed – and raise a confusing plethora of issues. Before shaking the kaleidoscope of concerns once again, those insights identified as having a bearing on the relationship between lawyers and capital may be summarized as:

1 The role of corporate counsel in directing the development of a company.
2 The way in which recursive and self-expanding claims to professional autonomy and monopoly make possible new forms of relationship with capital, either by the use of these experts-in-neutrality on state committees, or by the ideology of expertise which gives power within professional organizations to those lawyers who have close ties with capital.
3 The inability of professional ethics to control the lawyer–capital relation.

Studies of legal deviance: Capital as a tempter

The same concern about the professional autonomy of lawyers, and the same presumption that such autonomy is a defining characteristic of the lawyer as an archetypal professional, can be found in studies of legal deviance. Here capital is cast as the villain, subverting the professional from the true exercise of his or her calling. Lawyering in itself is conceived as good and pure, but as distorted by a growing association with and dependence on big business. As long ago as 1933, Karl Llewellyn cogently expressed this position:

> Any man's [*sic*] interests, any man's outlook, are shaped in greatest part by what he does . . . His sympathies and ethical judgments are determined essentially by the things and people he works on and for and with . . . Hence the practice of corporation law not only works for business men to business ends, but develops within itself a business point of view – toward the work to be done, toward the value of the work to the community, indeed, toward the way in which to do the work.
>
> (Llewellyn 1933: 177)

Rostow (1949/1955) and Kennedy (1971) were similarly concerned. Rostow thinks the association with business is fine so long as 'failures to utilize power in the general interest' (p. 56) are avoided. Kennedy feels like Llewellyn, that if lawyers serve 'the wrong clients', they will be tainted.

In recent years, the extreme dependence of law firms on each particular massive client has been re-emphasized. Indeed, branch offices may be opened to serve the needs of just one client (Stewart 1983). These writers, then, consider that because of their association with big business or corporate capital, these lawyers have lost their way. Lawyering *as such* is a valuable, even a noble, pursuit. Its relationship with large-scale capital is extrinsic. If lawyers' services can be reclaimed for the person in the street, then all will be well with the law.

The presumptions of this approach, then, preclude any serious questioning of the law as such or of the role of lawyers as traders in legal symbols. Certainly there could be no room for a suggestion that the relationship with capital is constitutive of lawyering. Rather, reforms may be necessary, after which lawyering will be back on tracks for social good. By not questioning the commodity to be purveyed by law work, the approach reinforces the assumption that it is an obvious and unquestionable good.

Reviewing these studies makes it possible to highlight a major weakness in all the approaches discussed so far. The eulogies, the studies of lawyers as professionals, and the studies of capital as temptation all approach the world without a theory, believing that reality can speak directly to them. *All fill the theoretical void with commonsense assumptions that are riddled with legal ideology about the value of law and lawyers.* Because these assumptions underpin the ensuing argument, all possibility of questioning them is closed off. From the conservative eulogists, with whom we started, to the liberal reformers who are concerned about legal deviance, this closure of the most important question is complete.

Careers of lawyers: The so very useful zig-zag

Studies spanning the last thirty years reveal a caste-like divide in the USA between elite lawyers in large firms which have mainly corporate clients and the country lawyers, solo practitioners, divorce lawyers and criminal lawyers whose work was described in a series of rich ethnographies in the 1960s (Carlin 1963, 1966; O'Gorman 1963; Handler 1967; Wood 1977). Now, as then, race and class (these authors omitted gender) connect with the law school attended, which connects with the opportunity to shine on an Ivy League law review, which connects with the young lawyer's first job. Bright young black people, in contrast, go to night school still (Lortie 1959; Ladinsky 1963; Heinz and Laumann 1982). Indeed, Heinz and Laumann suggest that changes in the structure and size of law firms, and intensification of professional organization, have created more rigidity, and that opportunities for young lawyers who start in the wrong place are declining.

A rather short summary can be provided of these studies of the careers of American lawyers, which are so entirely consistent with one another. First, lawyers from upper middle-class backgrounds and high-status universities get jobs in the large law firms in the USA, those which are directly employed by capital. Secondly, women lawyers tend to be marginalized after recruitment by a series of informal exclusionary processes ranging from their absence from the after-hours bar (Epstein 1970, 1981) to active abuse. The situation in other countries is no better in this regard (Podmore and Spencer 1982; Murray 1987; Boigeol 1988). (Whether access to the corporate bar is the best place for feminists to direct their efforts is another question.)

It also seems to be the case that the largest law firms operate an 'up-or-out' policy invented by the Cravath firm (Swaine 1948; Auchinloss 1955;

Smigel 1964/1969; Galanter and Paley 1991). In these firms, associates (employed lawyers) who do not succeed in the firm or who choose not to gamble on a partnership move out to senior posts either as executives or in the law departments of large client companies.

In this way, the thinking of the law firm and the thinking of the corporate client are closely intertwined: their universe of discourse is brought into alignment. In addition, 'the proportion of corporate chief executives with backgrounds in law is now increasing' (Priest and Rothman 1985: 143). These are men (not women) who achieve very senior positions in relation to corporate capital after a long and successful private career. The up-or-out people are presumably those whom Priest and Rothman characterize as 'semi-practitioners', moving into the big corporations at middle level after ten years or so in private practice – and then going on up. Their numbers are increasing too (Priest and Krol 1986).

In the UK, Malcolm (1966), a solicitor, recounts how he and his local bank manager made friends and moved upwards and inwards from the suburbs to the city centre. They both had the 'right' class background. However, with the expansion of large downtown firms of solicitors in England and the lifting of restrictions on the number of partners (Abel 1988a), this particular career path may no longer be typical.

The focal concern of these studies is the legal career, but the evidence they provide about the patterns of connection between the controllers of capital and their lawyers is invaluable. To those living their careers, simply maximizing their quality of life must be the presumed goal. And, indeed, the difficult decision about whether to play safe and move out or pass up a good opportunity in the hope of moving up is thoroughly presented. To the large companies, having someone they can trust and depend on who also understands the firm's strategies for the management of its capital and enterprise must be the prime objective. How precisely these movements of personnel mesh with the possibilities for capital is not explored in these pages, however. Their taken-for-granted assumption that we all know what a lawyer is, their deliberate choice of a lawyer's eye view as he moves through his career preclude the larger questions from being raised.

So although these works bring the law–capital relation quite straightforwardly into view, they too can only provide a collection of clues for those who wish to call that relation into question.

What lawyers do when they work for capital 1: Lawyers, politics and inventing institutions

The same law firms whose associates move out to become captains of industry rather than moving up within the firm supply government in the USA with a flow of specialist advisers. The substantial literature on these connections in the USA leads to a search for the influence of lawyers in politics elsewhere. The precise mechanisms are very different in each nation. However, the American data are so rich that it makes sense to treat the USA as an exemplary case study in this regard.

Brown (1948) was the first to point out that lawyers not only have a monopoly of the judicature, but also hold more than half the seats in each House of the American legislature and a sizeable proportion of influential executive positions. Abel (1988b: 227) supports this view. Moreover, recent work indicates that lawyers are to be found on both sides of the struggle as to where the powers of the Legislature and the Executive should be divided (Salokar 1992).

From Blaustein and Porter (1954) to Miller (1992), it seems that the proportion of lawyers in the House of Representatives has stabilized at around 42 per cent, and in the Senate at around 61 per cent. They also hold around a quarter of the seats at state level. Moreover, although lawyers are always found on both sides of the House, in a covert way they wield a disproportionate amount of power. They hold more than their share of leadership positions, particularly those of Speaker and chairperson of rules committees and judiciary committees to which they are appointed precisely because they are lawyers. Lawyers also sponsor more than their share of bills, and the bills which they sponsor are more successful than those put up by other people. Finally, although legal solidarity is rare, occurring only on matters affecting the occupation as such, such solidarity is always, invariably, successful (Derge 1959). The overall influence of a legal culture on these bodies can only be guessed at, rather than measured.

An intermediate position of influence within the legislature, although an executive appointment, is that of bill drafter. When Jones (1952) described the advisory and policy-making aspects of this task, he was advocating an expansion and professionalization of these appointments, such as has indeed occurred. For us it is enough to note that drafting is an influential activity in its own right, not simply a neutral application of a technical skill:[8] 'Legislative research and drafting work that is technically sound can contribute notably to wise legislative decision' (Jones 1952: 442).

This brings us to the Executive where, despite her now out-of-date figures, Brown's (1948) account is still the most complete. As she wrote, twenty-three of the then total of thirty-three presidents had been lawyers, as were 27 per cent of the forty-eight state governors at that time. In her day – and how much since then have civil services expanded worldwide – each of the following state agencies employed between four and five hundred lawyers: the Bureau of Customs, the Bureau of Narcotics, the Bureau of Federal Supply and the Bureau of the Comptroller of the Currency. In Foreign Funds Control, lawyers' work included: drafting legislation; preparing reports; making applications before committees; reviewing executive orders and proclamations; preparing formal and informal opinions and memoranda for the guidance of departmental administrative officers; litigation work involving officials; recommendations for settlement or compromise concerning 'general claims of the United States, legal problems concerning gold and silver transactions, and the administration of the stabilisation fund' (p. 49); the insurance of public debt obligations; the re-negotiation of war contracts; '. . . the formulation of proposals for an international monetary fund and an international bank for reconstruction and development' (p. 50); and representing the government in corporate reorganization proceedings (p. 52) – to name but some of the tasks she lists. Citing a Press Committee document, Brown affirms 'the lawyer . . . is inevitably thrown into the heart of the policy-making process and of necessity has an important, and often a controlling, voice in the major issues of his [*sic*] department or agency' (p. 78).

Brown's concern is that lawyers lack the proper training for these major policy-making executive jobs, since law schools fail to 'admit' that this is where so many of their graduates end up. On the contrary, their training is entirely appropriate, for the most influential categories of lawyers whom she identifies are 'political appointees', mainly with short tenure who advise about programme and policy formulation (ibid.: 61) and 'top flight career men' who move into government from private practice or academe, and are in 'frequent motion' between government agencies. Of these men (one must assume there were no women) Brown says, 'Their judgment is sought by executives in other than legal matters' (p. 63). A third influential group is the 'temporary government lawyers', hired from private practice on short contracts to troubleshoot, or give highly specialized advice in the early stages of a new policy or a newly devised institution. Later, lower-grade legal staff are employed. These might come from Brown's largest and least influential category, the permanent career service, people who rise through the ranks and whose maximum realistic aspiration would be to head up a Division of a less strategic department.

A more recent study (Horowitz 1977) documented considerable tension between the bright young lawyers of the Justice Department, needing to make their way as professionals, and who still have virtual monopoly of litigation, and the more immediate and substantive concerns of the longer-serving agency personnel. This, too, supports Brown's analysis, and suggests that the extent and direction of influence remains the same as when she wrote.

So, the policy makers among the lawyers are mobile and move out of, and afterwards back into, private practice. These private lawyers represent foreign governments as well as the USA (Kraft 1964: 105), and the forces of progress as well as those of reaction. It was, Kraft tells us, a lawyer with Covington Burling who thought up the scheme to use federal referees to judge voting lists in the South rather than local officials prone to racist bias. It was a Washington counsel for the drug industry who handled the delicate three-way negotiation between the industry and two governments which made it possible for drugs to be included in the ransom the Cubans demanded for those captured at the Bay of Pigs. Moreover, says Kraft, *these lawyers also create new forms of relationship*, for example a new style public–private corporation to manage a communication satellite (ibid.: 105). Let us hold that knowledge steady, while we see what else goes on in Washington.

The political aspect of lawyers' work which is most debated is their lobbying. Horsky (1952) claimed that Washington, D.C. had one lawyer for each 183 people; twelve years later, Kraft (1964) had the figure down to 1: 60. [It was 1: 530 for the country as a whole in 1976, according to Auerbach (1976).] What many of these lawyers are about is what Horsky calls 'influence peddling'. Their task is to know 'government intimately – not as a vast amorphous remote force, but as a grouping of individuals and offices'; . . . 'To represent the United Fruit Company, as the Corcoran firm does, is to know something about the State Department in general and a great deal about the desk officers in the Latin American field . . .' (ibid.: 104). These lawyers must know the ways of thinking of government so that they can anticipate policy and 'advise' in the course of friendly informal encounters how their client would be likely to react; they can communicate this pre-policy to the client and vice versa. In this way, the client's interests are there as implicit knowledge in the policy-making discourse. Sometimes, it seems, a lawyer-lobbyist may even suggest legislation, although by the 1950s, lobbying no longer took the form of the introduction of private bills. By knowing what is in the pipeline on both sides, these lawyers are able to work backstage for their corporate clients. There is no need in these days for the professionally abhorrent fix (Klaw 1958). On the contrary, today such lobbying is high-status work. These lawyers only become publicly known, however, when they represent their clients before governmental commissions and committees. This is a politics which succeeds best by not attracting political or public attention. These are the practices Llewellyn is talking of when he says that legal realists seek to follow 'the trail . . . into the wilds of government and politics, and queer events in both' (1930–31: 1248).

The more recent work of Nelson and Heinz (1988) has called the extent of this influence into question. Either it has declined through time, or this is just one more case of sociologists swallowing wholesale lawyers' propaganda about themselves. Horsky, of course, was himself a lawyer. The Nelson and Heinz data indicate that lawyers function more as technical specialists in those areas where litigation and formal hearings are frequent. They are neither the most numerous nor the most notable of interest group representatives in other areas.

Those data are challenging, but they do not challenge the argument that lawyers have an especially *creative* role in the drafting of constitutions (establishing of institutions) and in formulating agreements of all kinds. No other occupational group has claimed this skill. It is perhaps only as lobbyists that lawyers are less important than some of their apologists have led us to believe.

This mass of insights into the structure and content of lawyers' work can be summarized in two brief points. First and most crucially what lawyers do is creative. Their influence on legislation is creative; but more than that, their backstage influence *as lawyers*, not as lobbyists, is creative. Secondly, therefore, lawyers *think of new forms of relationships*. And these relationships are not innocent. One lawyers' invention, the International Monetary Fund, has continued to impact profoundly on the standard of living in the Caribbean where I live and work, insisting on policies of structural adjustment which have worked to the advantage of industry and high-income earners, but have guaranteed increasing impovishment for low earners and the unwaged.

Lawyers are *par excellence* institutional inventors for their clients. The best and most sought after and most influential social inventors work or have worked for corporate capital, before and after the period in which government buys their inventing skills. Their ties with both government and capital are close and personal, they are mediators, they ensure a unity of discourse or at least inter-discursive comprehension between the two.

A similar position appertains in Britain, although the numbers of lawyers involved in creative policy making are fewer, and one suspects that people with other kinds of training do it too. In the nineteenth century, a permanent legal adviser to the Foreign Office, for example, was a novelty (Jones 1971). By 1958, jobs in the Foreign Office Legal Department, the Lord Chancellor's Department and the Treasury Office of Legal Draftsmen were all reserved for barristers (Cecil 1958), whose ideology and style could be the more closely vetted (see p. 20). That restriction is no longer in force. The job, however, remains the same. The Civil Service Legal Department already employed 500 or so lawyers when Cecil wrote, but had lower status. There was, I would guess, less creative institution building in their more public legal role.

These are only leads, not data. My interpretation is that the creative institution building which is done in England is the same; although it is more often done by other people as well as lawyers. The links with corporate capital, as Sugarman's chapter in this volume suggests, are less direct and are changing rapidly in character, from the days when an indigenous high bourgeoisie met with barristers in London clubs to the more recent, post big-bang years of the twentieth century when firms of solicitors are growing rapidly to meet the needs of international finance houses and corporate productive capital.

What lawyers do for capital 2: Creative dependence

In this last stage of the empirical account, I argue that creative institution building is not occasional work done for government but regular work done for capital; and that it has always been so. In making this point, I lean largely on Hurst's brilliant histories (1950, 1970), seven accounts of large-scale law practices in the USA (Swaine 1948; Mayer 1966; Goulden 1971; Hoffman 1973; Stewart 1983; Mann, 1985; Nelson 1988), one legal biography (Fifoot 1936/1977) and the recent seminal work of Bob Gordon (1983), as well as Doreen McBarnet's and Sally Wheeler's chapter in this book. Other sources will be mentioned as I go along, but these I will somewhat cavalierly amalgamate. I also depend on the data presented in Cain (1976, 1979), which are not reproduced here.

De Tocqueville argued that 'The special information which lawyers derive from their studies ensures them a separate station in society' (cited in Hurst 1950: 250). He goes on to argue that lawyers are the 'aristocracy' in the USA because they are united by this common tie and the rich are not. Mills (1956) argues similarly that 'the higher cliques of lawyers and investment bankers are the active *political* heads of the corporate rich and members of the power elite' (p. 291; my emphasis). This view must, I think, be displaced in favour of a more adequate resolution of the contradictory evidence which has emerged from this selective reading of the wealth of materials available. The contradictory evidence is that lawyers do, in the course of giving advice in all kinds of strategic sites, help to formulate policy. Legal advice is not innocent and 'simply' technical. On the other hand, as Heinz and Laumann (1982) and Nelson (1988) argue, and as revealed by the inside stories of Hoffman (1973) and Stewart (1983), large law firms are in a relation of extreme dependence on their one, two or three large corporate clients. That is why after winning a prolonged anti-trust case for IBM, the partner in charge, at Cravath, Swaine and Moore, 'entered to applause'. A separate office had been set up and staffed for the duration of the case. That is why the loss of Kodak as a client, following the loss (later reversed on appeal) of an anti-trust case was a major disaster for the firm of Donovan, Leisure, Newton and Irvine, despite the fact that their other corporate clients included American Cynamid, Mobil, Ford and Walt Disney. They were 'saved' by gaining the massive new client, Westinghouse (Stewart 1983).

How, then, do lawyers 'make policy' as dependants? They do it crucially by (1) translating the objectives and demands of clients into an acceptable legal discourse and (2) by expanding that discourse – by the well-tried means of distinguishing their client's situation from that of decided cases or from that apparently described in a statute, or alternatively by likening their case to those in which an outcome that would be acceptable was achieved, by the processes of negotiation of 'sameness' and analogy. Goodrich (1986) has admirably described these modes of reasoning which are acceptable within and which constitute legal discourse.

Lawyers therefore receive from clients instructions of the order 'find a defence for me within the ambit of "I did it" ' (Mann 1985: 48). They may offer an initial resistance, as did the lawyer for the bank in my 1979 study, when pressed to find a way in which a bank could legally secure the eviction of an apparently protected tenant. But at least they can discover that 'the decided cases relative to the question all turn on the individual facts' (Cain 1979: 351); in other words, that there is legal room for manoeuvre.

This is to say that lawyers are imaginative traders in words. But these symbol traders are also creative. They *invent categories and these categories are constitutive of practices and institutions* within which their clients can achieve their objectives. As Hurst (1970) argues, the law, or as we might say lawyers' symbolic inventions, contributed to the 'pacification' of stockholders in the USA. Between 1890 and 1930, the law 'weakened' the shareholders' capacity for effective oversight of productive and financial activities; for example, shareholder voting power was whittled away by corporate articles which elaborated the share structure so that only one class of stock had voting rights. Or wide discretion, for example to effect mergers, could be vested in a simple majority of shares, so that the company could be led from the centre if holdings were diffuse (ibid.: 93). While the Securities and Exchange Act of 1934 set limits to this discretion, crucially by establishing rules (which have given rise to much lucrative litigation) about the information which should be made available to shareholders, lawyers' constitution building had already established the basic framework of the company within which capital would for the time being exist and expand, and by which it would be constituted. This implies that capital does pre-exist its legal constitution, at least in the minds and intentions of those who would constitute it as somehow available for their use. The need for capital is imagined by its potential users. They may even identify a possible source. But the constitution of that source *as* capital requires a practice which is, these days, largely a legal practice. And if *new* kinds of guarantees and inducements are given, then we may speak not only of the legal constitution but also of the legal invention of a new form for capital. Lawyers *invent relationships*. This is their special skill, their indispensable contribution to capital. As Gordon has expressed it, lawyers have devised:

> . . . new forms of security financing (the trust receipt, the equipment trust certificate, the 'open end' mortgage that secures an indefinite amount of issueable bonds); new forms of corporate securities (preferred stock, no part stock convertible debentures) which offered

diverse risks and opportunities and thus attracted many different kinds of investors; and new forms of corporate organisation (the trust, the pool, the joint traffic association, the holding company, the patent agreement).

(Gordon 1983: 80)

He argues further that 'it has yet to be established that this technical contribution was of causal significance in determining strategies and structures of enterprise', indicating that the business world itself does not accord it such a place. In this regard, the business world may well be right. The business world's experienced need for investment and resources in order to compete and expand is anterior to the legal inventions, and these inventions themselves are responses to very specific investment problems, arising in a particular socio-economic and a particular political situation – a situation with specific tax laws, specific potential resources seen to be available, unmobilized investments of the particular types and durations required and, as Hurst argued, investments carrying or able to demand (for the world external to the lawyer's office is not still and passive) control rights over their resource after it has been constituted as capital.

Indeed, there is ample evidence that since both capital and the lawyers began their rapid expansion (Auerbach 1976), this creative relation has been crucial. From the early days of the eighteenth century, particularly after the death of Lord Chancellor Holt, judges might, like Judge Lee of the King's Bench, 'invite the assistance of the merchants to ensure decisions which, while in harmony with legal principle, should foster and not retard their trade' (Fifoot, 1936/1977: 23). It took Lord Mansfield, however, to realize the importance of creating more or less generalizable rules from the mass of particular decisions. Sometimes, as in the case of contract, this involved the creation of a general framework 'not to dictate but to interpret and sanction' (ibid: 118), because Mansfield 'realised that the merchant was more competent than the lawyer to prescribe the form of a charter-party, or to direct the incidence of paper credit' (p. 118). But I do not wish to construct my own teleological account. The merchants might have found the authoritative-imaginative support they needed elsewhere; the quasi-feudal aristocratic bar might have been successful in its resistance to this new class alliance [as it was, ultimately, in the case of conveyancing, which most nearly touched the landed interests (ibid.: ch. 6)]. But Mansfield had patronage as his weapon in securing the support of other judges, plus the wealth-giving business which alliance with the merchant-capitalist class carried in its train. He organized the discourse of judgment away from scholasticist attention to outward signs of conformity (details of technical observances) towards general but malleable principles or rules, and streamlined procedure (processes of decision making) as a means both of securing the business of the new client class and securing the position of his supporters. It was a century before the sites of judgment were fully brought into correspondence with this new discourse (the Judicature Acts of 1875). And it was also a hundred years before the ideology of 'the profession' – of *the autonomous servant* – developed to express the contradictory relation then established between lawyers and their increasingly needed new clients. But Mansfield and the new-wave judges, finding their arguments where they could (from continental lawyers, from the clients, from the past) had secured the contradictory place of the symbol traders in their creative and dependent relations with capital.

I am not saying that this relation was necessary for capitalism: capitalism need not have got off the ground, could have taken different organizational forms, could have relied on (as in part it does) different groups of people for the innovative symbolic work which, in the event, enabled it to expand. Indeed, we have two modern examples revealing the non-determined character of the relation. First, we have Hadden's (1983, 1984) impressive analysis of contemporary international corporate enterprises. Apart from gasping at their size and complexity,[9] Hadden hints in his text that the legal form of the relationship between strings of subsidiary and affinally related companies does not any longer correspond to their operating practice. This practice is functionally structured, and now largely bypasses the apparent quasi-autonomy which the legal form of each subsidiary company supplies. In other words, at this level, lawyers may no longer be those who invent the form within which capital can exist and expand: the new inventors may be other executives and administrators, while lawyers perform a more defensive role in relation to tax laws and so on. I do not know. But in the light of Hadden, this is one plausible guess. The connections with the lawyering occupation, I am saying, can be shown to have existed and to have played a vital role. This does not mean that these connections between capital and lawyers as an occupational category are necessary or inevitable. Moreover, it is clear that capitalists themselves have increasingly come to prefer that some of their disputes should be settled by fellow capitalists rather than by lawyers (Ferguson 1980; Sarat and Silbey 1992; see also Dezalay, this volume). Yet professional justice is still used when legal inventions are challenged, or need to be secured.

The second modern example is the expanding European Community (EC). Here a new political vehicle is daily being created, with an explicitly *economic* purpose. But in this emergent enterprise, lawyers have an ever-increasing role as 'harmonization' of laws affecting trade continues apace. As Donner said:

> . . . in the movement of the enterprise [the EEC] to which he [*sic*] has put his shoulder, he will swiftly sense the right direction if not the

right words and expressions. If he does not he will soon meet economists and politicians who will tell him what aims to follow and what
role to play.

(Donner 1968: 58)

Let me belabour an important point. This does not mean that the EC will
be successful (whatever historical success may mean); nor does it mean
that lawyers will continue always to have a central place within the
processes of its development. But they do seem, at the moment, to be
inventing symbolic forms which are not only constitutive of new economic relations, but which also create a new kind of political expression
compatible with and encouraging of these new relationships.

None of this, of course, is what most lawyers do most of the time,
although if I am right it is given to far more people than had been supposed to be the architects of the structure of emergent history. But there is
evidence (Cain 1979; McBarnet 1984) that lawyers do translation work as
a matter of routine, and that they do at least quasi-creative work – constituting the facts of their case and showing how it 'therefore' falls within a
rule or does not (Rodell 1939; Goodrich 1986) – very often indeed. Mann
(1985) has also shown incontrovertibly that these techniques can indeed
be activated by those with adequate resources in relation to more everyday law work than raising and securing new forms of investment (capital). For well-heeled white-collar offenders in the USA, procedure is
adversarial up to and even *after* conviction. By a skilful constitution of the
facts of the case (control of information) and exploitation of the 'ambiguity' (ibid.: 203) in the typical white-collar crime statute, successful defences can be mounted and the law itself expanded.

The argument, therefore, is that this characteristic relationship of
creativity plus dependence was itself invented in eighteenth-century Britain
(and doubtless elsewhere – by diffusion or spontaneous generation) as a
means of securing and adequately responding to the requirements of a
particular class of clients who were both making persistent demands for
assistance, coupled with (later) threats of taking their business elsewhere.
The needs of capital meshed with a career opportunity (see, in particular,
Larson 1977). So were two configurations of very different scope (a class
and an occupation) articulated. The complexity of this articulation was
such that it was not secured until a century or more later when 'the
profession' was invented (by the members) as a means of holding on to a
creative space, a space which is not capable of being discursively closed
from outside, while at the same time remaining client-powered. *'The profession' resolved the contradiction between creativity and dependence*, a process
in which the particular formulation of its ethical rules remains crucial. In
so doing, it also reaffirmed the privileged connection between lawyering
and that part of the state which is constituted by activations of the law, for

the site of creativity was also the site of autonomy, the site which allegedly no client could penetrate, the space in which lawyers are neutral if inventive technicians. Professionalism secures the legitimacy and 'neutrality' of authoritative legal inventions on behalf of capital, as it makes professionals ideal discursive goers between two key configurations: capital and the state, the economy and the polity.

SECTION 2   SYMBOL TRADING AND REPRESSED KNOWLEDGES

Can anyone play? Lawyers, capital and the poor

This account, for all of its kaleidoscopic nature, describes the relationships between lawyers and capital. Most lawyers and most capitalists would probably agree with it, and also add 'so what?' What the account so far does not do is explain whether or not lawyers can do the same job for other groups of people. Is capital just one client, or a particularly favoured client, or is the lawyer–capital relation constitutive of lawyering itself? From the standpoint of the downsiders, an answer to this question is absolutely essential, and for that answer it is necessary to turn first to the classical theorists to get ideas for an elaborated explanatory map.[10] It is also helpful to abandon scholarly chronology and to begin with Max Weber.

Weber's work is, of course, far too complex to be captured in a summary. But no more is appropriate in the context of the present discussion. He argued that capitalism and the formally rational form of law developed together, but that neither caused the other. Capitalism needed predictability over time in its commercial relationships. Lawyers, already available in the environment, were harnessed to this enterprise. But most importantly in the context of this chapter, he discusses two critical relationships: that between the way lawyers are trained and the form the law takes, and that between the organization of practice and the content of law.

In mainland Europe, the institutionalization of legal training in academic departments led to 'pure', formal, logical legal rationality. The lawyers developed an academic orientation to conceptual purity as their main objective. There were, indeed, sometimes difficulties if the real world did not fit the categories thus elaborated. The 'emancipation of legal thinking from the everyday needs of the public' could produce anomalous and unworkable outcomes (Weber 1954: 205). None the less, Weber considers this mode of reasoning, generated in this context, to be the most advanced form of law.

The paradox which he himself identified was that the Common Law mode of formal extrinsic rational law was ultimately better for capitalism.

Not only did capitalism develop first in England where the Common Law system prevailed, but in Canada where both alternatives were available in the environment, the Common Law mode was chosen:

> . . . the essential similarity of the capitalist development on the Continent and in England has not been able to eliminate the sharp contrasts between the two types of legal system. Nor is there any visible tendency towards a transformation of the English system in the direction of the continental under the impetus of the capitalist economy. On the contrary, wherever the two kinds of administration of justice and of legal training have had the opportunity to compete with each other, as for instance in Canada, the Common Law has come out on top and has overcome the continental alternative rather quickly. We may thus conclude that capitalism has not been a decisive factor in the promotion of that form of rationalization of the law which has been peculiar to the continental West ever since the rise of Romanist studies in the mediaeval universities.
>
> (Weber 1954: 318)

In exploring the explanation of a finding so damaging to his theory, Weber points to a special relationship between the law and its users in the UK, a relationship in which capitalists as clients bring problems to the legal profession, and legal solutions are developed in a 'bottom-up' way. Thus new law is developed which is exactly attuned to the needs of the clients, who happen to be an expanding user class, emergent capitalists.

This case-by-case method was extremely expensive, so a second, non-rational system developed alongside it for those who could not pay – the courts of the lay magistrates – where 'finding' a decision could be done cheaply and expeditiously, without all this regard for predictability. But the development of the legal discourse itself was 'aimed at a practically useful scheme of contracts and actions oriented to the interests of clients in typically recurrent situations' (Weber 1954: ch. VII).

This sounds very like what has been described here, and it certainly shaped my own thinking as I read the eulogies, the professional studies, and so on. But as a theory it has both problems and implications. It lacks a more general concept for the kind of work that lawyers do. This inhibits any theorization of their practice, accepts lawyers' own conception of their uniqueness, leaves them for ever separated theoretically from other occupational groups, and implies that such a unique theorization is necessary for all other occupations too.

The Weberian view also assumes that any users with 'continually recurrent problems' can activate the legal system in their interests. This is precisely the question of course. It implies that if the unemployed or black mothers or the urban poor were given sufficient legal aid to turn them into repeat players (Galanter 1974), then the law would be elaborated to suit their needs in exactly the same way as it has come to fit the needs of capital. Weber's view expresses the conventional liberal position and we need to know whether or not that approach could work in order to decide where to direct our energies. A further implication of this Weberian position is that both the legal form and the legal process are neutral. Power lies *outside* them. The law is a neutral apparatus, to be used by whomsoever has the wherewithal.

Surprisingly (given his fall from intellectual grace), it is Marx who provides us with a concept which both links lawyers to other occupational groups and enables us to grasp their creative work. His concept of 'conceptive ideologists' is coined in *Theories of Surplus Value*.[11] He did not apply it to lawyers (whom he regarded as 'unproductive') and he did not develop the idea. He applied the concept to scientists and others who do creative thinking which is intrinsic to the production process, although he argues too that, as it becomes stronger, the bourgeoisie gives 'recognition to the ideological professions as flesh of its flesh' (Marx 1905/1969: 301). In this respect, Gramsci's (1972) conception of the 'organic intellectual' is extremely close. Distinguishing the organic intellectuals from traditional intellectuals (who are politically maverick and not to be trusted), Gramsci argued that organic intellectuals maintain institutionalized or regular relationships with a particular social class, such that they are integral members of it and have regular experiential knowledge of that class and its problems. These are also their own experiences and their own problems, demanding a solution. For Gramsci, administrators and managers – as well as scientists – are organic intellectuals of the bourgeois class, making it possible for class problems to be solved and so for the class to advance. Managers and administrators invent organizational solutions to problems; they invent methods of record-keeping; in modern times they have invented rapid international communication. Crucially, they are creative. They develop new forms of relationship, new practices and, of course, new names for them and ways of thinking about them. They literally *think* the advance of the class they are related to.

Lawyers, it seems, stand in precisely this relation to capital. They invent new forms of relationship and new forms of existence for capital, new practices, new institutions, from the IMF to a trust fund, from an executive director to a holding company.

Gramsci saw the work of the organic intellectual or conceptive ideologist (I prefer the latter term, but used in relation to Gramsci's concept) as creative. Thus Gramsci solves the first of the Weberian difficulties – for now, a lawyer, a chemist, an accountant and a chief executive can all be seen in terms of the same theory, as conceptive ideologists. The occupations have their specificities too, but we have a way of articulating them. We are beyond occupational nominalism. But the second question, as to whether anyone can use lawyers to do conceptive ideological work for them remains open.

The third question, too, remains open, for while the elaborations of conceptive ideologists plainly produce solutions to class-specific problems, does that necessarily mean that other classes and groups cannot use these inventions? A fax machine would work just as well for a shop-floor worker if she had the need and opportunity to use it, as it does for an executive. Is the law like that? These two questions cannot be answered from within classical theory. I will turn to Michel Foucault, the first of the post-moderns and in some ways the last of the classical modernists,[12] for some further insights before proposing a realist resolution.

Foucault (1970) argues that 'the fundamental codes of a culture', such as what it means to say that you know something, are constituted by communication rather than revealed by it. They are discursive constructions. So sexuality is different in classical Greece from the empire; our own assumptions about what is natural have a very short history (Foucault 1978, 1985, 1986). These are not different ways of speaking about a sexuality that already exists. They constitute it as what it is, give it its emotions, its practices, its abnormalities and its silences. Whatever else they are, the ways of speaking, the discourses, are not neutral. Discourse, on the contrary, is always powerful, a device in which each term constitutes a value, in which each name implies a course of action in relation to the named, in which statements take their meaning from their place in a field of statements, from their relationships within the discourse itself.

Foucault also posits an intimate connection between a discourse and the site of its enunciation. Such sites are constituted within the discourse itself as places from which the discourse may be spoken. The court is integral to the discourse of law, not a separate, independently existing place to which the law and the issues are brought. In the same way, the procedures of law constitute its being; they, too, cannot be separated from the substance they express. Foucault himself (1977: 217) argues that popular justice cannot be possible with a procedure that 'belongs to the bourgeois ideology of justice' and a discourse that calls judges into being. For the discursively constituted judge and court are precisely that: enunciators of a specific discourse which excludes the populace from judging and authorizes someone else – a judge – to do this on their behalf. A discourse may form the objects of which it speaks, but equally systematically it excludes the objects of which it cannot speak. Court room ethnographies from Carlen (1976) to Cain (1986) have shown how what is relevant to many plaintiffs and defendants cannot be heard, cannot be made sense of, cannot be allowed to be spoken in legal discourse. That you thought what you took would not be missed is not relevant, that before you were forced to migrate from Uganda you were a respected citizen is not relevant, and so on. The discourse of law does not correspond with everyday thought except in those areas of life, such as the stock exchange, where the legal form has constituted what is everyday.

Add to this the much earlier insight that the subject of law cannot be a person-in-relationships but must be a person lifted out of the relational context which constitutes her (Pashukanis 1980); the arguments that the law is intrinsically gendered, that 'a reasonable woman . . . with her sex eliminated is altogether too abstract a notion for my comprehension' (Allen 1987: 23); that the law is endemically racist (Fitzpatrick 1992); that the discourse of collective justice where it can be found constitutes quite different objects, subjects and theories from the professionalized mode (Cain 1985) – and it begins to be clear that lawyers cannot simply be hired to do conceptive ideological work for any old body. The very procedures which they have constituted as the law shape who is most likely to appear as a defendant (those vulnerable to the on-street exercise of police discretion) and who as a plaintiff (those whose dispute has some 'real law' in it).

These are the considerations which a reading of Foucault prompts: discourses constitute a field in which statements can be made and can mean; in so doing they exclude. Once madness has been medicalized, people who release toxic substances into the environment in the course of production processes are not mad. The discourse of insanity is not constituted by and cannot be expanded to contain such acts. So with the law. The uncertainties which beset the poor cannot be rendered predictable by law as can the uncertainties of capital. It is only selectively that the law can deal with the problems of the poor. It can deal in general with the problems of capital. And the reason for this is that the law has either constituted or recognized the modes of existence of capital. What capital 'is' at a point in time and what the law is are the same. There is an integral relationship between law and capital, brought about by lawyers. But *there is no such relationship of reciprocal constitution between the law and poverty.* The being of poverty lies elsewhere.

Foucault, and the considerations prompted by his approach, enable us to answer the two outstanding questions posed by the presumptions of Max Weber. Is the legal form neutral? No: no discursive form is neutral. Is the legal process neutral? No: the legal form and the legal process are intrinsically not extrinsically related. In this situation, can people other than agents of capital activate lawyers to do conceptive ideological work for them? One reading of Foucault says yes: wherever there is power there is resistance; at all points in the web of discursively constituted relations resistance is possible, changes can be made.

This reading can be challenged empirically, by a recognition that the law specifically allocates unsatisfactory places to the urban poor, forever vulnerable to the licensed discretion of police officers, officially unscrutinized procedural practices, devices constructed at a range of sites in order legally to silence them.[13] Other downsiders often fare similarly. And the gift of the gab, discursive facility, the argumentative skills of a Clarence Darrow or a D.N. Pritt do not seem capable of putting that right. It seems that that unexpected 'extra discursive', so frequently invoked in Foucault's works, after all has a part to play (e.g. Foucault 1972).[14]

This is a depressing picture, albeit convincing. Is there a ray of hope? Is there anything to be done? People have, of course, found their own solutions:

1 Using law selectively in those areas where it *can* help (making wills, buying houses, claiming recompense for injury, discrimination).
2 Developing alternative ways of resolving issues, some of them pre-figurative of an alternative 'legal' form.
3 Creating situations of dual power wherein alternatives may be developed.
4 Avoiding anything that smacks of the law at all costs.

But radical lawyers still ask: what can we do? I am not as pessimistic as the logic of the Foucauldian argument requires. But to move beyond pessimism it is necessary to allow for the existence of intransitive relation-ships, that is relationships which exist independently of anyone's 'knowl-edge' of them. Some discomfort in the working environment must have been experienced before women, gathering courage to try and share these unspoken experiences, invented the object of sexual harassment as part of a discourse of feminism. Once the discursive recognition/invention has occurred, the relationships become transitive: amenable to discursive or practical intervention. The conceptive ideologists here were feminist women, not lawyers. It seems that experienced needs (e.g. for money to maintain an army) lead to the invention of a relationship (like 'taxpayer' in this era). The relationship which generates the experience may be intransitive (not previously present to anyone's consciousness) or it may be transitive and sedimented, or it may be transitive and new.

With these rather rudimentary understandings in our discursive armoury, let us now look back at what we have garnered up about lawyers from the empirical and theoretical kaleidoscopic excursions. While it is impossible to add concepts from different theories or dis-courses, it is inevitable that ideas will be gathered from all over the place as one reads, and it is more fruitful as well as more honest to display that process of both accretion and rejection. It is fruitful because knowledge is not lost if the rich connotations of the terms are re-situated and given new meaning in the context of a new theory.

Playing a different game on the old court

From a realist perspective, discourse has potency but not primacy. Since discourse and discursive practices are social in character, discourse and discursive practices themselves are constituted in and by relationships. Not only, then, is discourse constitutive of relationships and institutions, as lawyers' discourse has been shown to be in these pages, but also relationships are constitutive of discourse, as well as conditions of existence for its emergence and persistence. Capital, for example – the potential for capital – is produced in a productive relationship which exists independently of legal discourse. Lawyers, because of their monopoly of judging and thereby access to the use of state force, and their historical experience as land and property agents (Birks 1960; see Sugarman, this volume), proved ideal allies in providing capital with forms of existence in which it could both expand and be adequately protected. Both lawyers and capitalists it must be supposed, identified advantages for themselves in the relationship or it would not have happened. This is where Larson's (1977) and Abel's (1985a, 1988b) argument about the profession seeking to expand the market for its services becomes relevant, as well as Lord Mansfield's accumen and foresight (cited at pp. 34–5). Hurst captures the argument:

> The corporate instrument proved useful to economic growth and materially affected its character by encouraging multiplication of ventures and by assisting the larger scale of enterprise for which technology and expanding markets supplied the prime dynamics.
>
> (Hurst 1970: 156)

There are three points to make about these developments which enable us to theorize them without imposing the notion of cause.[15] First, it has become clear that law is constitutive of the forms of existence of capital. But the discursive forms are not all that there is to be said about the matter. Capital can also be understood as a configuration of relationships which enables surpluses generated in the processes of production and exchange to be used to produce further surpluses. It is not static.

These relationships are mostly not lived independently of the discourses in which they are variously expressed, in which legal discourse plays a considerable part. But the fact that relationships are expressed in discourse does not mean that they are only discourse, and certainly does not mean that discourse 'causes' them or calls them into being. The relationships and the discourse must be understood both separately and together. Each has its own potency. Good arguments alone will not change relationships. Copernicus' ideas needed a technical invention – the telescope – a climate of opinion open to challenges to the established order, and a Galileo before they were accepted (Feyerabend 1975; Diamond 1986). And new forms of relationships alone may not survive unless an adequate discursive form for their existence can be elaborated. It is more helpful, I believe, to think of micro- or local hegemonies rather than *either* discourse *or* relationships, a choice which leads to an unanswerable chicken-and-egg question. These micro-hegemonies, moments of synthetic unity between discourse and relationships, may be better termed *discrels* to avoid the negative connotation of indestructibility imported by later usages of Gramsci's concept.

Such a line of reasoning helps us to understand Hadden's (1984) point, that international conglomerates increasingly function independently of their legal forms of existence. Their capital may be constituted legally, but the managerial line is increasingly independent of the companies' legal form. Since managerial decisions are also part of what capital 'is', it would seem here that relationships have developed independently of legal discourse, albeit perhaps in terms of another one.

This is my second point. Conceptualizing the situation in terms of local hegemonies makes it possible to map the interplay between discourses and patterns of relationships, between struggle and change. And it is not discourses or knowledges alone which give power, but also the relationships which they constitute, certainly, but in which also they are embedded. I am suggesting that a relational network can hold back a discourse, or facilitate its elaboration; that a discourse can hold back the development of relationships, or facilitate their elaboration. In the Hadden example, it seems that the company (legal) structure could have inhibited the development of relations of capital.

Thirdly, once moving beyond giving causal primacy to discourse (surely in itself a contradiction in the post-modern position) it becomes possible to see capital and law as *reciprocally* constitutive. It is not just capital which is given its form by law, but law is given its form also by capital. And law, too, should be conceived as a complex set of relationships shaped and constituted by a discursive practice, but not consisting only of discourse.

The developments and relationships mapped and variously formulated in this chapter can now be seen as a continuous movement to establish a discrel, an isomorphism between relationships and discourse, which forever threatens to break apart. For as well as the substantive changes in law to which so much attention has been given, there were also, in this process of discrel creation, changes in the form of organization of the occupational group, as the situation of autonomous dependence was discursively and relationally invented.

The large law firm in the USA and the up-or-out zig-zag were relational inventions doubtless thought through in terms of commonsense discourses of obvious convenience. The political zigger-zagger was also connected, it seems, with the international expansion of capital and the production of international political conditions of existence which could facilitate that expansion. Practices were established which closed not only the resultant contradiction between autonomy and dependence, but also the discursive rift between creativity and constancy, brought to light by the eulogies. There have also been changes in the sites of judgment, and continuous struggle over these, although in the UK the Judicature Acts of 1875 brought them into temporary alignment with the rest of legal discursive practice. The relations constituting the courts, the professional relationships, the relationships of practice, all served to foreclose by efficient policing of the discursive boundaries the ruptures which those two massive discursive contradictions might have brought about.

Discourses, then, have constitutive potency but not primacy over relationships. Relationships constitute but do not cause discursive practices. It is necessary instead to think of reciprocal constitution and partially independent potencies.

It is now possible to return to the issue of whether lawyers can be conceptive ideologists for those situated outside the relationships which constitute capital. The realist position I have elaborated, because it is explicitly non-causal, allowing no primacy even to discourse, offers more room for manoeuvre.

If we are thinking in terms of micro-hegemonies, in specific fields or configurations of relationships, then it seems that downsiders, too, need their conceptive ideologists, their discursive inventors, not to take on the law – often not central to their worries – but to meet their needs as best they can by conceptual and institutional creativity. Such inventions already include cooperatives, credit unions, ethnic schools, women's groups, trades unions, law centres, reciprocal child minding and neighbourhood tea parties. The discourse of Marxism did not turn out to be an appropriate vehicle for understanding these developments. The emergent discourses and institutional inventions of feminism seem likely to do better, despite the dangers of class co-optation. Ex-colonial societies are struggling with, against and through European forms of law. They are needed for trade, but undermine indigenous forms of social order. Some societies, such as Mozambique, are attempting to produce new legal forms which will help develop new indigenous culture from the old (Sachs and Welch 1987).

What is involved in this process of constructing relationships and a discourse that works towards justice as the underprivileged, the downsiders, see it? Plainly they cannot simply activate the institutions and discourses that exist. The structure of the courts, the organization of the practitioners, the procedures, the rules, the rules about the making of rules, the whole discursive and relational apparatus that constitutes the law militates against the routine use of the system by downsiders. Sometimes this appears to have been purposive, as in the creation of legal spaces for police discretion to make public order arrests. Sometimes this exclusion of downsiders appears more as the inevitable corollary of the integrity of law and capital. So while the system is indeed capable of occasional use by downsiders with spectacular effects, this *cannot* be what the system is about in its day-to-day work. If downsider outcomes were produced every day, the system would be a different one, an unrecognizable one, in which courts, procedures, rules, rules about the making of rules, and practitioner organization were all different. If every case went for trial, if all the rules and procedures were elaborated to achieve outcomes chosen by downsiders, there would be administrative chaos, capital would take its business elsewhere, and doubtless cries of loss of legitimacy and unreasonable behaviour by professionals – at the least. Integrity between law and capital would be broken.

This fantasy tale reveals both the possibilities and the problems in producing a form of justice appropriate to the needs of downsiders. Let us go back again to the new theoretical premise, concerning the integrity of relationships and discourse, and the potency of both. The implication is that change can begin with either relationships or discourse, but that since they are reciprocally constitutive, they have to be brought along together in mutual support and ultimately into 'obvious' alignment. If an attempt is made to change one without the other, it will be short-lived. If an attempt is made to change the discourse without changing relationships, only exceptional cases can get through. If an attempt is made to change relationships without changing the discourse, then the changes are vulnerable to attack as unprofessional or to co-optation (Cain 1985). So political work to produce change must engage with each and both. All the organizational relationships constituting rule making, decision making, legal services, procedures and occupational organization can be changed, as can the discourses which in part constitute them. The law *can* be made to work for downsiders. We are never stuck with what is. But changing the discourse is only one essential part of what is required.

Secondly, it follows that if both relationships and discourse are changed, whatever follows will not look like 'law' as we know it. Something else will have been brought about, even if it is still called law. This has happened before, of course, within the European legal system. In the British example, the royal prerogative court of the Star Chamber, and the later decision making by magistrates in the studies of their houses, would not be recognized as legal now in either form or substance, discourse or relationships. The rules, procedures, institutions, adjudicative sites, and the organization of practitioners were so completely different as to signify a discursive and relational rupture between seventeenth-century and nineteenth-century law, yet we have no evidence that the reformers saw their changes in this way. Indeed, the new system was and is constantly legitimated by reference to tradition.

Seron's (1992) work suggests that nothing so radical is happening today in alternative law practices in the USA. Indeed, those she studied appear to be bastion's of tradition. Theoretically, this should not surprise us, since resistance to changes in form from below is located both in the profession and in those sections of society which are major users and beneficiaries of the existing system, and who would prefer themselves to steer and monitor the shape and direction of change. However, the belief that no alternative is possible or conceivable, that the structural and legitimacy problems are insurmountable, itself acts as a brake or downsider initiatives (Cain 1985).

The second point, then, is that changing relationships and discourses is not only possible but very radical in its consequences. There are also reverses and alternatives. Each struggle has a range of possible outcomes, and almost infinite possible modes of discursive constitution. The trick is to find *both* a good way of saying *and* a possible relational nexus to target for change.

Social scientists as well as lawyers, religious, ethnic and other community leaders, and the organizers of women have a part to play here. Lawyers as presently constituted may lose their precedence, for the direction must emerge from downsider organizations. But their defensive function will remain necessary, and their contribution to producing collective and creative ways of understanding downsider justice will be their deep understanding of the present system and its limitations.

Such movements already exist, and are working towards that moment when the integrity of the law–capital relation will be broken. 'Law' then will not look like THE law; nor will it relegate the same people to silence.

Acknowledgements

I wish to thank all my friends and colleagues at the Institute of Criminology in Cambridge where I completed the research for this paper before leaving to live in the West Indies. I also wish to thank Ms Helen Alexander and Ms Yvonne Narinesingh for their forbearance when the disks, the fax machine, the printer and the author ceased to function, as well as for their energy and skill.

Notes

1 For a theoretical elaboration of the concept of standpoint as I deploy it, see Cain (1990) and Smith (1987).
2 I owe this term to Val Kerruish, who developed it as a useful generic for those 'on the downside of social relations' (Kerruish 1991).
3 This term, too, is borrowed, this time from Liz Stanley (1987).
4 The famous historian E.H. Carr (1961) pointed out that it is impossible to read the past without a vision of the future. In the same spirit, it is impossible to read the present unless one has a similar vision.
5 Sources used in formulating my account included Bancroft (1939), Birkett (1961), Bowker (1961), Ffyfe (1964), Grimshaw and Jones (1958), Hyde (1964), Macmillan (1937), Maugham (1954), Morris (1930), Pollock (1934) and Ward (n.d.). A recent American source that supports the argument is Clifford (1991).

6 I do not mean to imply that all the studies discussed in this section are empiricist; simply that the concept of the professional has an empiricist foundation.

7 Similar arguments from this period can be found in Shanks (1949), Burck (1957a, b), Hickman (1957), O'Meara (1962) and Grahame (1963).

8 Gordon's (1983) work elaborates on this position. It is discussed, however, in the next section of this chapter.

9 The Bowater Group, for example, consisted of 283 active as well as many dormant companies at the time of Hadden's study.

10 See Cain (1990, 1992) for a discussion of theoretical mapping as an alternative to causal theory.

11 As indicated earlier (p. 16), this Marxist concept has played a considerable part in my own account.

12 See Cain (1993).

13 See McBarnet (1981) and Lees (this volume) for a discussion of how the discretion secreted within the spaces purposively or accidentally constituted by legal rules makes it impossible for poor people or women to use law effectively.

14 Dreyfus and Rabinow (1982) argue that the extra-discursive plays a more considerable role in Foucault's later works than in the *Archaeology*, where such practices are none the less involved as the environment of discursive practices.

15 See note 10 above regarding discussions of the possibility of non-causal theory.

2 Outlining a theory of
legal practice

Christine B. Harrington

Introduction

In his introduction to Benjamin Twiss' study of how *laissez-faire* came to the Supreme Court, Edward Corwin turns to Judge Baldwin's famous dictum on how law is developed: 'The development of law . . . is primarily the work of the lawyer. It is the adoption by the judge of what is proposed at the bar' (Twiss 1942: x). Lawyers as a group, Twiss argues, forged the critical link between *laissez-faire* political philosophy and constitutional categories, such as property and contract. In this view, lawyers figure heavily in 'the stuff the law is made of'.[1] Surprisingly few books have been written since about the role of lawyers in the development of law. On the one hand, political scientists and historians, in biographies and accounts of Supreme Court decisions, have placed the judge at the centre of law-making, emphasizing judicial decisions over the work of lawyers and their litigation strategies.[2] On the other, traditional American legal scholarship speaks of doctrinal formation as the development of logically related concepts, autonomous from politics, formulated and practised by disinterested professionals. Critical histories of legal structure, however, describe the development of doctrine differently, emphasizing contradictory concepts embedded in liberal legalism. Karl Klare (1978), for example, argues that New Deal labour jurisprudence was an uneasy merger between nineteenth-century legal formalism and a result-orientated Progressive era politics. Yet similar to traditional doctrinal studies, critical legal histories pay little attention to the role of lawyers in shaping or maintaining doctrine.[3]

Recently, social scientists, particularly those closer to a law and society perspective, have moved away from looking at law simply in terms of judicial opinions or doctrinal formulations, the law-centred approach. In contrast, the legal pluralism approach views legal developments as a product of more than just what the judge says or what lawyers are able to get past them. For legal pluralists in general, law includes the 'unwritten yet well understood codes defining standards of behaviour in industrial enterprises and business transaction, among neighbours, and within universities, churches, or public bureaucracies' (Arthurs 1985: 2).[4] A range of social institutions and interactions that were once treated as informal and private are now viewed as sources of legal authority.

Although we now consider material that has been traditionally cast as private parties or outside the law in our investigations of law, like the old law-centred paradigm, the new legal pluralism framework tends to de-emphasize what Twiss and Corwin believed to be important in the development of law – lawyers. This is not to suggest that lawyers have been ignored altogether. On the contrary, frequent reference to de Tocqueville's thesis regarding the political power of lawyers in the USA[5] testifies to the fact that social scientists are interested in the *power* of the legal profession in American politics. We remain fascinated with the extent to which lawyers have or have not retained their hold on American politics.

Studies of lawyers as decision makers in state legislatures (Derge 1959) and the American Bar Association's (ABA) impact on national legislation (Melone 1979), for example, point to the leadership role lawyers play in American politics.[6] Studies of ABA efforts to gain influence over the federal judicial recruitment and selection process suggest that the legal profession is a privileged private actor in American politics (Grossman 1965), if not a private government (Gilb 1966). As part of the research tradition seeking to broaden our understanding of law beyond the decisions of judges or the rules of law expressed in doctrine, this work refines, in important ways, the common wisdom that American lawyers are a powerful group in national policy making (Nelson and Heinz 1988).

These efforts to investigate the role of lawyers and their professional power in politics, however, exclude the obvious – information on what lawyers do, the content of the law they forge. It is therefore perhaps not surprising that the divide between 'law in the books' and 'law in action' remains alive and well. Studies of doctrinal formation lack sociolegal significance and studies of lawyers lack a comprehension of the content of the law lawyers create.

This may also be due to the fact that Judge Baldwin's assertion – the development of law is primarily the work of lawyers – begs the question. It leaves open the issue of what lawyers do in the development of law. To answer the question, to get at that sociolegal significance of law, one might examine doctrines from particular fields of law, like administrative law, to see if they reflect interests similar to those of the legal profession. Yet, even if we were able to reduce the challenge to a mechanical task of connecting lawyers with doctrine,[7] we would be approaching the problem from the wrong angle. My research has convinced me that the legal profession is central to the development of administrative law, but professional interests are not 'found' in the law.[8] Interests are rooted in and transformed by the political struggles of pre-established institutional arrangements both internal and external to the legal profession.

This chapter is part of a larger project investigating the connection between the practice of law and the content of doctrine through an analysis of political struggles and institutional arrangements that shaped the administrative state. In administrative law, the primary struggle is over who (lawyers and non-lawyers) will represent the government, corporations and individuals affected by administrative regulation and in what settings (agencies and courts). This struggle frames the institutional position and ideological boundaries of administrative law. It reveals the formation of administrative law practice, its constitution in the institutional arrangements of the legal profession and the administrative state.

My starting point in this investigation is to articulate theoretical foundations for an alternative view of legal practice, one that does not separate those engaged in legal practice from the substances of legal and political development. I begin by describing functionalist and structuralist accounts of the organization of legal practice and analysing the views of professional power that are rooted in these theories. By incorporating some aspects of the structuralist perspective into an ideological interpretation of legal practice, I then argue that we can build an alternative theory of professional power, which looks at the formation of law as a historical construction.

The organization of lawyers' work

The term 'legal practice' is used often in both ordinary and scholarly discourse to refer to the work that lawyers do. Every day we hear lawyers' work referred to as the 'practice of law' and their jobs described as a 'practice'. The term often refers to the amount of time lawyers spend on particular tasks, such as speaking with clients, researching cases and appearing in court. It indicates the characteristics of a lawyer's routine – do they use pre-printed forms and if so for what portion of their work?[9] Lawyers' practice is characterized by the extent to which 'the law' is important in their work – do they mediate between parties in disputes more often than litigate?[10] Answers to these questions vary according to the type of clients lawyers represent and what fields of law they practise.

Studies of the structure and organization of lawyers' work have developed a concept of legal practice that describes more than the mechanics of work in various fields – it focuses on the organizational requirements of practice (Nelson 1981: 101). In the large-firm context, organizational requirements include 'getting and keeping clients; recruiting new lawyers and keeping the old; dividing labor among partners, associates, and nonprofessional staff; coordinating the efforts of lawyers specializing in different fields of law; protecting against conflicts of interest; and the like' (ibid.). These requirements structure the day-to-day practice of law in corporate firms and they secure the conditions for sustaining that practice over time.

This concept of legal practice has been used to study the power of lawyers in terms of their control over their work. In particular, it has been employed in a number of recent studies focusing on lawyer–client relationships.[11] Does the organization of legal practice give lawyers power over their clients? Who is in charge, lawyer or client?[12]

In their book on the social structure of the Chicago Bar in the mid-1970s, Heinz and Laumann (1982) argued that the clients' interests determine the organization of practice in large law firms where the corporate sector of the profession practises law. Nelson (1985: 505) agrees that in large firms, 'the direction of their law reform activities and their approach to the issues that arise in ordinary practice ultimately are determined by the position of their clients'. This work confirms what a number of historical studies of corporate law practice document – the loss or exchange of professional autonomy for money (Llewellyn 1933; Auerbach 1976; Gordon 1984b).

In contrast to the hired gun image of corporate lawyers, Abraham Blumberg (1967) and others argue that the legal practice of criminal defence lawyers is determined largely by the organizational incentives of the criminal court system, not their clients.[13] The main organizational requirement of practice for defence lawyers is that they work closely with district attorneys and plea bargain most of their cases. Large caseloads in criminal courts establish production norms, placing demands on lawyers to manufacture 'assembly line justice'. As a consequence, clients are secondary figures. Yet the intangible nature of lawyers' work,[14] Blumberg argued, requires that lawyers play a 'confidence game' in order to convince clients that their knowledge of how the system works is what makes their advice worth paying for and following. To fulfil the organizational requirements of this practice, the defence lawyer plays a 'double-agent' role.

Somewhere in between the images of the corporate lawyer as hired gun and the criminal defence lawyer as double agent is a third view of lawyer–client relations. Stewart Macaulay's (1979) study of consumer protection lawyers in Wisconsin suggests a more mixed view of legal practice. He found that the lawyers representing individuals in consumer protection cases were more likely to play:

. . . nonadversary roles without great knowledge of the contours of consumer law, while the lawyers for corporations act more traditional parts – lobbying, counseling drafting documents, and defending cases after complaints are filed. However, lawyers for corporations are at least occasionally pushed out of the character of legal technician.

(Macaulay 1979: 153)

His description of the relationship between lawyer and client in this field does not make a sharp distinction between types of clients and the nature of professional power. All of these lawyers mediate rather than adjudicate, and according to Macaulay they all 'seek to educate, persuade and coerce *both* sides to adopt the best available compromise rather than to engage in legal warfare' (p. 117).

Together, these studies describe a range of legal practices, organized to represent, manipulate and compromise the interests of clients. Varying prestige of legal specialities (corporate or criminal)[15] and varying types of clients (individuals or organizations), may affect the power of lawyers in lawyer–client relationships. Furthermore, these relationships are multifaceted, with a number of underlying dimensions (professional, business and social) working to organize the practice of law (Kritzer 1984). In the large law firm setting, one dimension may be more salient than in other kinds of practice (Macaulay 1979: 421). In particular fields of law, a certain style of practice (i.e. mediation) may also be more prevalent.

While it is becoming clear from the growing number of studies of lawyers' work that the organizational requirements of practice are themselves highly variable, the theoretical perspective that has driven this body of empirical research remains relatively unchanged. Underlying these studies is a concern with the function of lawyers' power, which stems from Talcoltt Parsons' (1954, 1962, 1968) and Erwin Smigel's (1964/1969) writings on professional autonomy. Parsons argued that legal training and specialized knowledge enable lawyers to act as intermediaries between their clients' narrow self-interests and the legal system. Similarly, Smigel argued that Wall Street lawyers were able to moderate the demands of their corporate clients by defining their clients' problems in relation to broader, social standards of justice. Their essential function, Parsons (1962: 57) maintained, is to integrate conflicting elements in society and to 'oil the machinery of social intercourse'. This traditional functionalist view of legal practice casts lawyers into a role where their professional knowledge functions to maintain the rule of law, protect private interests, and acquire professional power and prestige for lawyers all at the same time.[16] Clearly, the functionalist model incorporates normative prescriptions into its description of professional power.

Contemporary studies of lawyer–client relations begin with this idealtypical model of the legal profession's function, test its validity in ent legal practices, and show how structural conditions of legal practice affect the scope of professional autonomy. Evidence of professional autonomy is the ability of lawyers to define their clients' problems and offer solutions without relying on clients' interpretations or accounts. In essence, lawyers' power lies in their autonomy from clients. However, where the traditional functionalist view of legal practice found autonomy in professional knowledge and supported its social control function, recent studies of the organization of corporate legal practice argue that lawyer autonomy is limited.[17] These findings are presented as a challenge to Smigel's theory about professional power: 'dominance of client interests in the practical activities of lawyers contradicts the view that large-firm lawyers serve a mediating function in the legal system' (Nelson 1985: 504–505). Looking more broadly at the role of lawyers and non-lawyers in the representation of private interests before the federal government, Nelson *et al.* (1987) empirically test the Parsonian model. They conclude that lawyers 'now occupy a relatively specialized niche in this system, one that allows them to reproduce themselves economically and to maintain a sense of independence and autonomy in their work, but that sharply limits the nature of their influence over the formation of policy' (Nelson and Heinz 1988: 241). Further they argue that increased competition among Washington law firms encourages firms to develop a 'posture of zealous advocate for the client' (p. 295). Specialization and competition, trends they see in the organization of legal practice among Washington lawyers, undercut both the descriptive and normative claims associated with Parsons' model.

Arguably, attention to the social structure is an important contribution to theorizing about legal practice. It transcends the universalist perspective of functional theory and specifically its characterization of lawyer-as-mediator. Yet by focusing on the organization of lawyers without attention to the law they produce, the structural approach does not advance the concept of legal practice far enough. It leads us towards a very sophisticated map of how practice is organized, recognizing diversity among clients, fields of law and styles of practice, but the conceptual framework for legal practice is not captured in this particular view of its organization. Nelson and Heinz (1988: 244) acknowledge that they have ignored the 'qualitative significance of lawyers' work in the policy-making process and the fact that law or legal consciousness (whether held by lawyers or nonlawyers) is a critical, constitutive element of policy-making institutions'. And they warn us to exercise appropriate caution in interpreting their findings for this reason.

This limitation exists not merely because social scientists have chosen to study the social structure of legal practice instead of legal consciousness, but because their perspective on legal practice *separates* legal consciousness from social structure. For example, in his discussion of his

research on large firms in Chicago, Nelson says that lawyers maintai
ideology of autonomy but the 'changing organization of work ir
corporate sector continues to increase the divergence between that ideology and practice', and thus this 'ideology has little bearing on their
practice' (Nelson 1985: 543, 504). Analytically, he treats legal consciousness, or ideology, separately from the 'realm of practice'. Thus legal practice is conceptualized in traditional positivist terms – ideas about law are
separated from the material organization of its practice.

While contemporary analyses of the organizational requirements of
legal practice go beyond mere description of the work lawyers do, we
need to develop an interpretive perspective which takes seriously the
meaning and conception of law *in* the organization of legal practice. Legal
practices have content, not only functions and corresponding social structures. The development of legal specialities, such as administrative law,
as well as the tendency for lawyers to 'occupy a relatively specialized
niche' in larger systems of political representation, are examples of organizational forms and practice that embody an ideology about law and legal
work.[18]

Legal practice and ideology

An alternative view of legal practice examines the ideological content and
political significance of the work that lawyers do. Work is shaped by how
lawyers construct legal ideologies as they work with them. Lawyers are
engaged in the task of 'trying to explain and rationalize what they see
happening in the world in terms of some general normative conceptions'
(Gordon 1982: 72). As Maureen Cain (1979) argues, lawyers are 'conceptive ideologists'[19] whose work includes the creation of the language with
which they translate political issues and economic concerns; 'discursive
translation is a lawyer's defining skill' (p. 339). In this sense, lawyers'
work contributes to the development and support for a 'general ideological scheme or political language' that arises from their constructive acts
(Gordon 1982: 72).

Different interpretations of professional autonomy follow from the
view that lawyers produce ideology and ideology is a defining characteristic of their practice. The conventional interpretation is that the constructive acts of lawyers are the job of an advocate. Clients, whether they
are corporations or political activists, hire lawyers to translate their interests into a legal language that will make sense and hopefully establish
legitimacy for their claims.[20] Lawyers in this view are the hired guns.
There is little doubt that this instrumental view of lawyer-as-advocate
was predominant among legal service reformers in the 1960s and 1970s,
where expanding access to lawyers for those without representation (e.g.
the public interest law movement[21]) or for those without the economic

means to afford it (e.g. the poverty law movement[22]) was a strategy to democratize politics through law.

This purposive interpretation of legal translation marginalizes professional autonomy in ways that are similar to how the structural analysis minimizes the constitutive character of legal consciousness in its description of the organization of legal practice. The substance of what is being translated by lawyers in their practice is reduced to 'client interests'. An alternative view of legal practice, which avoids the path of instrumentalism and comprehends other aspects of practice than just the dynamics between lawyers and clients, leads to new ways of understanding the complexities of professional power and legal practice.

Lawyers are not politically significant only because they translate disputes into legally intelligible arguments; a resource some groups are able to purchase and others are denied. Legal practice is not that clear-cut. The political significance of legal practice cannot be fully understood if it is treated as an instrument for advancing interests 'precisely because there is a second tier to lawyers' work' (McBarnet 1984: 233). Lawyer's also *work on the law*, as Doreen McBarnet points out, 'to interpret it, to make the law fit the facts of their client's activities and interests. Lawyers are not just translators but transformers and transcenders of law' (ibid.). That corporate lawyers represent or fit their clients' interests into a legal discourse does not necessarily mean that lawyers' autonomy is lost. Autonomy, like power, is not zero-sum. When a case is over and the client goes home, the practice of law continues. Lawyers' language remains operative after their relationship to a client has ended.

The continuous nature of legal practice is, in part, what gives lawyers some degree of autonomy from their clients and control over legal consciousness. Their authority over a language, through its creation, translation and re-creation, establishes a 'meta-language'.[23] Events are converted into legal claims with the language of pre-established categories. Through this interpretative process situations are constructed. For example, in 1983, when the US National Highway Transportation and Safety Administration (NHTSA) rescinded its rule mandating that the automobile industry phase in passive restraint systems (i.e. airbags or seat belts), lawyers representing car manufacturers translated this event into a violation of Section 553 of the Administrative Procedure Act's (APA) rule-making procedures.[24] They argued that the agency's decision to rescind its own rule must be approved by the same procedures used to make rules. These lawyers constructed an interpretation of rule-making that incorporated acts of deregulation under the rubric of the APA's rule-making process. This interpretation prevailed in the Supreme Court. But the significance of this constructive act does not necessarily turn on the outcome of the case. That is, it is not necessary that a lawyer win the case in order to demonstrate authority over a meta-language. It is important to recognize that to 'trade in categories and interpretations must necessarily be to trade a way not just of perceiving but also of constructing situations' (Cain 1979: 333).

The power to trade in legal categories, whether certain arguments prevail in court or not, is based on the status of professions. In his work on professions, Eliot Freidson (1970) argues that the potential for producing ideology is inherent in the status of professions. This potential, Larson suggests:

> . . . exists not only because cognitive and normative elements are used ideologically, as instruments in an occupation's path toward professional status, but also because, once reached, this structural position allows a group of experts to define and construct particular areas of social reality, under the guise of universal validity conferred on them by their expertise.
>
> (Larson 1977: xiii)

In this sense, the structural position of professions and their work are closely related to one another. Lawyers work on both.

Lawyers construct ideologies about law for different audiences. Lawyer–client relationships are one arena for the creation and translation of law. Most research, as previously noted, has focused on lawyer–client interactions in order to determine 'who's in charge'. However, some of this research touches on the image of law lawyers create for their clients. Studies of the day-to-day interactions between divorce lawyers and their clients, for example, tell us that lawyers try to socialize clients into a view that lawyers are insiders in the legal process, a process riddled with irrationality and disappointment (Sarat and Felstiner 1986). From this stance, lawyers seek to ascertain information they need from their clients. Sarat and Felstiner describe encounters with divorce lawyers and clients as marked by competition and accommodation between lawyer and client expectations about law.

The struggles between professions and within the legal profession over work are other sites for the production of ideologies about law.[25] Lawyers compete with other professionals for control over work. Inter-professional competition is one way lawyers differentiate themselves from other professions (Larson 1977; Abel 1981a, 1989). Struggles over the control of work put professions in conflict with one another and at the same time define what is at stake in the status of professions.[26] Traffic engineers, city planners and businessmen were among those with whom government and private lawyers competed for work in federal administrative agencies. Similar to other areas when non-lawyers originally dominated the practice of law,[27] administrative practice was and still is to a certain extent a contested terrain.

Intra-professional competition over work is also one way in which members of the bar distinguish their work from what other lawyers do. In the 1930s, for example, there were conflicts within the bar between New York City tax, patent and custom lawyers and the ABA over whether a federal administrative court[28] should be established to hear challenges to agency decisions. The tax, patent and custom lawyers opposed such efforts by the ABA on two grounds. On the one hand, they objected to the proposed administrative court because they did not 'wish "their" courts consolidated into the undistinguished mass of administrative jurisdiction' (Jaffe 1939: 1225). On the other hand, they argued that the legitimacy of lawyers as a group would be threatened by such a proposal. They claimed that in the mist of growing political support for New Deal agencies, the President and members of Congress would perceive the removal of adjudicatory powers from agencies and the concentration of power in courts as purely a self-interested move by lawyers, not an action on behalf of the 'public interest' (ibid.). In their opposition to the ABA, these lawyers, who had established practices in the tax, patent and customs fields, articulated an ideology about administrative practice that was not in opposition to agencies or even the existence of non-lawyer practitioners. This particular ideology constituted a view of lawyers as policy specialists working with agencies and other professions to formulate administrative procedures and advance legislative policies in these fields. Although they were confronted with considerable opposition from other members of the legal profession, their fears were echoed in speeches by members of Congress and in President Roosevelt's veto message.[29] At the same time, tax, patent and custom work was defended as specialized administrative law work – it was defined as lawyers' work. The point is that lawyers maintain and create new services, and demands for those services, in competition with other lawyers (Abel 1981a, 1986b, 1989).

In the competition over work, lawyers construct legal ideologies about the nature and boundaries of law. Abbott (1986a: 190) argues that the creation of these boundaries, or what he calls 'jurisdictions' between professions, is the central phenomenon of professional life. He argues that jurisdictions are constituted by new technologies and new developments in knowledge and in organizational structures affecting work. The ideologies that are established in struggles over work constitute an arena of law-making that has yet to be examined. Preoccupation with lawyer–client studies has led to important work on lawyers, but it has also drawn attention away from other arenas where lawyers, as a profession, construct law. The making of administrative law through the struggles over professional boundaries focuses attention on how lawyers construct ideologies about who can practise this law (lawyers and non-lawyers) and in what settings (agencies and courts).

Questions about the formation of legal ideologies in these struggles cannot be answered in the abstract. There are, however, important theoretical debates about the extent to which professional ideology is determined by clients and/or the legal system that influence how empirical studies of legal practice are framed. So far, we have discussed the traditional functionalist perspective, the socio-structural view, and an ideological analysis of legal practice. To some extent, all three perspectives have implications for a theory of professional autonomy. The functionalist and the socio-structural perspectives differ over the degree to which lawyers are autonomous from their clients. The *amount* of control lawyers have over their clients is not, however, the central concern in an ideological approach. Instead, this approach directs attention to the conditions for and content of constructive acts, such as struggles within and between professions over work.

The use of the concept of ideology in this alternative theory needs further elaboration because in the context of the professions, where the use of formal knowledge is an exercise of power (Freidson 1986), ideology has a number of different implications. Even among those who agree on the importance of studying constructive acts of lawyers, there is some debate about the extent to which these acts are determined by other social forces. William Simon, who writes from a critical legal studies perspective, argues that the vision of practice in traditional legal thought is an ideal

> . . . notion that lawyers mediate between the determinate, articulated interests of a client and the determinate, articulated constraints of a legal or social system. Both the client's interests and the constraints of the system are seen as constituted prior to the lawyer's activity. The basic message of the professional vision is Stoic: the lawyer achieves fulfillment by participating in a world that is largely (though not entirely) already made.
>
> (Simon 1984: 469)

He disputes this vision and calls for an alternative account that includes both the 'unavoidable reality' and the 'moral and political opportunity' of client and system interests being *indeterminate*. In his view, history has not decreed the place of lawyers in our society, nor can their role be derived from science or legal doctrine. The constitutive tendency of legal practice is for some critical legal scholars, who are themselves lawyers, indeterminate and autonomous from doctrine – made up by lawyers. Acknowledging the extent to which his own enterprise is in part like the traditional one,[30] in that both have a 'utopian quality', Simon interprets the constitutive tendency of representation as a positive opportunity for practitioners rather than a danger to be guarded against (pp. 470, 487). For those who study legal practice, Simon suggests that deconstructing legal practices and uncovering constructive beliefs will enable us to see the arbitrariness of legal categories.

However, if legal categories, invented in legal practice, are simply arbitrary, then it is hard to understand how this deconstructionist approach can identify *interests or politics* in legal ideologies. Simon's deconstructionist approach rests on a hyper-indeterminacy claim that leads to a voluntarist vision of legal practice. In response to a related 'anti-professionalism' argument put forth by others in the American critical legal studies movement, Stanley Fish (1986: 676) adopts what he calls a 'strong interpretivist or conventionalist view, a view in which facts, values, reasons, criteria, etc., rather than being independent of interpretive history, are the product of the history' – a view which points out problems that are apparent in the voluntarism of Simon's vision as well. Fish says, 'in short, the ideology of anti-professionalism – of essential and independent values chosen freely by an independent self – is nothing more or less than the ideology of professionalism taking itself seriously' (ibid.). This result is ironic, if not unfortunate, for a vision that intends to be critical of the dominant notion of professionalism. It demonstrates some of the problems that a constitutive approach should avoid and that can be avoided if the political forces that both shape and are being shaped in the constructive acts of lawyers are not ignored.

Another problem that a constitutive approach should avoid is the implication that ideology, in this case the ideology of administrative law practice, is itself coherent and monolithic. Constitutive theories that use the anthropological conception of cultural systems as being synonymous with ideology have been criticized on these grounds. Theda Skocpol (1985) argues that the anthropological conception of cultural systems, assumes that cultural idioms and ideological activities are 'integrated patterns of shared meanings, total pictures of how society does and should work' (p. 90). She argues that studies that use this concept to examine the role of ideology in revolutions, for example, tend to 'read entire systems of meaning into particular documents' and 'treat fundamental cultural and ideological change as the synchronous and complete replacement of one society-wide cultural system by another' (ibid.). For these reasons, she contends that social scientists and historians 'are not well served by supporting the notion that sets of ideas – whether intellectual productions or cultural frameworks of a more informally reasoned sort – are "constitutive of social order" '.[31]

Thus to argue that ideologies of legal practices are constitutive of political institutions and professional arrangements is not necessarily to imply that these frameworks are coherent and monolithic systems of meaning. What Skocpol has claimed for political ideologies in the reconstruction of state power, sociolegal scholars have found to be the case in studies of legal ideologies, such as informalism (Henry 1983; Fitzpatrick 1988; Harrington and Merry 1988). There are multiple legal ideologies (formalism and informalism) which co-exist in liberal societies and among different types of organizational settings (hierarchical and participatory). Administrative law is no exception. A continual tension between managerial control and individual freedom represents but one set of contradictory themes underlying theories of bureaucratic legitimation in administrative law.[32] How legal ideologies rise, decline and intermingle in different tempos needs to be explored (Skocpol 1985). It is in this sense that ideology provides a theoretical basis for locating doctrinal developments in the practice of law.

In addition, ideological structures might themselves have a dual character, which means that they are at once constraining and enabling (Giddens 1976). Ideologies about who can practise administrative law have blocked some possibilities for non-lawyer practitioners. In the debates over who should be allowed to practise before the Federal Communications Commission, for example, lawyers as a group argued that the constitutional right to a fair hearing requires that individuals be represented by lawyers. Yet this ideology cuts against claims by other groups of lawyers (e.g. Occupational Health and Safety practitioners) who have stressed the importance of legal expertise in policy making and argue that it should be the basis for privileging lawyer practitioners yet not excluding non-lawyers altogether. Certain ideological structures may be biased against non-lawyer practitioners in some instances, yet it is important, at least theoretically, to leave open the empirical possibility that ideological structures themselves undergo continuous reproduction and/or transformation as a result of struggles over professional boundaries and within the legal profession. My research shows ideological structures are neither indeterminate or arbitrary. And as Skocpol (1985: 91) notes, 'it will make a difference which idiom or mixture of idioms is available to be drawn upon by given groups. Indeed, the very definitions of groups, their interests, and their relations to one another will be influenced by cultural idioms.'

The choices and uses of available idioms and the particular potentials within them that are elaborated, are influenced by the political conditions under which ideologies develop, are sustained and transformed. Ideologies about administrative law practice are not autonomous from political structures, nor are they completely dependent on it. This sociolegal study of the development of administrative law follows a suggestion made by Roger Cotterrell to 'seek knowledge of the *conditions* under which ideologies develop, are sustained and disintegrate because of the sociological and politically practical significance of this knowledge' (Cotterrell 1983a: 70, emphasis added). The conditions of legitimacy as well as the jurisdictional claims, to use Abbott's phrase, are matters of sociolegal analysis. The particular political opportunities and constraints government and private lawyers and non-lawyers confronted is the focus of the next chapter. Here, however, my purpose is to advance an alternative theory of legal practice that articulates elements (structural and ideological) of what lawyers do so that we can better analyse their role in the development of law and hence the legal construction of politics.

This perspective builds on Freidson's (1970, 1983, 1986) and Larson's (1977) path-breaking studies of the professions and Abel's (1989) elaboration of a political economy approach in his studies of the legal profession in the USA. In Freidson's (1986) study of professional power, he argues that 'the professions can exercise some powers by virtue of their place in the political economy' (p. 210). Thus, from this scholarship on professions we draw the view that cognitive knowledge and the skills of lawyers are tied to the political economy. Because there are 'systemic sources of variation in the use of formal knowledge', we cannot assume that the relationship between all constructive acts by lawyers is uniform and consistent in shaping the political economy (ibid.). Rather, I interpret this view as compatible with my position that legal ideologies are constructed in the material realm of work which itself is a contested terrain. The concept of ideology I draw on, therefore, refers to the structure of values and cognitive ideas presupposed in and expressed through struggles over legal practice. In addition, a legal ideology is politically 'significant in so far as it influences the manner in which individuals conceptualize and evaluate social relations and their place and aspirations within society' (Cotterrell 1983a: 84). Larson and Abel focus specifically on the market sources of professional power, arguing that professions organize themselves to attain market power and that the structure and organization of the profession is 'shaped by the relationship which these special occupations form with a type of society and a type of class structure' (Larson 1977: xv). Together, Freidson, Larson and Abel have broken ground for a new theoretical perspective on professions. They theorize a relationship between professional jobs and the political economy which looks beyond, or perhaps behind, the structure of lawyer–client interactions.

The alternative theory of legal practice, outlined above, is an interpretative perspective. It takes seriously the meaning and conception of law in the work that lawyers do and in the way the profession defines that work through competition with other professions and within the legal profession. The focus encourages us to explore the *political* content of the relationship between professional work and the political economy in a field of law closely tied to the reorganization of state power in the twentieth century – administrative law.

Legal practice and political development

With this outline of a theory of legal practice, I would like to conclude by addressing the problem of developing interpretative frameworks for understanding the role of legal practice in the political development of law

and the state. The ideological conception of legal practice, which I p¹
forth as an alternative to functional and structural definitions, rests on the
claim that law and legal practice are social and political constructions.
Therefore, the concept of legal practice, like the concept of profession,
should be treated as a historical construction. What Freidson stresses in
his approach to the professions, I also find compelling for interpretative
studies of legal practice and political development. He argues that we
should:

> . . . not attempt to determine what profession is in an absolute sense
> so much as how people in a society determine who is a professional
> and who is not, how they 'make' or 'accomplish' professions by their
> activities, and what the consequences are for the way in which they
> see themselves and perform their work.
>
> (Freidson 1983: 27)

By treating categories like 'legal practice' or 'profession' as folk categories,[33] we can look at the political development of law from the outside, as
it were, and determine the importance of its content in securing the conditions for the exercise of political power.

With the emergence of interpretative social science,[34] historical
methods for studying law are becoming more central to sociolegal research. The recent movement within the social sciences towards doing
more historical investigations is predicated on a fundamental rethinking
of the relationship between theory building and historical analysis. Historical work in the social sciences fell to disfavour in the late 1950s and
1960s largely because of the strong connection between historical analysis
and theories of political evolution (Schwartz 1987). In political science,
historical work was often associated with a narrow definition of politics
as statecraft and a formal description of institutions. The turn away from
historical sociology was similarly a rejection of what C. Wright Mills
called the 'twin orthodoxies of "grand theory" (i.e. Parsons' structural
functionalism) and "abstract empiricism" that dominated sociology until
the late 1960s' (Skocpol 1987: 19). This rebellion against historical analysis
was never as strong or so complete in the study of law. Alongside
behavioural studies of judicial decisions in the 1960s, there was a steady
flow of doctrinal studies that relied heavily on historical analysis. Yet
both behavioural and doctrinal traditions in law were based on grand
theories of law and social development arising from functionalist interpretations of Weber and the influence of Parsons.

The contemporary movement to build theory from history fits well
with interpretative analyses of law-making, in part perhaps, because of
the unbroken ties between historical work and legal studies. The atem-
poral character of evoluntary functionalism and social development theories, which characterized earlier historical analyses, however, minimizes

the context of law such that theory ends up determining historical processes rather than the other way around. In his review of social history and social sciences' use of history, Olivier Zunz (1987: 38) notes that another tendency of such grand theorizing is to minimize the context of what is an *interdisciplinary* discourse. There is evidence in the current law and society debates over legal history to support Zunz's claim.[35] Historical studies of law that are framed by social development theories view law as a product of modernization. This framework tends to provide an ahistorical explanation of legal processes.[36] As Charles Tilly (1980: 55) notes, when knowledge is dehistoricized in grand theory, the taken-for-granted becomes that basis on which predictions are made and trends are 'established' (see also Edelman 1988).

Skocpol (1987: 4–5) defines the current work in social science history as a 'continuing, ever-renewed tradition of research devoted to understanding the nature and effects of large-scale structures and fundamental processes of change. Compelling desires to answer historically grounded questions, not classical theoretical paradigms, are the driving force'.[37] Her work on state formation and revolution has inspired political scientists to join with historians and put historical analyses back into social theory and social theory back into history (e.g. Skowronek 1982).

Political scientists who study law can draw on history to develop interpretative frameworks for understanding the legal construction of politics. Specifically, we need to develop methods that are sensitive to temporal processes (Abbott 1983; Skocpol 1987). Breaking from the law and modernization theory, which rest on a linear conception of legal development and change, requires that we question whether in fact legal practices change over certain time periods or whether they remain the same. Political meanings are not only constructed in periods of transformation; we should be cautious not to overlook the role of legal practice in maintaining existing forms of political power. This means that historical analysis may respecify the forms and periodization of the relationship between law and political development.

There are two distinctive discourses about administrative law practice I am interested in. One deals with doctrinal discussions, centring around particular regulatory disputes (e.g. constitutional and statutory interpretations of agency authority to make rules and adjudicate and the appropriate scope of judicial review). This discourse is carried out in agency opinions, lawyers' briefs, judicial decisions and scholarly commentaries. The second is professional discussions, addressing the role of lawyers in society, what administrative law practice means and entails, and who should do this work. These discussions appear in a variety of places, such as debates and policy statements from the bar, non-lawyer practitioner associations, government lawyers, agencies, and in congressional hearings.

We often think of these two types of discourse as carrying different 'legal' weight and authority. What the ABA Committee on Administrative Law or non-lawyer practitioners say about administrative practice is given less 'legal' weight than what the US Supreme Court says in a majority opinion on administrative rule-making. While it is the case that the Supreme Court has acquired a substantial amount of institutional authority over law-making, this situation was not inherent in the nature of the Court nor was it inevitable (Brigham 1987). And for a field of law like administrative law, which was premised on the notion that administrative policy and administrative practice are at odds with traditional legal procedures, it is even more puzzling how lawyers and courts come to play a predominant role in shaping administrative law.

Despite the outcome of struggles between non-lawyers and lawyers and agencies and courts, discourse about doctrine and practice in the field of administrative law both deal with developing what might be called 'rules about creating rules', or a practice for constituting doctrine. My concern, therefore, is not to define the ideology of administrative law solely in terms of who prevails in the struggles over this work, but rather to examine the conditions under which struggles over this work take place, how they shape the political meaning and institutional organization of administrative law. I am interested in how terms like 'administrative law' are negotiated in the struggles over work; what is included, excluded and emphasized in both realms of legal discourse.

Conclusion

This theory of legal practice focuses attention on the historical development and significance of law *in* politics. Yet alone the theory does not tell us what kind of role legal practice plays in political development. Studying the formation of legal practice involves an analysis of the development of professional boundaries and how they are negotiated under certain political conditions. Focusing on the discourse about legal work is one way of building an interpretative framework for studying the meaning and content of law. This discourse has a history and it also contributes to making histories. How legal language is constructed in work and how it is employed in the development and support for new institutional arrangements, such as federal agencies and the administrative state, is therefore my primary concern.

Rather than treat social structure and ideology as separate modes of analysis, the theory of legal practice I begin with links structure and ideology together; legal practice is viewed as a historical construction of sociolegal relations. This interpretivist perspective seeks to study the past for insights into the origins of contemporary sociolegal phenomena. The formation and generation of legal ideologies provide the context for understanding lawyers' work.

Acknowledgements

I would like to thank John Brigham, Maureen Cain, Howard Gillman, Frank Munger and Susan Sterett for their comments on an earlier draft of the manuscript.

Notes

1 Twiss entitled his chapter one, 'The Stuff the Law is Made of' (1942).
2 Peter Irons (1982) notes this absence as well and points to Richard Klugar's (1975) study of the litigation strategy in *Brown* v. *Board of Education* (1954) as an exception. Since Klugar's book, there have been several important case studies that examine the impact of litigation strategies on judicial decisions. For example, see Susan Olson's (1984) book on the disability rights movement, Timothy O'Neill's (1985) study of litigation in the *Bakke* case, and Donald Downs' (1985) book on the *Skokie* case.
3 Robert Gordon's (1983, 1984a, 1984b) study of corporate lawyers in the nineteenth century is an exception.
4 See Fitzpatrick (1983) and Merry (1988) for an overview of legal pluralism.
5 See de Tocqueville [1835–40] (1945).
6 See Eulau and Sprague (1964).
7 I am reminded of Justice Robert's famous description of the Supreme Court's mandate in *United States* v. *Butler* (1936), where he said 'the judicial branch of the Government has only one duty – to lay the articles of the Constitution which is invoked beside the statute which is challenged and to decide whether the latter squares with the former'. This legal formalist view of law is present in social science research as well. As this research relates to assessing interests, see Brigham and Harrington (1989) on the difficulty of evaluating the impact of judicial background in a positivist framework.
8 Although Auerbach does not examine New Deal administrative law doctrine, his thesis that professionalism prevailed over political discord between government and corporate lawyers does imply that the law reflected the values of professionalism. He argues that professionalism provided a 'common bond' between lawyers, a set of values in which process is divorced from substance (Auerbach 1976: 224–9). The problem with Auerbach's view of professionalism is that his definition is so broad and general that it is hard to determine when, if ever, the law does not reflect professional values.
9 See Kritzer (1988) for a description of lawyers' routine in 'ordinary litigation'.
10 For example, see Macaulay's (1979) study of legal practice. Based on interviews with a non-representative sample of Wisconsin consumer protection lawyers, he challenges the classical model of legal practice in which lawyers apply the law. He finds instead that lawyers mediate between buyer and seller.
11 An exception would be Hagan *et al.* (1988). Instead of focusing on power in terms of lawyer–client relationships, they analyse the class structure of the Toronto Bar, describing the nature of control lawyers have over their work in relation of their position in an occupational class structure.
12 This question framed Douglas Rosenthal's (1974) study of personal injury lawyers.

13 Eisenstein and Jacob (1977) develop this thesis further in their organizational analysis of three urban criminal courts. See also Feeley (1979).

14 See Freidson (1986: ch. 1) for a discussion of formal knowledge and legal work.

15 See Laumann and Heinz (1977) and Heinz and Laumann (1982) for a discussion of the sociological literature on lawyers and professional prestige, internal hierarchies of the legal profession, and the nature of social stratification in the legal profession.

16 That the American Bar Association finds these models attractive should be of little surprise. As Nelson and Heinz (1988: 239) note: 'The prospect of an autonomous professional stratum capable of maintaining a normative framework for legal and political discourse continues to excite contemporary analysts. The legal professions' most recent manifesto on professionalism, the report of the American Bar Association's Commission on Professionalism (1986), repeatedly asserts that the autonomy of lawyers from their clients is an essential condition of their ability to serve the public interest.'

17 In contrast, Cain (1979) argues that some radical critiques of lawyers show that lawyers perform a repressive social control function (see Johnson, 1972; Bankowski and Mungham, 1976).

18 For example, see Heydebrand (1977, 1979) and Harrington (1985) for an analysis of how technocratic and bureaucratic rationalizations structure legal organizations.

19 Cain associates her notion of lawyers as conceptive ideologists with the work of Antonio Gramsci and Max Weber. She argues that these theorists 'provide the basis for a model of lawyers as both agents of the bourgeoisie and translators' (Cain 1979: 335).

20 J. Woodford Howard's (1986) description of the *Cramer* treason cases, 1942–45, is a good example of law making from an advocate's perspective.

21 See Handler (1978) and McCann (1986) for discussions of the organization and meaning of advocacy in the public interest law movement.

22 There are several good descriptions and analyses of the lawyer-as-advocate role in the poverty law movement. In particular, see Stumpf (1975), Handler *et al.* (1976), Katz (1984) and Kessler (1987).

23 Cain (1979), Abel (1979) and Macaulay (1979) use this term. For other important works on law as language and linguistic analyses of law, see Scheingold (1974), Bankowski and Mungham (1976) and Brigham (1978).

24 See *Motor Vehicle Manufactures Assn.* v. *State Farm Mutual Automobile Ins. Co.* (1983).

25 By drawing attention to these different arenas of discursive translation (client interactions and professional competition), I do not intend to imply that there is a hierarchy between micro- and macro-levels of practice. There is indeed an interplay between the development of legal discourse in client interactions and the framing of professional boundaries (Harrington and Merry 1988). Although claims are made to different audiences, the construction and legitimacy of what lawyers do goes on in both arenas.

26 Andrew Abbott (1986a: 187) argues that inter-professional competition is a 'determining fact' in the history of professions. I agree that professions are shaped in part by the boundaries they create between one another. However, these boundaries are not themselves absolute or fixed.

27 The existence of non-lawyer practitioners suggests that the phrase 'practice of law' does not necessarily mean that lawyers are doing the work. Marie Provine's (1986) study of non-lawyer judges is a good example of this point.

28 Senator Logan's 1936 bill to establish a US Administrative Court was endorsed by the ABA Special Committee on Administrative Law, Section 3787, 74th Cong., 2nd session.

29 Eventually, the Administrative Court proposal was passed by Congress in 1940 (Walter-Logan Bill), and then vetoed by Roosevelt.

30 By 'traditional', Simon is referring to idealized views of lawyers, similar to those presented in Parsons' functionalist perspective of the legal profession.

31 Skocpol's critique of constitutive theories is at the centre of a scholarly debate over her view of the significance of ideologies in social revolutions. William Sewell (1985: 61) argues that:

> . . . ideologies inform the structure of institutions, the nature of social co-operation and conflict, and the attitudes and predispositions of the population. All social relations are at the same time ideological relations, and all explicit ideological discourse is a form of social action. What all of this suggests is a very different and far more complex object of study than Skocpol takes up in her fairly cursory discussion of revolutionary ideology. It is not enough to treat ideology as a possible causal factor explaining some portion of the change wrought by revolution. If society is understood as ideologically constituted, then adding ideology to the account will also mean rethinking the nature, the interrelations, and the effects on the revolution of state, class, international, and other structures. Moreover, the replacement of one socio-ideological order by another also becomes a crucial dimension of the change that needs to be explained, one no less important than the replacement of one class system by another or one state apparatus by another.

Sewell's emphasis on looking at how social relations are ideologically constituted may ignore the extent to which ideologies are themselves problematic – enabling and constraining, mobilized by certain groups, under certain circumstances and not others, etc. If ideology is understood as itself an arena of contests, then the ways in which it constitutes social relations will lead to a far richer and more complex analysis.

32 See Frug (1984) and Edley (1990), for example.

33 Freidson (1983: 27–8) elaborates further on the idea of folk conceptions of the profession:

> This is not, however, a simple undertaking, for we cannot realistically assume that there is an holistic folk which produces only one folk concept of profession in societies as complex as ours. There must be a number of folk and a number of folk concepts. Surely it seems likely that rather different concepts of profession would be advanced by occupations seeking the rewards of a professional label than by other occupations attempting to preserve the rewards they have already won, or by sets of employers or clients seeking to control the terms, conditions and content of the jobs they wish done, or by government agencies seeking to create a

systematic means by which to classify and account for the occupations of the labour force, or by the general public.

34 For a general overview of interpretative approaches in the social sciences, see Rabinow and Sullivan (1979). See Harrington and Yngvesson (1990) for a discussion of contemporary debates in interpretative sociolegal research.

35 In particular, see Hartog (1983) and Gordon (1984a), who critique evolutionary functionalism as a framework for interpreting legal history (e.g. Friedman 1973).

36 For an example of this tendency, see Munger's (1988) critique of longitudinal studies of litigation.

37 Having identified historical sociology as a tradition, it was recently established as a section of the American Sociological Association. Skocpol (1984: 4) describes the new section as dedicated to fostering comparative and historical sociology and reconsideration of the methodological ideas and historical works of Max Weber.

Constituting capital and the state

3 Legal creativity: law, capital and legal avoidance

Doreen McBarnet

Introduction

The relationship between law and capital has been explored more through the study of legislation and the political process than through the study of lawyers' work. Yet the owners and managers of capital may use creative legal services just as readily and more routinely than political power to achieve their legal goals. These goals may involve the innovative construction of legal forms – 'legal entrepreneurship' and 'private lawmaking' (McBarnet 1987; and see McBarnet 1984; Powell 1987) – or they may involve the creative legal avoidance of legal impositions. This chapter focuses on the latter, on creative avoidance. It shows how lawyers' work – and the work of others dealing in law – can sabotage regulatory impositions and regulatory control.

Laws have been introduced ostensibly to provide individual rights for the less powerful in society or to protect collective interests against the absolute rights of property or the absolute right of business to pursue profit maximization. Health and safety codes, pollution regulations, rent control and anti-discrimination legislation are good examples. The effectiveness of such legal control of big business has been the subject of extensive socio-legal research and analysis. The findings have not been optimistic. Although the tendency to critical assessment in the social sciences may often underplay the measure of real progress achieved by legal reform, it is none the less the case that research has tended to highlight the limitations of the legal control of capital rather than its success.

The failure to control 'capital' – big business or 'high net worth individuals' – through law has been largely ascribed to four factors: the failure of legislators, the failure of law enforcers, the failure of drafters, and the failure of the whole cumbersome apparatus of law itself, destined always to lag behind dynamic social practice.

Those who make the law have been criticized as succumbing to powerful lobbies and fatally weakening legislation as a result, or as being necessarily a 'captive state' by virtue of social networks, economic powerplay or the blackmail of multinational business able to threaten to damage the economy by turning elsewhere if regulation is overdone. The substance of the law itself is thus often seen as an inadequate compromise riddled with exemptions and loopholes and lacking the teeth to give it any chance of success. This in turn affects enforcers. What can they do with inadequate powers? How successful can bluff be against sophisticated violators? Enforcers are seen as 'captured' too. Organizational pressures intrude. There are too few enforcers, too many people and organizations to be policed. Negotiation, compromise, under-enforcement result. At a more technical level the drafters are blamed. How can law be effectively implemented when it is overcomplex, unclear and riddled with loopholes? At the most general level of all is the notion of lag: law is just too slow to keep up with the pace of changing social and economic reality.

But there is another problem, one which has been ignored in the analysis of why regulation fails – not how the law makers *make* law, not how the regulators *enforce* it, but how those on the receiving end *use* and manipulate it. Political lobbying over the content of law is one way in which capital can actively influence the effectiveness of law. But this active role does not stop with the passing of legislation. Rather, legal techniques are brought into play to create strategies for emasculating the law by legally *avoiding* it. Aware that new law does not suit their interests, the owners and managers of capital may well lobby against it. But at the same time, armies of Wall Street and City lawyers will be working to construct devices which can render the law irrelevant anyway. The success or failure of pressure groups or subtler economic pressure in the political process is not the end of the story. It is merely part of the manipulative process. Just as important is the creative legal practice which seeks to achieve the same end by quieter means (McBarnet 1984). In short, even if one could imagine a legislature so committed to egalitarian policies that it would not compromise in its law-making, armed with an enforcement agency with the commitment and powers to fully control violations, effective control of capital would only meet further barriers in legal creativity.

Enforcers cannot enforce laws unless they can claim rules have been violated. What regulation studies have underplayed is the extent to which the regulated do not violate but merely avoid legal controls. The options available to the regulated in response to law are not merely 'compliance' and 'non compliance'. They may also engage in 'creative compliance' to comply with the letter of the law but none the less render its declared purposes ineffective. Despite the legislature, despite the enforcers, law through the active work of the regulated and their advisers, becomes merely symbolic.

Focusing on legal avoidance prompts re-examination of the two other factors conventionally blamed for the failure of law: drafting and lag. Faulty, hasty and overcomplex law may well create problems for regulators. But much of the complexity of law and the convolutedness of its wording is not the cause but the result of avoidance. Specific devices to avoid law result in more law and more verbose law in the attempt to close the loophole. As for the notion of lag – the inevitable inability of the rusty apparatus of law to keep up with thrusting dynamic practice – it may also confuse cause and effect. It may be less a matter of law lagging behind practice than practice quite deliberately moving out of the reach of law. Regulation is not so much lingering behind the practice of dynamic business as a major motivation for its dynamism. 'Capital' adapts to law not necessarily by complying with its aims but by changing its form to keep outside its ambit. Those allegedly subject to the law can turn law upon itself and render it ineffective.

Avoiding, manipulating and using law in this way is achieved through use of legal techniques. Access to the techniques and skills of creative legal work thus becomes a key factor in the effectiveness of law, and in the scope for those with such access successfully to avoid control. Given market forces, and despite exceptions such as organized labour (Genn 1988), the clientele of creative legal work is dominated by private and corporate capital. The result is that legal creativity is more likely to be used to avoid than to implement the legal control of capital. This chapter, based on empirical research in the field of taxation,[1] explores the processes of legal creativity and legal avoidance at work.[2]

Tax avoidance in action

The world of taxation – corporate and private, national and international, capital and income – is riddled with avoidance devices: indeed, there is a whole sophisticated tax avoidance industry specializing in creating, marketing and disseminating legal methods to minimize or avoid tax. It is not just lawyers who are involved, but accountants, bankers, and a whole range of consultants, and there is a vast range of tax avoidance techniques.

Take UK capital gains tax. In 1965, the Labour Chancellor of the Exchequer introduced capital gains tax in the interests of greater equity. Is was to be an effective tax on the rich, 'an attempt to make speculators, property developers and well-advised financiers pay a fair share of tax on their profits'.[3] But creating effective law that impinges on the interests of the 'well advised' is a difficult task. Being well-advised includes being well-advised on how to avoid tax. Capital gains tax has been successfully avoided over the years by a series of creative devices which have rendered it, according to specialist commentators, the 'most legalistic and least cost-effective major tax in the government's armoury'.[4]

One can, of course, avoid tax simply by taking property out of the jurisdiction altogether by going offshore to one tax haven or another. Or, indeed, one can evade tax by criminal action, by simply not disclosing assets – the world of secret money, numbered Swiss bank accounts and safe deposits. But there is the less drastic option – though it involves the transaction costs of professional fees – of taking advantage of one creative device or another to *avoid* the law in a way which may break the spirit but does not break the letter of the law, and thus leaves the avoider quite immune from either paying tax or the risk of punishment (McBarnet 1991). There is a whole range of techniques available to avoid capital gains tax. The devices known as 'bondwashing' and 'offshore roll-up funds' used the law by manipulating the definition of income and capital and playing on exemptions.

Bondwashing played on two exemptions: the exemption of government bonds (gilts) from capital gains tax if held for over a year, and the tax exempt status of particular categories of market actors, notably pension funds and market jobbers.

Gilts realize income twice a year with a dividend. The practice was to sell the gilt just before the next dividend was due for a price which reflected the value of the coming dividend. The dividend would have been subject to income tax but by selling the gilt at a value that included the dividend rather than actually realizing the dividend, the dividend value became a capital gain rather than income. The capital gain was exempt from tax. The security was sold to a tax exempt organization which took the income without paying the tax and resold the security for the process to begin again. No tax at all was therefore paid.

Offshore roll-up funds enjoyed a heyday in 1983–84, when some £2 thousand million was invested in them. Again the interest (subject to income tax) on deposited funds 'converted' into capital by taking it to a fund offshore (out of United Kingdom jurisdiction), 'rolling up' the interest due by adding it to the capital sum and reimporting the money as capital not income. At the time, higher rate income tax was 75 per cent compared to 30 per cent capital gains tax, so that for the higher rate taxpayers who normally used this device the tax savings were enormous.

Tax avoidance schemes attained a certain notoriety in the hands of the Rossminster Group in the 1970s. For example, a major specific capital gain, perhaps resulting from a one-off situation such as the sale of land for development, would be offset by a paper loss, artificially created by a marketed tax avoidance scheme. These schemes were often inordinately complex, using devices relating to several areas of law – different corporate entities constructed solely for the purpose of playing some role in the scheme, trusts, charities, offshore elements. Financial transactions never intended to be fulfilled would cancel each other out in substance but in legal form would stand to create a situation where effectively 'nothing' became $+ x - x$. A positive paper gain was created but fell into an exempt category, and was therefore irrelevant. A corresponding paper loss was left and this could be used against the gain in the real world which the scheme was designed to offset.

Vendors of such schemes have tended to be portrayed as the black sheep of the tax world, yet it is difficult in practice to see any qualitative distinction between these schemes and much routine, 'respectable' tax planning in City institutions, such as – to give a simple example – 'bed and breakfasting'. This had been practised on a large scale and seen as 'a staple investment practice'.[5] Bed and breakfasting refers to a way of creating artificial losses on shares to set against real capital gains and thus reduce or totally avoid paying capital gains tax.

Bed and breakfasting

In a portfolio of shares there may at any given time be some shares which stand at a higher value than when purchased, some which have dropped in value. If shareholders' judgement is that the high value shares have gone as high as they are likely to, or if they simply want to cash them in for some other purpose, they may want to sell them. However, the sale will incur capital gains tax on the amount gained since the shares were bought. At the same time, the portfolio may include shares currently standing at a loss. The capital gains tax on the gains would be wiped out by selling these shares at a loss. This would be 'tax efficient' but totally pointless; making a loss would defeat the object of buying the shares in the first place. Unless the shares that have dropped in value appear to be a lost cause, the investor would normally want to hold on to them until they, too, rise in value and a gain can be realized.

What bed and breakfasting achieved was the *effect* of selling the loss-making shares without actually losing the shares or losing on them. Shares showing a current loss were sold on to a broker, thus 'crystal-lizing' the loss, but repurchased the next day at virtually the same price, so that they could be retained until they rose in value. The artificial loss could be used to offset the gains made on the other shares, the net capital gain was reduced or eliminated, and capital gains tax avoided.

Bed and breakfasting has been used for a number of purposes varying with changes in the organization of the tax in different British Finance Acts and ranging from ensuring full take-up of exemptions, through deferral of payment of tax, to reduction or elimination of tax altogether. Bed and breakfasting could be used to crystallize gains as well as losses, and this could be useful for ensuring full take-up of annual exemptions. Since these could not be carried forward to future years, gains up to the value of the exemption had to be cashed in in the current year if the benefit of exemption was to be utilized. A shareholder might not wish to cash in rising shares, however, so bed and breakfasting allowed the gains to be crystallized and tax saved without losing the shares themselves.

In the era of tax bands, the same technique allowed full utilization of low bands, so that a little tax was paid now rather than a lot later. Less was paid on later gains because the repurchased shares would have a higher value at the time of repurchase than at the time of original purchase so that the next time they were 'sold' the gains would be calculated from a higher cost price and would thus also be less than if the interim 'sale' had not taken place. Bed and breakfasting need not be a one-off; shares could be dealt with each year in this way so that gains, declared in small doses, attracted low rates of tax. The progressive nature of the tax was thus undermined.

Losses could be carried forward, so another tactic was to bed and breakfast in order to build up 'banks of losses' for use in the future. The value of this lay, in particular, in the likelihood that in years when there would be high gains, the market as a whole would be high and there might be no shares in the portfolio which would show a loss if bed and breakfasted. Having artificial losses 'in the bank' could deal with the dilemma of how to cash in on a high market without paying tax. After the Stock Exchange's 'Black Monday' in October 1987, bed and breakfasting was recommended in order to minimize the effects of the crash via the saving on tax, present or future, which the losses would allow.

Bed and breakfasting avoided capital gains tax, but it could also avoid income tax if used alongside 'laundering' techniques like offshore roll-up funds. Income would first be rolled up into a capital gain, then the capital gain in turn avoided via bed and breakfasting.

Non-resident trusts

Another technique using offshore structures to escape tax is the non-resident trust, a more expensive technique for bigger deals and bigger fish.[6] It is easy enough to escape tax simply by becoming a tax exile in a tax haven. But not everyone wants to do that, perhaps least of all those with stately homes and large family estates or businesses in the UK. Trusts are brought into play to provide the legal fiction of emigration. They separate real people, liable to pay tax, from the capital gains on which they would be liable to pay it. The taxpayer stays home, the assets emigrate, and, if all the legal technicalities are observed, a potential tax bill disappears. Capital assets are safely out of the tax net without any need for taxpayers to become tax exiles themselves.

This is fine as far as it goes, but what if you want to use the money back home? It will then become a capital gain or income received by a UK resident and liable to tax. The non-resident trust has become the foundation for further avoidance techniques to circumvent the problem of getting the money back into the country without attracting tax. Where one beneficiary could be domiciled abroad the technique was to pay him or her first. Tax would be due only on the gain. If an amount equivalent to the gain was paid out to the beneficiary domiciled abroad, the tax would be liable on that and only on that. Beneficiaries back home could then receive payments out of the general trust funds without tax being charged. However, since the first beneficiary was not domiciled in the UK, he or she in reality received the gain free of tax. The trust could thus pay out, even to UK residents, without tax being paid by anyone. Other more general techniques have involved paying out to UK residents in the form of interest-free loans. The aim here was to cut tax to a fraction of what it would otherwise be, since tax would be due only on the benefit, i.e. the equivalent of the interest, rather than on the whole sum.

Getting the money out of the UK could also pose problems. If you could anticipate a major gain well in advance of it occurring, you could set up a non-resident trust, insert the currently nil value assets and realize the gain tax-free in the trust. Long term planning in very wealthy families might allow just that to happen. More usually, however, assets with major potential would have already gained some value before the trust was set up. The answer then was a two tier trust structure, initially resident in the UK, but with the power to appoint non-resident trustees and so 'emigrate' the trust. The initial UK residence of this 'freezer trust', allowed for deferral of tax on the gain so far. But the big gain took place after transfer of the trust offshore and was tax-free.

These examples demonstrate just some of many devices routinely in operation; many are far more elaborate. But tax avoidance is not just based on standard techniques. It is also based on highly complex one-off schemes, tailor-made for the specific needs of a specific client. These are extremely costly in terms of professional fees, but are undertaken because of the vast sums of taxation they can save. The tax bill involved in multi-million pound corporate transactions can be managed, minimized or avoided by complex one-off structures. Such tailor-made schemes may remain one-off, exclusive to the single client, or they may in turn become practised more widely, eventually to become themselves standard tools of tax avoidance.

Beyond tax avoidance

Avoidance is not confined to tax. Techniques to use and to avoid law crop up across the range of law. Rent legislation can be taken as another example. Nelken's study of landlords, law and crime describes the harassment techniques used by landlords to exploit tenants despite the legal rights established by the Rent Act 1965. He points to the scope provided by the Act which sought to 'encourage as a priority "freely negotiated" agreements between landlords and tenant' (Nelken 1983: 56) and underlines the fact that many of the methods used by landlords, such as 'winkling' (offering financial inducements to leave tenancies) were quite legal. The substance of the law is therefore seen as allowing, by policy or by silence, the practices which made it ineffective.

It is vital to recognize that the ineffectiveness of regulation is often written into the law itself. But the law has also been used in much more subtle and technical ways in an endeavour to create loopholes. Loopholes may not be explicitly written into the substance of law but may have to be constructed *post hoc* by creative legal work. In short, even if the law-makers should positively seek to be unambivalently effective, legal avoidance techniques could still be brought into play to try to undermine their efforts.

The crucial technique is the manipulation of definitions. For example, exceptions to rules recur through law on equity grounds. Yet as soon as an exception is recognized in law, the way is open for those whose activities the law is seeking to bring within the ambit for its control to redefine those activities to fall within the exempt category. Just as in tax law a more favourable rate of capital tax over income tax spawns devices to redefine income as capital, so the distinction between tenants and licensees created the 'potential . . . for wholesale avoidance' of the Rent Acts by redefining ordinary tenancies in terms of licences (Farrand 1978: 379; Farrand and Arden 1981; Haley 1985: 1053; Yates and Hawkins 1986). Indeed, precedents soon become available for 'judge-proof licences' achieved, for example, by renting through a company specially created for the purpose with memoranda and articles of association which permitted the company only to license not to lease. Anyone renting accommodation from the company could be by definition only a licensee not a tenant (Adams 1976: 5). Likewise exemptions in the Rent Acts for holiday lettings or lettings with board led to a rash of 'holiday lettings in sunny Kilburn' (Shelter 1975) or the provision of board 'consisting perhaps merely of a sandwich'.[7]

Legal avoidance techniques are routine and permeate the range of law. The tax examples cited above largely involve private capital and investment institutions. Large scale business is also heavily into legal avoidance, not only in tax but in relation, for example, to financial controls and corporate governance (McBarnet and Whelan, forthcoming).

Our research on insolvency law also shows how financial institutions have constructed devices to secure priority for their claims over the scarce resources of insolvent companies (McBarnet and Whelan 1987; see also

Wheeler, this volume). In the face of statutory attempts to provide basic equality among creditors or indeed priority for particularly weak creditors such as employees, devices such as the floating charge have been adopted to keep the lenders in the most powerful position. Even in areas such as health and safety regulation, one can see examples of avoidance in action. Brathwaite's study of multinational pharmaceutical companies, for example, mentions in passing a US company involved in its eleventh lawsuit over a drug declared by the enforcement agencies to be in contravention of the Food and Drugs Act. Each time the drug was banned, its ingredients were minutely adapted to make up a 'new' drug, and it was marketed until successfully challenged again (Brathwaite 1984).

Adaptable creativity

Creative avoidance devices which become standard and routine generally provoke a regulatory response. All of the tax avoidance devices discussed above provoked legal action of one sort or another in an effort to control them. But many standard devices also have long histories of such attempts to control them without great success. The specific form of the device aimed at by the law may cease to be used but only to give rise to another remarkably similar but formally different method which technically escapes the law. Bondwashing has been the subject of regular legislation and litigation since 1927 and has featured in the majority of Finance Acts since 1965. Its history demonstrates sixty years of careful adaptation of the device to meet new controls without essentially losing its effect. The announcement on 15 September 1983 that offshore roll-up funds were to be subject to new methods of assessment was followed in the financial press within two days by advertisements for roll-up alternatives, some of which at least have proved effective.

Between 1982 and 1985, old-style bed and breakfasting was rendered ineffective as a routine tax avoidance device because of changes introduced in the 1982 Finance Act. In its original form, bed and breakfasting never straddled two stock exchange accounts, for two reasons. The first was further tax avoidance. Keeping to one account avoided stamp duty which would otherwise have arisen. Second, it kept the non-tax costs down, since it meant stockbroker commission was charged on only one transaction, not on two. The identification rules introduced in 1982 meant that shares sold or purchased in the same stock exchange account were identified with each other and each transaction cancelled out the other. These rules were subject to strong but vain protest from the financial community, who found the change doubly frustrating because other provisions in the Finance Act would have increased the scope for tax avoidance through bed and breakfasting. In fact, further changes in the 1985 Finance Act opened the door to bed and breakfasting again.

In the interim, however, the result of the 1982 legislative changes was not mere acceptance of the situation but adaptation to it, or perhaps more accurately, adaptation *of* the situation to tax avoidance purposes. New ploys were floated, to take advantage of what limited scope was left for old-style bed and breakfasting. One was 'cash and new', using the old bed and breakfast formula but combining it with the practice of paying in cash for 'new shares'. This escaped Finance Act identification because cash settlement was normally the day after the transaction so that sale and repurchase would have different settlement days. The sale would thus be identified with the original purchase rather than the repurchase.

Old-style bed and breakfasting was itself adapted, being replaced by 'weekending'. Weekending did exactly the opposite of bed and breakfasting; instead of ensuring that sale and repurchase fell within one stock exchange account, weekending straddled two accounts, thus avoiding identification of the two transactions. The sale would take place on an end-of-stock-exchange-account Friday at the close of business, and the repurchase, at the start of business on the Monday of the new account. It was, of course, more expensive, since two commissions and stamp duty were payable, and the circumstances in which it was advantageous, more limited. In the right circumstances, however, it was still worth doing where large holdings were involved, so capital gains tax continued to be avoided by the creation of artificial losses through a technique different in specific form, but the same in substance, as old-style bed and breakfasting.

To some extent the judges look through the legal form of the activity to its substance. For example, in an effort to uphold the spirit rather than the letter of the law, the judges in *Street* v. *Mountford*,[8] in *Ramsay* v. *I.R.C.*[9] and *Furniss* v. *Dawson*[10] recognized the need to look through devices and see them as merely means of avoiding in the first instance the Rent Act, and, in the second, taxation.

But as new criteria are established for what *is* acceptable, devices are adapted to fit these criteria and stay on the right side of the fence between illegitimate and legitimate practices. The new emphasis in tax law on a need for commercial purposes as well as just tax avoidance in transactions which result in reduced tax led, for example, to tax planners advocating that commercial purposes should be built into schemes.[11] Regulation founders on creative adaptation.

Creative avoidance and lawyers' work

What these examples demonstrate is that the 'regulated' need not passively accept law meted out by legislators, or judges, but can themselves act upon it, manipulate and use it to suit their own interests. Behind avoidance devices lies creative legal work. Sometimes lawyers play a key creative role in the original idea behind an avoidance device. Sometimes they are the technicians, the engineers or developers for ideas that come from clients themselves or from other advisers.

Research on the legal profession has tended to focus on access to it rather than on what it actually does. Lawyers offer two classes of service – off-the-peg and tailor-made, routine and creative. Access is a vital aspect of the issue of legal avoidance, but it is not so much access to lawyers as access to the *creative* – and circumventory – role of lawyers that is at issue. Lawyers' work is not simply a matter of applying law; it involves creating and constituting law. Lawyers are not simply a means to the implementation of statutory or other ready made rights, but creators of legal techniques, definitions and devices including devices which *avoid* state impositions and *obviate* other people's 'legal rights' if they impinge on the interests of their clients.

The legal profession, in short, is as much geared to the avoidance of law as it is to its implementation. Nelken, observing the legal advice necessary for some of the Rent Act avoidance strategies he describes, sees them originating in the readiness of 'tame solicitors, barristers' and others to participate in shady dealings (Nelken 1983: 56). But avoidance is not just the prerogative of a few marginal 'tame' members of the legal profession: it is a normal routine part of the legal profession's role. Indeed, it is the creative side of the lawyer's job that is its most prestigious aspect and attracts the highest fees.

It is important to give due emphasis to the active and creative role of lawyers in working *against* the spirit of the law. There is little point in merely laying the blame for loopholes in the law at the door of legislators or drafters. Exemptions or faulty drafting may provide scope for legal creativity – they may leave the chink open for the thin end of the wedge. But it takes the active hammering of the profession to split the law apart.

Lawyers may not of course see themselves as working against the spirit of the law. Their role is merely the pragmatic one of interpreting and applying and working with the law as best they can in the light of their client's interests – any client's interests. But the nature of the law allows considerable scope for legal creativity,[12] and the nature of access to the law means that that creativity is more likely to be used to avoid than to implement law aimed at controlling capital. So long as there is unequal access to the creative role of lawyers, avoidance techniques are likely to be available only to those with the resources to buy legal expertise to work on law in their own interests.[13]

Conclusion

Law is multi-faceted and contradictory. Creative legal work takes advantage of its substantive, institutional and ideological contradictions to produce routes through the maze of regulation which minimize its undesirable effects for clients. Law is not just a body of state pronouncements, diktats to be passively received by the regulated, but 'a raw material to be worked on' by those on the receiving end and their advisers.

Lawyers' work, at its most prestigious, is not the mere application and dispensing of ready made reified law, but the creation and constitution of law. Lawyers create new legal forms and adapt old forms for new purposes on a pragmatic basis, in response to clients' needs, and to solve clients' problems. These problems include tax, state controls and the legal rights of others. A key part of lawyers' creative work is finding legal routes for circumventing or removing such legal obstacles to and constraints on clients' activities.

If, then, law tends to be less than effective in controlling economic elites, it is not simply because favourable or weak law is handed over on a plate by a captive, incompetent or constrained state. It is also because of the circumventory work of lawyers creatively constructing techniques by which their clients can escape legal control.

Acknowledgements

My thanks to the ESRC whose funding helped initiate our research on tax evasion and avoidance, and to the Jacob Burns Socio-legal Fund, which has provided the support to develop and continue work on 'creative compliance' in tax and more generally.

Notes

1 This chapter draws particularly on research on tax evasion and avoidance, conducted with Dr Graham Mansfield.
2 A preliminary version of some of the analysis has appeared under the title 'Law, policy and legal avoidance: can law effectively implement egalitarian policies?' *Journal of Law and Society*, 15 (1), Spring 1988.
3 *Financial Times*, 2 May 1985.
4 Ibid.
5 *Financial Times*, 20 April 1982.
6 For further details of these and other sophisticated techniques, see Mansfield (1987) and McBarnet (1992).
7 *R. v. Battersea etc. Rent Tribunal ex p. Parikh* (1957) 1 WLR.
8 (1982) 2 WLR 877.
9 (1981) STC 714.
10 (1984) 2 WLR 226.
11 For deeper analysis of attempted control by looking through form to substance, and how the regulated react, see McBarnet and Whelan (1991).
12 For detailed analysis of the contribution of structures of law and the use of ideology, see McBarnet (1988) and McBarnet and Whelan (1991).
13 But see McBarnet *et al.* (1993).

4 Capital fractionalized: the role of insolvency practitioners in asset distribution

Sally Wheeler

Introduction

This chapter looks at the struggle over assets in insolvent companies. It draws on a study conducted as part of a larger research programme[1] on business and finance, which has analysed, among other things, the role of loan finance/credit within the company form and the legal devices used to protect it. These issues have hitherto received surprisingly little attention from the sociology of law movement,[2] despite their obvious implications for capital interests. The conventional view is that law works in the interests of capital. The research programme has questioned this relationship by focusing on capital and state in conflict and on intra-capital conflicts (McBarnet 1984, 1988; McBarnet and Whelan 1987). McBarnet and Whelan focus on the struggle between fractions of capital for the scarce resources of an insolvent company and the role of law and legal devices in that struggle. This chapter focuses on the operation of one of these devices, the retention of title clause, on the role of lawyers, and on the practical tactics employed by insolvency practitioners in enforcing conflicting claims.

Background

To set the empirical material presented in this chapter in context, it is necessary to look briefly at the legal forms and institutions open to those who intentionally or unintentionally provide loan finance for companies. The term finance is used to mean financial assistance provided by outsiders – not that provided by members of the company through share purchase. Traditionally, loan finance is thought of as being mainly assistance provided by institutional investors, in exchange for a security interest in the company's assets (i.e. the right to resort to those assets in the event of default). Indeed, this particular interest has received legal recognition and protection for over 100 years in the form of the floating charge.

The advantages of the floating charge as a form of security and the forces which gave rise to its creation are well documented (e.g. Pennington 1960; Gower 1979). Briefly, its non-specific nature enables a security to be given by the company without any interference in the management of the company or the conduct of the company's business. The security is taken over a class of assets and fixes on specific items only when the charge is crystallized (expressed colloquially 'called in'). This involves the appointment of an insolvency practitioner as administrative receiver to realize the assets to satisfy the security. In the past, stock in trade has been a principal asset used to satisfy the charge. Quite frequently this stock has not been paid for. It has been supplied on credit by other manufacturers (the suppliers as they will now be termed). These goods can be caught within the floating charge secured on the company's property, despite the fact that they have not been paid for, by virtue of the UK Sale of Goods Act (SGA) 1979. Under s.17 of the SGA, title to goods (i.e. ownership) is deemed to pass on delivery unless the parties agree otherwise (s.19); for example, perhaps they might agree that title will not pass until payment for the goods has been received. This particular type of agreement between the parties is known as a Reservation of Title (RT) clause.

The right to contract out of the s.17 presumption was little used prior to 1976.[3] Suppliers of goods seemed content to be unwitting, unprotected purveyors of loan finance in the form of credit for other companies. However, in 1976, *AIV BV* v. *Romalpa Aluminium*[4] was decided by the Court of Appeal. It was a case concerning the supply of aluminium foil by a Dutch company to an English company and the Dutch company's terms and conditions of sale contained a RT clause. The purpose of the clause was clearly to defeat s.17 and retain title to the goods until payment was received. The Court of Appeal allowed recovery of the unsold foil. This decision has generated an enormous quantity of academic debate (Goode 1982, 1985; Milman 1984; Bradgate 1987) devoted to working out its implications. Evidence presented to the Cork Committee (1984) by financial institutions described the enormous growth in the use of RT clauses by suppliers. However, all this interest has generated only nine or so reported cases.[5] The rapid growth in the use of RT clauses since 1976 can be attributed to two related factors: first, the economic recession of the late 1970s and early 1980s provided an incentive for unsecured creditors to actively seek protection from customer insolvency and, secondly, the 'Romalpa' case itself received a great deal of publicity in financial journals and newspapers.[6]

The next section will look at the importance of RT clauses for institutional finance capital and subsequent sections will seek to show why there have been so few litigated cases on a development as important in credit finance as the establishment of the floating charge in the previous century.

The importance of Reservation of Title clauses

The effect of a successful RT clause is to remove the supplier from the creditor distribution list altogether. The suppliers' goods, left on the insolvent companies premises, are returnable on the basis that they never formed part of the assets of the insolvent company. The goods will not then be available for realization towards the amount owed to the debenture holder and this clearly decreases the prospects of satisfying the security completely. The distribution list looks like this:

1 Fixed charge, i.e. similar to a mortgage, taken over one particular asset.
2 Preferential creditors, e.g. state bodies such as the DSS and Inland Revenue.
3 Floating charge.
4 Unsecured creditors, e.g. suppliers of goods and services.

A RT clause creates a division in the class of creditors that is traditionally found at the bottom of the list.

Holders of floating charges can deal with the threat to their position of priority in two ways. They can 'take advantage of one device or another to avoid the law in a way which may break the spirit but does not break the letter of the law' (McBarnet 1988) or they can defend vigorously all RT claims submitted. McBarnet and Whelan (1987) focus on the first. They show that the history of insolvency law is littered with attempts by one or another form of capital to gain priority over others. The floating charge was one such successful attempt. The distribution list of creditors given above sits uneasily with the principle purporting to underlie UK insolvency law – *pari passu* distribution of assets. New devices created to avoid loss of priority are not suitable for all companies and all lenders and there is also the problem of companies which have already given floating charges secured on stock; hence the development of the second method of dealing with RT clauses. It is that second method, the strategies employed to defend RT clauses, that is the subject of examination in this chapter. The process of making a RT claim involves going through various stages of proof as set up by the insolvency practitioner; the process taken as a whole can be viewed as the 'enforcement process'. This study reveals law as indifferent to, or unable to deal with, a dispute within capital; both to suppliers of goods who feel compelled to use the machinery of RT clauses by the failure of law to recognize the priority of their claims on the insolvency of trading partners, and to insolvency practitioners who regard the very existence of RT clauses as detrimental to the speedy disposal of insolvencies and as an erosion of the debenture holder's prioritized security. It also reveals capital as unconcerned by the impotency of law: the intra-capital conflict is won by the class which capitalizes on all its advantages and realizes the strength of its position.

Methods

The study was based on field research; the methods were interviews, documentary analysis and observation. Three principal groups of actors were involved: suppliers, insolvency practitioners and their lawyers. Insolvency practitioners and their lawyers were selected on a 'snowball' sample basis. This was necessary because of the problems of obtaining access in the business community. Suppliers were selected on a purely random basis with efforts being made to cover as many different types of industry as possible. The geographical area of study was primarily the West Midlands in the UK. As a highly industrialized area, this was likely to generate company insolvencies and suppliers of goods rather than services. The number of actors contacted and interviewed was eighteen insolvency practitioners, thirteen lawyers and twenty suppliers. It is not suggested that these numbers are large enough to generate quantitative data. The interviews were kept as unstructured and reflexive as possible and lengthy observation (i.e. two months or more) and documentary analysis of entire claims failed was also undertaken. This is sufficient to enable valid conceptual generalizations to be made.

The documentary analysis was particularly important as it was based on complete receiverships or liquidations. The idea was that each insolvency turns to a certain extent on its own facts and this factual basis affects both the supplier's and insolvency practitioner's perspective on the claim. It was thought that a claim could only be treated as representative of the enforcement process if it was looked at in the context of the whole insolvency. For example, decisions about stock and methods of dealing with RT claims will differ depending on whether it is intended to carry on the company's business and sell it as a going concern or simply wind it down and dispose of its assets in a piecemeal fashion.

Formal law

'Formal law' is here being used as the term to describe judicial decisions or statutory intervention. The judicial decision which created so much interest in RT clauses has already been outlined. A feature of any method of law-making is the room for manoeuvrability that it leaves the parties it is seeking to regulate – the uncertainty element. An examination of any area of law reveals that there is no such thing as 'certain law'. This view is by no means one which is universally accepted. Treitel, for example, (1981) takes the view that contract law, for example, needs and indeed creates legal certainty through its rules. Weber (1966) held the view that a predictable, consistent set of laws was essential in the commercial arena if capital was to develop. To take the view that certain law exists is to ignore the role that lawyers and para-legals play in legal practice. They serve their clients' interest by working on the law to ensure that their interests do not conflict with its demands.

Lawyers do not serve the interests of their clients by simply translating particular interest or particular disputes into legal terms (cf. Cain 1983); they do much more than that. Either as in McBarnet's work, the letter of the law is manoeuvred around by using more formal law, or formal law is evaded by the creation of administrative rules within its own framework. In the case of RT clauses, case law requires that three elements be present for a clause to be successful: a clause must be part of the contract of sale made between the now insolvent company and the supplier, it must reserve legal title to the goods and the goods must be identified as unpaid for. No guidance is given as to what must be shown in order to satisfy these elements; this is a matter for the parties and if they disagree, then they can resort to litigation to solve their differences. In practice, the administrative structure is designed and imposed by the dominant actors – in the case of RT clauses, this is the insolvency practitioner and his lawyer – and the administrative structure designed reflects the gap between the requirements of the formal law and what is required at the practical law level to fulfil these requirements.

This is not to say that formal law developments have no impact at all on the claims enforcement process. They do, because the process with its administrative rules cannot exist in a vacuum oblivious to the legal environment to which it owes its existence. Formal law (case law in the main, as there is very little legislative input in this area) is seen by insolvency practitioners in terms of the game analogy – case law sets the goalposts in the claims enforcement process but the rules of the game are the administrative rules that they themselves impose and which they may have to change or adapt as the impact of particular cases filters through.

An emphasis of this chapter is that satisfying the formal law is a meaningless concept. A claimant supplier must satisfy the formal law as interpreted by the dominant actor and illustrated in the administrative rules. The insolvency practitioner is the dominant actor for a variety of reasons; first, he is in possession of the goods; secondly, he knows whether he wishes to use the goods in future production or whether he needs to order more from the supplier; and, thirdly, there is a significant power imbalance between the two parties in terms of their financial capacity, legal competence and familiarity with the problem. In short, insolvency practitioners display all the classic characteristics of repeat players (Galanter 1984) in relation to this particular type of highly specialized commercial work.

Starting blocks

To make a claim, each supplier has to go through certain stages, perhaps more appropriately described as filters, as their effect in practice is to discourage potential claims. To understand the enforcement process, it is important to look at the mental set with which the parties begin the process.

The insolvency practitioner (IP) begins with his mind firmly set towards rejection of every RT claim if possible, while recognizing that in some cases it may be financially advantageous to settle the claim and avoid the legal costs of defending it. In the words of IP2:

> I would not describe myself as setting RT claims or even administering RT claims. I reject RT claims whenever I can. If I have to admit them, then I do so as cheaply as possible. You have to be careful that the costs of rejection do not exceed the costs of the claim . . . I don't deliberately try to diddle these suppliers, you know . . . If their internal credit control is so bad that they supply so much on credit then that's tough, they deserve to lose out.

Similar views were expressed by IP4:

> RT claims have to be rejected whenever you can commercially and sensibly do so. Why should suppliers of goods get themselves to the top of the tree – what about the chap who supplied the canteen? It's a small cake and everyone ought to get some.

Laudable sentiments indeed! However, a glance at Table 1 shows that this is merely a public relations front, at least in relation to administrative receivers. They are appointed by debenture holders and are often from one of the ten major accountancy firms. They take their fee out of what is recovered and Table 1 shows that insolvency is a profitable part of business for these firms. Coupled with this, there is the incentive of future appointment to make sure that the debenture holder's security is successfully satisfied. Liquidators are not under the same pressure directly from debenture holders, as they are appointed on behalf of and act for the general body of creditors. However, there is often little liquidity left in a company in liquidation and the liquidator has to be paid his fees out of the assets that he is able to recover and realize. Obviously, the less that is taken out of the meagre assets of the insolvent company on an RT basis,

Table 1 Insolvency fee league table for financial year end March 1992

Firm	1992 income £m	% of total income 1992	1988 income £m	% of total income 1988
KPMG Peat Marwick	49.47	10	13.1	5
Coopers (1)	46.16	8	16.5	9.6
Touche Ross (2)	41.96	12	6.8	5.8
Price Waterhouse	36.04	9	8.4	4.7
Ernst & Young (3)	35.90	9	–	–
Grant Thornton	26.04	22	–	–
Arthur Andersen	16.54	5	4.5	4
Stoy Hayward	14.34	21	4.1	11
Pannell Kerr Forster	12.85	15	2.4	5.1
Robson Rhodes	9.80	2	1.6	6.3
BDO Binder Hamlyn	6.86	6	3.6	5
Kidsons Impey (4)	6.61	11	–	–

A number of mergers between firms and acquisitions of firms by others have taken place within the accountancy profession. Those movements as they affect the fee table are noted below.

1 Coopers' figures include those of Deloitte Haskins and Sells, which was the fourth highest earning firm from insolvency in 1988.
2 Touche Ross' figures include those of Spicer and Oppenheimer, which was the seventh highest earning firm from insolvency in 1988.
3 Ernst & Young were formed from Ernst & Whinney and Arthur Young, consequently no figures are available for 1988.
4 Kidsons Impey were formed from Kidsons and Hodgson Impey.

the more there is available to satisfy the liquidator's fees. Although liquidators are usually appointed from smaller accountancy firms than administrative receivers, there is still a need for liquidation work to be profitable.

The claimant supplier begins the enforcement process with feelings of hostility towards the administrative receiver. All the suppliers interviewed referred to either previous unsatisfactory dealings with administrative receivers or cited instances that they had heard of. These instances may not have been true, or may have been told from only one viewpoint, but they illustrate the point that claimant suppliers felt that the administrative receiver had other interests at heart and would avoid acknowledging claims if possible.

The point raised by IP2 about credit control goes to the heart of the organizational structure of the firm. All the suppliers interviewed had some form of internal credit control and all agreed that the need to make a RT claim indicated that these credit checks had failed. A study of credit control is really beyond the scope of this chapter, but some points have relevance to stances taken during the claims enforcement process. The focus of suppliers is forward looking towards new customers. Every company can withstand a certain amount of bad debt and all the suppliers felt that the possibility of incurring bad debts was better offset by striving to attract new customers than spending time checking the credentials of existing ones. This forward-looking perspective left suppliers in some difficulty when asked by insolvency practitioners to document their trading history with the insolvent company, as required by the administrative rules of the claims enforcement process. These were not records that could easily be produced. The forward-looking perspective also accounts for the fact that suppliers do not either as an entire group or as individual industry-based groups band together to form repeat player organizations (Macaulay 1966; Galanter 1974), despite the fact that in the industrial recessions of the late 1970s and 1980s there must have been opportunities to do so. Information sought from bodies like trade associations, etc., suggests that the only centrally co-ordinated information for suppliers reflects their own commercial perspective; it concerns the quality of the product and specifications.

Making a claim

1. Notification

This is the first stage involved in bringing a claim. Whereas insolvency practitioners now have to inform creditors of their appointment,[7] at the time this research was conducted that was not the case. Notification to creditors of the company was made on the basis of the company's own records. A claimant supplier depends on the correctness of these records to be informed of the possibility of making a claim. As far as this part of the administrative structure is concerned, this is not a filter controlled by the insolvency practitioner, but it is still one over which the claimant supplier has no control. Notification is very important for a potential claimant – the longer he remains unaware of an insolvency, the more difficult he will find it to make a claim. Insolvency practitioners maintain, and indeed this was confirmed by observation, that they keep records of stock that is used for continued production and stock that is moved to rationalize space and ease security worries. However, this is of little assistance to the claimant supplier who needs the physical evidence of the goods themselves in their original packaging with serial numbers, etc., to assert the validity of his claim, i.e. to show that the goods are his and can be identified as supplied on invoices which have not been paid.

The creditor's letter
Unless the supplier hears of an insolvency through local press reports or from other manufacturers, as was the case in some instances, then he is

reliant on the creditor's letter to inform him of his right to claim. The form and content of the letter are a matter for individual insolvency practitioners or their firms, because it is not unusual for standardized documents to be used within firms to deal with RT claims. The same letter is circularized to all creditors and can take one of two forms: it can either ask that potential RT claims be submitted to the insolvent company, or it can simply request that any claim against the company be brought within a certain time limit without specifically alluding to RT clauses. The rationale behind the use of the second form of letter can be seen from the comments of IP14: 'I don't actually want to encourage these claims . . . If you put "claims against the company" half of 'em don't know what you're talking about.'

The first form of letter was used by insolvency practitioners who felt either generally or in the context of a particular insolvency that it was better to know the potential level of claims as soon as possible. The second form of letter can be seen as denying a right created by the formal law; the formal law creates or confers a right to claim but fails to create a mechanism whereby someone has the right to know of their rights. It leaves this to the parties and the structure imposed by the dominant actor who uses the manoeuvrability within the formal law to his own advantage.

2. Access

A supplier who receives and correctly interprets his notification letter, then has to gain access to the premises of the insolvent company. While notification belonged partly to the formal law model, access belongs to the administrative structure. Only three claims in the 259 examined raised questions of the denial of access and each of these can be explained on the grounds of internal confusion on behalf of the suppliers. It is clearly impractical for access to be denied completely in a large receivership. A far more important issue is the manipulation of the timing of access. The sooner a supplier can gain access to the premises and identify his goods, the sooner he can begin to pressurize the insolvency practitioner for their return. By delaying access, the insolvency practitioner can ensure that he knows exactly which goods he needs and which he does not and what the most effective defence strategy will be.

The insolvency practitioners interviewed put forward the idea of three types of opponent at this stage: first, suppliers and inexperienced lawyers whose protests could be ignored as there was no immediate threat of litigation; secondly, experienced lawyers who because of their frequent involvement in this area were part of an informal club network. Here insolvency practitioners knew how far they could exploit the power imbalances between the two sides: if they had plausible reasons for delaying access, then these reasons would be accepted; if not, the opposing lawyer would seek an injunction, and the result was normally a compromise. Thirdly, there were the experienced lawyers who were not part of the club. This category was most difficult for the insolvency practitioners and it appears that a rather more acrimonious compromise was reached. Here insolvency practitioners are identifying the area as one of difficult legal practice; only those who exhibit the external features of legal expertise will give any cause for concern.

3. Inspection

From the viewpoint of both parties, inspection is essential: for the insolvency practitioner, it indicates the maximum amount of any successful claim; for the supplier, it identifies whether there are any goods that can be the subject of a claim and whether that claim is economically worth pursuing. Despite the steady increase in the use of RT claims, it was clear that many suppliers had no idea of the significance of the inspection stage. Some thought that the purpose was to allow them to collect their goods – these ideas were rudely dispelled by the insolvency practitioners involved. This ignorance is probably due to one of two reasons: either the supplier had taken his RT clause from the sales documentation of another manufacture – 'the trickle down effect' (Macaulay 1979) – and so had no idea of the administrative structure surrounding the enforcement of his clause, or the quality of legal advice sought at the clause drafting stage was such that the lawyer involved had no idea of the demands of the enforcement process.

The insolvency practitioner uses the inspection stage to emphasize to the supplier that he regards his claim as a very small part of a much larger process. This is done by using a dramaturgical perspective. The supplier is shown around the premises by a junior member of staff who often appears uncertain of the procedure. Requests to see the administrative receiver or 'someone senior' are denied on the grounds that they are all too busy and that much more information will be required before a decision can be reached. This is often the first time that a supplier has contemplated the possibility that his claim will be rejected or heard that further evidence will be needed. The attitude shown is one of disinterest – 'it's somebody else's decision'.

This front is maintained to the extent that obvious discrepancies in identification are not pointed out at this stage, but left to become grounds of rejection at a later stage of the enforcement process. In claim 8, it was clear that although an item was found in its original packaging, and was greeted with great acclaim by the supplier concerned, conversely the number of the only unpaid invoice was not the same as that on the item. The whole process, whether intentionally or not on the insolvency practitioner's behalf, has a disconcerting effect on the supplier – recovery is not going to be the easy matter he had in mind and he does not receive any positive indication that the matter will be settled quickly.

4. The questionnaire

The final element involved in making a claim is the completion of the questionnaire. This is provided by most insolvency practitioners and like the creditor's letter usually exists as a standard document within their particular firms. When completed, it underlies the insolvency practitioner's treatment of the claim. Broadly speaking, all questionnaires request the same information. They ask for documentation of the supplier's entire trading history with the insolvent company, the date of supply of the terms and conditions of sale, and the name of the person within the insolvent company who accepted them, and the means by which the supplier links his goods found to the unpaid invoice.

The questionnaire asks for information which the supplier regards as irrelevant and difficult to obtain. He has a distrust of the insolvency practitioner based on structural reasons and the questionnaire entrenches this distrust (cf. Hawkins 1984). The information sought by the questionnaire cuts across the internal organization of the firm. The forward-looking perspective of the supplier dictates that this information, if available, will be stored in several different departments under the control of several different people. Insolvency practitioners justify the information sought on the grounds that they need to build up a complete picture of the pattern of supply and on what basis that supply was made. The questionnaire enables an insolvency practitioner to see at what points the claim does not fit into the administrative structure and so what will be possible grounds of rejection. It also provides a valuable insight into how likely the claim is to be pursued; missing information has a certain negative value, it shows that the claim is unlikely to be followed up vigorously or, if it is, that it will be easily defeated – the supplier either does not possess the information or does not understand why it is needed.

The administrative structure set up by insolvency practitioners results in some possibly legally valid claims, in the sense of formal law, dropping out at each stage: some suppliers will not realize that they have a right to claim; others will not do so on the grounds of cost and time; still others will be discouraged by the inspection process or the questionnaire. The fact that the administrative agenda is created and adhered to emphasizes the insolvency practitioner's dominance over the whole situation. A significant feature of making a claim is that there is virtually no formal law involved at all – only the interpretation of its requirements offered by the insolvency practitioner's administrative structure.

Negotiation of claims

This is the next step in the enforcement process. Negotiation in the context of RT claims is different from that assumed in the traditional analyses of negotiation,[8] where there is bi-party dialogue moving towards some sort of agreed settlement. The nature of RT claims is that negotiation is zero-sum. If a claim is admitted, then generally it has to be admitted and satisfied in full.[9] It has already been established that the insolvency practitioner is in a position of control. Consequently, negotiation between the parties takes the form of the establishment of defence strategies by the insolvency practitioner. These strategies are imposed on the supplier as part of the administrative structure of the claim process; the successful supplier is the one who overcomes these strategies. The defence strategies are formed by reference to four interrelated policy factors, which are largely in the control of the insolvency practitioner.

The development of case law has altered considerably the range of defences available to insolvency practitioners. Now defences frequently rest on incorporation points (whether the terms and conditions of sale of the supplier containing the RT clause ever became part of its contract with the insolvent company). The arguments on this issue are based on fact rather than law and call for a knowledge of the claims process, in that the supplier needs to know why the information sought is important. The insolvency practitioner simply picks from the current case law the part of the decision which will benefit him the most.

Circumstances of the insolvency

The records and practices of the insolvent company will have a part to play in the formulation of a defence:

> If you know that they stored their goods with the packaging removed in large bins all mixed together . . . then you can state with more conviction that they [i.e. the supplier] have not adequately identified their goods . . . knowing the company and the supplier greatly increase the chance of success (IP6).

This policy factor may operate to remove a supplier from the application of defence strategies and enable him to be treated differently from other suppliers. A supplier supplying specialist goods that are difficult to obtain elsewhere or a very large supplier in an administrative receivership that is continuing to trade for the time being may receive different treatment to ensure that he continues to supply the insolvency practitioner. Once again, the insolvency practitioner is in control, as he knows which goods he needs; the supplier has to realize the strength of his position and communicate this to the insolvency practitioner, otherwise he will receive the same treatment as the other suppliers.

Self-presentation of the supplier

This is the only factor over which the supplier has any control. All insolvency practitioners felt that any defence put to a claim must have some foundation in fact and law. As lawyer 7 put it:

> . . . you have to be careful about the points you raise. A good experienced lawyer will spot a spurious defence a mile off and then you lose credibility. Even the good points you have will be ruined.

A differential is being drawn here between suppliers; uninformed suppliers can be deflected by the use of false counters that insolvency practitioners and their lawyers know would be ineffective in negotiation with informed suppliers. Legal representation does not necessarily equate with 'informed status' – this only happens if the lawyer used is identified, by the insolvency practitioner and his lawyer, as an experienced commercial lawyer with knowledge not only of the formal law but also of the administrative structure.

Claims defence policy

These four factors result in the formulation of the claims defence policy. It is presented to suppliers in the form of an initial rejection letter demanding better evidence of a particular factor like identification of the goods. The letter is an objective exercise for insolvency practitioners. Cost, time and their degree of control mean that the vast majority of claims are not at this stage considered on an individual basis.

The initial rejection letter presents a problem for the supplier; he realizes that proving his claim will be difficult but often does not understand why. In response to the rejection letter, he can often only reproduce all the documentation that was produced in relation to the questionnaire. The rejection letter often asks for the relevance of the produced evidence to be explained, but the subtlety of this is not apparent to the supplier. Other choices for the supplier at this stage include writing to the insolvency practitioner and demanding to know what is required or simply dropping the claim.

The effects of the rejection letter can be seen from administrative receiverships 4 and 5. In 4, there were 23 claims, the total value of which was £95,477.29: 17 per cent of suppliers with claims to the value of £16,140.05 dropped their claims. In 5, there were 44 claims with a total value of £461,927.84: 31 per cent of suppliers dropped their claims, which were valued at £94,103.04 after the first rejection letter. Lawyer 2, who was acting for the insolvency practitioner in both these instances, summed up their attitude as:

> . . . tell them all to go away at first, just fob them off with the usual stuff about identification, and wait and see who comes back. Then keep the claim running as long as possible and hope that they go to sleep on it.

The initial rejection letter takes effect as a further claims filter, and emphasizes the control of institutional capital.

Delay

The suggestion is that delay is used by the insolvency practitioner and his lawyer as part of the administrative structure for dealing with claims. Their rationale appears to be that delay 'takes the heat out of a claim' – that suppliers with their forward-looking perspective, as time passes, will forget about the claim. Lengthy delays in communication support the idea conveyed at the inspection and questionnaire stages that the insolvency practitioner is not particularly interested in speedy settlement of the claim and regards it as unimportant. Delay is used as a tactic even when the claim is clearly one which can be rejected on other grounds. Claim 132 was such a claim. The RT clause involved was one which, according to the decision in *Re Bond Worth*[10] was legally invalid – the claim could have been rejected straight away. A file note on the claim reads:

> Five mins speaking to Y . . . to ask him the position with regard to the claim which is invalid . . . Y is to find out whether all of the supplies we want have arrived. If so we can write immediately and say that their claim is bad. If there are further supplies to be made then we should write a stalling letter.

The lawyer sample interviewed did not view delay as a blanket tactic, it was something that had to be used selectively. If it annoyed suppliers or their lawyers to the extent that they issued proceedings, then it had failed its purpose. They recognized that in some claims delay exhausted its purpose and had to be abandoned. In claim 52 (value £19,520), the claim comprised goods that were loose and stored with others and goods still in their original packaging. In relation to the first category, there was clearly an identification problem. After protracted delays, a settlement figure was offered by the insolvency practitioner's lawyer. The supplier's lawyer negotiated this figure up to £7674. The lawyer wrote to his insolvency practitioner client in the following vein:

> Their solicitors are clearly getting exasperated with all the delays. If we do not settle . . . they might litigate . . . for the full amount. They

would not get that much but they would get substantially more than the £7,674 they are prepared to settle for now.

The supplier here was left feeling relieved that he had recovered any of his claim. The whole process took two years and two months. The insolvency practitioner was left feeling that his tactics had secured him a bargain.

Belts and braces[11]

The picture presented here is of the ever-changing question. Whatever evidence the supplier produces, the insolvency practitioner will always produce another question to be answered. For example, in claim 61, evidence as to the links between unpaid invoices and goods was asked for and supplied; without admitting the validity of this evidence, the insolvency practitioner then asked for evidence of incorporation of terms and conditions of sale. The supplier did not pursue the claim further.

The supplier can find himself on a never-ending treadmill of questions, where his answers are either not accepted or supplanted by further questions. For example, the supplier has to show that the insolvent company traded on the basis of his terms and conditions of sale. If the insolvency practitioner says that the supplier's terms and conditions of sale cannot be found at the insolvent company's premises, then the supplier has to accept this. The next step for the supplier would be to produce a signed copy of the terms, at which point the insolvency practitioner will question the authority of the signatory to bind the insolvent company.

Bluff

Bluff, as a device, is used by insolvency practitioners to bolster their position. Its use emphasizes their superior knowledge of the whole process. A common example was a general bluff presented to all suppliers in the hope of convincing them that there was an insurmountable hurdle to recovery; all suppliers of high-volume, low-cost goods (e.g. nuts and bolts) might be told that identification of each item will be impossible because of their type. This is not viewed as a spurious defence by insolvency practitioners but as a simple inquiry as to whether the practices of these particular suppliers differ from others in the same industry.

The bluffs used by insolvency practitioners were in no way non-legal or extra-legal, simply their interpretation of the facts of the insolvency. Their use of bluff in relation to formal law is quite different from the way in which this relationship is found in other contexts (Hawkins 1984). They did not portray the formal law as having greater powers than it in fact did. This would appear to be for two reasons: first, their dominance over the process is so complete that this is not necessary and, secondly, the risk of loss of credibility is too great. If the supplier were to purchase good quality commercial legal advice from an experienced lawyer, a spurious bluff would have the same effect as the presentation of a spurious defence.

The role of external factors

A point made at the outset of this chapter was that law always contained an element of practical uncertainty or manoeuvrability and that the insolvency practitioner's administrative structure capitalizes on that uncertainty in this context. Galanter (1974) takes the view that litigation will be avoided to preserve this element. Any decision which would offer clarification of the position in favour of suppliers would be detrimental and so settlement would be offered:

> If a repeat player is interested in maximizing his tangible gain in a series of cases . . . he may be willing to trade off tangible gain in any one case for rule gain (or to minimize rule loss) . . . We would then expect repeat players to settle cases where they expected unfavourable rule outcomes.
>
> (Galanter 1974: 98)

However, this is not found here. The administrative structure is considered to be a flexible process which can adapt to any changed situation. Factors like possession of the goods, premises and insolvent company's records are considered to be cards which will overcome any change in the formal law. There are other external pressures which mean that settlement is viewed as a last resort. Settlement is seen as something which can result in a precedent being set for that particular insolvency. Other suppliers hear of it and demand settlement – settlement is seen as a sign of weakness. Bargaining reputation is viewed as more important than the administrative structure. Settlement of claims that do not merit it may result in opposing lawyers/ suppliers viewing that particular insolvency practitioner and his lawyer as a 'soft touch' in any future insolvencies or related commercial work.

Insolvency practitioners take the view that a claim in which formal legal proceedings are commenced will not necessarily end up being adjudicated by a court. This view is reinforced by the small number of formal law decisions in RT claims. They often have greater resources in terms of finance than suppliers and are prepared to go along with litigation in the hope that cost factors dictate that it is dropped at a later date.

The role of legal advice

There are two issues here – the importance of the legal advice received by the insolvency practitioner and that received by the supplier. Dealing with RT claims is almost everyday work for insolvency practitioners; they deal with a lot of the day-to-day claims administration without consulting a lawyer. They are often supported by large technical directorates within their own firms who produce standard documentation to be used throughout the process and briefings on the latest case law. The questions raised by the insolvency practitioner–lawyer relationship are really beyond the scope of this chapter and can be found elsewhere (Wheeler 1991b). It is sufficient to say that the insolvency practitioner has the status of a para-legal because of his familiarity with the process and that para-legal experience enables him to choose an experienced and competent lawyer from a commercially orientated practice to act for him.

Only 24 per cent of suppliers used any form of legal representation and, as has already been mentioned, lawyer use does not equate with recovery. Suppliers seem to have an inherent distrust of law and lawyers. There appears to be several reasons for this (cf. Macaulay 1963; Beale and Dugdale 1975). Cost is a major factor in determining both the decision to go to law for assistance and the type of lawyer sought. Large commercial practices present an image of affluence and 'fat cats' to a manufacturer. Manufacturers distrust anyone who does not make something or provide a service closely connected with industry. They see lawyers as parasitic; their offices and equipment must be paid for by exorbitant and unjustified fees and the misfortunes of others. Claim 221 provides an interesting example of this.

This was a claim for £25,000 and the supplier sought the assistance of an experienced lawyer from a large commercial practice as soon as he heard of the administrative receivership. He represented to the lawyer that his company was in dire financial straits and would probably become insolvent itself if the money was not recovered. The lawyer achieved recovery of the stock in five days. It was a labour-intensive exercise involving fifteen telephone calls and six telexes to the insolvency practitioners and several to their lawyers. The lawyer then wrote to the supplier advising him that his credit control needed to be examined and of the consequences of the Insolvency Act 1986, s. 214.[12] The supplier replied thanking him for his concern, but assuring him that his company was financially secure and that loss of £25,000 was not that serious. The reason for his story of imminent closure was that he believed the lawyer would not handle the claim speedily or forcefully without that extra spur. The lawyer involved here knew that success depended upon the amount of pressure placed on the administrative structure.

Suppliers frequently fail to see the drawing up of terms and conditions of sale and the enforcement of RT clauses as situations which may give rise to complex problems. In their view, RT clauses can be enforced in the same way as a neighbourhood boundary dispute – a solicitor's letter will put everything right. There is no real conception that an insolvency practitioner is part of a highly professional organization, and will not concede anything unless he is forced to; more than one letter is required to do this. The overwhelming tendency among suppliers is to approach small general practice solicitors, whom they might have become familiar with in another context, e.g. domestic conveyancing. RT claims are not regarded as a problem which demand a higher level of skill. As far as the supplier is concerned, the law gives an absolute right to recovery and one letter should be enough to enforce that right.

As can be seen from the preceding discussion of the administrative structure imposed on claims negotiation, the choice of a general practice lawyer is not a good one. Successful claims negotiation requires knowledge of the administrative structure as well as the formal law, as can be seen from claim 221. General practice lawyers do not possess knowledge of either of these factors. RT clauses are not a frequent source of work for them. However, they take these cases (1) because it is part of the ethos of general practice that the lawyer undertakes whatever work the client requests and (2) because a case of this type may lead to future work (Bankowski and Mungham 1976).

The general practice lawyer's inability to deal with the requirements of the administrative structure is traded upon by the insolvency practitioner and his lawyer. They regard these lawyers as missing open goals in the enforcement process; for example, they treat with amusement the failure to ask for stock records which would be helpful in the linking of goods to unpaid invoices. One lawyer went so far as to suggest that 90 per cent of the lawyers dealing with claims in an administrative receivership where he was representing the insolvency practitioner should be reported to the Law Society for their gross incompetence in asserting their clients' claims.

The use of experienced commercial lawyers may provide the key to success for suppliers as in claim 221. However, the cost of pursuing the enforcement process through a lawyer of this type may take all of, or even exceed, what is recovered, so giving only a Pyrrhic victory to the supplier. This lawyer group may not pursue claims with particular urgency, although they are fully cognizant with the process. They are aware of the problems of obtaining payment when the cost of recovery exceeds actual recovery. RT claims are labour-intensive, in that if success is to be achieved it requires constant pressure on the insolvency practitioner in the first few days of the insolvency and this is expensive in terms of man hours. Demand for payment on account is standard practice in large commercial firms; the supplier is faced with the prospect of paying for a by no means certain recovery. Experienced commercial lawyers are of most assistance to large national or multinational companies which have either their own legal departments or regular contact with large commercial law firms. In that instance, claims will be pursued as part of a continuing service, at a competitive price to ensure the continuance of the relationship. RT claims may not be profitable but other aspects of commercial law are.

Conclusion

It would seem that formal law offers support to neither side. Institutional finance capital wins the day because it is able to take the formal law and add it to its structural advantages to present an almost unassailable position of control. Knowledge of the formal law alone is insufficient for the supplier. Success for the supplier is dependent upon an understanding of the administrative structure, which can then be used to dilute the control of the insolvency practitioner. Even an understanding of and pressure upon the structure will not necessarily give the supplier success, as he is still dependent to a certain extent on the practices of the insolvent company, over which he has no control.

Notes

1 The research programme was conducted by McBarnet, Whelan and Wheeler at the Centre for Socio-legal Studies, Oxford. The material presented here was collected in 1986 and is discussed more extensively in Wheeler (1991a).
2 See Rubin and Sugarman (1983: p. 43f). The studies cited there are mainly historical in perspective, detailing the growth of investment in the corporate form and changing views of debt enforcement.
3 There are several nineteenth-century decisions which make it clear that the seller of goods has long been able to retain title until he is paid: *McEntire* v. *Crossley Ltd.* (1895) AC 457 and *Helby* v. *Matthews* (1895) AC 471. McEntire is a deferred sale agreement and Helby is a hire agreement with an option to purchase; however, the principles which can be extracted are analogous to the principle of RT clauses.
4 (1976) 1 WLR 676.
5 *AIV* v. *Romalpa, supra* note 4; *Re Bond Worth* (1980) ch. 228; *Burden Ltd.* v. *Scottish Timber Products* (1981) ch. 25; *Hendy Lennox Ltd* v. *Puttick (Grahame) Ltd.* (1984) 1 WLR 485; *Re Peachdart Ltd* (1984) ch. 131; *Re Andrabell Ltd.* (1984) 3 All ER 407; *Clough Mill* v. *Martin* (1984) 2 All ER 982; *Specialist Plant Services* v. *Braithwaite* (1987) BCLC 1.
6 An indication of the level of comment passed can be gauged from this comment of Professor Roy Goode: 'doubtful whether any case decided this century has created a greater impact on commercial law' (*The Times*, 5 November 1977).
7 Insolvency Act 1986, s. 46.
8 Genn (1987) provides a comprehensive review of the negotiation and bargaining literature.
9 Unlike personal injury claims, for example, where it is quite normal for a claim to be admitted but negotiation to continue over the quantum of recovery in one part of the claim, e.g. pain and suffering.

10 *Supra,* note 8.
11 A traditional term used by lawyers meaning that every eventuality has been thought of and covered.
12 Insolvency Act 1986, s. 214. If a company continues to trade when on an objective standard insolvent liquidation can be the only result. The directors become personally liable for the debts of the company, from that point onwards, unless they can show that they did all they could to avoid this.

5 Blurred boundaries: the overlapping worlds of law, business and politics

David Sugarman

Introduction

Are lawyers professionals, constrained by public service limitations on their work, or free-wheeling businesspeople? So the current debate surrounding professionalism *vs* commercialism is articulated (American Bar Association 1986; for its historical antecedents, see Gordon 1988). All too often this controversy is grounded in a sort of *Gemeinschaft-Gesellschaft*: a golden age of the lawyer as public servant which has given way to the ethics of the marketplace. The starting point of this chapter is that this way of thinking about the work of lawyers is unhelpful in so far as it encourages a belief in stark divisions between a pure realm of 'lawyering' and the grubby world of 'business', and between the 'private' and the 'public' dimensions of lawyers' work. In practice, both lawyering and business and the public and private roles of lawyering are, and probably always have been, imbricated within each other. This chapter seeks to demonstrate this coalescence from historical materials. In particular, it describes and analyses the high-profile involvement of lawyers in business enterprises, and also their significance in state and civil society.

Transcending the divisions between lawyering and business and the private and the public roles of lawyers in society helps to focus attention on a related set of connections that are often neglected within the history and sociology of the profession: namely, the relationship between the ideas and culture of the profession, the work lawyers undertake, the organization of legal practices and their economic context, how these change over time, and the larger cultural and political significance of lawyers in society (cf. Gordon 1983; Brooks 1986; Prest 1986; Lemmings 1990; Nelson *et al.* 1992b). This opens the way for a new agenda for the history and sociology of lawyers and legal institutions, one which recognizes the role of lawyers in creating and transmitting some of our most important political discourses (Sugarman 1992b). An examination of these issues also illuminates the in-built conflicts of interest and the plurality of voices, logics, 'traditions', audiences and spheres of action that are an important feature of legal work, thought, culture and authority. From this broader perspective, we can investigate the relative elasticity of the ideology of legal professionalism and the ways in which that ideology sustains apparently divergent conceptions of the profession, while asserting a common culture and history binding lawyers together as a community (Sugarman 1991; Sarat 1992).

This chapter attempts to summarize some of the manifold tasks undertaken by lawyers for business in England between 1750 and 1950. Hopefully, this synthesis will assist and encourage more work in this important field of research. In addition to presenting a selective overview of this fledgling field, the chapter elaborates a prospectus for future work. It suggests some ways in which the cultural, political and economic dimensions of lawyers' work, and the professional ideologies that lawyers bring to their work, might receive more sustained attention. In particular, it seeks to illustrate some of the close and on-going connections between the overlapping worlds of law, business, politics and political discourse, thereby enriching our understanding of law in history.

Tasks lawyers performed for clients

Until well into the nineteenth century, the provision of legal services was not highly institutionalized. Most lawyers had no standardized training or formal paper qualifications, nor did the profession demand a full-time working commitment. Thus, until the late nineteenth century, English lawyers were extremely heterodox and variegated, wearing several occupational hats at once – rather than professing a single calling.

Despite their often low reputation, lawyers proved indispensable to their landed and business clients. Let us take the work of London attorney Robert Andrews. London's house-building boom of the 1720s and 1730s generated a considerable amount of business for attorneys. Much of it was straightforward conveyancing, but a great deal of business was triggered by the builder's need for capital and for quite complex arrangements for financing the building:

[Andrews] not only drew up the formal instruments, such as bonds and mortgages, through which loans were secured, but also rapidly established himself at the nexus of an intricate network of credit. The builder looked to him as a source of capital and the widows or spinsters with modest annuities or tradesmen with surplus profits and the merchants entrusted him with their savings to find the best outlets for their investment.

(Belcher 1985: 78)

Thus, attorneys and solicitors performed many functions for their clients including the collection of debts, conveying land, money lending and investment brokerage, estate management and the keeping of accounts. In the public domain, they managed elections and clerked for local commissions governing turnpikes, railways, general public works and enclosure. 'Inside the 18th century attorney, half a dozen later professional men – accountant, company secretary, and others – were struggling to get out' (Reader 1966: 43).

Lawyers as lenders, investors and financial intermediaries

A substantial literature now exists on the role played by attorneys as money lenders, professional investors and financial intermediaries. The pioneering work of Anderson (1969), Holderness (1975) and Miles (1984) has highlighted the increasing use of the mortgage and, therefore, the significant extension of credit from the late seventeenth century onwards, a century before the major industrial changes of the late eighteenth century. Crucial here was the local attorney who channelled funds from those with savings to those needing capital. In the late eighteenth century, attorneys were also the most important professional investors.

Attorneys and solicitors combined two specialist knowledges. First, a thorough knowledge of the locality, the opportunities it afforded for investment, and the financial activities of its residents; second, a legal expertise that could draft and police mortgage arrangements. Regional networks of attorneys performed the function of banks. These credit markets spanned both rural and metropolitan society; and they were widely used by most sections of society, notably the landed and middling sort.

From the 1870s to the turn of the century, British investors played a leading role in the funding of colonial and overseas railways. Here, too, City solicitors acted as conduits of capital and generally encouraged such investment (Slinn 1984: 84–5, 111–12, 116). In these diverse ways, lawyers made a signal contribution to capital formation in the early modern period.

Railways

The expansion of railways provided a new and highly lucrative income for the legal profession. The establishment of every railway company required a private Act of Parliament. Here was a veritable lawyers' paradise: complex and antiquated procedures were allied to time-consuming and costly lawyering (Kostal, 1994).

Solicitors and barristers drafted legislation; and the bar created a new market for its services as specialist counsel who argued the pros and cons of each bill before Parliament. Having secured statutory power to expropriate private property, lawyers played a crucial role in the often delicate negotiations with landowners, as well as conveying the land. Moreover, the railways generated many new legal problems in such areas as accident compensation and commercial law (Kostal, 1994).

The coming of the railways precipitated an accident problem of hitherto unimagined proportions. Lawyers were centrally involved in the legal and social problems that arose from these mishaps. Solicitors like Sir Thomas Paine, whose major clients included the North London Railway Company, were also called as witnesses before House of Commons Select Committees by counsel representing their clients. Concern at the social consequences of railway construction on the provision of working-class housing was becoming a matter of public disquiet:

> In the 1850s and 1860s Lord Shaftesbury had publicly criticised the eviction and displacement of thousands of Londoners . . . [Paine's] detailed knowledge of the area, derived from visits he had made . . . enabled him to reject suggestions which would have involved the North London Company in greater expenses . . . and to offer . . . [a] compromise.
>
> (Slinn 1987: 64)

Partnership and company law

For much of the nineteenth century, the partnership was the dominant form of business organization. Although partnerships could be and frequently were created without the help of lawyers, lawyers none the less played an important role in rationalizing business organization through their innovative use of partnership and later the limited liability company.

The limited liability company created much new work for solicitors. They were required to draft the companies' major constitutional documents, the articles and memoranda of association; and where companies failed, they were obliged to oversee the winding up. Legal confusion concerning the jurisdiction of the Courts of Bankruptcy and Chancery during the period 1848–57 produced more rich pickings for the legal profession.

The Companies Acts of 1856 and 1862 removed or watered-down earlier statutory provisions designed to protect the general public. From 1856 until the turn of the century, England was 'blessed' with the most permissive of regimes for regulating companies – a regime that was more abstentionist than its counterparts on the Continent and in North America (Sugarman, forthcoming). There was concern about improving the protection of investors, limiting the extension of limited liability and so on. While City solicitors acknowledged the weight of some of these criticisms, there was a strong tendency to favour the permissive *status quo*. Two arguments in particular repeatedly recur in their evidence and writings. First, the charge of 'impracticality'; that is, an emphasis upon the very limited role that the law (especially statute law) can play in preventing the dishonest from perpetrating a deceit. Secondly, it became an article of faith that England's liberal laws had made the City a haven for commerce and banking, and that any additional regulation would drive much of the City's highly profitable business to other parts of the world. In this way, a *laissez-faire* company law, the boosting of trade and industry, the abundant supply of capital and corporate lawyering were assembled, *en masse*, self-evidently working in the national interest. Company lawyers played an important role, naturalizing and sanctifying the limited liability company. Incorporation and limited liability were reclassified from a privilege to a right (Sugarman, forthcoming).

Lawyers were also a powerful pressure group within and beyond Parliament. On the publication of the Joint Stock Companies Bill of 1888, for example, seventeen leading City firms published a pamphlet opposing the Bill. They also served as 'expert witnesses' before parliamentary select committees. When discussions were under way for the reform of company law, the partners of major corporate specialists would submit written and oral evidence as well as sit on the committees responsible for making recommendations. Lawyers also sired numerous missives, pamphlets and lectures, from letters to *The Times* to public lectures on such worthy subjects as 'Bankruptcy and Liquidation'.

Knowledge is power. Nowhere is this more evident than in the diverse ways that lawyers used their specialist expertise and their wealth of contacts to shape the form and content of company law and, therefore, the organizational structure of the business corporation. Practitioners were the oracles of company law. They authored the basic textbooks and (very importantly) those collections of precedents that were used, re-used and re-worked in the everyday world of corporate practice. As with other areas of facilitative law (such as contract, property, trusts and family law), company law provided a skeleton for individual choice:

> In varying degrees, this facilitative power afforded the parties concerned the opportunity to make their own law (private law-making),

and even the opportunity, on occasions, to by-pass or attenuate the state law or equitable obligations established by Parliament or the courts, that otherwise would apply . . . Facilitative laws illustrate the way in which the *form* of law itself may, through its enormous flexibility and the legal principles that sanction that flexibility, mediate or avoid the legal order. Thus, use and avoidance of the law go hand in hand.

(Sugarman and Rubin 1984: 10–11)

The inventiveness of England's major company lawyers may be illustrated by way of a brief example. City solicitors constructed modern-style investment trusts from the 1850s. It was thought that spreading the risk within a broad-based portfolio would be especially attractive to smaller investors. However, the poor reputation of the market in shares continued to detract from a major development of this market until the 1880s onwards, when limited liability companies became more acceptable. As the USA eclipsed Britain in trade and manufacture, so new American techniques designed to market shares, or to facilitate the preservation and accumulation of wealth were selectively transplanted to England by City solicitors. One instance of this transatlantic borrowing was Linklater's adaptation of the American fixed trust for their clients, M&G. Thus, the unit trust movement (as it came to be known) arrived in England. By 1936, it was estimated that some £50 million had been invested in some sixty-seven unit trusts (Slinn 1987: 139).

A dimension of the lawyer's role in business largely neglected in the English literature, but illuminated in the work of Chandler (1977) and Macaulay (1979) on America, is the role of lawyers as rationalizers *within* the corporation, causing new structures of business organization to be created in response to legal imperatives. For instance, the advice of corporation lawyers has been credited with encouraging the trend away from horizontal mergers towards the integrated operating company after 1890. The influence of lawyers on business organization is certainly a topic worthy of greater attention.

This is but one instance of a phenomenon explored by sociologists of the legal profession, namely, the way lawyers transform their clients' objectives and strategies by telling clients what they can obtain from the legal system which, in turn, is significantly influenced by their clients' own resources (Sarat and Felstiner 1986). As John Griffiths (1986) puts it, lawyers seek only as much 'justice' as the client can afford and persuading clients to accept what the law offers becomes an important facet of lawyer–business relations.

Taxation

The mitigation of tax liability became a vital concern of lawyers' clients, especially with the increase in death duties after the Finance Act 1919.

From the 1920s onwards, the larger firms of solicitors were expected to report to their clients on the implications of each year's tax changes announced in the annual budgets. In the case of solicitors Boodle Hatfield, this was done by the following day. Boodle Hatfield, one of London's oldest law firms, became leading tax specialists to Britain's wealthiest landowners. Its leading in-house expert on tax law in the 1920s and 1930s was Carlton Smith. Smith was a non-conformist, socialist, teetotaller, renowned for wearing spats, travelling everywhere by taxi and carrying a copy of the *Daily Worker* under one arm and a pile of briefs tucked under his other arm. There is a particularly British irony here: Smith devised the tax avoidance scheme for the Duke of Westminster which triumphed over the protestations of the Inland Revenue in a leading House of Lords case in 1935, thereby reducing the tax paid by the richest man in England (Belcher 1985: 146–7).

The election of a Labour government in the period 1945–51 and the higher personal and corporate taxation associated with it and the post-war era, created additional demands for an in-house tax specialism. At Linklaters, for instance, it was only in the mid-1940s that they recruited a chartered accountant, Malcolm Christopherson, who was admitted as a solicitor and a partner in 1951. At this time, he was their taxation specialist. Within the next decade, he had overseen the expansion of the firm's taxation expertise, establishing important links with the Law Society's Committee on Revenue Law and the leaders of the Revenue Bar (Slinn 1987: 181).

Conveyancing

For most solicitors, provincial as well as metropolitan, their bread and butter was earned not from company and revenue work but from conveyancing:

> It was in the period 1660–1750 that the true family attorneys were born. This was largely as a result of their acquisition of the conveyancing business. The creation of a situation in which attorneys were consulted not only on lawsuits, but on wills, trusts, marriage settlements, the buying and selling of land, as well as on the procuring or lending of money, ensured that such men could never be the mere givers and receivers of instructions. Conveyancing work (and especially that undertaken for the more prosperous local inhabitants) meant regular attendances on clients and receiving information on their personal affairs. The attorneys had the chance of becoming the confidential and trusted advisers with whom, as with the local physician, it was perfectly natural to dine and be on first name terms. Such positions with the more illustrious families, could confer extra benefits in the way of agency work, manorial stewardship or even a

match of marriage. If anything contributed more to the growth in respectability and status of the eighteenth century attorneys it was this infiltration of themselves into the confidence of the wealthiest persons in the neighbourhood.

(Miles 1984: 501–512)

Since the eighteenth century, conveyancing has been the single most important source of income for attorneys and solicitors. The solicitors' pre-eminence in this area was finally consecrated in 1802, when the younger Pitt granted them a monopoly over conveyancing. As the *Law Magazine* boasted in 1868, the legal profession had 'the custody of an immense percentage of the property of the State' (cited in Kirk 1976: 97). The information gleaned from conveyancing was a valuable commodity, since it enabled solicitors to secure investment opportunities for themselves.

Conflicts of interest, and lawyers as an unpopular and economically inefficient hindrance

Conflicts of interest were omnipresent in the lawyers' everyday work. Attorneys and solicitors were entrusted with their clients' monies. They also had access to a cornucopia of inside information and opportunities not generally available to the public. Lawyers transformed this information into opportunities for themselves and their clients which, in turn, gave rise to new information, new opportunities and new clients.

Surprisingly, the rich literature on British entrepreneurship and the evolution of the structure of British business enterprise has little to say about the important role of lawyers as entrepreneurs, managers and directors in their own right, or on behalf of clients. As many lawyers saw it, they were entitled to profit from possible conflicts of interest. Thus, many solicitors regarded themselves as free to invest their clients' money to their own advantage, a view that the law condoned until well into the nineteenth century. Sometimes the song of the siren proved irresistible. Scandals were commonplace, with the problem of the bankrupt solicitor arousing considerable disquiet. In fact, most solicitors failed to maintain separate accounts for their clients' monies until well into the present century.

Public scepticism as to the integrity of the profession was not wholly unjustified when the unscrupulous were employed as attorneys and solicitors. One such individual was John Williams, a Liverpool attorney, who in the 1820s was convicted of forgery: 'The Bill of Indictment at the trial was "30 feet long and contained 16 counts and 500 law folios of words"!' (Williams 1970: 162–3).

While business might find lawyers useful, it also found them expensive, technical and time-consuming. In some quarters of the economy,

there was a strong preference for forms of regulation and dispute resolution which circumvented lawyers, which relied instead upon the
conventions of the business community, guild or trade association concerned, or simply the imperatives required when creating and sustaining long-standing business relations. Here the maintenance of a good
reputation and the operation of custom and informal sanctions might be
more significant than legal regulation, at least in the short term (Sugarman and Rubin 1984: 4–12; Arthurs 1985). Indeed, throughout the Industrial Revolution, the legal system did not operate like an efficient
slot-machine, providing speedy, certain and rational solutions to problems as they arose. Instead, the businessperson was often confronted by
an unpredictable body of rules and procedures, and competing and
overlapping jurisdictions (extra-legal, local, customary, equitable, common law, statutory and so on), which on the face of it may have hindered the rise of a market economy (Atiyah 1979: parts I and II;
Sugarman and Rubin 1984; Sugarman 1987). The technicality and expense of going to law turned litigation into a game of chess which put a
premium on tactics and the wearing down of one's opponents. Usually,
only those with sufficient financial resources could take on a dedicated
and well-resourced adversary.

The dominant traditions in history and social theory (both liberal and
radical) have exaggerated the capacity of legal regimes to facilitate certainty and predictability for business and the businessperson's need for
such a legal regime. In practice, flexibility – a flexibility that put you in the
position of an entrepreneur if you desired it, that gave you the legal
regime you wanted, the adjudicators you wanted, that allowed you to
avoid the state legal order when you wanted to, but to use its coercive
might when you needed it – was the pre-eminent virtue of the English
legal system, albeit that this flexibility was often facilitated by and mediated through the expensive, Kafkaesque world of the law (Sugarman
1987: esp. p. 46). In other words, traders, entrepreneurs and lawyers
might, on occasions, actually have a stronger interest in a legal system
characterized by confusion and complexity which they could exploit (at
least if they had the resources to do so), rather than the certainty and
calculability which historians and social theorists have assumed enterprise required of the legal order.

Public and political roles

So far, only some of the better known areas where historically lawyers have
acted for their business clients have been discussed. But lawyers also performed important public and political roles. Indeed, to attempt to separate
out their public from their private functions is doomed to founder.[1] For
example, one of lawyers' most important roles has been to provide clients

with knowledge about, and contact with, influential people – a role that was both private and public.

Lawyers represented their clients in public arenas. For instance, the final decade of the nineteenth century and first decade of the present century witnessed tenacious efforts to restructure landownership in a more equitable fashion; and to limit the enormous powers of landlords over tenants. The solicitors for England's wealthiest landlords, Boodle Hatfield, defended their propertied clients against these attacks. They did this through their lengthy submissions of evidence to Parliament, written and oral; and the campaign that they waged in the letters page of *The Times* (Belcher 1985: 112–19).

Those solicitors who acted for major government institutions played a special role in economic development. Freshfields, for instance, were solicitors to the Bank of England. In the 1890s, they played a crucial part in the rescue of the House of Baring, the merchant bankers, whose collapse would have generated a national financial crisis (Slinn 1984: 124–5). In the 1930s, they assisted the Bank of England in its efforts to reorganize British industry (Slinn 1989: 29).

The profession also exercised important public roles through the professional associations that represented lawyers, the Inns of Court, the Law Society, the provincial law societies as well as other pressure groups, such as the Social Science Association. The bar had a large constituency in Parliament, both in terms of the number of Members of Parliament who were barristers, and also with respect to their in-built influence in government, through the offices of the Lord Chancellor and the Attorney-General (the head of the bar). A parliamentary seat was also a valuable stepping stone for those members of the bar seeking high judicial office.

While solicitors were not so well represented in Parliament and government, they were none the less significant lobbyists. The Law Society in London and the provincial law societies in the country together exercised considerable influence on legislation and legal practice, an influence that extended to matters not exclusively relating to solicitors. The Society's intimate links with the City, government and the judiciary were established soon after its formation in 1825 and have remained an enduring feature of its power and influence. In essence, the Society made itself an essential and intrinsic co-partner in the formulation of state policy (Sugarman, 1994).

Here are instances of a much wider and important phenomenon; namely, the multiple roles, the many arenas of struggle, that were open to lawyers. It was the opportunity to be key players in many spheres – often straddling private practice, public office and politics – that significantly added to their value to business and to their consequent influence and power. Indeed, in one of their roles, lawyers might undertake certain tasks for specific interests; and, in another, they might seek to negate their previous work and, therefore, the interests they were supposed to serve.[2]

The growing number of histories of law firms neatly illustrate the close interplay between the personal, professional and political. For example, James Freshfield, as well as being solicitor to the Bank of England, also acted for Sir Robert Peel and other politicians, was a Peelite and Member of Parliament who was appointed High Sheriff of Surrey. Additionally, he was a member of the Carlton and Athenaeum Clubs and Royal Society. Last but not least, he was the Chairman of Divorce Commissioners and a director of the Globe Insurance Company (Slinn 1984). It would be easy to provide a list of similar examples but, more generally, three points can be made.

First, we cannot understand significant tracts of the history of English law unless this dynamic is acknowledged and mapped out in some specificity. Secondly, lawyers were able to capitalize on their work experience of, and their contacts within, governmental institutions. Most sectors of state administration were relatively small-scale until late in the nineteenth century, so 'face-to-face' relations were possible. Thirdly, the role played by lawyers in public life has been largely neglected in England. Services to voluntary organizations brought increasing prestige to individual lawyers and the legal profession generally. Such appointments might bring the opportunity to meet potential clients and increase local influence.

The success of a few lawyers in holding major public offices – for instance, solicitor C.G. Beale, who served as the Mayor of Birmingham three times during the 1890s – generated various benefits to many other solicitors. Not only was the election of a solicitor to the Mayoralty proof of the stature of the profession *as a whole*, it was also used to good advantage by the legal press to show the value of lawyers as opposed to businessmen running vast municipalities. An examination of over two thousand solicitors in Birmingham for the period 1880–1900 shows that they were extensively involved in public works, social clubs, educational institutions and sports, especially cricket (Rowley 1988).

The public life of the lawyer: local and executive government

Lawyers have played other important roles in local and national government. Traditionally, it is barristers who have filled the major legal posts in central government. Attorneys and solicitors have tended to monopolize most of the posts held by legally qualified employees in local government since at least the eighteenth century (Offer 1981: 19–20).

Solicitors also played a significant role in the work of political parties and the overseeing of elections. Until at least the late nineteenth century, the offices of registration and election agents were largely performed by local solicitors. Here was yet another area of employment which brought solicitors new contracts and closer links with the major families and local centres of power.

Law and ideology: Towards cultural, social and political histories of the legal profession

Until recently, the dominant traditions within the history and sociology of the professions tended to conflate the growth and importance of the professions with the coming of industrial society. One corollary of this approach was a tendency to treat lawyers as little more than the instruments of their clients' economic dictates, which in turn were conceived of in attenuated and simplified terms. In other words, the professional consciousness of lawyers and other professionals – how they constructed, understood and interpreted their responsibilities, interests, specialist knowledge, work organization, professional identity, relations with the state, clients and other professionals, and how these changed over time – were usually ignored or treated as axiomatic. Similarly, the role and importance of professional ideologies beyond the field of professional work has often been conceived in an overly functionalistic fashion. How did they influence and reflect the work of legal institutions such as courts and the everyday practices of lawyers, and what was the relationship between legal, economic, religious and political thought? In the remainder of this chapter, I want to suggest some ways of addressing these sorts of issues, ways that acknowledge the intellectual, political and cultural dimensions of the profession and their larger cultural and political significance.

Some historians have sought to understand the profession in terms of a struggle for cultural authority as well as for immediate financial rewards (cf. Starr 1982; Bourdieu 1984a, 1987). According to this notion, lawyers stake out a claim to represent certain cultural practices and ideas. For example, Robert Ferguson (1984) argues that in revolutionary America, 'the lawyer [was] at the center of republican literary activity . . .'. Ferguson brings to light:

> . . . a now-forgotten configuration of law and letters that dominated American literary aspirations from the Revolution until the fourth decade of the nineteenth century, a span of more than fifty years. Half of the important critics of the day trained for law, and attorneys controlled many of the important journals. Belles Lettres societies furnished the major basis of cultural concern for post-Revolutionary America; they depended heavily on the legal profession for their memberships. Lawyers also wrote many of the country's first important novels, plays and poems. No other vocational group, not even the ministry, matched their contribution.

Ferguson also examines:

> . . . the importance of the courtroom as a ceremonial forum in re-
> publican culture. Formal legal argument drew large audiences
> throughout the period, and practicing attorneys had much to do with
> the rise of a literature of eloquence and oratory.
>
> (Ferguson 1984: 9)

To enquire into these issues is to investigate the efforts of the profession,
to translate economic power into moral and cultural authority, which, in
turn, were dependent upon the profession's claim to be independent.

One facet of this phenomenon is that vein of legal culture which assumed that only the courts and lawyers were the proper arbiters of legal
attainment and the proper institutions for dealing with the law, with its
corresponding tendency to deprecate or ignore other forms of ordering
and organization in society (Arthurs 1985). In some cases, this discourse
led to the implication that in certain mysterious ways, lawyers were
above the law itself, and that only by being outside the law could the Rule
of Law and civilization as we know it be preserved.

A related issue is the role of the legal profession in sustaining
the middle classes, its values and its importance within local communities. Most lawyers were of, and dealt primarily with, the middle
classes and gentry. Lawyers together with teachers, doctors, the clergy
and writers:

> . . . spent their lives manipulating words, explaining the middle
> class to itself. As a legal writer claimed in the mid[-nineteenth]
> century:
> > 'The importance of the professions and the professional classes
> > can hardly be overrated. They form the head of the great English
> > middle class, keep up to the mark its standard of morality, and
> > direct its intelligence.'
> Within this group were found some of the most prominent in exhort-
> ing their peers about [right conduct, the meaning of life and] the
> appropriate role for men and women. For example, a lawyer using
> the trust, a doctor advising a woman against any worldly or intellec-
> tual excitement, the vicar's sermon on family life, the schoolmaster's
> talk on manliness and work, as much as the artist's or writer's por-
> trayal of idealized ringleted maidens and stalwart youths, contrib-
> uted to the creation of middle class values [and the restrictive roles of
> men and women].
>
> (Davidoff and Hall 1987: 264)

Of course, there was no monolithic middle class. This has been underlined by recent work which describes the rich and contradictory ideas and
values that they imbibed:

The 'oppositional culture' of the provincial middle classes cannot be understood outside a religious context. Middle-class men and women were at the heart of the revivals which swept through all denominations. The cold-blooded pursuit of profit was as deeply suspect on moral grounds as was the desire to shed the taint of trade. A wealthy shopkeeper's son started the process of mobility which ended with the marriage of his own son into the Essex gentry by choosing to train for the law. He framed his decision on ethical principles, claiming that a legal profession, being free from 'perpetual attention to profit and loss', had fewer temptations to vice and 'the most intimate connections with morality'.

(Davidoff and Hall 1987: 21–2)

The UK was the centre of the British Empire; and the Empire was a valuable source of business and connections as well as the provider of a host of careers opportunities, public as well as private (Duman 1983: ch. 4). Moreover, the common law was their mutual heritage. The elite lawyers of the common-law world saw themselves as cultural attachés, sharing and constituting a common language, world view and history. English solicitors, so it was said, had 'first demonstrated' how to rise to the needs of commerce and finance, thereby securing Britain's world leadership. And, wrote John Foster Dulles, 'as America came of Age, and particularly as New York became increasingly a centre of finance, commerce and industry, a comparable need arose and was met' (Dulles 1957: iv).

Some commentators have argued that among other things, lawyers were a great stabilizing force within society. They knitted together bases for social solidarity; and constituted a vital ballast or counterweight against the despotic elements in society (Sugarman and Rubin 1984: 96; Gordon 1988: 14–19; Sugarman 1992a). In market towns such as Ipswich and Colchester, it has been shown that the wealthier lawyers 'were a power in the local community helping to bind together the commercial, trading, manufacturing and farming interests and many were active in local politics . . . Law was the platform where the middle classes and upper classes might meet' (Davidoff and Hall 1987: 262, 265). The more powerful attorneys mixed with bankers, wealthy farmers, manufacturers and even gentry.

To what extent did England's lawyers help to consolidate an uncertain order, creating new certainties (in the guise of old certainties), constituting a new basis for order, stability and community, with their notions of history, national and class identity, Englishness and statehood? Many judges and lawyers asserted that they did perform a stabilizing function; but it is a dimension of the history of the legal profession that has not yet received much attention. To focus upon these questions is to investigate the role of lawyers, judges and jurists in creating some of the important languages through which community, solidarity and the moral foundations of social life were articulated and transmitted (Durkheim 1957; Luhmann 1979).

Thus, lawyers were important retailers of ideology. For example, they fitted their clients' projects into an overall ordering of social life (Gordon 1990). As Maureen Cain has argued, lawyers translate and reconstitute everyday discourses:

> . . . in terms of a legal discourse which has trans-situational applicability. In this sense law is a meta-language . . . [It] is also the workaday language for certain state . . . [servants] . . . Lawyers are translators – that is their day-to-day chore. They are also *creators* of the language into which they translate . . . To think for the first time, a debenture share, say, is a creative act . . . It is in this sense that lawyers are conceptive ideologists.
>
> (Cain 1979: 335)

Legal discourse constituted legal subjects (for example, the reasonable man, married women, lunatics), creating a space from which they could speak but only as permitted by the law.

The close involvement of lawyers and professional bodies like the Law Society in the formulation of legislation, law reform and legal practice suggests that they exercised an important influence on the available normative languages and therefore the presuppositions of the legislative and decision-making process. One might hypothesize that by helping to define the perimeters of what was proper for the authorities to undertake – what got on the agenda, and what did not – they were influential in setting the limits of political innovation (Sugarman, 1994).

Bodies like the Inns of Court, the Law Society, the provincial law societies, and the new university law schools helped to explain the profession to itself and construct (and reconstruct) its sense of identity. They also helped to constitute 'legal professionalism', that is, what distinguished 'proper' from 'illegitimate' legal services, whereby certain individuals became defined as a threat to society – 'sham lawyers', arbitration, 'ambulance chasers' and legal aid committees (Pue 1987, 1989, 1990; Sugarman, 1994).

Lawyers were important producers of political discourse, rights talk, conceptions of polity and so on, both constraining and potentially liberating, which are deep-rooted in the institutional structure of society (cf. Kammen 1986). The new histories of intellectual and political thought point to the ways we might investigate their gravitational pull as a body of tradition and as a way of organizing the world.

None the less, the importance of legal discourse as political discourse is an empirical question rather than something that can be taken for granted. For example, in England, one is confronted with a paradox. The importance of the Western legal tradition stemmed in part from its existence in written form (Clanchy 1979). Writing enabled lawyers to claim to be, and sometimes to appear to be, above and beyond the individual acts of power involved in legal practice and the application of the law (cf. Dezalay 1986a). In manifold ways, the written form of law abrogated power to those lawyers claiming specialist expertise in the 'interpretation' of the law (Goodrich 1986, 1990). From this perspective, the history of the common law tradition operated within the general traditions of hermeneutics and rhetoric usually associated with continental philosophy. All this directs our attention to the special power of lawyers to do things with words. For example, English law was an important constitutional discourse; and English society in the late sixteenth and early seventeenth centuries was 'intensely legalistic' (Brookes 1981: 58).

On the other hand, contemporaries 'thought it unneighbourly to take disputes into court, and in practice there was frequent resort to compromise and arbitration' (Brooks 1981: 58). Moreover, the languages of the law co-existed alongside other equally important discourses such as religion, the natural sciences, history and political economy. The extent to which these operated in tandem, or mediated, refracted and attenuated the law and the claims of its priesthood are difficult but important questions that merit greater attention.

The influence of lawyers as a pressure group was also mediated by the divisions within the profession (common lawyers *vs* civilians, barristers *vs* solicitors, the Law Society and elite London solicitors *vs* country solicitors and the provincial law societies, practitioners *vs* academics) (Pue 1987, 1989, 1990; Parrott 1991). In fact, the nature and scope of legal professionalization were constantly contested. Were lawyers independent of particular interests or dependent upon particular interests; gentlemen with privileges and duties or men of business; scientists or practitioners; guardians of public interest or guardians of private interest; aristocratic and anti-commercial or contractual and self-interested; officers of the court or the hired-hands of the client? Only by reconstructing the world as lawyers saw it, experienced it and made sense of it, can we understand how that world was organized so that lawyers could claim to be 'gentlemen' or 'businessmen' or both.

The power and legitimacy of the profession depended, in part, upon how these contradictory images were synthesized and delineated, both within the profession and in its relation to society. One way to analyse this process is to subject 'the lawyer's somewhat ambivalent moral and social position' (Prest 1981a: 12) to greater historical specificity than hitherto. In what ways, if any, did the profession reconcile these contradictory images?

From one perspective, the struggle between these dualisms represented the attempt of certain groups within the profession to dominate. From this vantage point, the structure of the profession was the result of a series of compromises between its various factions and fractions. But this struggle also testifies to the contested nature of legal professionalism as an ideology and to its relative elasticity. As a result, the ideology of legal professionalism could be used to justify a variety of contradictory and competing images of professional behaviour and thereby help to create and justify different interests within the profession, while simultaneously laying claim to shared notions of learning, judgement and culture (Sarat 1992; Sugarman 1994).

In addition to studies of intra-professional conflict, competition between lawyers and other occupational groups, investigations of how lawyers were displaced in some fields but moved into or created new ones, would greatly enhance our knowledge of the relationship between law, business, politics and political discourse (Abbott 1988; Dezalay and Sugarman 1994). On what basis did lawyers fulfil certain roles but not others? What were the processes and conditions which caused lawyers to elevate social, moral and status concerns over immediate financial advantage (and vice versa) when determining the nature and parameters of its province? After all, barristers did not have to scorn the notion of a direct, contractual relationship with their clients; and solicitors need not have spurned accountancy, tax planning, investment advice, and so on, thereby creating a vacuum filled by accountants and banks.

The supposed 'individualism' of the common law mind is largely correct, but it is of limited value as an explanatory tool (Hedley 1987). This is because the notion is so indeterminate that it could often embrace very different value positions. 'Individualism' has become a short-hand which often obscures the complex interplay between personal, professional, religious, moral, economic and political factors. Why certain features of individualism prevailed over others in specific situations is something that has yet to be explained.

Lawyers, business, the family and women

One area where the traditional divide between the public and the private has overly circumscribed the historiography of the legal profession is in the interconnections between law, business, the family and gender. We know little about how sex roles were structured through the everyday work of the legal profession. Historical studies of law, economy and business have tended to be based upon a conceptual separation between family/business, family/lawyers, family/economy. But the role of the lawyer's family, especially the role of the wife, requires serious attention. The new histories of the middle classes increasingly stress the interrelationship between the family and the firm. It has been emphasized that not only consumption decisions, but the structure, activities and success of firms, were structured by family·matters as well as business needs. Most law firms were family enterprises heavily dependent on family capital, family members, family connections and the unpaid work of wives and children. The family, law firms and legal work were not separate spheres but elaborately conjoined in ways that have yet to be explicated.

Towards an analysis of the conditions underlying effective legitimacy

The widespread acceptance of the legitimacy of the legal profession is now assumed to be axiomatic of successful capitalist development. But does it require more empirical work than has been the case to date? How might we analyse the conditions underlying effective legitimacy?

The strength (and weakness) of the profession has stemmed from its propensity to express several contradictory tendencies side by side. First, it claimed to act in the general interests of society; and its much-asserted autonomy derived from its claim as a major bulwark against tyranny and despotism. Secondly, while the profession had a strong interest in welding its disparate interests into a harmonious confederation, its members were likely to differ over fundamental objectives. Moreover, the profession's capacity to act in unison was also circumscribed in that it was an arena of struggle. Diverse factions, strong and weak, endeavoured to use the profession to fulfil their specific goals. Thirdly, the profession tended to be an instrument of domination. Its intimate relationship with both the state and the most powerful groups in society meant that this was a tendency from which it was difficult to cut loose. In sum, the power and legitimacy of the profession were contingent upon the way these contradictory tendencies were fused, both within its internal structures and in relation to the society at large.

While these questions could be addressed in future research in terms of abstract theoretical assertions concerning the relative autonomy of the profession and so on, their complex contingency is more likely to be understood through comparative research both within and between national legal professions. This work might analyse how and why and to what effect 'law jobs', and 'public' and 'private' roles, changed over time in different nation states (Rueschemeyer 1973; Abel and Lewis 1989). It would have to be sensitive to the heterogeneous nature of the profession and the diversity and specificity of the fields of action within which legal work is undertaken. Divorce lawyers, for example, may operate somewhat differently to those specializing in tax avoidance.

Conclusion

Three images of lawyers pervade much of the popular and scholarly literature. First, there is the lawyer as the self-serving pettifogger, propagating litigation and increasing the complexity and, therefore, the expense of the law. As Charles Dickens put it, 'The one great principle of the English law is to make business for itself' (Dickens 1971: 58). No wonder, then, that an attorney in *Bleak House* is called Vohles: a 'vole' in a card game is a situation in which the dealer gets all the winning cards.

The second image of the lawyer is that of the larger-than-life advocate of public-interest matters – quick-witted, statesmanlike and fair-minded – much celebrated in TV series, notably, *Perry Mason*, *LA Law* and *Rumpole of the Bailey*. Thirdly, lawyers sometimes see themselves as neutral technicians, offering the characteristically 'legal' skills of counsellor, drafter and advocate. Here the core of lawyering is the private world of private law-making, usually performed behind closed doors on a one-to-one basis.

All of these images have an important grain of truth. Yet each is, of course, a caricature of what lawyers actually do. A more appropriate perspective for analysing the role of lawyers in business would be to explore the rich polyphony, the collisions and inter-penetration of cultural galaxies, the plurality of roles, voices and forums, some merged, some independent, that constituted the way lawyers made a living and constructed their personal identities, and the complex bearing of these factors on issues of power, authority and community. From this vista, the traditional separation of lawyers' 'private' and 'public' roles is easily subverted because in practice the lines of demarcation between the private and the public were regularly crossed with ease. This is not only to assert that the private and public coalesce. It is also to see how the legal profession is constituted by a double discourse which both claims that the public and private are separate and that the public and private cannot be separated. The history of lawyers undermines that tenet of legal formalism that only those distinctly 'legal' tasks, separate from 'society', 'business' and 'politics', are what lawyering is really about.[3]

Notes

1 On the public roles of English lawyers, see Duman (1983: chs 4–6), Brooks (1986: ch. 10), Holmes (1982: chs 5 and 8), Prest (1986: ch. 8) and Sugarman (1994).
2 This capacity to do one thing with their right hand (as it were), which they undid with their left hand, is well illustrated in Gordon (1984b).
3 When viewed from the perspective advocated in this chapter, Osiel's (1989) valuable discussion of American lawyers as capitalist entrepreneurs and European lawyers as aristocrats seems to exaggerate the undoubted differences between American and European lawyers.

6 Lawyers' work as constitutive of gender relations

Sue Lees

Introduction

This article focuses on the way women are treated both as victims and defendants in criminal justice trials. It portrays how sexism continues to dominate a criminal justice system whose official ideology is that the Rule of Law and the equal treatment of individuals is axiomatic. It involved attending selected murder and rape trials between 1987 and 1990 at the Old Bailey, the Central Criminal Court in England, and the analysis of newspaper cuttings for the 1980s. It reveals how lawyers and judges use the law to support a particular cultural convention about how gender relations should be. Thus the work of lawyers can be said to constitute gender relations.

No major study of homicide has been carried out in Britain since Blom-Cooper and Morris (1964) conducted their research. While magistrates' courts have been well studied by women researchers (Carlen 1976; McBarnet 1981; Eaton 1986; Allen 1987), only Susanna Adler (1987) has studied rape trials. Most of these studies were undertaken as doctoral research, and were therefore carried out on 'shoestring' finance. Research foundations tend to exclude criminal law from their remit, so funding is hard to come by.

Access is also a problem. Justice has to be seen to be done in most countries and in the UK anyone can gain access to the public gallery. However, it is often difficult to hear, space is limited and access cannot be guaranteed, nor notes easily taken, so access to the press seats is essential, which can take a long time to negotiate.

The doctrine that all individuals who stand trial shall stand equal before the law seems clear and unambiguous, but there are considerable grounds for judicial manoeuvre within the law. Legal ideals of impartiality and objectivity, ideals which are so often invoked by the Bench to establish its essential neutrality, may be neither achievable nor desirable goals as they are currently conceived by law. It is, however, important to be clear about the criteria which courts use to differentiate between individuals. My research will show that the law's construction of women is such as to exclude them from the conception of the judicial subject. It shows how in recent murder trials men and women, both as defendants and victims, have been viewed very differently.

The earliest recognition of the limitations of legal rationalism as a critical tool was that the law, which impartially applies to both rich and poor, can be, in its very universality, a form of discrimination against the poor and weak. Formal equality at law has severe limitations as a device for the elimination of substantive structural inequalities between people. It may even, as the critical legal theorists argue, consolidate them (see Fitzpatrick and Hunt 1987). Additionally, any universal principle can be formulated in a particularistic way, either with reference to the definition of the actor or to the act. Thus if all men who commit murder or assault shall stand equally before the law, anyone not defined as a man for legal purposes need not stand in the same relation. Women, children, slaves, non-whites, etc., can be treated differently without violating the properties of formal equality as long as the differences in sex or age or whatever are believed to be morally relevant. There is nothing in the formal properties of law itself that provides these criteria of moral relevance. For this reason in the last century, the denial of equality to women co-existed alongside the rule of law. Husbands could legitimately beat their wives for non-compliance, whereas similar action by women would be defined as assault. These husbands' rights of coercion weakened during the nineteenth century, though the courts are to this day, for example, still reluctant to concede physical violence as a valid excuse for a woman leaving a marriage (Atkins and Hoggett 1984). The infamous exclusion of marital rape from legal protection gave British husbands the right to rape their wives until as recently as March 1991.

Hilary Allen (1987: 23) records the ambiguity of English law in relation to the 'equality' of men and women. Citing a 1987 decision, she documents the official inconceivability of 'a reasonable woman with her sex eliminated'.[1] An invitation to lawyers and judges to interpret what is reasonable is an invitation to them to fall back on their common sense, their culture, their class, race and gender-based stereotypes. Thus to decide that what would be reasonable for a man would not be reasonable for a woman, and vice versa, does not breach the requirement of equal treatment. The same rule is being applied – but of course in a different way.

So we shall find in the case of murder trials that the law often constitutes gender relations in its discretionary spaces rather than in-its explicit rules. Not only does this make these practices difficult to research and uncover, it also renders these practices virtually immune to political action.

In terms of the content of legal statutes concerning criminal behaviour, most historians would argue that the trend has been towards the elimination of particularism and differences in favour of equal treatment for all citizens. As far as women are concerned, however, it is still the case that laws are made and implemented overwhelmingly by men and it is male conceptions that have been uppermost. These conceptions serve to keep women in their places and consolidate male domination. It is also why many statutory provisions in the criminal law exhibit an ideology of female passivity, as with rape. However, the ideological vision of female passivity embodied in statutes conflicts with the conception of women as precipitator and provocateuse or provoker that emerges in the court proceedings which are the focus of this study. This contradiction results in women who take an active stance by defending themselves against a husband's violence often being regarded as evil or vengeful. They do not conform to the vision of passivity. Similarly, women who do not fit in with the conventional model of domestic wife and mother are frequently seen as provocative.

Grounds for the commutation of murder to manslaughter, such as the criteria used to establish the defence of provocation, and grounds for mitigating circumstances, bear an uneasy relationship to the rule of law. The advance of law involves the abolition of particularism and exceptionalism in favour of the consistent application of rules. The growth in the use of mitigating circumstances in a legal defence and the widening of defences for murder indicate a recognition that this cannot be done. Justice cannot be achieved by the application of formal rules. It is ultimately a substantive, not a formal, issue. No sooner are formal rules announced, than justice requires their modification in particular circumstances or as regards particular categories of people.

The basic difference between the recognition of provocation or self-defence on the one hand and the arbitrary exceptionalism of the pre-legal system on the other, is not a matter of the formal structure of legality. What separates the refusal to try a king for a murder or an under-age juvenile or a person regarded as insane, is a question of moral and political convention. Because it is just such a question, those older forms of arbitrariness that have survived the growth of civil and legal rights can find their point of re-entry into the modern legal system through the discretionary spaces embedded in the law, not least those involved in pleas of mitigating circumstances (see also Mitra 1987).

Moral responsibility

This Achilles' heel of the modern system of law and right was recognized in essence many years ago by Max Weber (1964). As classically formulated, guilt implies moral responsibility for action and moral responsibility implies the freedom to have acted otherwise. If it can be shown that the person could not have acted other than he or she did in the circumstances, or other than he or she could reasonably have been expected to do, then moral responsibility and hence guilt is negated. It is important to recognize at the outset that the dichotomy of 'free will' *vs* 'determinism' is one of the central and philosophically unresolved dichotomies of Western culture and there is no methodology for identifying whether claims of free will or determinism are valid in particular cases. Thus what are considered valid forms of determinism, forms of constraint on the agent regarded as sufficient to make the exercise of moral responsibility impossible, are always conventionally defined. In such situations, predominantly male interests and ideologies will make their presence felt.

Two types of situations in which it might seem that reasonably objective judgments can be made in murder cases are when the killing was the unintended consequence of other actions or when it was undertaken in self-defence. With unintended consequences in a typical case of a manslaughter charge (i.e. where a motorist runs down and kills a pedestrian on an icy road), there has to be some judgment as to whether the motorist was driving with reasonable precautions. But in such cases this affects only the severity of the sentence. The charge of murder legally, if not philosophically, is reserved for cases where intention can be shown.

Killing in self-defence is more clearly associated with intent and the definition of what exactly self-defence involves has been criticized by feminists who have argued that to demand that the danger must be imminent overlooks the disparity of strength between, for example, husbands and wives, where the wife considers she is in imminent danger and kills her husband when he has, for example, passed out with drink or is asleep. The present definition limits the question to the extent to which the defendant's life was actually in danger *at the time of the killing* and whether any other evasive action could reasonably have been taken.

Mental illness might seem to be a similar case. If it can be shown through the assumed precision and non-ideological nature of psychiatric evidence that the person was suffering from mental abnormalities sufficient to interrupt the process of rational thought, then a case for non-responsibility for action can be made. This was the conclusion in the Yorkshire Ripper case. The main ambiguities in such judgments centre around the problems of *post facto* psychiatric investigation, coupled with the ever-present danger of tautology, whereby the fact of the crime (e.g.

hideous and multiple murder) is taken as supporting evidence of insanity. The assumption 'no rational person would act thus . . .' is inevitably coloured by conventions which may have a sexual, class or ethnic particularity (see Blumberg 1967; Allen 1987).

Provocation

The UK Homicide Act of 1957 amended the law so that a category of homicide such as murder by shooting and in the furtherance of theft carried the death sentence, but the remainder carried a mandatory sentence of life imprisonment. The death penalty was suspended for murder in 1965 and abolished five years later. All murders were then made punishable by life imprisonment. Under sections 2 and 3 of the Act, the grounds for extenuating circumstances were widened – by introducing grounds of diminished responsibility by which murder could be commuted to manslaughter (section 2) and by widening the defence of provocation (section 3). The former depends on medical evidence, but the latter derives its validity from the behaviour of the victim, who must be shown to have precipitated his or her own death to some lesser or greater extent. Before the Act, only limited types of conduct were sufficient to constitute provocation: physical violence or detection of a spouse in the act of adultery were almost invariably required in order to found a defence of provocation. The House of Lords in *Holmes* v. *DPP* (1946) stated that save in circumstances of a most extreme and exceptional nature, a confession of adultery by one spouse to another could not constitute sufficient provocation to justify a verdict of manslaughter if the injured spouse killed his [*sic*] spouse or adulterer. Section 3 of the Homicide Act changed this and provided for a manslaughter verdict on the grounds of provocation where there is evidence of a sudden and temporary loss of self-control:

> Where on a charge of murder there is evidence on which the jury can find that the person charged and provoked (whether by things done or by things said or by both together) to lose his or her self control, the question whether provocation was enough to make a REASON-ABLE MAN do as he did shall be left to be determined by the jury; and in determining the question, the jury shall take into account everything both done and said according to the effect which in their opinion, it would have on a reasonable man.
>
> (Homicide Act 1957, s. 3)

Juries must therefore take into account:

1 The events which have happened/anything done or said (or a combination of acts and words) will suffice.

2 The relevant characteristics of the defendant which may result in loss of self-control.

The difficulty with these guidelines is that both the jury's view of the events which happened and the relevant characteristics of the defendant are often ambiguous. As Susan Edwards comments:

> Whilst provocation might well appear as a relatively clear legal category bound by rules and procedures, what precise forms of action, behaviour, mannerisms, speech and situation, and relevant characteristics a jury may consider constitute provocation, is both arbitrary and ambiguous.
>
> (Edwards 1986b: 138)

The most important exhibition of sexist ideology surrounds the way in which provocation is used. Provocation is at best a very fluid and difficult defence. Is provocation being used as a psychological or as a moral factor? The difficulty of any hard and fast rules for the use of the defence of provocation in murder trials derives, first, from the fact that a large number of murders could be described as crimes of passion which from the subjective standpoint of the defendant are the result of intolerable provocation. The question for the court to decide is whether the action is a justifiable response to its antecedents: whether a particular set of reasons can be construed as justifying a homicide. Within this framework, ideological conceptions of 'normal behaviour' will inevitably be brought to bear.

Sexist assumptions and prejudices colour these conceptions of normality in at least two respects. First, this occurs in what is considered legitimate behaviour to women. Studies of rape trials, for example, have shown how evidence relating to the prostitute status of a victim as a construction of the latter's promiscuity, is frequently allowed in cross-examination, and in the formulation of verdicts. Similarly, any prior relationship between the victim and the accused is used to argue tacit consent to rape on the part of the victim (Edwards 1981: 58; Adler 1987). The sentencing of women to prison has been shown to be more dependent on their non-marital status or unconventional lifestyle than the gravity of the actual offence. Pat Carlen (1983) found that women who resisted the oppression of their gender role were particularly at risk of imprisonment. Women who resist being beaten up by their husband by attacking him as he sleeps, or women who take to alcohol, find themselves in danger of a prison sentence if charged with quite petty offences.

Similar constructions of legitimate (i.e. non-provocative) female behaviour surfaced in those murder trials which I observed. Here evidence that the victim was seeking a divorce or unsubstantiated evidence that she was in any way promiscuous, is cited and frequently accepted as grounds for her husband's defence of provocation. Part of what is considered as legitimate behaviour on the victim's part in these cases is derived from a view of the responsibilities of the normal wife. Similarly, as we shall see, when women kill in self-defence after years of brutal beatings, they generally face much harsher treatment by the criminal justice system than men who kill in jealousy or in response to marital difficulties (see Jones 1991; Browne 1987). Without a doubt, it can be said that if the men in these cases had achieved a 'reputation for promiscuity' and this had been cited by defence counsel for their wives where the latter were on trial for the murder of their husbands, the court would not have given it a moment's consideration.

The second criterion of normal behaviour involves an evaluation of whether the behaviour was 'exceptional' for the defendant (i.e. atypical compared with past behaviour). This is brought to bear as evidence for whether or not the murder was an understandable response to provocation. As Mary Eaton (1986) points out in her study of magistrates' courts, pleas of mitigation invoke a consensual social world in which the defendant's relationship to the family is presented as the benchmark of normality. Should this relationship follow an acceptable conventional pattern, it will be used to show that the defendant is not really a criminal, since the social identity in question is basically conformist. Criminal activity will be presented as a temporary aberration and must therefore be due to some form of exceptional provocation. The family is therefore at the centre of the model of social normality that is used to differentiate 'real criminals' from others. A good family member is not really a criminal but criminal behaviour on the part of an individual with an unconventional lifestyle is unsurprising. An independent woman is just not acceptable (Eaton 1986: 44). Where the woman is a victim, likewise, in the Old Bailey trials which I watched, the lack of conventional behaviour is taken as evidence for her provocation. Whether as victim or defendant, in trials where women are involved, it is therefore a woman's reputation that is focused on. In my earlier research on adolescent girls, the only security against verbal sexual abuse and a bad reputation was for girls to confine themselves to the 'protection' of a male partner. The law can be seen as an extension of processes of control that affect all girls and women in their everyday lives (Lees 1992, 1993).

For Asian women appearing in murder trials in the UK, there is an added dimension. *Izzatt* is the notion whereby women are seen as the upholders of the honour and tradition of their family and in-laws. *Izzatt* is prevalent in all major Asian religions and is central to keeping women under control and within the confines of the family. If she deviates from the accepted norms by choosing her own partner in marriage, marrying outside her caste or religion, or separating from her husband, she commits the ultimate crime, dishonours her family, culture, religion and will

be labelled as unrespectable (Wilson 1978). If she steps outside her pre-
scribed role, she is considered tainted, promiscuous and treated with
contempt. She is seen as coming under the influence of Western immoral
values which have had a corrupting influence on her. No wonder that she
is regarded as doubly unconventional should she be involved in a court
case. The reasons that led to her crime are irrelevant; it is the action itself
which is the focus.

Notions of normal and reasonable behaviour are thus always involved
in any decision as to the presence of 'provocation'. The other major problem with any attempt to assess provocation in murder trials is that the
victim is not available for questioning. This gives an almost unobstructed
terrain for commonsense conceptions and stereotypes deployed by the
defence (usually male) to construct the victim (usually female) as precipitator. It is arguably even harder here than in rape cases for the prosecution to challenge these constructions.

Feminist philosophical considerations

The history of modern philosophy appears disproportionately obsessed
with establishing rules by which mind, reason, self and will can legitimately control body, the emotions, the external world and desire.

(Gould 1984: 56)

During the past ten years, feminist philosophers have proposed that sex
should be the variable of interest in the scientific examination of such
human characteristics as rationality (Harding 1983; Lloyd 1984; Ruddick
1989). Genevieve Lloyd, for example, traces the history of the double
association between reason and masculinity and emotion and feminity.
She shows how this association has taken different forms from the seventeenth century onwards, but that rationality has been seen as a way of
controlling emotions and passions. Masculinity and rationality have also
been seen to be closely connected. Philosophers such as Descartes distinguished the sensuous, imaginative and emotional from the rational
and argued that women were somehow lacking in respect for rationality.
The idea that rationality could be attained by training which involved
gaining control over emotion and imagination led to the perverse argument that, since women were incapable of rationality, they should be
educated differently. Such discriminatory ideas about women's education were expressed by Rousseau in his tract *Emile*:

To be pleasing in his sight, to win his respect and love, to train him in
childhood, to tend him in manhood, to counsel and console, to make
his life pleasant and happy, these are the duties of woman for all time
and this is what she should be taught while she is young.

(Rousseau 1762/1974)

Lloyd argues that faith in the 'victory of reason' has declined now that threats to humanity can no longer be said to be posed by the forces of unreason rather than by having their source within reason itself. Nevertheless, these ideas about male rationality and female emotionality are still embedded in the legal process.

Allison Jagger (1989) agrees that from Plato until the present, with a few notable exceptions, reason rather than emotion has been regarded as the indispensable faculty for acquiring knowledge. She too argues that the 'rational' has been contrasted with the 'emotional' and linked to other dichotomies, such as that between masculinity and feminity. It appears that there are different conceptions of rationality, which may be determined partly by the social and gendered background and experiences of individuals as well as the really different possibilities which exist for men and women. Thus the most rational action for a woman may well indeed be different from the most rational action for a man, even if they could be imagined to be in apparently similar circumstances.

Feminist sociologists have also attacked the neutrality of scientific rationality (see MacKinnon 1987; McNeil 1987; Smith 1988) and have argued that objectivity is little more than male subjectivity. MacKinnon suggests that whether we are regarded as the same or different from men, the standard by which we are judged is male:

> Concealed is the substantive way in which man has become the measure of all things. Under the sameness standard, women are measured according to our correspondence with man, our equality judged by our proximity to his measure. Under the difference standard, we are measured according to our lack of correspondence with him, our womanhood judged by our distance from his measure. Gender neutrality is thus simply the male standard, and the special protection rule is simply the female standard, but do not be deceived: masculinity or maleness, is the referent for both.
>
> (MacKinnon 1987: 84)

Feminists do not claim a feminine point of view that is objective abstract, or universal. Far from it. They recognize that woman's perspective will vary under different political systems and that bias is inevitable. They reject the ascendence of the universal, abstract point of view. They do not believe that this is possible for men either. What feminists do argue, however, is that the human rationality has been defined from a distinctively masculine perspective which is not only one-sided but also in some respects perverse (Gould 1984: 44).

It is important to examine these arguments and conceptualizations in order to understand our present legal system and the extent to which it rests on a male standpoint and on male interests. The evidence suggests that conceptions of 'rationality' underpinning legal definitions protect patriarchy and condone male violence. This chapter demonstrates that, first, our traditional masculine conceptions of humanly rational belief must be revised and, secondly, that the dichotomy between conceptions of emotion and rational behaviour needs to be questioned.

My research at the Old Bailey

Between September 1987 and October 1988, I attended fourteen murder trials at the Old Bailey (the Central Criminal Court in London). In addition, I sat in on one 'child destruction' case. I was unable to attend trials between October and December 1987, but I attended selected trials throughout 1988. The names of the defendants and the dates of the trials are presented in the Appendix. I also sat in on ten rape trials and four re-trials. Newspaper cuttings for the years 1985–89 were analysed. However, my research applications to the Equal Opportunities Commission, the Gulbenkian Foundation, the Leverhulme Trust, the Nuffield Foundation, the Law Society and the Rowntree Trust were all unsuccessful. The area of research was not looked on favourably by research committees. I do not believe that being a feminist means being un-methodical. Far from it. The newspaper files alone merited a systematic and statistical treatment. But I had only £5000, squeezed out of a research budget for another study. I have therefore used the data expressively and illustratively, although I hope convincingly enough not just to prove my point, but also to demonstrate the importance of adequately funding research of this kind.

The judge's direction

Judges normally begin their summing up with a statement such as 'You must put your emotion aside', implying that sympathy will disrupt the 'rational' process of decision making. He (or she) then goes on to direct the jury that in cases of provocation there must be two elements:

1 The defendant must lose his self-control.
2 The provocation must have been such as to make a reasonable man lose his self-control.

Justice Pain (1 March 1988, Old Bailey) described this as follows:

> You have to look to see if there was a complete loss of self control to the extent to which you really do not know what you are doing. Simple anger is not enough. Then you have to consider if the provocation would have made a reasonable man lose his self control. You apply the test of a person of similar age in a similar situation. Rational people do irrational things. The prosecution has to show that this was murder. You might be satisfied that this was a case

where there was no provocation. Then there is no problem. You might be satisfied that this was a case where there was provocation. Again there is no problem. If you are not sure then he is entitled to the benefit of the doubt and you return a verdict of manslaughter. To argue that rational people do irrational things, and that simple anger is not enough, is to suggest that there are certain emotional responses that are out of control of the rational person.

However, irrationality is a relative rather than an absolute concept. Studies of some alien categories show them to be culture specific interpretations of apparently irrational beliefs, and to 'make sense' in the context of culture specific views (Sperber 1989: 47). What is regarded as 'irrational' behaviour by judges may be little more than the judge's failure to acknowledge the reality of male violence as a means of social control and domination over women. To prove the crime of murder, there have to be two features, the act of killing and the intent to kill. It is, however, argued in trials that if the 'intent to kill' is 'irrational', murder is commuted to manslaughter. Evidence of intention is therefore sometimes overruled when the judge does not regard the act as 'rational'. The problem is how to draw the line between an angry response that involves elements of intention and an angry response which is uncontrollable. It is debatable whether any violent response is ever uncontrollable in the way judges suggest. The examples English judges often use in their summing up to juries to describe provocation are of the soldier, returning either from the Falklands or Northern Ireland, to find his wife *in flagrante delicto* (in bed with another man). This is curious as judges sometimes point out in contradiction that in Britain we do not have a legal category of crimes of passion. In reality, such cases are extremely rare, but giving such examples provides a rationale for the whole defence. Once the jury has accepted the idea of provocation where a man is beside himself on confronting his wife in bed with someone else, then they are more likely to accept the idea of provocation for bad housekeeping or insubordination or nagging: simply not being a 'good wife'. It is a slippery slope. It could be argued that it is not rational to kill someone under any circumstances except self-defence, or for some nefarious gain. The rational action on confronting your partner in bed with someone else would seem to me to be to discuss it together over a cup of tea. Not so according to British justice. In this way, almost any behaviour can be regarded as provocative. The most common scenario in murder trials is where the woman is seeking a separation or divorce, does not wish to continue living with her husband, does not wish to have sexual relations with him, yet this very wish is presented as provoking her own murder! Legally, it is regarded as grounds for the defence of provocation.

Shortly after the definition of provocation was widened in 1957, Justice Thesiger at the Essex Assizes – in finding Kenneth Burrell not guilty of murder but guilty of manslaughter on the grounds of provocation for killing his wife who was in bed with a lover – recognized this problem when he commented:

> The accused undoubtedly had very severe provocation but on the other hand the large number of divorces do indicate that this sort of situation, though not quite in such a dramatic form, is apt to arise and it would be a terrible thing if all people who commit misconduct while their husbands are away were subjected to a violent attack like this.

Such reservations are rare and, as the following cases show, provocation is often accepted far too readily without any evidence that the woman has even been unfaithful let alone actually in bed with someone else.

There are three problems about the defence of provocation. First, as we have seen, the woman is dead and cannot therefore answer false allegations that may be presented by the defence. The defence counsel can therefore paint a picture of the deceased that is far from the truth. It is possible for the prosecuting barrister to present evidence 'in rebuttal' of allegations (to refute them), but in the cases analysed this rarely occurs. Therefore, entirely false allegations can be presented without anybody contesting them.

Secondly, the whole rationale of the defence is debatable. Can a man be driven 'beyond his senses' to kill someone and then return unscathed to the 'rational' human being he was before? If he can't take her nagging any more, why doesn't he just leave? This way of resolving marital difficulties is never considered. For example, in the Boyce case, discussed below, his wife had left him and had moved to the country with the children, but had been persuaded to return on a visit for Christmas when she was killed. Yet this was never mentioned in the court case, where as we shall see, his wife was falsely presented as a provocative woman. Stark contradictions emerge in the way that violence is regarded in court cases. As Lee Ann Hoff points out in her book *Battered Women as Survivors*, if women have violence used against them and fail to leave, they lack self-respect. If men are stressed by non-violent behaviour (e.g. nagging), their use of violence is justified as necessary. This reasoning presupposes the traditional belief that a man's self-respect depends on the use of violence in such a case (Hoff 1990: 125). In the Boyce case, this was exactly the argument. No mention was made that she had left him and was living apart. No mention was made of her plans to divorce. All the focus was on the extent of her conformity with the expected role of wife: on whether she was a good housekeeper, mother and sexual partner, both in terms of fidelity and as a provider of sexual services. This was – and customarily is – used as a benchmark against which to judge the man's responsibility for killing her. If the victim does not conform to the expected role of wife and mother, she is seen as provoking her own death. The defendant, on the other hand, is presented as reacting to intolerable pressure. The victim is then presented as the real culprit in pushing the man to violence.

Thirdly, the prosecution rarely refers to the male defendant's behaviour prior to the killing even when this has involved violence. This is partly due to the fact that the victim is dead and therefore is not there to make allegations against the killer, and partly due to the failure of the prosecution to seek evidence from relatives and friends.

The following four cases are typical. In all of them, a manslaughter verdict was returned. In all cases, evidence that the woman had been subjected either to violence or to considerable pressure before her death made no difference. Instead, all sorts of uncorroborated allegations were made regarding the dead woman.

Christobel Boyce

Nicholas Boyce was released on parole in February 1990 after serving four years of a six-year sentence for manslaughter. He was tried for the murder of his wife, Christobel, by head-banging and strangulation. He had dismembered her body in the bath, cooked parts of it to disguise them and dumped them in plastic bags. By a unanimous verdict, he was acquitted of murder and found guilty of manslaughter on the grounds of provocation.

Boyce had been a student for six years at the London School of Economics and Christobel had been the sole breadwinner for two years when her husband's postgraduate grant had finally run out. She had worked as a full-time senior social worker at the London Hospital as well as taking the main responsibility for looking after the couple's two children. At the time of her death, she had decided to seek a divorce.

The jury apparently accepted that Boyce had been the subject of, to quote his defence counsel, Michael Wolkind: 'a non-stop form of humiliation and degradation which drained every bit of self-respect from a grown man'. It was alleged that he used to sneak home terrified to his wife, that she constantly bullied him and remorselessly ground him down until he finally snapped and strangled her with an electric flex, and that what he wanted, all he ever wanted, was some peace and time to spend with his children. He was:

> . . . not even allowed in the marital bed irrespective of whether or not his wife was there at the time. He could not even take a bath at

home . . . He finally broke down in circumstances in which an ordinary man might also have done.

Pronouncing sentence, Sir James Miskin commented: 'Before these events you were hard-working, of good character, devoted to your children. You were simply not able to get on with your wife.' This was not true according to Christobel's friends and relatives. Even if it were true, it would scarcely be relevant to whether or not he was guilty of murder.

The law provides that murder can be commuted to manslaughter where the victim precipitated his or her own death. As outlined above, a plea can succeed where there is evidence of a sudden and temporary loss of self-control on the part of the defendant which shows the crime is not premeditated. Allegations relating to the provocative behaviour of the victim may be uncorroborated and untrue. In this case, Christobel's friends and relatives were horrified at the outcome. They believed the picture painted of her and of Boyce to be totally false. The whole trial had revolved around the assumed character of the victim. 'Christobel was on trial, not Nick', a friend of the couple said.

Part of the problem lies in the view that the Crown Counsel's role is that of an impartial prosecutor, not protector of the victim. Evidence to rebut the allegations of the defendant is not collected from relatives and friends and is rarely called by the prosecution. This is mandatory in some civil justice countries where the deceased and her relatives are represented by a lawyer to counter false allegations. For example, in France, *crime passionnel*, a defence whereby as long as the accused could prove his spouse's adultery he stood a good chance of a manslaughter verdict, was abolished as grounds for defence following protests by women. Now the family and deceased are represented in court. This contrasts with the situation in Britain where relatives are often not even informed of the date of the trial until the very last moment and are often not involved in plea bargaining at all. In cases where men have killed their wives in horrendous ways, there are grounds for believing that premeditation may have preceded the killing. But they are treated leniently by the courts, serving around three years in prison with remission.

The Boyce case is not unusual. Three other recent trials where the women victims have been seeking divorce after violent episodes in the marriage ended in manslaughter verdicts.

Caroline Schofield

Caroline Schofield's mother was not informed that plea bargaining between the prosecuting barrister and the defence barrister had reduced the charge of murder of her daughter to manslaughter until days before the trial. Richard Schofield was not therefore charged in court with murdering his wife, Caroline. She was found battered and strangled at their house in Gloucestershire, shortly after she had split up with her husband. She had started a new business and had wanted to start a new life. She and her husband had parted before, and however hard they had tried it had not worked out.

The murder charge was dropped and Richard Schofield pleaded guilty to a lesser charge of manslaughter on the grounds of diminished responsibility. None of the evidence of his previous violence came out in court. None of the prosecution evidence was heard, neither did Caroline's family have any chance to speak. The hearing only took an hour during which five psychiatric reports were read out. He was sentenced to four years. Caroline's mother commented after the trial:

> It left me feeling as though my daughter had committed a crime. After her death I discovered that when she had left Richard a few years ago, she had taken out an injunction against him on the ground of violence. That did not emerge nor did we have any say in whether or not there should be a trial. Because he spent 9 months on remand, Richard could be out at the end of the year with good behaviour. I just cannot believe it.

Why do prosecutors doubly silence the dead victim in this way? Why does a long history of victimization not count as relevant evidence? The law, in its rules of evidence, in its exercise of prosecutorial discretion, condemns such victims and their families to carry responsibility for their own deaths. In so doing, it establishes that non-compliant women are beyond its effective protection.

Sandra Midlane

The third case also went to court in January 1990. Stephen Midlane went on trial for strangling and cutting up his wife Sandra. Police had toiled for weeks looking for her remains on an Essex rubbish tip and had found everything except one leg. The Crown Prosecution Service accepted his plea of guilty to the manslaughter of Sandra and attempted murder of the couple's two sons, aged four and five. Judge Neil Dennison QC sentenced him to five years which, with remission, meant he would be released in three years: he is free now as this book is published.

In a plea in mitigation of sentence, the defence claimed that Midlane attacked Sandra in the middle of an argument over Sandra's infidelity, accidentally hitting the vagal nerve on her neck. The manslaughter plea ensured that evidence contained in police statements, of the breakdown of the marriage and of prolonged violence, was never put before the court. Enough has been said.

Kohila Baig

In the fourth case, Mumtaz Baig stood trial in September 1987 for allegedly murdering his wife Rohila by strangling. The couple had married in 1980. Mr Baig had left and returned to Pakistan shortly before the birth of their second son in 1982, following what he described as arguments with his in-laws. His pregnant wife had already returned to her parents after her husband had beaten her up. In his absence abroad, she had obtained a transfer of the house to her name and a legal separation. Between 1982 and 1986, his only contact with the children was to send birthday and Christmas cards. In January 1986, he returned to the house and later that year his wife made it clear she wanted a divorce. He killed her in December.

He pleaded provocation, alleging that Mrs Baig had admitted in graphic terms being unfaithful with one of his friends. The friend vehemently refuted any indiscretion in the witness box, maintaining he had never been alone with Mrs Baig let alone had a sexual relationship with her. The likelihood of a devout Muslim woman making the admission was not raised, nor the horror with which her family would react to such an allegation. As Baig's English was poor, he had an interpreter in court, though he managed twice to murmur: 'I wasn't in my senses.' He also stated: 'Because she wanted to take away the children, I intended to kill her.' The prosecution did not draw out the contradictions between the two statements. The jury found Baig not guilty of murder, and he was sentenced to six years for manslaughter. Even if the issue is decided at trial rather than in a backstage bargain, the victim's character remains posthumously in jeopardy. This is the outcome of lawyers' work.

Male reason *vs* female unreasonableness

There are profound objections to the way the defence is allowed to operate. Different criteria are applied to male and female behaviour. For provocation to be argued in aid of a woman who has killed her partner, the man must be persistently violent; in the reverse situation, the women need only be insubordinate. Such criteria reflect a double standard. 'Rational' men are able to avoid their responsibility by pointing to sexual or irrational behaviour, 'woman trouble' or other feminine influences which can be used to blame the victim. The unfairness, and the untold distress caused to victims' relatives, will continue as long as the courts allow pleas of provocation to open the door to unverifiable allegations which are neither sought to be proved by the defence nor rebutted by independent evidence. Libel laws do not cover the deceased, so relatives are not able to seek redress from false allegations made in homicide trials. Violence from wives is met with a quite different response, as shown in the following case.

Susan Goddard-Watt

Susan Goddard-Watt shot and injured her husband with a Magnum revolver as he was finally leaving her. The evidence of provocation (that he was leaving for good) and the absence of any long-term injuries did not save her from an eight-year prison sentence. Her husband, a nineteen-year-old RAF serviceman, described how he was 'duped into marrying her, lured by steamy sex sessions and snared by lies'. He said:

> I hate her. She turned out to be a cunning vixen who would do anything to get what she wanted. When she got into a rage she was like a snarling wild beast.

Four months after their wedding day, he continued: 'She had imposed a sex ban. She had satisfied her appetite for me. She said that for £1000 she would get out of my life.'

Described as a trained markswoman, she had 'loaded her Magnum and blasted his car' as he drove past with a friend after he had walked out on her for good. They were injured but had both made a full recovery.

On hearing her sentence, she sobbed:

> I think I would rather be executed than sent to prison. I cannot take any more of this, being ripped to pieces while inside. I never meant to cause anybody any pain.

She hardly fitted into the conventional feminine stereotype. She had married a man considerably younger than herself, was sexually experienced and a trained markswoman. She got eight years, and the victim was not even dead.

What should be done?

How can it be argued that it is reasonable to murder your wife or husband if they wish to leave, are unfaithful, let you down, fail to be a 'good' partner or nag you? We may all have murderous feelings, but this has nothing to do with the immorality of actually committing murder. It is not rational to argue that men cannot control their anger, and are not responsible for killing women. To argue that men kill their wives because they cannot help it, are driven beyond their senses, are provoked into it by insubordinate behaviour, is a convenient way of condoning male violence. It also fails to address the prevalence of violence against women in the home which serves the function of maintaining women's subordination. It fails to take into account the women who are killed in the process of divorce proceedings where violence is the main ground for the breakdown of the relationship. The defence of provocation should be abolished. Originally designed to protect men and women who were 'provoked' by being attacked, it is now used to condone men for murdering wives who are often seeking a divorce in response to years of violence.

There are three ways in which violence is condoned. First, judges frequently sympathize with the male assailant. Judge Pickles, for example, in a 1989 TV interview, referred to the 'Jekyll and Hyde' within all men. He regretted that sometimes he 'had to send a man down' and added that he 'was basically pro-women'. Bochnak makes the same point in regard to the sympathy judges show for men who have committed violence against women:

> The man's act while not always condoned is viewed sympathetically. He is not forgiven, but his motivation is understood by those sitting in judgement upon his act since his conduct conforms to the expectations that a real man would fight to the death to protect his pride and property . . . The law however has never protected a wife who killed her husband after finding him with another woman. A woman's husband simply does not belong to her in the same way that she belongs to him.
>
> (Bochnak 1981: 14)

This sympathy for the murderer even extends to cases where the wife has not been unfaithful, contemplating divorce, or allegedly failing in her wifely duties. In one case, a man had killed his wife 21 years before and was only discovered after he bragged to his second wife, Selena, that he had committed the 'perfect murder'. He 'hit his first wife twice with a heavy stool' and then pushed her downstairs after a furious argument over his passionate affair with Selena. Summing up, Mr Igor Judge QC said:

> He has lived his life with the appalling threat of exposure to the world and to his adored sons. In one sense he has served a life sentence in prison in his own mind, trapped by his own fears.

A defence counsel will, of course, use any argument he or she can think up to use as mitigation, but will only use arguments that the jury are likely to accept. The fact that this man murdered his first wife cold bloodedly in order to marry Selena is not considered sufficiently important to preclude such a plea for clemency. One cannot imagine a defence lawyer putting forward such an argument in defence of a woman who had killed her husband in order to marry someone else. It is literally unthinkable in the setting of the court. In the above case, the defendant was acquitted of murder and found guilty only of manslaughter for which he received a six-year sentence; less be it noted, than poor Susan Goddard-Watt who did not even kill her husband.

Secondly, when a husband uses violence against his wife, it is regarded by the judiciary as a random irrational act or in the final analysis the woman's fault. She must have provoked it. That men use violence when they are fully in control of their senses to prevent women from leaving, getting a divorce, through jealousy, or to coerce them is not on the agenda. The power they hold over women, the fact that they may have a motive, financial or other, for getting rid of these women, is often hidden, denied and rationalized away. The feminist analysis which sees male domination as a crucial factor contributing to the maintenance of wife abuse is disregarded. As Radford (1987) has suggested, the law is concerned with defining the limits of violence appropriate for the control of women. Even after a conviction for murder, the 'irrationality' of the act can be used to excuse it. Take the case of Graham Sherman, a Royal Marine who on 28 February 1990 was convicted of culpable homicide of his wife and month-old baby with a shotgun. He walked free from the High Court in Aberdeen after Lord Dunpark rejected imprisonment with the following words: 'In my opinion, you have punished yourself more than enough by what you did. You will have to live with this for the rest of your life' (*Guardian*, 28 February 1990). He added that Sherman had no idea why he had killed his family scarcely two years after his wedding and no one had been able to offer any explanation. He continued:

> It is obvious to me your state of mind at the time must have been very disturbed indeed and you acted for some inexplicable reason. It has been established you were a good and loving husband and father who assisted your wife with the care of your baby.

The evidence that he assisted his wife with the baby is only based on his evidence as his wife was not there to testify.

If the murder had been seen in the context of Sherman's service in the armed forces (he had served in the Royal Marines since he was sixteen, in Northern Ireland and elsewhere) and in the context of the prevalence of violence against women in the family, rather than dismissing the behaviour as inexplicable, Sherman's behaviour could have been understood. To be cynical, his silence about the reason for his attack and his assumed incomprehension made good sense in terms of his defence. Lord Dunpark offered the defendant his deep sympathy, adding that he hoped it would not trouble his conscience:

> There is no point in deferring sentence for good behaviour. You have no previous convictions . . . neither is this a case in which, in my opinion, a probation order would help you. It would just keep on reminding you of what you have done and the sooner you try to forget this the better.

Not only did he let Sherman free for the horrendous killing of two innocent people, but he also advised him to forget about it as soon as he could.

There are shades of culpability even in non-deliberate killings, but the judge is denying him any culpability at all by his statement.

Thirdly, implicit within the context of the defence of provocation is that male violence is *uncontrollable* and therefore men cannot be held fully responsible for it. In this way, male violence is condoned by the judiciary. Anger is a reasonable response when displayed by men but only rarely when shown by women. We have already seen in the case of Susan Goddard-Watts how her aggression was treated harshly by the judge.

Provocation as a defence for women who kill

There are homicide cases where provocation is put forward successfully as a defence for women. These cases fall into two groups, the first where there is evidence that the woman was a conventional, devoted wife and the second where there has been a history of violence. Take the case of Gillian Philpott, aged 28, who was not charged with murder and pleaded guilty to manslaughter on 8 January 1991 on the grounds of provocation for strangling her husband with a dressing gown cord after a party on New Year's Eve 1989. She then dragged his body to a landing and tied another dressing gown cord round a bannister 'to indicate he committed suicide'. She then made two attempts to kill herself, once with painkillers and once by trying to drive over Beachy Head. After her arrest she told police: 'I begged him to love me. I said he would never find another woman who would do all the things I did for him.'

Immediately before the killing, friends and neighbours still believed they were a devoted couple according to her defence counsel. Her marital difficulties had started after she had begun to suspect that her twin sister whom she had invited on their honeymoon in the Far East and to share their home in Kent, was having an affair with her husband. The twin sister had left but Mr Philpott had banished his wife to a separate room. Plea bargaining was accepted by the prosecution presumably due to her suicidal attempts and evidence of her devotion. However, diminished responsibility would appear to have been a more appropriate plea.

Secondly, since the Maw sisters were imprisoned in 1980 for killing their father who had subjected them and their mother to years of violence, there has been some move in Britain to take into account cumulative provocation. This typically involves a course of cruel or violent conduct by the deceased, lasting over a substantial period of time which culminates in the victim or someone acting on his or her behalf intentionally killing the tormentor (Wasik 1982). In such cases, there need be no apparent final provoking event. An example of such a case occurred in November 1986 when Valerie Flood, described as a devoted wife, killed her husband after years of drunken beatings, and was found guilty of manslaughter rather than murder on the grounds of provocation. The court heard how she had been frequently beaten, hit with hammers, cut on the legs with a machete, had her nose broken several times and had been burnt with cigarettes. She had finally snapped when he had tried to strangle her and attacked her with a carving knife which she had snatched from him and used against him. Though in this case provocation was used as a defence, I would argue that this was much more a case of self-defence than provocation. All the evidence pointed to self-defence. He was attacking her and she snatched the actual knife that he was using against her. Had self-defence been successfully argued, she would of course have been acquitted rather than found guilty on a reduced charge. It seems that provocation may work against women even when used in their defence. So does the law constitute and reward 'appropriate' gendered behaviour, by policing the inappropriate.

It seems extraordinary that provocation should be argued in such a case. This may be due to the unacceptability of women defending themselves against male violence (see Lees 1992). Even here, although provocation was accepted, Mrs Flood's reaction is totally reasonable in view of the attack she was sustaining. She does not fit into the category as a man would, where so-called 'unreasonable' behaviour is followed by a return to rationality. No one could argue that her snatching the knife from his hand to avoid sustaining an injury was not sensible, rather than caused by anger. Anger is not an acceptable response to frustration on the part of a woman.

The unacceptability of anger

If anger is not regarded as an acceptable response on the part of women, how then is it conceptualized? Since a woman is never regarded as really reasonable, it is not possible for her to lose her reason. In law, therefore, it does not appear that a 'reasonable' woman can be driven 'beyond her senses' and remain 'reasonable' unless she is suffering from premenstrual tension (PMT) and is, as Dr Katherine Dalton put it, 'at the mercy of her hormones' (cited in Eaton 1983). This fits in with the idea that non-conformity in women is due to biological imbalance rather than rational choice. She is either suffering from diminished responsibility, which means she is then confined usually for an indefinite period to a mental hospital, or she is deemed to be suffering from PMT, or she is acting in revenge and is guilty of murder. This implies that, unlike a man, she can never be 'provoked' into violence and remain a reasonable person.

In 1981, for example, Mrs Khristina English killed her lover by driving her car at him, after he had told her that he was going out with another woman. She claimed that something had snapped when he had made a 'V' sign at her. Medical and psychiatric evidence diagnosed her as suffering from PMT on the basis of PMT pointers. Following pregnancy she had suffered from post-natal depression, she had been sterilized and had gone some hours without eating. Failure to eat in PMT sufferers, it is said, could produce hypoglycaemia, in turn producing aggressive uncontrollable behaviour. Her plea to diminished responsibility was accepted and she was banned from driving for a year and given a one-year conditional discharge (see Luckhaus 1986).

As Bel Mooney argued in *The Times* (18 July 1981):

> The courts did not give her a reduced sentence because her boyfriend was a cad . . . she was conditionally discharged because she convinced the court that PMT had led to diminished responsibility – even though she had threatened to run the boyfriend over earlier in the day, which might have been taken as evidence of premeditation.

When women do express anger at men, men often accuse them of 'being emotional', so denying their anger.

The unacceptability of female anger as a response to provocation is mirrored by the lack of understanding about the predicament of victims of violence. Bochnak, in her study of women subjected to male violence in the family, found judges often fail to understand what living under the threat of attack involves. As one of the trial judges commented:

> Given your domestic troubles, which as I find were present but are not to be accepted in their entirety, the law itself is not without remedy and was not without remedy to you. There are friends: there are relatives: there are community and Church and other avenues of advice: there are policemen: there are Chamber Magistrates: there are solicitors: there are means of protection in the community.
>
> (Bochnak 1981: 33)

All the evidence suggests that these forms of protection are in fact not widely available in the community and that it is very difficult for women to get help. In the UK, the women's refuge movement, rape crisis centres and victim support schemes provide some skeletal service, but this is underfunded and rudimentary. Extensive financial support would be needed to provide the kind of help judges assume exists.

The concept of provocation embodies the idea that murder is precipitated by the victim, in effect that the victim is to blame for her death. The arguments used in court by the prosecution reflect a strong gender bias that not only allows some men to go free or be leniently punished, but also serves to condone violence against women. This sympathy for male defendants is not confined to homicide cases. The idea that sympathy for the victim can distort judgment, whereas sympathy for the defendant does not, arises from an identification of male judges with male defendants, and is illustrated by a case heard in June 1990, discussed below.

Social worker John Hall, convicted of raping a sixteen-year-old girl in his care, was cleared and freed on 25 May 1990 from his seven-year jail sentence by three appeal court judges because of a 'misdirection' by the trial judge. Hall was sentenced by the Recorder of London in July 1989 following an alleged offence against a girl at a hostel for adolescents in care, run by Southwark Social Services. He claimed the girl had consented to sex but she alleged rape. Lord Justice Neill said that the original judge in the case, where Hall had been found guilty, had made too much of the victim's distress in his summing up, and this amounted to a misdirection. In summing up, a judge had to be selective and ordinarily could only be expected to cover the aspects of the evidence which appeared to him to be important. Said Lord Justice Neill:

> We have been much more troubled, however, by the submission that the appellant's defence was not put adequately and fairly to the jury. It was argued that there were constant references to the distress of the girl which seriously damaged, even if it did not completely undermine, the credibility of the appellant's account of what happened . . . We have read and reread the summing up in this case several times. We have considered the submissions of unfairness in the light of and in conjunction with the submissions on corroboration. We are satisfied that the several criticisms of the summing up have to be looked at together. The case could perhaps have been left to the jury on the basis that there was no corroboration. But this was not the course which the judge took: we feel bound to say that we have found the directions on corroboration less than clear. Moreover, the failure to give a plain warning to the jury as to how they could regard evidence that the girl was distressed and incoherent when she arrived at the grandfather's house was, in the present state of the law, misdirection.

In the case the girl had been severely traumatized by the alleged rape, and a woman police officer and a police surgeon had given evidence to this effect.

Directions to the jury

The myth of equal justice for all is never more blatantly exposed than in a rape trial. Not only is the woman's account of her experience dismissed and trivialized, but the whole procedure loads the dice against her. Not only her testimony, but her very life up to her complaint of rape and her motives in making that complaint are brought into question – and often aggressively or mockingly so. The judge pulls together this bias against the complainant in his directions to the jury. People lie more about their sexual behaviour, he warns, than about any other area of human conduct.

Here, for example, is how judges put that questionable proposition to the jury in two cases I attended:

1 There is in all cases of sexual allegations a special warning. Experience has shown that people who say they have been the victims of sexual attacks do not always tell the truth. Such allegations may be very easy to make and very difficult to refute. It is dangerous to convict on the evidence of the complainant alone.

2 What is the most difficult and the most intimate part of our lives? It is our sexual life. It is not only the most difficult but the most unstable part of our lives. It has become a rule of law that some supporting evidence is needed that is wholly independent.

It is only with sexual crimes where this warning is given. The judge combines it with the usual direction that it is not up to the defendant to prove his innocence, but for the prosecution to prove his guilt beyond any reasonable doubt. As one judge put it: 'He does not have to prove anything. The proof has to be so strong that you are sure that the defendant is guilty. Then it is your duty to convict. But the defendant gets the benefit of the doubt.'

Put in opposition, these two directions make it very difficult for a jury to convict. Only in sexual cases does the defendant get this double indemnity. The Common Serjeant of London set out the thinking which lies behind this judicial caution in September 1989:

In complaints of sexual matter, made by men and women, it has been found that whether out of spite, excitement, jealousy, sexual gratification or malice, false allegations are made and once made are extremely difficult to disprove.

Jennifer Temkin (1987) points out that if a woman reports a burglary, or makes an insurance claim, her word is not automatically doubted, though of course investigation would take place to substantiate her report. But her integrity would not be questioned, her statement would not be picked to pieces, her whole life would not come under investigation. In a rape trial, since it is 'known' that under the influence of sex women lie so convincingly that they will not only fabricate a story of rape, say to avoid being honest with their partner, but to substantiate it they will run naked into the street, cry compulsively, spend the night in a police station, change their name or even move home, the judiciary remains ever alert against a miscarriage of justice. Only if she contrives to be physically assaulted, too, can a woman be sure of fooling them. The judge fails to warn the jury with equal solemnity that experience has shown that accused men lie to escape conviction. Nor does he draw the jury's attention to the fact that most women who have been raped cannot face the ordeal they will have to go through if they complain to the police (many, indeed, cannot face telling anyone) or to the fact they are often threatened with retaliation if they do go to the police. In a case I attended, J.S. when asked why she had not gone at once to the police replied: 'Because he told me that if I told anyone or went to the police, he'd come back for me and the children.'

One main barrier to gaining convictions in rape cases is the belief that rape can never be corroborated; since the act takes place in private and rests on the presence or absence of the woman's consent, it is argued that independent corroboration is impossible. This is not wholly true as trials often rest not simply on the question of consent but on two different accounts of what actually happened. Evidence to back the man's or woman's story is often given but is often not treated as corroboration. For example, Mr Y said he had never been on the wasteland where the complainant claimed rape had taken place. A can of beer with his fingerprints was found close to where the grass had been flattened as though two people had lain there. In several cases, evidence was given by witnesses that the complainant had been in a state of shock when she had rung desperately, half clad in the middle of the night at a neighbour's door. This, however, was not regarded as corroboration, nor did the defence lawyer find it necessary even to explain why else she should have been in this state. The argument was put forward that she could be faking it. A rape victim will usually show signs of distress or other psychological reaction, but this is at once suspect. In one case I saw, rather as in the case just discussed where John Hall was so successful, several police officers, including a police surgeon, gave evidence that the woman was shaking with fear and distress, tears were streaming down her face, she wanted to wash herself frequently and was afraid afterwards to go out alone. They all agreed she was in acute distress showing every sign that she was suffering from what has been identified as the rape trauma syndrome. The prosecuting counsel failed even to mention her distress in his summing up. When I questioned him about it later, he responded that it was absurd to regard the woman's state as corroborative.[2]

Forensic evidence is relevant only in establishing that intercourse took place, not intercourse with or without consent. In the absence of vaginal injuries, which are rare, forensic evidence is often used by the defence to argue that the woman consented. The prosecuting lawyers seemed very inept at countering these claims. This should be an area where the judge explains that since most women who are raped are in a state of panic due to the threats on their life that often accompany rape, they may not struggle, but this does not mean they are consenting. Much confusion surrounds this question. Two police officers I spoke with, working with sexual assault cases, believed that forensic tests could ascertain from the fluids whether or not the complainant had consented. If police believe this, jurors are often equally confused by the lack of injuries and taken in by the defence's spurious arguments.

Judge Dean, who told an Old Bailey jury in April 1990, which subsequently cleared Peter Kemp, a London property consultant, of rape, 'As the gentlemen of the jury will understand, when a woman says "no" she doesn't always mean "no" ', is voicing a common view which is used to support the argument that women are prone to make false allegations. The focus should, however, not be on the myth that women do not know their own minds (so how is a poor man to understand when he should make advances). Rather, the focus should be on how such a misunderstanding could have arisen, if it did, or why the woman has gone through all the trouble of reporting the rape to the police.

Conclusion

The dichotomy between reason and emotion as illustrated in the law and practice of homicide and rape trials is clear. It parallels the dichotomy between masculinity and feminity, where rationality is associated with men and emotionality with women. Not only has reason been contrasted with emotion, but it has also been associated with the mental, the cultural, the universal, the public and the male, whereas emotion has been associated with the irrational, the physical, the natural, the particular, the private and the female.

Both Plato and Freud considered that women had a lesser moral sense than men. To quote Freud:

> I cannot evade the notion (though I hesitate to give it expression) that for women the level of what is ethically normal is different from what it is in men. Their super-ego is never so inexorable, so impersonal, so independent of its emotional origins as we require it to be in men . . . They show less sense of justice than men . . . they are less ready to submit to the great exigencies of life. They are more often influenced in their judgements by feelings of affection or hostility.
>
> (Freud 1925: 257)

Though to be fair Freud did emphasize that he was talking about the construction of feminity, he still clearly considered that for whatever reason, women were not able to think 'rationally' to the same extent as men, that their views were too easily coloured by their emotions, that they employed less abstract categories. Philosophers on the whole agree with Freud's views that emotions and personal feelings are an impediment to thought. In contrast, Susan Sherwin (1989) argues that feminists who consider direct personal experience an important component of truth, pay particular attention to the emotional content of thought. It is certainly true that consciousness-raising has used emotional experience as a starting point from which to move to a more abstract analysis of personal experience. But is talking about personal experience the same as talking about emotions? And what are philosophers saying when they argue that emotions interfere with rationality?

Surely this is a false dichotomy in that there is no such entity as 'raw' feeling which is not constructed by cognitive categorization. We learn to label certain emotional sensations in the same way that we label physiological sensations, such as hunger, thirst and pain. This involves a cognitive process that is dependent not only on cultural concepts but may also be gendered. Feminists grasped this many years ago in pointing out that sometimes cognitive categories did not exist to describe their emotional experiences. We spoke of the 'silencing' of women's experience and the lack of vocabulary to describe it. Betty Friedan (1963) talked of 'the problem that has no name' and terms such as 'sexual harassment' were coined and have now passed into everyday usage. The lack of a language to express experience may well lead to women sounding incoherent, and being dubbed irrational as a result. The distinction made between reason and emotion is fundamental to the law on homicide. Where men behave violently in rape or homicide, their behaviour is often seen as being 'uncontrollable', and it is argued that their 'rationality' is *temporarily* overcome usually as a result of some kind of provocation from the woman. After this they return to their natural state of reason. It is posited in law that, under provocation, it is reasonable for men to behave in a violent or irrational way. This is based on the assumption that men are temporarily not in control of their emotions if sexually aroused or aroused by jealousy or insubordination. Violence in such circumstances is seen as a *temporary aberration*, rather than the responsibility of the perpetrator. This shifts the responsibility from the man to the victim who is seen as provoking her own death or her own assault. It is the woman's reputation which is the focus of both homicide and rape trials. It is often said that it is she who is on trial, even after death. When women themselves are on trial for murder, however, provocation is rarely successful as a defence unless she is herself physically attacked and, as we have seen, its use may be only in preference to a more complete defence. Women can successfully plead diminished responsibility, especially on the grounds of premenstrual tension, but this only colludes with the ideology of femininity as resting on an emotionality divorced from 'rational' behaviour. Lawyers in their defence of clients collude in the ideology of gender bias and the law itself perpetuates gender inequality.

The defence of provocation illustrates the way the rules for establishing appropriate relationships between mind and body, reason and the emotions, are geared to male interests. We have seen that in homicide trials, the concept of provocation rests on a certain conception of 'rationality' which denies that men can rationally use violence to control their wives.

This is not to say that they always intend necessarily to actually kill their wives. However, the definition of murder embraces not only intention to kill but also intention to do some serious harm, and there is little doubt that in most of the cases where provocation is presented as a defence, evidence exists that this second intention was present. By regarding their violence as momentarily 'irrational' or 'provoked', men avoid responsibility for their violence and retain their so-called rationality unsullied. Thus male irrationality, as far as the law is concerned, is temporary and understandable, whereas female irrationality is biologically given and so always immanent and never available to male comprehension. The dichotomy between emotion and rationality, and its connection with dichotomies of feminity and masculinity, results in a denial of emotionality and desire as important determinants of human conduct and has far-reaching and perverse consequences. Lawyers have to work within the framework of these interpretations of the law.

Feminist standpoint philosophers argue that there is a need to redefine reason and restructure its priorities. They argue for an alternative moral and epistemological vision that would not only question the condoning of violence in the family but also call for a different vision. Nancy Hartsock, for example, has developed and transformed the Marxist notion of a privileged political and epistemological standpoint. A standpoint is an engaged vision of the world opposed and superior to dominant ways of thinking. As a proletarian standpoint is a superior vision produced by the experience of oppressive conditions of labour, a feminist standpoint is a superior vision produced by the political conditions and distinctive work of women, such as is involved in caring (see Hartsock 1983; Ruddick 1990: 129). Conversely, a male standpoint when embedded in the law and supported by myths of universality, constitutes women as *properly* vulnerable to male strategies of domestic control: even to the point of murder.

The Rights of Women (1992) in their *Submission to the Royal Commission: Proposed Amendments to the 1957 Homicide Act* put forward two recommendations. They advocate a redefinition of 'reasonable' in a way that makes sense for women as well as the 'reasonable man' and put forward the idea of a new defence of 'self preservation'. In regard to the former, they argue for a subjective criterion for reasonableness, based on honest belief. Quoting the case of Yvonne Wanrow, a US Indian woman who shot and killed a known child abuser who had broken into her house at night and made advances towards her child, they cited the following extract:

> The impression created – that of a 5 foot 4 inch woman with a cast on her leg and using a crutch must, under law, somehow repel an assault by a 6 foot 2 inch intoxicated man without employing a weapon

in her defence. Unless the jury finds her determination of the degree of danger to be objectively reasonable – constitutes a separate and distinct misstatement of the law and, in the context of this case violates the respondent's right to equal treatment of the law. The respondent (Wanrow) was entitled to have the jury consider her actions in the light of her own perception of the situation, including those perceptions which were the product of a nation's 'long and unfortunate history of sex discrimination . . .' Until such time as the effects of that history are eradicated, care must be taken to be sure that our self-defence instructions afford women the right to have their conduct judged in light of the individual physical handicaps which are the product of sex discrimination.

(Gillespie 1989: 117)

Secondly, they argue that the new defence of self-preservation should be a partial defence, similar to provocation resulting in a manslaughter verdict, in recognition that taking a person's life is never justified, yet is a very different situation from that worthy of a finding of premeditated murder. This defence would be open to a person who has been subjected to continuing sexual and or physical abuse and intimidation combined with psychological abuse to the extent that 'they honestly believe that they have reached a point in which there is no future, no protection and no safety from the abuse and believe it is a question of only one of them being able to survive' (Rights of Women 1992).

Notes

1 The judge remarked that 'a reasonable woman with her sex eliminated is altogether too abstract a notion for my comprehension' (cited in Allen 1987: 23).
2 Cain (1979) has characterized this response as a 'refusal to translate'. The situations in which such a refusal occurs are clearly patterned by gendered presumptions.

Appendix: Homicide cases attended at the Old Bailey, 1987–88

Name	Charge	Date	Victim	Judge	Plea	Result
Virgo	Child destruction	September 1987	Girlfriend's foetus	Hazan	Not guilty	Murder, life
Baig	Murder	September 1987	Wife	Lowry	Manslaughter, provocation	Manslaughter, 6 years
Name not published	Murder	September 1987	Rapist	Hazan	Not guilty, self-defence	Acquitted on direction of judge
Gemmel, Sarah	Murder	September 1987	Violent cohabitee	Pigot (Common Serjeant)	Manslaughter, gross provocation	Manslaughter, 2 years (1 year suspended); plea accepted by prosecution
Taylor	Murder	June 1988	Mother	Pigot (Common Serjeant)	Manslaughter, diminished responsibility	Section 37, no bed available; adjourned 28 days
Cohen, Bette	Murder	August 1988	Woman friend	Rougier	Manslaughter, diminished responsibility	Manslaughter, plea accepted by prosecution
Connolly, Kathleen	Murder	n.d.	Violent husband	Rougier	Manslaughter, provocation	Manslaughter, plea accepted by prosecution
Fares	Murder	March 1988	Wife and two children	Rougier	Manslaughter, diminished responsibility	Manslaughter, 6 years
Irwin	Murder	February 1988	Wife	Petrie	Manslaughter	Section 37

Appendix: continued

Name	Charge	Date	Victim	Judge	Plea	Result
Fyvies	Murder	May 1988	Boyfriend	Rougier	Manslaughter, killing accidental	Manslaughter, 3 years, plea accepted by prosecution
Kavusi	Murder	March 1988	Wife's lover	Rougier	Manslaughter, provocation	Manslaughter, diminished responsibility
Pilgrim	Murder	September 1988	Wife of close friend (possible affair)	Rougier	Not guilty	Guilty, life
Name not published	Murder	July 1988	Violent ex-cohabitee	Rougier	Not guilty	Acquitted
Richens	Murder	March 1988	Girlfriend's rapist	Pain	Manslaughter, provocation	Murder (10:2 majority)
Thompson and Doyle	Murder	February 1988	Ex-girlfriend's neighbour (blamed for end of relationship)	Pain	Not guilty	Thompson, murder; Doyle, acquitted (jury invited to consider possibility of self-defence and provocation)
Hopwood	Murder	October 1988	Violent husband	Petrie	Not guilty	Unknown

7 The forum should fit the fuss: the economics and politics of negotiated justice

Yves Dezalay

Introduction

This chapter takes as its starting point two central hypotheses. First, negotiated justice represents an area of professional struggle between two methods of intervention in a dispute which are indissociable, complementary but competitive, and which correspond to two types of competence and knowledge. The actors in this struggle are the judge whose decision is based upon ritual, legal technique and the letter of the law, and the mediator who contributes a combination of social and legal resources in order to have the parties agree to a compromise that is more acceptable because it is more reasonable.

There is an infinite redefinition of the market between those two types of official. The boundaries are perpetually challenged, and it is in and through such processes of redefinition that the legal field is transformed. However, the ceaseless struggle and opposition between these two concepts of justice must not be allowed to conceal their complementarity. This is a division of labour which allows simultaneously for the autonomy of the law – its transcendence within time and social space – and its permanent updating in accordance with social transformations. Both modes of justice, no matter how antagonistic they appear, represent essential components of the belief in law, and therefore of the very survival of a field of professional practices.

Secondly, a theory of negotiated justice implies taking into account the diversity of the fields of disputes in which negotiation operates: from the internal conflicts of capital to the problems of the lower classes. Negotiated justice, like justice itself, is endlessly traversed by contradictions between 'high' and 'low' justice. The contradictions divide everything – the clientele as much as the legal operators – but cohabitation is necessary both for the legal order to be transcendent, and for a justice that claims to be above class distinction, because in this cohabitation lies the system's claim to legitimacy and credibility.

Negotiated justice is a terrain which highlights in particular the contradictions between high and low justice. Its structural position on the margins of courts drives it towards an amalgamation of both 'high' disputes (where the stakes are too important to be entrusted to the hands of ordinary judges) and disputes which are 'below' ordinary litigation because the legal costs exceed the parties' resources. But both high and lowly disputes have to cohabit because mediator notabilities – even more than judges who can shelter beneath ritual and legal form – could not be deemed legitimate if, side by side with the greater notabilities of capitalist mediation, there did not exist lesser notabilities willing to provide paternalistic mediation for the lower classes. These petitioners may be either lay notabilities or experts, but they must admit allegiance to the authority of law and of judges.

This chapter uses these hypotheses to explore the history of mediation in selected Western legal systems. At the same time, it exclusively seeks to avoid an internal analysis in terms of professional stakes, which neglects the political stakes of society as a whole.

Following Bourdieu's (1971: 75) theory of symbolic fields, I argue that the two dimensions – internal and external – permanently mirror one another in accordance with the principles of homology. The competitive game played out in a particular field, between operators whose complementarities derive precisely from their differences, transforms a professional field such as that of law. It is also through these struggles that innovations produced in the field of law can be brought to correspond with other changes in society.

Transformations affecting the political field modify the balance of forces within the legal field between the holders of different forms of symbolic capital. For example, the political upheavals of nineteenth-century Europe weakened the position of the *juges de paix notables* whose authority in the legal field was based mainly on heredity, and advantaged the new professionals whose legal competences were acquired by scholarly training. Inversely, today, the place experts have carved out for themselves in the field of negotiated justice conforms with the technocratization of political power, whose holders must now accumulate social authority and scholarly competence. In broader terms, the transformation of legal norms called for by a new economic and social order, has, as its corollary, a restructuration of the field of professional practices where legal norms are endlessly redefined.

Within these transformations, operators of negotiated justice play a determining part because the legal field's division of tasks assigns to them the role of reformers as opposed to guardians of dogma and tradition. This role suits them, corresponding as it does to their position overlapping the legal and the social fields. But here again, in this permanent *querelle des anciens et des modernes* that lies behind the ceaseless *aggiornamento* of the legal field, the position of each party can only be understood in relation to its contradictor. It is their opposition, eternal and eternally renewed, that constitutes the legal field as an autonomous entity, just as capable of playing on the register of sacred authority and tradition, as on that of modernization and innovation.

Informal, alternative, negotiated justice cannot dissociate itself from the formal justice it opposes because, quite often, it is but a stage, an instant in the redefinition of the legal order, which inevitably passes through moments when established legal forms and institutions are challenged, and moments when they are gradually reconstructed by and through negotiation.

In a structural approach such as this, if it is obvious that mediation cannot be isolated from the adjudication it opposes and complements, it is also obvious that competitive struggles between professionals to improve their positions in the field of law are the place and the means whereby the legal field takes account of social changes. The history of negotiated justice can only be understood when taken as a whole – politically and professionally. Hence its interest and its difficulty.

The text which follows attempts such a holistic understanding of negotiated justice, in which both the external-political and the internal-professional accounts are seen to complement each other. The paper deals with the following topics:

1 A sociology of professional stakes: the staging of mediation as a political discourse.
2 A play of interconnected political and professional solutions.
3 Negotiated justice seen as a stake in the professionalization of the legal field:
   - the economics of a dual system of justice and the disqualification of notability mediation by schools of law;
   - the 're-invention' of mediation within a professional framework.
4 A new professional elite – business lawyers:
   - business arbitration as a happy marriage of interests between elite lawyers and business people;
   - social justice: delegation of the 'civilizing function'.
5 Negotiated justice seen as a renegotiation of the division of labour within the market of social peace:
   - paternalist mediation on the terrain of social justice: a mediation within norms;
   - capitalist mediation in the field of business justice: a mediation about norms;

- business justice as the domain *par excellence* of negotiated justice;
- from an extra-normative negotiation to a negotiation about rules;
- the judicialization of negotiation: a professional territorial strategy;
- litigotiation as a valorization of a legal services strategy: a new figure of dual justice, and of an economy of rarity.

Elements for a sociology of negotiated justice

Mediation, conciliation, arbitration, transaction – all those para-legal practices that have been labelled 'social justice', 'informal justice', 'negotiated justice' – are by their nature atypical, if not paradoxical practices within the symbolic field of law, in which a 'justice without law' is as inconceivable as a society without law.

The strength of law, as Bourdieu (1987) has shown, is for the most part, its form: rules of procedure, codification and, more broadly speaking, the whole internal ritual, which give it its universal value and its unequalled performative force. This form, specific to law, is produced and managed by rules, institutions, the *habitus* specific to the field. Fruit of its own relative autonomy, it is also the basis of its legitimacy because it transcends the conflicts of interest it aims to resolve.

Legal formalism thus represents an incomparable resource; it is the very cornerstone of the legal field's constitution, autonomy and social power. It is actively sought after by disputants who wish at all costs to demonstrate publicly that they have 'the law on their side' (Boltanski 1984). Such usage and recourse to the strength of legal form by the profane is strictly monitored by those 'clercs' whose pre-eminent situation within the field of dispute processing depends upon their monopoly of the production of the legal form. It is precisely the complexity, if not the esotericism, of legal ritual and the authenticated forms that is the best defence of legitimate producers of legal formalism, when faced with other competitors attracted by the profits of the market of social peace, be they lay mediators hoping to benefit from their personal charisma, their moral rectitude or their social capital of relationships, or yet again, other professionals attempting to transform dispute situations into 'social problems' to apply their own therapeutic skills.

If such is the logic of the legal field, mediation practices cannot but have a marginal place, inevitably contested, if not more or less considered occult. This 'shadow justice' (Harrington 1985) represents a tactical argument that re-emerges from time to time, in reaction to excesses of legal formalism (Abel 1982: 2), but which is denounced and condemned as soon as it has achieved the desired political and strategic adjustments it was deployed to obtain. Weber himself did not exclude a re-emergence of these 'Khadi justices', on the margins or just outside of 'modern', 'rational', 'bureaucratized' legal institutions.

But is this the main problem? If neighbourhood justice can – at a stretch – be subsumed under the same concept as the paternalistic mediation by 'notables', that which Weber called 'Khadi justice', can this concept also be applied to the negotiation of rules between government agencies and the big corporations described by all observers of economic law? (Jeantin 1985; Winter 1985; Lascoumes 1986).

Unfortunately, this diachronic and synchronic double dimension of negotiated justice – the different façades it adopts within legal space and time – is, for the most part, not discussed in professional literary output (Dezalay 1991: 121). The learned stage for the debate on mediation is practically monopolized by two sets of good fellows, each of which finally sends the ball back to the other's court:

- those who insist upon a natural, pre-existing need for community justice that modern state jurisdictions refuse to acknowledge or satisfy;
- those who are more concerned by the extension of state social control, which, in the guise of a second-class justice for second-class citizens, has taken over a neglected terrain, abandoned by traditional community structures.

But both groups, with some rare exceptions (Auerbach 1983; Cain 1985; Harrington 1985), ignore the diversity of mediation forms, as if these practices of negotiated justice were limited to the field of petty neighbourhood disputes. So it is hardly surprising to find them shocked by the arrival of a third group of good fellows on the scene: the 'new formalists' (Sarat 1987), whose aspirations are to enrol in the name of their doctrinal competences, and annex to the service of capital, a field of practices previously considered the prerogative of militant practitioners and advocates of social justice.

The great merit of the few studies that touch upon this diachronic and synchronic dual dimension is to demonstrate that these practices of mediation – and the competing knowledges they are the object of – constitute the tactical arguments of a global political debate where the authority, the legitimacy and the territorial claims to competence by the different categories of competing law professionals are played out (Harrington 1985: 15). The promotions or criticisms of these negotiated justices serve as tactical supports, or as pretexts, for a plethora of competing reformist strategies which all aim to transform the image of justice and of its professionals: their methods of intervention, their territories of competence and their methods of legitimation.

The corollary of these competitive struggles around the practices of mediation is the relative blindness of all these committed, if not militant, students to the complexity of the stakes involved or to the system of political and professional sites from which, at a given moment, and in a given place, these practices of mediation are formed and learnedly produced.

*Towards a sociology of professional stakes: the staging of mediation as
a political discourse*

These observations define my object – a diachronic and synchronic analysis of negotiated justice and, simultaneously, of the diversity and the
specificity of these successive or simultaneous forms of mediation. Likewise, these preliminary observations define my method: since the learned
discourse on mediation is a political discourse which challenges explicitly
or implicitly the territory of competence and the hierarchy of professionals, the answer to this dual interrogation on the diversity and histor-
icity of mediation practices implies re-situating the protagonists of these
negotiated justices into a system of political and professional strategies.

Indeed, the sociologist cannot pretend to an exteriority denied to those
observed. The one defence for us all is to openly acknowledge involvement in the learned stakes surrounding mediation and to sharpen our
awareness by a kind of sociology of sociology – what Bourdieu (1980)
calls a 'socio-analysis' – of the positioning system that classifies us.

Furthermore, systematic confrontation with other legal fields, even
other symbolic fields (see, e.g. Bourdieu 1971, 1978, 1984b), can at least
reduce the risks of being caught in a trap where the object is indissociable
from the professional discourse. The raw materials of the sociologist of
law – be they dossiers or interviews – are already prefabricated data.
Mediation, much as is the law, is at the same time a practice and a learned
representation of that practice, produced by and for the professionals
(and their clientele!).

This sociology of professional stakes, if it tries not to be a banal objecti-
vated reproduction of professional discourse, does not tend either towards a denunciation or desacralization (Bancaud 1987) of professional
ideology by the unmasking of the particular interests that might lie behind this, that or the other strategy of reform. It is, indeed, imperative to
describe the game of these interests in order to understand where, when
and how these innovations are produced. But we cannot stop there. The
specificity of symbolic fields such as that of the legal – or the religious
(Bourdieu 1971) – is precisely permanently to subject individual interests
to the collective logic of the whole field; in this instance, the production of
belief in the universality of the law.

The promotion of a negotiated social justice by a professional business
elite – the municipal courts of the progressive era or today's neighbourhood justice centres – is not a simple ideological disguise of their own
negotiation practices in the world of business, but also a recognition by
these dominant groups that even they feel obliged to submit to imperatives proper to the legal field.

The ideology of mediation, like the ideology of law, *is a component of the
legal field*. It is certainly not, as a superficial derivation of Marxism would

have one believe, a vague disguise, a veil that it would suffice to draw away in order to expose the 'true' reality of legal practices (Thompson 1975: 258). Learned representation of the game of law by professionals for their own use and purposes and that of their public, not only camouflages these practices but serves to redefine them. It is a 'prescriptive discourse' (Bourdieu 1981: 69). This legitimate and legitimizing representation that the law gives to and of itself (Stewart 1981) imposes rules of behaviour that apply to the professionals themselves.

The problem – and hence the interest – of a sociological approach to law and mediation consists of taking a serious view of this self-production of knowledge, without paraphrasing and thereby objectivizing the account the professionals give of their practices and the virtues extolled within them. Our objective is to extricate from the stakes of mediation the rules of the game of law: not only those imposed upon those in search of justice, but those such as internal protocols and assumptions, behaviours and values, which the professionals impose upon themselves in order to create a legal field that is also a field of belief and a closed market (Cain 1976).

The stake of mediation practices – or, more precisely, of the accompanying learned discourse that both denounces or valorizes them – is in fact to define and endlessly redefine the legitimate producers of 'commodities of social peace' (to paraphrase Weber) and the reserved market for their specific products. Whether it be to exclude or disqualify the *juge de paix notable* or, on the contrary, to assign new markets to a particular category of professionals (for instance, commercial arbitration to elite business lawyers, or social justice to social workers and psychologists), these very different strategies have, however, a common denominator in that they are inscribed in the logic of a professional field which has two contradictory logics permanently running through it. These logics, co-existing in tension, are:

- an expansionist logic which aims to spread the market of legal goods and services, by following social demand, or even arousing it by diversifying products and producers;
- a logic of hierarchical closure of the field, in order to valorize these goods and services, by strict control over the production of these producers (Abel and Lewis 1989) and of the competence specific to them: the handling of form and legal technique.

My methodological approach – a comparative history of selected Western legal systems in relation to the practices of mediation – was determined with the aim of unearthing the invariants that define the legal field as a symbolic field. Naturally, the intention is not to produce in a few pages a broad outline, a synthesis of the evolution of these systems, but simply to employ the varieties and similarities observed, past and present, drawn from here and there, in order to explore or refine the hypotheses presented above.

A play of indissociably political and professional positions

One of the fundamental postulates of the field theory (Bourdieu 1972) deployed in this analysis is, in effect, that homology/hierarchization and the division of labour within the field of law reproduces the position of these different groups of professionals in the market of disputes, and, by extension, in the political field or the social field. The territorial confrontations between professional groups (Abbott 1986a) on the question of practice, or of clientele, are indissociable from political positions and options in society as a whole. Hence the interest and the difficulty of the question of mediation which necessitates a combining of these two large systems of variables that are the legal structures and positions in the political field, into a diachronic approach, a system of endless redefinition.

Both of these explanatory systems are soon revealed to be inadequate, and far too simplistic. Let us consider first of all the classical opposition between common law countries and those following the romano-germanic tradition. Indeed, mediation practices do not carry the same weight in common law countries and countries of codified law. Differences in statutes and stakes reflect the relative strength of the theorists and practitioners in these different systems. But, this explanation by structures, though pertinent, is still insufficient if only because it does not take into account historical aspects proper to each of these legal systems, and, in particular, the diversity of the forms, sites, and statutes of mediation. Parallels drawn between England and the USA demonstrate that the status of such practices – in or beyond the margins of courts – is closely linked to the strategic options of an elite of law professionals in relation to the Welfare State and its corollary, social justice. For all that, negotiated justice cannot be reduced to a by-product of the Welfare State as some authors have tried to make out (Garth 1982; Ost 1983), if only because, as recent history has shown, such options are easily recalled into question.

Broadly speaking, what characterizes this double play of positions – political and professional – is that they are endlessly redefined as the result of a multitude of individual, competitive, contradictory, but also complementary initiatives. This continuous evolution is the cornerstone of the legal field's durability, its credibility, its appropriateness to a social order which, in order to perpetuate itself successfully, must submit to never-ending change. And so, a reading of mediation history must simultaneously take into account its political and its professional background. The logic behind this professional game is dual. It is essentially, as Abbott (1986a: 191) suggested, a territorial struggle which can be spatial (to extend a field of competence) or hierarchical (to reassert

last instance authority over a territory temporarily or partially dele-
gated to other categories of operators). The two movements are often
combined: the extension of a field of jurisdiction presupposes a revalorization of competences, an investment in the learned field, producer of
legitimate authority. But they are also contradictory. As Larson (1977)
demonstrated, the process of professionalization is fundamentally a
process of market closure: the control by a small elite of professionals of
the production of producers – recruitment, selection, the definition of
competences – in order more successfully to control the production
of legal goods, imperative to market valorization. Closure of the market
and an economics of rarity go hand in hand in limiting the numbers of
producers and their intervention techniques in the field of disputes. In
order to avoid possible takeover by potential competitors of a terrain
scorned by producers of 'high' law, it is partially and temporarily dele-
gated to operators who would recognize the last instance authority of
law professionals.

The history of mediation is inscribed into these contradictory stakes of
field closure and the extension of markets. For example, the disqualification of the *juge notable* mediation, and its re-invention by the reformers of
the progressive era as sub-technology, are two indissociable aspects of a
professionalization process which marks the emergence in France of
modern professions, controlling and limiting their market by the transformation of a know-how into a scholarly knowledge. Or, conversely, the
development of negotiated justice in the field of business, within the
framework of arbitration, where lawyers and merchants gain mutual
profit, is quite clearly oriented towards an opening of the market to
professional services. However, the same would be said for the field of
social justice, where mediation simultaneously covers the activism of
judges widening their range of intervention, and that of auxiliaries such
as educators, psychologists and social workers, who therein see a way
towards emancipation from the authority of law professionals.

This history of mediation is thus the difficult, although inevitable, cohabitation between two systems of justice responding to very different
professional and social interests. In a recent study, an interviewee,[1] an
haut magistrat, qualified (in private!) this contradictory structure as *justice
en dentelles* (crepe-covered justice) and *justice de l'abattage*.[2]

Dual justice where professionals and lay notabilities – the justice of the
rich and the justice of the poor – cohabit, represents the classical solution
to this problem and can be found in all legal systems in the early years of
industrialization. It is in a way the first form of negotiated justice. But we
could ask ourselves if the instrumentalization of judicial recourse, a sort
of colonization of legal space by practitioners of negotiation that Galanter
terms 'litigotiation', is not simply a modern form of this dual gear justice
system.

The combination of an economical, routine and informal treatment of everyday disputes, and of a more costly and sophisticated attitude to business affairs, selected by professionals to call into question and re-define norms, thus representing the modern, rational and professional form of this economy of rarity, is at the very basis of this symbolic field. The division of tasks and the hierarchicalization of competences is no longer inscribed in paraphernalia and rituals. These modern factories for processing disputes and producing law (the big business law firms and, to a degree, the legal services of private and public corporations, or the neighbourhood law firms and public law firms) allow the professional elite to combine and control cheap, mass-produced processing of dis-putes, while at the same time constituting 'rare' cases destined to receive 'first-class' legal services.

In all truth, such a short cut should not elude the variety of mediation practices that lie sandwiched between those two rather extreme examples of the division of labour in the field of law. If the avatars of negotiated justice respond to the structural logic of a symbolic field, they are also themselves the contingent and precarious results of struggles for influ-ence that are simultaneously played out on the fields of law and of state power.

The field of law plays a central role. It maintains and reinforces the field's autonomy by obliging political motivations to fit into the mould of professional and legal strategies. But also, the structures produced by and within these struggles for influence can be employed in their turn as support tactics in the game that aims to redefine them.

Even when the promoters of a professionalization strategy manage to have their domination ratified by inscribing it into a codification of the division of labour and hierarchicalization of competences, this institu-tionalized equilibrium remains a precarious compromise that those sub-ject to domination try to challenge by leaning on the transformation of social relations, in order to contest the orthodoxy of those dominant. The 'rhetorics of crisis' (Harrington 1985), the denunciation of the 'end of the law' (Ost 1983), is the central argument of these *aggiornamento* strategies that contest the authority and orthodoxy of those dominant, by pointing out the inadequacies of the law they produce – and therefore their own inadequacies as leaders – in the new order of social relations.

If these strategies are played out on the field of law, it is fundamentally the political terrain that determines the outcome. The promotion or de-nunciation of mediation cannot escape from this broad principle that governs political transformations in the legal field, corollaries of the trans-formations of legal norms in the social field. For example, the history of Germany indicates that by using state support, the legal professional elite were able to eliminate their main competitors – the lay justices of the peace – from the field of dispute processing, and have ratified a position of quasi-monopoly for those producers recruited solely on a basis of scholarly selection (Gessner and Plett 1989).

The difficulty and the interest of a political and legal history of mediation is that these practices are themselves in the image of the legal field: changing and variable, but conserving in essence their identity. Thus, mediation takes on various forms according to whether it is inscribed into the territory of justice for the poor, or that of justice for the rich; according to whether it addresses itself to the marketplace – making understood its independence from state norms – or to the state itself as a means of elaborating new norms. Lastly, it is the hinge upon which hangs the central episode of the history of the professions which is the process of professionalization: the closure of a market by excluding the laity has been succeeded today by a play of competition, within the framework of a state-controlled market, between different complementary figures of expertise. This does not mean to say that we are speaking of separate and distinct histories. The fundamental principle of negotiated justice always and in every domain remains the same: that of combined legal and social resources in the processing of disputes. Above all, as Auerbach and Harrington have shown, all these dimensions interpenetrate on all levels.

Rather than take these factors one after the other, according to the classification principles presented above – social mediation *vs* capitalist mediation, mediation without legal norms *vs* mediation to constant norms – it would seem more pertinent to draw from a series of key moments in the history of Western legal systems where these different figures are combined and transformed.

Legal form is produced by and within a ritual. Stability of norms and stability of positions in the field go hand in hand. This 'justice without law' within the field of law, that is negotiated justice, represents a necessary area of freedom which allows professional positions to fluctuate. It is the condition and support of the transformation of norms. This 'shadow justice' functions in close symbiosis with the official legal scene. Its dual structure allows for change in the continuity of things, a cardinal virtue of the legal field, because it reinforces belief in the law.

Negotiated justice seen as a stake in the professionalization of the legal field

During the nineteenth century, and until the First World War, the history of negotiated justice could be better described as the misadventures of notability justice: the replacement of lay judges, 'natural' mediators drawn from the social elite, by second-class professionals, in the field of justice for the poor. This is closely related to the arrival of the middle classes in the field of law and thus the replacement of quasi-hereditary methods of producing judges by the scholastic formation of legal competence and authority.

The determining factor in the diversity of local histories such as the permanence of dual justice in Great Britain, its irradication in Germany, or its 're-invention' in a professional context in the USA, appears to be the position of professional elites in the *political* field, because it is this position that dictates their strategies in relation to this internal problem of the field of law: the definition of legitimate practices and of legitimate producers of justice.

However, no matter what solution is retained, it only displaces the field of law's structural problem: that of managing the contradictions inherent in the necessary co-existence of a low and a high justice. 'Aristocratic' justice resolved this in its own fashion by reserving 'noble' legal services for the disputes of the wealthy, and delegating to lay notabilities the costs and the profits of maintaining order among the dominated classes. This central problem still confronts the would-be democratic judicial systems, because the recruitment of producers is a little more meritocratic.

The economics of a dual system of justice, and the disqualification of notability mediation law schools

The economics of a dual justice is that of a system which encourages the exchange of legal and social resources – to put things more precisely, which helps economize on recourse to 'noble' legal resources, where rarity has created value, by the use of social resources, personified by the *juge notable*, mediator *par excellence*, whose authority in the field of lower-class 'petty' disputes derives from an inherited social position. The coherence of such aristocratic means of producing justice – where mediation plays a large part – came from the fact that the professionals also derived most of their legal authority from their social background.

The disqualification of mediation is related to the transformation of the means-producing producers of justice: the replacement on the field of dispute of a quasi-hereditary line of social peace producers, who were endowed with an authority that transcended the law, by a new group, produced and formed by schools. Mediation is a difficult 'art' to teach in schools; on the other hand, the manipulation of legal technique and texts upon which the new professionals, stemming from the middle classes, are going to base their authority, can be taught with ease.

The weakening of aristocratic means of producing justice is linked to the underlying contradictions between high and low justice, and even more to the position of the legal elite within the dominant class. The emergence of law schools has resulted in, and been the means of, weakening the position of the *noblesse de robe*, in the political field.

In this respect, Germany and Great Britain represent two antinomical situations. In Germany, the schools over-produced jurists from middle-class backgrounds who, with the control of the state machinery, have managed to eliminate the *juge notable*, whose disqualification in the field of law is the corollary of this political disqualification since the setting into place of the Bismarckian state. In Great Britain, on the other hand, the peaceful co-existence of a small professional elite and a justice of notabilities, is probably linked to the tight control professionals maintain over their own reproduction, and their area of competence.

France presents an example of a potpourri situation, where one can retrace characteristics of British justice – the withdrawal of the professional elite into 'pure' law and legal technique, and a division of labour entrusting the more commonplace tasks of mediation to subprofessionals, if not to lay people, combined with scholarly means of reproduction. The ambiguous, if not downright difficult relations of the professional elite with the political powers, are probably a key element of this evolution. The French case has been discussed in detail elsewhere, most notably by Karpik (1988). The political ambitions of the *noblesse de robe*, and their relative failure, led Napoleon and successive regimes to restrict the judiciary to a strict and limited role as enforcers of the letter of the law. Pushed to the defensive by frequent beheadings, they colluded by emphasizing the 'purity' of law and legal technique. At the same time, a separate branch of the judiciary, the *Conseil d'Etat*, was developed to deal with administrative and policy matters. Only with the advent of the Third Republic did the advocates (but not the courts or the judges) regain some political power. As a result, practices of mediation have become the prerogative either of the political *haute justice* of the *Conseil d'Etat*, or of the disqualified professional categories such as the notary, the semi-professional judge who, in specialized jurisdictions, takes charge of clearly defined terrains of dispute – commercial, agricultural, industrial relations.

Even if the process is slower than in Germany – doubtless because of the relative isolation of jurists in the social field – the progression to scholarly recruitment favouring a rise of the middle classes in the field of law has brought about the progressive disappearance of the practice of mediation by notabilities, characteristic of aristocratic justice, in France as well.

The re-invention of mediation within a professional framework

The evolution of the American legal system is unlike any of the European instances outlined above. There is no question, as in Great Britain, of conserving a dual justice where delegation of authority to lay notabilities is the corollary of a policy of scarcity of producers and of selectivity of disputes. There is no question either, as in Germany and to a lesser degree in France, of eliminating the lay judges and their practices of mediation to the benefit of legal technique and its duly ratified producers. The history of American mediation at the turn of the century is that of skilful re-invention of the practice of mediation within the frameworks of a new form of social justice, destined to take the place of the paternalistic mediation of the *juge notable*.

The conciliation advocated by the progressive era reformists was a rationalized, formalized, codified practice, set entirely within the scope – albeit in a subordinate position – of the professionalization projects of the legal field (cf. Harrington 1985). Far from being a semi-tolerated relic of former times, mediation is the prefiguration of a modern attempt at a mass-produced processing of disputes through a rational division of tasks. On this account, it represents an innovation of comparable importance to that of the great law firms which place concentrated, specialized legal services in the service of capital. Furthermore, the two social inventions are related.

The negotiated, but rationalized, social justice which occurs in the municipal courts, is a sort of prototype that may, in the future, serve as a model for the European juvenile or family courts (Platt 1969). It is completely inscribed into the professionalization process, since it simultaneously makes war against lay justices of the peace, who are discounted and disqualified as archaic, irrational and partisan. The modernity of negotiated justice stems also from the fact that it appears at one and the same time on two terrains related by a concentration of capital and of people, by production and mass consumption: the terrain of the internal disputes of a capitalist class, and the terrain of the problems of the workforce, now taken in hand beyond the boundaries of workplaces.

The final characteristics of this modernity stem from the connection between the mediation of the internal disputes of the upper classes, and the development of a subordinate and controlled mediation that processes working-class disputes. This is in fact one of the keys to the evolution of mediation in its modern form: its simultaneous existence on two terrains, and the determining role played by the field of business in the redefining of these practices of mediation.

A new professional elite: business lawyers

Why did the professionalization process that drove Germany and France to eliminate notability mediation result, in the USA, in its re-invention? This is the central question. The answer seems obvious. The alliance system that dominates the legal field is not the same; and the dominant tendencies in the field of professional practices are radically different from those prevailing at that time in Europe. Even in the nineteenth century, the elite of the bar in the USA drew support neither from the state, nor from the proper-tied classes, but from a business clientele with which it was more or less totally assimilated. The development of industrial capitalism transformed the activities and the production method of this elite of urban practitioners. As large law firms were established, negotiation and the mediation of business affairs became more widespread and valorized than pleading in a court room, which was abandoned to young newcomers. 'By mid-century, lawyers for the major economic interest . . . were beginning to replace the brilliant court-room pleaders at the top of the emergent professional hierarchies' (Larson 1977: 126).

Indeed, this new professional elite, like its European counterpart, considered it important to invest in the field of learned law by encouraging the creation and the development of the first law schools (Auerbach 1976: 76). But this promotion of learned law could not be done to the detriment of the business practitioners because they dominated the professions and controlled the schools. The science of law and American legal doctrine could not be, as in Germany, pure and exclusive legal theory, a negation of social determinants of law and a disqualification of the mediation practices that combine legal and social resources in the processing of disputes.

Business arbitration as a happy marriage of interests between elite lawyers and businesspeople

The development of commercial arbitration is a happy marriage of convenience between lawyers who thereby gained access to a profitable market, and a business community that wished simultaneously to escape state control and possibly embarrassing publicity while retaining the benefits of legitimate legal sanction on its compromises (Auerbach 1983: 105).

Arbitration could certainly not be termed an informal justice, or a justice without law. But recent research has shown that when arbiters are nominated by parties, they are perceived more as mediators concerned by the impact and the reception of their sentencing, than as judges solely preoccupied with applying the law of the books (Dezalay 1986b). Above all, this form of dispute processing gives the parties and their representatives more control over the course of operations. At any time, proceedings can be interrupted in favour of a compromise.

As much through the choice of the arbiter as through its operational methods, arbitration achieves that combination of social and legal resources that we define as a practice of mediation. Moreover, it foreshadows two developments characteristic of the contemporary legal landscape: that of the judge as a mediator (Galanter 1985) and that of 'litigotiation' (ibid.: 1) defined as the strategic deployment of procedural resources by the parties, the eruption of negotiation on the legal scene. This early private justice heralded the arrival of a more general movement of privatization of state legal institutions in the service of dominant social interests in the USA.

The initial success of mediation in the field of business was a determining factor for its future as a legitimate professional practice. Its prestige is in relation to that of its producers. Far from being the sorry privilege of a despised category of sub-professionals, as in Europe at that time, to be a mediator was the attribute of the professional.

The concentration and the division of labour in the law firms permitted this new elite of professionals to play simultaneously on the two scenes: that of learned law, by recruiting the elite of the law schools (Kennedy 1985: 193) and by a continuing investment in the terrain of jurisprudence and doctrine in order to affirm their pure legal authority; and that of mediation, which presupposes the existence and maintenance of the notability's social authority, of a network of political influences and relationships (see also Harrington 1985).

Social justice: delegation of the 'civilizing function'

The social concerns of the professional elite in the USA are perfectly inscribed into a professional logic that obliges them to assume a paternalist and sanctimonious role in relation to the abuses of capitalism – which marries well with their 'WASP' protestant ethic. The object of this 'civilizing function' (Larson 1977: 59) was not only to improve the profession's public image, it also went towards creating the political and moral authority of these notabilities-of-law on which they based their professional practice of mediation (Harrington 1985: 22).

University lawyers, anxious to set themselves apart from their rather cumbersome and bossy 'big brothers', the business lawyers (Auerbach 1976: 75) – and for this reason prompted to claim the title of 'keepers of the professional conscience' (Larson 1977: 172) – played a determining part in the development of these new social jurisdictions. In this case – but it often happens – their political ideals and their reformist strategies were in comfortable agreement with the role that the division of labour in the field of law assigned to them.

The history of the municipal courts has already been written (Harrington 1985), and we will not come back on it except to underline that mediation in this new terrain was inscribed in its turn into a professionalization strategy that had three objectives in mind: to discipline the producers of justice, control their production, and promote a rational and economical management of legal and judicial commodities.

The disqualification of the justices of the peace and the legal commodities they produced, goes hand in hand with control established by the new bars over the recruitment of the presiding judges of the new municipal courts (Harrington 1985: 52). As Auerbach (1983: 99) writes: '. . . indeed the elimination of lawyers from the unsavory breeding ground of the municipal petty foggers' Court was a blessing that would enhance professional prestige' (cf. Larson 1977: 139; Harrington 1985: 45).

This movement, which replaced lay notabilities with professionals, reflects what we have already observed in Europe. What is novel and different in the American experience is the setting up of a new economy of the judiciary, a new economy of rarity, that replaces dual justice: the presiding judge, professional of law *par excellence*, supervises auxiliaries of lesser legal competence who strive for conciliation and prevention with a minimum amount of procedures and formalities, but, on the other hand, by calling upon social resources (Platt 1969: 42; Galanter 1974: 128; Harrington 1985: 33): psychological techniques of investigation, support groups, relay associations. Through the hierarchicalized division of tasks, a new means of production that refers explicitly to the Taylorian theories (Harrington 1985: 48), provides a less costly legal service that is better adapted to working-class resources: 'It is perfectly feasible to administer a much higher grade of justice in petty causes, than that dispensed by the Justice of the Peace, without recourse to the cumbrous and expensive machinery of our superior courts' (American Bar Association 1909, quoted in Harrington 1985: 47).

On the condition that these new techniques are put into operation within the framework of the courts and, above all, under the tight control of 'true' professionals, such rationalizations of the market of legal forms can only reinforce their monopoly by reserving this sophisticated and costly resource for the most deserving affairs. Conciliation and mediation should not be considered as competitive techniques in regard to law, but as Auerbach (1983: 99) writes, 'a new screening device to select those who will leave or continue through the Courts'. The task of these new gatekeepers was to eliminate cases undeserving of the 'full legal show', 'by early identification and diversion to other community resources of those offenders in need of treatment, for whom full criminal disposition does not appear required' (Harrington 1985: 27).

This system was too much the darling child of its professional elite promoters for it not to be endowed with every virtue, in particular those of efficiency and legitimacy. 'A litigious proceeding is destructive; it is calculated to embitter the litigants. A conciliation proceeding gives the court its only chance to repair, reunite and construct' (Smith 1919, quoted in Harrington 1985: 56). Are these the objective qualities of mediation, or a discourse of self-fulfilling prophecy which assigns to mediation its tasks and therefore its *modus operandi*? Whatever the reality, it is of little importance; the essential fact is that through this new economy of the judiciary, professional markets are being divided in a manner that is no longer horizontal – the classical division between notability justice for the poor and professional justice for the propertied – but vertical (Abbott 1986a) –

the setting up of a 'low justice' by sub-professionals, guaranteed and controlled by 'true' professionals.

The future of this new allocation of tasks will be durable. Harrington underlines aptly that it is the same logic that inspires the professional elite's slogan of the 1980s: 'the forum should fit the fuss' (Auerbach 1983: 124–5). Scandalous words, because they openly express one of the structural – and therefore hidden – constraints of the field of law.

This new division of labour is as yet precarious, recalled as it is into question by the very logic of the professional system: the judge's auxiliaries strive towards autotomizing their practices of prevention or therapy by insisting upon – with the very arguments of the 'fathers' of these new social jurisdictions – the 'perverse' effects of a 'sporting theory of justice':

> As their involvement with divorce cases through conciliation, counselling and court-ordered custody evaluations increased, social workers began to raise objections about the appropriateness of legal decision makers and the use of legal decisions altogether, representing a rejection of the lawyer/social worker partnership that they had initially espoused.
>
> (Fineman 1987: 151)

But, in their camp, the masses of minor professionals reacted to the threat of this new competition, all the more so in that their numbers have increased rapidly with the multiplication of small law schools (Abbott 1986a). Their counter-offensive was to invent new strategies to make up for their clientele's lack of resources, either by calling upon financial help from the state within the framework of systems such as legal aid, or by reducing the costs of reprocessing 'ordinary' disputes to a minimum; however, with the preservation of the value of 'noble' legal services in mind, in the legal clinics that allow them to combine routine and informal treatment of everyday affairs and 'noble' or 'ennobling' jurisprudential strategies for the more rare and exemplary affairs.

Negotiated justice seen as a renegotiation of the division of labour on the market of social peace

The stakes were not quite the same after the Second World War. It was no longer a matter of adapting methods of hereditary reproduction corresponding to an aristocratic justice to a new political order, but of managing the redistribution of tasks and of profits among the different operators intervening on the market of disputes. However, the basic problem remained the same: the execution of 'low' justice tasks by agents who are in a subordinate position in relation to the legal field elite. Although they have a legitimate authority conferred on them by acquired scholarly competences, their occupational gain in status is meagre. If, indeed, 'the forum should fit the fuss', it is because a revalorization of 'vulgar' legal services can only result in an inflation of legal commodities and therefore devalue their selling price. Low justice must remain a second-class justice for internal occupational reasons, under pain of bringing about a devalorization of those legal commodities produced by the elite, for the elite, commodities whose rarity creates their value.

The central pivot of this modern history also remains unchanged: that of the competitive struggle between different groups of operators to enlarge the share of the market allotted to each, but to keep the occupation's hierarchical place in the scheme of things. High status corresponds to high influence in the processes of legitimate norm redefinition, the ultimate of hierarchicalization in the fields of law.

In this new context, negotiated justice is no longer a behind-the-scenes justice, a 'shadow justice' that economizes on the ritualized forms that go hand in hand with respect for established norms; it is now venturing into the reserved terrain of legitimate norm redefinition, either to have advances in social law ratified, or to have new capitalist forms and institutions declared official. But, on this new playing field, the game is slightly modified according to whether the question is of social justice or of the justice of capital.

Whereas operators of paternalist mediation – the legal counterpart of the Welfare State – do not fundamentally challenge norms or the division of labour, operators of capitalist mediation wish to call the structure of the professional field into question, redefine it to their own advantage and to that of their clients. The emergence and recognition of a new law that conforms to a new post-Fordian economy, necessarily involves the setting into place of new positions and new internal rules within the field of law. This struggle is what links the internal explanation in terms of status-seeking with the external or structural and historical explanation. To re-employ a metaphor often used by labour economists, one passes from a 'negotiation within norms' (where the competing parties play the game according to the established rules in order to better their position) to a 'negotiation over norms' (where the rules even of war are called into question).

Negotiated justice in the USA is no longer content to prosper in the wings of adjudication. Its operators now demand that it be recognized as a legitimate legal practice, so that they may be considered fully fledged actors in the law game and thus add their weight to the redefinition of norms and to the political orientations within the field of law. Clearly, in the face of this new objective, neither the players nor the attending forces are quite the same.

Paternalist mediation on the terrain of social justice

Most commentators agree that the development of negotiated justice on the terrain of social justice is related to that of the Welfare State (Garth

1982). But European scholars add further that they foresee the 'death of the law' (Rippert 1949), or at least, the decline of the legal professional, condemned to be no more than one figure of expertise among others. Whereas in the USA there is strong reaction against the 'back wash' of 'common', 'petty' disputes, that are 'clogging' the 'noble' courts, the English, the French, and especially the Scandinavians are worried about the removal of cases from judicial jurisdiction to administrative forums, thus escaping the control of authentic and legitimate jurists.

The strength of these antithetic positions stems surely from the fact that they are part of a constant re-equilibrating process that helps to adjust the position of each professional category concerned in the field of dispute/resolution, either as a reminder of the advantages of a tightly framed delegation of minor disputes ('the forum should fit the fuss') or to forestall any vague desires for autonomy on the part of subordinates, by reminding legal professionals of the risks of losing control over the processing of such disputes, however minor they are.

These alarmist remarks are tactical arguments whose function is to manage a hierarchical sharing out of a naturally unstable market: under the cloak of mediation, each of the protagonists in the increasingly collective processing of disputes strives to extend its own autonomy at the expense of its fellow operators. By becoming mediators, the judges of lesser jurisdictions widen their range of means of intervention and adopt the colours of an effective and equitable interventionism. This is also a play for more autonomy in relation to a hierarchy reserving for itself the monopoly of legitimate norm interpretation. For their part, the judges' auxiliaries see in mediation the possibility of shaking off a burdensome tutelage that confined them to a minor role, by glorifying the virtues, but also the demands, of a therapeutic type interventionism.

These competitive interventionisms set limits for each other. Their boundaries were also tightly confined by the more prestigious professional categories – high judges, elite of the bar, law teachers – to the less valorized fields of legal practice. Negotiated justice – for instance, that of the juvenile courts – might be a 'justice without law', but it was also a practice within the norms, reinforcing the division of labour in the processing of disputes, and for all that its boundaries were not precisely defined, it was none the less stable. The bulk of the displacements that intervened in this field of negotiated justice were not the result of activity by the practitioners engaged in it, but of the political strategies of the professional elite. Rhetorical figures of 'dispossessed justice' or, on the contrary, 'submerged justice', should not hide the fact that this is a 'prescriptive discourse', meaning that its aim was to transform the reality it pretended to describe. If there were transformations of the position of courts and of 'high justice' professionals in the field of 'petty' disputing, such displacements were as much actively looked for on the one side as they were passively submitted to on the other.

Here again, it was the position of the professional elite in the political field that determined its strategies in relation to the Welfare State and thus towards negotiated social justice.

That practices of negotiated social justice have developed in Europe outside of the courts is due, in large part, to the reluctance of the professional elite to deal with common disputes, reservations that conform to the positions of this elite in the political field and which the public authorities ratified by creating new forums and methods of dealing with these problems, outside of and independent of the courts. On the other hand, the fact that these practices of paternalist mediation developed more or less in the sphere of influence of the courts in the USA results from the influence of the organized bar on the constitution of the New Deal in the inter-war period.

A comparative history of the two systems has the additional advantage of demonstrating that such political positions and options, although they determine the status as well as the locus of paternalist mediation practices, are never definitive. The advocacy of alternative dispute resolution can thus be employed as an argument, either towards a strategy of dispossession by the legal elite (i.e. further delegation) as in the USA, or of 'repossession' (i.e. reaffirmation of authority over previously abandoned territories) as in Great Britain.

The history of mediation in the field of social justice is written elsewhere. The field loses autonomy, that is what is demonstrated by the contrast between the American and the British examples cited above. At best, one can find there traces of the strategies of the professional elite in the field of power. This form of negotiated justice thus remains quietly in the place assigned to it by those dominating the field: that of a subordinate justice that reinforces established order because it is powerless to challenge a division of labour in the field of law that is the corollary of the place of law and lawyers in society.

Capitalist mediation in the field of business justice: a legalized negotiation challenging established norms

In contrast to what happens in the field of social justice, where mediation practices do not or are not allowed to challenge fundamentally the system of norms and the division of tasks in which they are inscribed, in the field of business justice it is precisely the norm system – and even broadly the system that reproduces these norms – that the practices of legalized negotiation aim to call into question. To paraphrase Galanter (1981), it is no longer a question of mediation in the shadow of the law, but of the law and the courts in the shadow of negotiation.

The essential stake of these boundary upheavals – internal as much as external – of the legal field is that, if they do not implicate legal autonomy, they imply a redefinition of relationships between the legal and the politico-economic sphere. Thus further misadventure of the figure of mediation takes us back in a way to our starting point: the *juge notable* as an agent of the inscription and setting into place of the political into legal forms and rituals.

Mediation, as has been shown, is no longer the prerogative of the notable but of the expert – or at least of a network of experts whose interventions complement, complete and combine with one another in the processing of 'mega-disputes' (Galanter 1983). But these experts, do they not represent the modern face of notability, its conversion into a framework for the scholarly reproduction of social elites? Control over the social network of elite business clients, which also produces the lawyer, and whose expectations the lawyer embodies, no longer guarantees a position within the elite – with the political power and social authority that position implies. Proof must be shown, as Middler (1986) notes, of that learned competence by and through which this network of influences is constructed.

The blossoming of such practices of mediation in the field of business indicates a reopening of the legal into the economic and the political, which is probably related to the need to define a new system of norms – and hence a new system of professions – adequate for dealing with economic upheaval, the crisis of the Welfare State and, to take things even further, with the displacement of what Keynes called 'conventions', i.e. social and legal institutions at the basis of the Fordian model of mass production and consumption (Piore and Sabel 1984; Boyer 1986; Sallais and Thevenot 1986).

The main transformations involve first the spreading of the American professional model of management consultancy (Dezalay 1989c). The European professional scene is marked by the appearance of large and highly specialized legal – but also audit or consulting – firms, a feature previously unheard of. The result is that one can begin to observe a *de facto* stratification not dissimilar to that in the USA (Heinz and Laumann 1982), and that these highly competent, well-connected and extremely powerful concentrations of practitioners play an increasing role in the redefinition of norms (McBarnet 1984).

The phenomenon is now multi-professional. The law and jurists can no longer pretend to monopolize the codification of social and economic relations (Eymard-Duvernay and Thevenot 1983). Other technologies and other experts also claim this function. This is particularly so in Europe where the absence of elite law professionals experienced in dealing with business disputes or management consultancy gave a chance to other categories of professionals to gain a strong foothold in this profitable market. One example is French elite audit firms, who claim the role of *magistrature du chiffre* (economic and financial bench) (ATH 1985). The linkage between socio-economic change and legal change, that professionals of law strove to master by a dual investment on the legislative and the jurisprudential level, has today been made more complex by the introduction of new actors. It is through these territorial struggles between different complementary and competitive categories of professionals that new rules and new institutions emerge to fit the new needs of post-Fordian capitalism (whatever they will be!). Negotiated justice tends thus to become the support and the forum of this permanent renegotiation of the division of tasks between jurists and other experts in the market of capitalist disputes, and from there, in the political field (Dezalay 1989b).

Clearly, the development of such hypotheses would extend far beyond the limits of a chapter such as this. The following section summarizes the argument as it derives from my own research (Dezalay 1989c) and other sources (Galanter 1983; Winter 1985; Lascoumes 1987).

'Litigotiation' – or the colonization of the judicial scene by professional negotiation

Analysing the recent promotion of mediation among American judges, Galanter (1984–85) notes that this new figure of negotiated justice is profoundly different from the paternalist conciliation extolled by the progressive era reformers. Whatever the underlying causes, he himself discerns a passage from a dyadic negotiation to a triadic mediation, in which the phenomenon of demand for an 'honest broker' has broken down barriers between negotiation and adjudication, and upset the division of labour between professionals of law.

The court case, a structured, homogeneous entity, playing a central and pre-eminent role in the processing of disputes, has been replaced by a series of procedural episodes that rarely conclude with a judgment, and that are so many elements of a disputing strategy, happening simultaneously on a multiplicity of registers. Instrumentalization of the legal procedure is a tactical argument in a negotiation strategy. Galanter proposes the term 'litigotiation' to describe this eruption of negotiation within litigation.

The redefinition of the role of the judge as a mediator – Ost (1983) used the word *juge-entraineur* (trainer), but perhaps he ought to have said *entraine* (somebody dragged along by his team!) – is an intrinsic component of this new division of labour: the judge is cited at the disposition of professional negotiation. In parallel with this transformation of the judge's function, the practice of the lawyer is also modified. Whereas for years, the elite of the bar abandoned the precincts of jurisdiction for the advantages of negotiation (Johnstone and Hopson 1967: 83, 103), today, it has been suggested, the personage of litigator (cf. *New York Times*, 1 June

1986) has been revalorized. Or perhaps one should say litigotiator to express in more precise terms the colonization of the judicial scene by practitioners of negotiation who are wending their way back to the courts by importing their own *habitus* and *modus operandi*.

But to understand the scale and moreover the implications of such a phenomenon, we need to examine the context that produced it: business disputes and the transformation of professional practices in this field. In the first place, this seems to be the terrain where it is all happening (or at least where it all started: Galanter 1983). It is not the small, independent practitioner who treats affairs like divorce in a routine and as informal a manner as possible (Sarat and Felstiner 1986), who is going to rediscover the delights of procedure, but the big law firm business lawyer, who is unique in the sense that he alone (there are few women) can set up highly sophisticated, but very costly legal strategies (Galanter 1983, 1985). In order to launch such strategies, the support of concentrated, specialized professional services is imperative and, in addition to this, the financial backing of a clientele capable of gaining from such costly investment. It is also in this domain, it would seem, that recourse to the judge mediator, in accordance with arbitration procedures, or under derived forms like 'rent a judge', 'mini-trial', etc., has developed the most rapidly (Dezalay 1991). This conjunction is more than pure coincidence in the sense that it corresponds to factors in this field of dispute that are both structural and conjunctural.

Business justice as the domain par excellence of negotiated justice

At the turn of the century, Weber had already observed the capacity of the industrial and commercial world to obtain privileged treatment from the field of law and of justice: a processing of their disputes by specialized experts, familiar with their specific needs and more concerned by the effects of their interventions than with strict respect for legal form or judicial ritual (Weber 1978: 882). But the development of state interventionism in the economic sphere and the increasing interpenetration between big economic interests and public administrative agencies – which does not boil down to a mere 'capture', except in that the 'captor' is transformed by the effects of his 'capture' and becomes in his turn more conscious of global, political factors (Bourdieu and St Martin 1978) that thus scramble the frontiers between the private and the public – has but extended this phenomenon (Scholz 1984; Shapiro 1985; Winter 1985; Lascoumes 1986). 'Cooperation, negotiation, bargaining, bartering are not only the rules in regulating law enforcement, but . . . they are the preferred way of dealing with regulatory problems' (Winter 1985: 237).

However, it is not enough to demonstrate the ancientness of negotiated justice in the field of mercantile law in order to understand a phenomenon such as litigotiation. If it is an instrumentalization of the judicial in

the service of negotiation, it is also a juridicalization of business negotiation. The forum imposes, to a certain extent, its own rules (Boltanski 1984;
Dezalay 1985b).

To account for these transformations, as Lascoumes notes, inspired by
Foucault, one must not forget that

> . . . the field of governmental instruments was diversified early on
> and disposes of a complete register of actions where various compo-
> nents are individually mobilized according to the needs of the histor-
> ical period in question and the socio-political context.

> (Lascoumes 1987: 151)

Today's calling into question of the nation state as much as of the Fordian
model of production and mass consumption, calls for a redefinition of
norms through and by negotiation, but with an inevitable officialization
by the courts of the results of such negotiations. As Powell (1987) argued,
the 'homologation' of new business devices by State Supreme Courts is
essential to the generalization of new rules, in this case concerning a
financial restructuring scheme known as 'the poison pill'.[3] This works
towards a recentring on the judge and the judicial, privileged places for
decreeing legitimate norms (Jeantin 1985). At least this is the case for the
important economic groups that possess both the means for and the
possibility of gain from the costly investment these jurisprudential strategies represent (Winter 1985: 244).

From an extra normative negotiation to a negotiation about rules

As Lascoumes (1987: 150) notes, one reaches a continuum where negotiation no longer stops at the legislative lobbying phase but becomes a
continuing process which plays on all levels of dispute processing, in
tight interaction with the defining of rules. Codified law becomes a 'bargaining chip' during negotiations and, reciprocally, disputes serve to feed
strategies aimed towards the redefinition of norms (Jeammaud and Lyon-
Caen 1982; Winter 1985).

As McBarnet (1984) and Dezalay (1989d) suggest, this continuum can
only be understood by taking into account this community of practitioners, reputed to be only applying legal rules, when in fact they also
contribute towards their redefinition, their reinterpretation, if not their
deformation ('avoidance by compliance with the letter of the law':
McBarnet 1987). It is in this decentralized and professionalized regulation, increasingly characteristic of modern economies, that new rules
emerge and legal change is linked to social change. 'Capture' theories are
inadequate here because the dispersion of central public authority can be
observed as well as the taking into account of political and global constraints by 'private' agents.

Litigotiation, more than the extension of the social judge's paternalistic interventionism, can therefore be seen as a spreading into the legal field of practices more characteristic of economic regulation (but less and less limited to this field). But these practices are themselves permanently redefined by intra-professional competitive struggles that find support from a specific historical environment: the economic crisis engendered by the 1973 oil price rise which ended 'the 30 glorious years' and encouraged the necessary (but painful!) reinvention of new economic conventions and institutions.

The judicialization of negotiation as a professional territorial strategy

A historical context of this sort exacerbates competition between the various professional categories for the market of codifying social relations. Sometimes this results from the appearance of new territories of intervention as yet not quite staked out and sanctioned in the name of a particular knowledge, and thus propitious to unfair competition, for example, the curing of failing firms (Dezalay 1989d). Or, more generally, because the margins between different knowledges and different operators are never rigorously defined, there is always room on the borderlines for a degree of uncertainty that freelance agents on either side will take advantage of and where many transformations of the system of norms and practices can be played out.

While analysing the field of industrial and financial restructuration, we became aware of a revalorization of legal rationality, which is rather paradoxical when you take into account the introduction of the new tools and new knowledges – auditing, management, commercial or financing engineering – that are supposed to replace the monopoly of legal and accounting techniques. In fact, competition with new professionals striving to impose new know-how, drives professionals of law to reinvest in that which creates the specificity of their professional field: the manipulation of legal technique, the public and ritualized processing of disputes in the field of law. By reintegrating into the courts, professionals of law remind potential competitors that their services are indispensable and that their authority is not to be questioned when disputing is transported into the terrain of rule interpretation.

Big disputing, characteristic of 'mega-law' (Galanter 1983), can also be interpreted as the argument of a territorial strategy (Abbott 1986a) employed by jurists to maintain their pre-eminent position in the field of dispute resolution. However great the concessions made to other professional categories, depending on the political and professional balance of forces, the hierarchical authority of elite law professionals, their monopoly of the redefinition of the law of the Law – and of the judge of judges – can always be reaffirmed. Because of their control over the courts, these elite law professionals can stand above other professionals. They, alone, decide what transcendental norm will be imposed upon social or technical particular norms; with, as a corollary, who will be deemed fit to decide upon the legitimacy of the various operators and mediators competing on the market of dispute processing. Investment in court procedures and pure law serves as a strong deterrent against potential competitors.

It would be erroneous, anyway, to oppose the development of mega-law with that of negotiated justice. The concentration and specialization of professionals in large units of legal goods and services production, permits them to combine informal negotiation and jurisdictional strategies within this new figure of litigotiation, by carrying them simultaneously, and by selection – through criteria that are as professional as they are economic or political – of those particular disputes that most merit the investment of partial or total judicial recourse.

This new form of legal practice first saw the light of day in the field of business, but today it is spreading to all fields of dispute, where the presence of 'repeat players' (Galanter 1974) makes a Taylorian division of labour worthwhile with, as a corollary, a stratification in the field of dispute processing between routine affairs deserving of negotiation, and affairs of principle justifying heavy legal investment. Legal clinics tend to adopt the same strategy, using mediators to treat routine, mundane disputes and concentrating any skilled resources, such as the few sophisticated young lawyers that they employ, to develop the few cases they consider to be socially, politically or legally 'interesting' (Katz 1978).

Litigotiation as a valorization of legal services strategy: a new figure of dual justice and of an economy of rarity

The success of this new division of labour and sharing out of the market, probably stems from the fact that it is a modern solution to the legal field's structural problem: an artificially induced production of rarity that conditions the value of symbolic goods such as law. In the primitive form of dual justice described by Weber, such rarity was achieved by the statutory limitation of professionals deemed fit to produce pure law, to embody the sacred authority of the law. Today, it is the wealth of investment, enormous in comparison to the criteria of artisanal justice production – but perhaps only proportional to the importance of the direct or indirect stakes of law in a modern economy – that guarantees an auto-limitation of the production and the consumption of 'noble' legal services, consubstantial with their value and their social authority. Marketplace rules have replaced the statutory and internal rules controlling the ability of producers to limit their total output. But the underlying logic remains the same: that of an economy of rarity, structural principle of a field of beliefs.

Acknowledgement

This paper is an expansion of a talk entitled 'Negotiated justice as a renegotiation of the division of tasks within the field of law: The French example', presented to the DRPP Conference on *Alternative Dispute Resolution in Europe*, Washington, D.C., 15 June 1987, and published in C. Meschievitz and K. Plett (eds), *Beyond Disputing: Exploring Legal Cultures in Five European Countries*. Baden-Baden: Nomos, 1989.

Notes

1 I am referring here to a series of interviews on the politics of mediation, conducted in the spring of 1987 with A. Girardet, among French 'Hauts magistrats'. See 'La conciliation, instance de reglement des litiges, enjeu professionnel et institutionnel. Rapport de recherches au Ministere de la Justice'. E. Le Roy, Y. Dezalay, A. Garapon and A. Girardet, Roneo Laboratoire d'Anthropologie juridique de Paris 1.
2 *Maison d'abattage* (slaughterhouse) is a production-line brothel mainly used by lines of poor immigrants.
3 The 'poison pill' was invented by New York lawyer Marty Lipton to protect a company from a hostile tender offer by issuing different kinds of preferential share to raise the cost to the would-be buyer (Wilson 1984).

PART 3

Towards prefigurative legal practices

8 Miners and lawyers: law practice and class conflict in Appalachia, 1872–1920

Frank Munger

Introduction

Sid Hatfield, small-town West Virginia sheriff in John Sayles's movie *Matewan*, gunning down Baldwin-Felts mine guards in May 1920, has become part of our contemporary folklore of resistance to powerful corporations. At the core of the image is an industrializing society deeply divided by class in which access to law and justice was not equal. After the final scene, a brief epilogue informs the audience of the inevitable consequences of law and order in mining towns. At the end of this true story, the winning law and winning lawyers were on the side of the corporations which owned the coal companies. The Baldwin-Felts guards shot down by Hatfield were legally entitled to evict striking miners from company-owned housing. The legislature enacted a law that allowed Hatfield to be tried by jurors from another county who were less sympathetic to him. Company lawyers in Charleston obtained court decisions upholding the companies' anti-union contracts with their employees and granting a sweeping anti-organizing injunction under the federal anti-trust laws. A little over a year later, while waiting for his second trial, Sid Hatfield was shot to death on the courthouse steps in neighbouring McDowell County by a Baldwin-Felts undercover agent who was immediately released on bond posted by prominent citizens of the community (Lunt 1979; Savage 1990).

This chapter describes the law practices of Appalachian lawyers after 1870 as industrialization transformed a southern West Virginia community into the landscape of 'Matewan'. A small, relatively homogeneous group of circuit-riding lawyers serving a slow-paced and isolated mountain community adapted to the rapidly changing conditions created by industrialization and the intrusion of a national market. The lawyers who continued their practices or who were drawn to the area had new clients to serve: an entrepreneurial class, a growing number of business organizations and a rural proletariat. The creation of a modern class structure brought bitter opposition and violent class conflict. Lawyers adapted their practices somehow to a community in which sharp differences of capacity and interest were emerging between groups of potential clients. How this occurred between 1870 and 1920 in Fayette County, West Virginia will be explored by describing which lawyers took on the new types of clients and legal issues and how the organization of law practice changed.[1]

Far from atypical, Fayette County was representative of much of late nineteenth-century America outside its metropolitan centres. In 1870, more than 80 per cent of the population lived in communities with fewer than 2500 inhabitants.[2] Americans lived in 'island communities' (Wiebe 1967) that were rapidly being integrated into a national economy and transformed by the rise of large organizations and institutions that possessed the power to alter American social structure, politics and culture (Israel 1972; Hays 1973). The experience of change that occurred in such communities, in which most Americans lived, has shaped the society out of which our contemporary culture has grown, leaving a residue of distrust of both big government and big business. 'Matewan' resonates with modern experience of the power of corporations and the precariousness of individual rights in the face of organizational and institutional power. Throughout late twentieth-century society, as well as in the seemingly remote events of Appalachian labour history, the opposing rights of individuals and corporations are represented by different defenders with unequal resources at their command.[3] If, in de Tocqueville's judgement, lawyers before the Civil War were an aristocracy helping to integrate a young pre-industrial democracy – embodying belief in practical self-governance, fair contention among private interests, and a respect for rights – in post-industrial America, lawyers have been increasingly identified not with preservation of community but with partisanship and loyalty to particular clients (Wilson 1910; Marbury 1912; Auerbach 1976).

Prior research has suggested that the changes in American society in the late nineteenth century, at least as they occurred in the largest cities, created a highly stratified legal profession that matched elite lawyers with clients that were leading businesses or institutions. Business corporations were primary actors in the transformation of the economy and in the resulting changes in the political and social life of the nation. Corporations employed the services of lawyers to give legal form to their power and to their transactions. Legal work created by corporations was conducted less and less in courtrooms. In a courtroom, a single lawyer sufficed in most cases to present a client's cause. Instead, legal work created by new methods of business management and new ways of transacting business was conducted in offices and could occupy many lawyers simultaneously. The profession as a whole felt the shift to office work as the increase in volume and routinization of business transactions emphasized drafting, negotiation and settlement of conflicts (Hurst 1950).[4] As business corporations grew in number and size, the first large law firms were formed in commercial centres like New York, Chicago and Philadelphia (Hobson 1986). Corporate law firms grew in size as corporations grew in power, and business lawyers assumed a pre-eminence over other lawyers, forming the first professional associations and articulating their views of the professional mission.[5]

The same economic transformation that created law firms and a corporate bar drew waves of immigrants to America, many of whom viewed entering the legal profession as a route out of the working class and into the middle class. Part of the mission of the emerging national leadership of the profession after 1880 was to interpret and react to the stratification (and proliferation) of lawyers which industrialization helped to create and which appeared to threaten both the status and the economic security of lawyers.[6] One such reaction by the elite was to define ethical professional behaviour and to criticize the unprofessional practices of the lower orders of the profession who represented primarily lower orders of clients (Auerbach 1976). The practitioners most criticized by the urban and national elite were members of the urban bar who routinely seemed to represent legal interests of the newly emerging working classes in personal injury, petty criminal and family cases (ibid.: 45). The economic marginality of the clients, and the volume of cases required to make this kind of practice viable, seem to have required both aggressive client-seeking and risk-sharing with clients by means of contingent fees. Perhaps because such practices demonstrated too clearly that law was just an ordinary business as well as a profession, they were among the first to be condemned as unprofessional. Further, the nature of the clients' interests often required litigation against clients of greater substance and standing – the employers, the common carriers, the sellers of goods on whom ordinary members of society were increasingly dependent. Cases of this variety were often labelled 'nuisance' cases, which were uninteresting at best and irresponsible at worst (Note 1902; McConville and Mirsky 1989), and young lawyers were advised to avoid them (Auerbach 1976). Because of these inherent difficulties in representing members of the working classes, it has been easy to conclude that only lawyers who were themselves economically and socially marginal might find such clients worth the effort.[7] Thus, much of what has been written about the impact of the rise of industrial society on the legal profession suggests that class divisions among clients were quickly reflected in the social and political hierarchy within the profession itself.[8]

Notwithstanding the apparently close correspondence between American class structure and the delivery of legal services, 'Matewan' suggests the possibility of other legacies. If the transformation of American society in the late nineteenth century has left us with a legacy of class justice, it may also have left a legacy of access to justice as well. On the one hand, if it is true that increasing partisanship by lawyers resulting from their social and economic dependence on corporate clients is a legacy of the corporate and class transformation that occurred during industrialization, this effect should have been all the more clear in a small community where there were few initial differences among attorneys and yet where industrialization created class differences and class conflict among potential clients.

On the other hand, the experience of lawyers in an Appalachian coal community may have evolved according to some other pattern. The homogeneity of the lawyers, the limited client base, or the opportunities for more close-knit professional and social networks may have made the changes in small town or rural law practice quite different from those in large cities. Notwithstanding the pressures from contentious labour relations and county politics, the closer integration of the professional community may have slowed the growth of differences among law practices. In particular, I shall be interested in whether smaller numbers or greater integration of the legal profession affected access to lawyers by social 'have nots' such as the poor and wage-earning classes, or by political and economic 'outsiders' such as unions.

Frontier law practice in Fayette County, West Virginia

In 1870, fifty years before the 'Matewan' events, the industrial revolution had not reached southern Appalachia. Before completion of the Huntington branch of the Chesapeake and Ohio Railroad in 1873 first made exploitation of the New River coalfield possible, Fayette County, West Virginia was wilderness. Its population of about 6000 supported a modest agrarian economy, for the mountainous region was not particularly suited to farming. The mail arrived with civilized frequency, about three times a week, although Fayette was still a long trip on horseback from Charleston (Peters and Carden 1926). The circuit court played an important role in the mountain community, not only as a resolver of conflicts, but also in administering government, much as the justices of the peace had functioned in the English counties a century before.[9] On the judicial side, land disputes and debts were important.[10] The circuit court's docket of civil wrongs was comprised of assault cases and an occasional action in slander, and it handled an assortment of misdemeanour and felony cases brought by an elected prosecutor, assisted by an elected sheriff and a few paid constables. Equally important were the court's other functions. The circuit court provided a rudimentary administrative structure for the county for taxation, collecting fees, running charitable institutions and licensing regulated activities such as preaching or carrying a pistol. For much of the frontier period and well into more modern times, 'court days' provided the county with one of its primary social diversions (Peters and Carden 1926: 208; Moon 1988).

In 1870, the practice of circuit-riding by lawyers still existed, a train of lawyers and clerks, and often clients, following the quarterly sittings of a circuit judge from county seat to county seat. Circuit-riding by attorneys was a practical adaptation to the scarcity of clients and the absence of demand for a continuous judicial or administrative presence in frontier counties. The laborious and often tedious journeys on horseback over mountain trails yielded lore of drinking, eating, practical jokes and wrestling matches that romanticized the life of the circuit riders. Alexander MacCorkle, a southern West Virginia circuit rider who became governor, later recalled the end of a long day's journey on the circuit in these terms:

> With all the weariness of travel over the rough, country roads, splashing through the creeks, climbing the hills, there was a sense of exhilaration which only touches those who are in the sunlight of the mountains. The rest by the roadside at night, or in the country farmhouse, was a joy never to be forgotten.
>
> (MacCorkle 1928: 279)

As MacCorkle concedes, the drinking, gambling and general rowdiness that gave the circuit riders a colourful reputation was as much a response to boredom and the privations of a long and difficult journey, broken only sporadically by the satisfactions of trial work. Indeed, frontier attorneys seemed ready to settle their practices in a single location if business would support it. Calhoun (1965) notes the disappearance of circuit-riding as soon as the population of each county supported resident attorneys.[11]

Retrospective accounts from Appalachia and other parts of the frontier tell of close-knit relationships among circuit-riding lawyers, and even if we assume that these memoirs have glamorized the law practice of circuit riders, close professional relationships are documented in the circuit court records by constantly shifting patterns of co-representation of clients by the attorneys on the circuit (cf. Calhoun 1965). Not only were there few social or professional divisions among the lawyers on the circuit, but there also appears to have been little specialization, the principal skills underlying a lawyer's reputation being oral advocacy and a broad knowledge of general legal precepts. The public attention which the pre-industrial circuit court commanded meant that the performances of both judges and lawyers on the circuit were widely reported and that lawyers were often public figures of sorts, making entry from law practice into politics a common occurrence. The proficiency of circuit-riding lawyers in trial strategy and oratory and their knowledge of general legal principles was contrasted rather contemptuously by its alumni to the lesser learning of lawyers of later generations whose in-office practices called for narrowly specialized knowledge (MacCorkle 1928).

Three practising attorneys resident in post-Civil War Fayette County were Theophilus Gaines, George W. Imboden and Henry W. Brazie. Gaines moved his practice from Washington, D.C. in 1867, and was twice elected Fayette county prosecutor, in 1867 and 1873.[12] Imboden's family had owned land in Fayette County for at least two generations. Brazie graduated from West Point, served in the Union Army in West Virginia and elsewhere and in the late 1860s returned to West Virginia, settling in Fayette County to take up the practice of law.[13] We do not know what drew these three to the area, but it is unlikely that it was the promise of a lucrative law practice, since there were few opportunities for new lawyers.

In this respect, the careers of Gaines and Imboden are different from those of the generation of attorneys that followed, who were drawn to Fayette in the 1870s at the opening of this particular frontier by the building of the railroad, the expanding opportunities to make a living, and because Fayette eventually became large enough to sustain resident lawyers. For later attorneys, Fayette would be the starting place for their careers as lawyers, its economy the source of their success and, for some, the springboard for their political aspirations. Unlike Theophilus Gaines and G.W. Imboden, the attorneys who arrived and settled in Fayette County after 1870 were committed to and dependent upon a new economic and political order that emerged with the opening of the first mines.

Law practice and the beginnings of industrialization

In 1873, the Chesapeake and Ohio Railroad completed a line between Richmond, Virginia and Huntington, West Virginia, making the New River coalfield in Fayette accessible to eastern ports.[14] The magnitude of the explosion that followed can be measured in part by the increasing volume of coal mined in Fayette in each decade after 1870 (see Table 1). By 1890, Fayette coalmines produced over a million tons each year, and by 1900 they were producing 4.5 million tons, making the county a major coal-producing county in a leading coal-producing state. The building of the railroad and the opening of the mines rapidly transformed Fayette County from an isolated mountain community to a boom town. The flood of new residents almost doubled the population by 1880, more than

Table 1 Indicators of the growth of Fayette County, West Virginia, 1870–1920

Year	Population[a]	Coal[b] (tons × 10⁶)	Miners[c]	Mines[d]
1870	6 650	0	0	0
1880	11 560	0.3	NA	5
1890	20 540	1.6	2 985	27
1900	31 990	4.5	6 392	86
1910	51 900	9.4	11 146	140
1920	60 380	7.8	9 666	166

[a] US census; [b] 1880, 10th census of the USA; 1890–1910, West Virginia Department of Mines Reports; [c] West Virginia Department of Mines Reports; [d] 1880, Peters and Carden (1926: 257–8); 1890–1910, West Virginia Department of Mines Reports.

doubled it again by 1890, and again soon after 1900 – an eight-fold increase in just over thirty years.

From an economic backwater in which mail arrivals and circuit court days provided local excitement, the county became a place where change occurred overnight. Old villages grew rapidly, new towns were established as camps for miners, and new businesses sprouted to supply mining equipment on the one hand and goods for the new wage-earning and entrepreneurial classes on the other. Existing villages and towns immediately felt the impact of change as the flow of suppliers, grocers, tradesmen and artisans of all descriptions, lacking the land and husbandry of indigenous residents, swelled the numbers of inhabitants. An even more dramatic change was the rapid emergence of a proletariat, wage earners not attached to the land who reshaped the social geography of the county. By 1890, miners constituted more than half of the adult male labour force and by 1910 they were nearly four-fifths. The new proletariat populated the county outside the established towns and villages, more than 80 per cent of them living in company-owned towns (Lane 1924; Althey 1990).

Transportation, commerce and people created an attractive climate for young lawyers as well as for labourers, merchants and artisans. For the first time, young men were drawn to Fayetteville intent upon establishing a law practice. No fewer than seven attorneys settled in Fayette between 1870 and 1880. James W. St Clair and W.D. Payne were typical. St Clair was born in 1853 in Roanoke, read law in the office of Judge D.S. Johnson in Princeton, West Virginia, and moved to Fayette County to establish his practice in 1875. Payne, also born in Virginia, moved to Fayetteville in the 1870s, where he remained until 1906, when he moved to Charleston. This pattern was followed over the next two decades, as other young men from neighbouring Appalachian communities read law with local attorneys while supporting themselves through other work, such as teaching school, and entered law practice in Fayette County.

Table 2 Lawyers' caseloads in Fayette County Circuit Court in 1885

| Lawyers | Type of case | | | | | | | | | | | Total cases | Tort (ER) | Tort (EE) |
| | Business/organization clients | | | | | | Individual clients | | | | | | | |
	C	L	T	CHY	O	B/O (%)	C	L	T	CHY	O			
Partnerships														
St Clair and Wilson	5	0	0	0	2	7 (21)	6	7	3	6	4	33	7	9
Imboden and Payne[a]	0	0	0	0	2	2 (15)	3	4	0	3	1	13	2	2
Solo lawyers														
Brazie	0	0	0	0	1	1 (8)	1	1	1	5	3	12	0	2
L.G. Gaines	2	0	0	0	1	3 (16)	3	4	2	4	3	19	0	2
L.D. Isbel	3	1	0	0	0	4 (29)	2	1	0	4	3	14	2	8
Van Pelt	3	1	0	0	1	5 (31)	2	4	0	5	0	16	0	2
Other solo lawyers	0	0	0	0	0	0 (0)	0	2	3	3	0	8	0	1
Other lawyers														
Charleston lawyers (3 firms, 4 solo)	4	1	4	0	1	10 (59)	0	4	1	1	1	17	5	3
Others (2 firms, 7 solo)	0	0	0	0	2	2	1	2	2	6	5	18	n/a	n/a

[a] Not partners, but always appeared as co-counsel.

Key: C, contract cases; L, land cases; T, tort cases; CHY, chancery other than land; O, other cases. B/O, total business/organizational cases; %, per cent business/organizational cases. Tort ER, employee accident cases 1872–1900 (one-third sample), client = employer; Tort EE, employee accident cases 1872–1900 (one-third sample), client = employee.

The young attorneys who began practising in Fayette after 1870 were on the threshold of upwardly mobile careers. A career typically included both law practice and other activities – either business or politics. Law practice, alone or in partnership with one or two other attorneys, was often interrupted by periods devoted to other enterprises. In some cases, this produced a bewildering pattern of short-term partnerships and re-alignments as attorneys moved between law and alternative careers.[15] The pattern itself suggests that among the principal attractions of Fayette for its first generation of lawyers were the business and political opportunities that an expanding frontier provided.[16]

By 1885, the number of attorneys had grown from seven to nineteen, all but one of whom resided in Fayetteville, the county seat. Among the group of nineteen, however, seven handled nearly two-thirds of all of the cases brought before the circuit court (see Table 2). These seven, whose practices were mostly established in the 1870s, were already the senior members of the bar, training many of the next generation in their offices and providing a nucleus from which new partnerships formed. No fewer than six of the remaining Fayette attorneys were in their first year of practice and handled at most one or two cases as co-counsel with a more experienced attorney. Thus, the concentration of cases in the seven leading Fayette law practices can be explained in part by the inter-generational differences created by the rapid expansion of the profession.[17] Three others were in public office, and two of the three remaining attorneys were relatives of the seven active attorneys who had elected not to engage in private practice. Thus, eleven of the twelve less active practitioners were either very new to law practice or had left it voluntarily for personal or career-related decisions.

What may be most striking after a second look is the *even* distribution of cases among active and relatively experienced members of the bar. With the exception of St Clair, each handled between twelve and twenty cases in circuit court. The distribution suggests that these lawyers may have promoted relatively equal sharing of business, maintained perhaps through co-counselling arrangements. If it is true that in 1885 the relationships among members of the legal profession promoted equal distribution of business, it is evidence that there was a professional community that remained close-knit even after circuit-riding had ceased.

St Clair's practice stands out because it was about twice the size of the others, and it marks the beginning of a transition to larger, partnership-based practices encouraged by the flourishing economy. As we shall see, by 1910, law practice in Fayette was dominated by small partnerships whose clientele reflected the industrial community. Still in the early stages of this change in 1885, it is important to examine how St Clair built his successful practice and how his clients might have differed from the clients served by the other, solo practitioners.

In the 1870s, we might expect Fayette law practices to draw heavily on the business of the growing economy. Historically, the business before the circuit court reflected the problems of the frontier economy, namely the uncertainties of transactions involving real property, as collateral or as a commodity, and small business transactions in contract or debt. When the opening of the railroad changed the economy, bringing the coal companies and many other related businesses and their employees to the county, a young attorney might have foreseen among his potential clients the operator/entrepreneurs, investors, suppliers, store owners, tradesmen and labourers, not to mention creditors, neighbours or customers of the new businesses.

Notwithstanding the changes in the economy, the immediate impact was not to flood the circuit court with cases directly concerning the new industries, coal and transportation, though between 1873 and about 1900 the total amount of litigation grew at about the same rate as the county's population (see Munger 1988: 80). Over 1100 civil cases were filed in Fayette County in the circuit court between 1872 and 1879. Well over 2000 plaintiffs and defendants took part in these cases, but only sixty-seven (about 3 per cent) were coal companies or railroads.[18] Although the number of court cases brought by or against a coal company or railroad was only a small proportion of the total, the indirect impact of industrialization on the business of the lawyers may be clearly observed in the increasing proportion of litigation over land. Litigation over land increased from 16 per cent of the civil cases in circuit court in 1872 to over 60 per cent in 1885, and this latter figure does not include private condemnation cases brought by railroads. By 1885, about 12 per cent of all parties to circuit court cases were businesses other than railroads or coal companies.

While the predominance of private litigation between individuals about land or contract disputes continued, by the end of the 1880s there were signs of important changes in the mix of business cases in the circuit court. Businesses remained about 12 per cent of all litigants, but coal companies and railroads grew from 3 per cent in the 1870s to about 5 per cent of all parties to civil ligitation in the 1880s, reflecting an increase in cases brought against railroads and coal companies for trespass to property, breach of contract and default on debts. Further, the number of personal injury cases brought by employees in the 1880s was rapidly rising. Between 1872 and 1880, only nine had been filed in the county, two against coal companies and seven against the Chesapeake and Ohio Railroad. Between 1881 and 1890, the number of accident litigation cases more than tripled, including five cases filed against Fayette coal companies and twenty-five against railroads. These changes in the parties and types of cases brought in circuit court, although involving relatively small numbers, provide some indication of the new clients and legal issues linked to the growth of the coal industry that might have been the foundation for the most successful law practices.

In 1885, as 'take-off' began, the in-court practices of Fayette's seven most active lawyers appear quite similar.[19] With the exception of Brazie, who, as county prosecutor in 1885, had a civil practice primarily as local counsel for estate litigation brought by out-of-state lawyers, a typical practice consisted largely of contract and land cases, with a secondary emphasis on estate and family suits in chancery. For five of the seven, individual clients with legal disputes over land provided the largest class of cases. Although St Clair's practice was far larger than the others, the proportions of land, contract and miscellaneous chancery cases were similar.

Notwithstanding these basic similarities among law practices in 1885, we can observe the emergence of differences in the relative proportions of business cases handled by each attorney. The differences are significant, because getting in on the ground floor by representing the new companies might well have been a key to the growth of a law practice, and thus a measure of a lawyer's success. Three attorneys, St Clair, Van Pelt and Isbel, handled over half of all of the cases for businesses. While businesses represented only about one-fifth of St Clair's circuit court clients, and 30 per cent of Van Pelt's and Isbel's, St Clair handled more litigation for businesses than any other lawyer. Ironically, however, only St Clair's practice survived into the second generation of Fayette law practices, casting doubt on the relationship between in-court representation of businesses and growth as a successful corporate law firm. Representing businesses in the early years of the coal industry might also have made a lawyer less willing to represent the adversaries of coal companies. The number of accident cases brought against railroads and coal companies was small but rising steadily during the 1880s. Table 2 shows the number of employee accident cases handled by each of the seven attorneys who were most active in 1885 over the whole period between 1872 and 1900. Not only are the cases distributed over the whole group of seven, but the two attorneys who represented the most businesses and the most coal companies, St Clair and Isbel, also represented the most employees in accident cases. Thus, in 1885, a larger than average business clientele neither foretold success nor led to exclusion of miners or railroad employees as clients.

Early business law practice

The amount of in-court work for businesses may be a poor indicator of the volume of business-oriented legal practice and of a lawyer's continuing relationships with businesses. Representing businesses in circuit court often meant litigating routine contract and debt actions against customers or suppliers and appealing similar cases heard before justices of the peace. The largest American businesses of the period were developing management skills to enhance their adaptability to larger and more competitive markets. Business planning in turn often relied on the development or modification of legal structures for both business organization and business transactions. The emphasis on planning transactions that could be successfully enforced in courts wherever a company did business, and later the development of government regulation, relentlessly pushed business law practice out of the courts and into law offices where the practice consisted primarily of research, counselling and paper work. This long-term trend occurred in the late nineteenth and early twentieth centuries, but for Fayette lawyers we do not have direct evidence of how quickly this happened and for which clients.[20]

There is evidence that St Clair's law practice had important links to the growing coal industry. Coal companies rarely appeared in court, even though the local economy was being driven by their activity, and when they appeared in circuit court, it was often as defendant in a debt or trespass action. In 1885, among Fayette lawyers, only St Clair represented a coal company in circuit court, and no fewer than three cases were brought against St Clair's client.[21] St Clair himself seems to have had a financial interest of some sort in the business, and as a result he also appeared as a defendant in one of the cases.[22] Equally important, among St Clair's individual clients in 1885 were at least two men who later owned large coal companies, who were in the early stages of their own careers. Confirming St Clair's early close connection with coal entrepreneurs, MacCorkle recalled settling a strike by Fayette miners in the early 1880s in which he (MacCorkle) represented the miners and St Clair represented the company (MacCorkle 1928: 187). Over their long careers, MacCorkle reflected, the two attorneys frequently met in these same roles. Another attorney, L.G. Gaines, Fayette's second leading lawyer in 1885, also numbered among his clients in that year at least one individual who became an important coal operator. Confirming the importance of closer connections to the emerging coal industry than those of other lawyers, we shall see that both St Clair and Gaines played an important role in producing the next generation of business-oriented lawyers in the county.[23]

Representation of coal operators in a few cases in court did not necessarily mean that a continuing relationship between a particular business and a particular attorney existed. Representing a business in a state circuit court might be a minor part of a large corporation's legal needs. For example, the Chesapeake and Ohio (C&O) Railroad corporation based in Baltimore, was one of the first large out-of-state corporations to have a continuing relationship with a Charleston-based West Virginia law firm, Simms and Enslow, which represented the C&O in many state circuit court cases. Only a few of the largest corporations appear to have had such a continuing link to West Virginia lawyers in 1885, and it is likely that these connections were made primarily with law firms in Charleston, where law practices were larger and located near both the state capital and the federal district court for the southern district of West Virginia.[24] Occasionally, however, the C&O appeared as co-defendant or co-plaintiff in an action represented by a Fayette attorney, on a one time basis.

Moreover, the entrepreneurial management style of most coal operators was quite different from the more refined management of the C&O and other large corporations. Management practices that enhanced business efficiency and predictability were a product of late nineteenth-century corporate growth, and included encouragement of continuing relations with lawyers that would yield swifter and more thorough planning of the legal structure of business organizations and the terms of business transactions. However, these practices began in specific industries where conditions were more conducive, especially railroads, retailing, oil and chemical production, and required many years to become standard in other industries or to trickle down to smaller businesses (Chandler 1977). It took time to turn generalist practitioners into corporate and business specialists who could advise about and arrange litigation across the range of problems and jurisdictions that concerned a large corporation. Such attorneys were not readily available anywhere in 1885, but especially not in southern West Virginia. Thus, leading Fayette coal operator Justus Collins, in 1907 alone, at the height of his power and wealth, employed fourteen different lawyers, four of them in West Virginia, while others that he consulted about matters that concerned his West Virginia interests were in Cincinnati, Washington, D.C. and Richmond.

Thus, to ask whether by 1885 St Clair was retained on a continuing basis by particular coal companies as a modern corporate lawyer is to seek evidence of a practice whose time had not yet come in Fayette. Most of the early coal companies were home-grown products created by entrepreneurs who resided in Fayette and who directed mining operations themselves, sometimes through a superintendent. Their legal needs were episodic, and lawyers were hired, as Justus Collins hired them, when circumstances called for a lawyer. Moreover, like the coal operators, St Clair himself was a product of the fertile soil the new economy provided for opportunism. His standing in the community did not depend on his law practice alone, since he was also a coal mine owner and an important political figure in the county. Nor does examination of his large in-court practice suggest that in 1885 he was financially dependent on the legal business brought to him by the coal operators. He was known among his contemporaries as someone who rose to prominence in part by having particularly close connections to the growing coal industry, but he was never identified solely as its spokesman. MacCorkle summed up his memories of St Clair with a eulogy to the self-made man:

> For twenty-five years he lorded it over the great and unique develop-
> ment of the New River, drawing leases, trying law-suits, defending
> and prosecuting murder cases, dominating policies, fixing wages and
> rates, shaking a perverse operator like a terrier does a rat, or knock-
> ing down a threatening miner, playing poker with all comers, and
> notwithstanding opposition from every side he was the last word in
> every important question involving this great field . . . he was an
> important factor in all the great political meetings in the old Third
> District and throughout the whole of West Virginia.
>
> (MacCorkle 1928: 188)

An attorney entrepreneur, St Clair's mixture of law practice, mine owning and political activism represents a highly successful adaptation to the opportunities and turmoil of the early industrial county.

Law practice in the industrial county

In 1910, the number of Fayette attorneys who appeared in circuit court reached twenty-seven, a little more than double the number who appeared in 1885. While the number of practising attorneys more than doubled, the population of the county more than tripled and the tonnage mined increased nine-fold between 1885 and 1910.[25] The civil caseload of the circuit court kept pace with the population of the county, increasing slightly more than three-fold over the same period. Thus, the average in-court caseload of Fayette attorneys increased substantially with time and reflected in other ways the changes that occurred.

The types of cases brought to the circuit court reflected the business and personal changes which industrialization brought about. Between 1885 and 1910, literally hundreds of new coal-mining operations opened, of which between 15 and 30 per cent failed or were absorbed by other companies within five years, providing additional business for lawyers (see Munger 1988). The percentage of in-court clients that were railroads or coal companies increased from about 5 per cent in 1885 to about 9 per cent in 1910, while businesses in general increased from about 12 to 19 per cent of all in-court clients. Businesses constituted a larger proportion of in-court clients, but the differences between 1885 and 1910 also reflect the impact of change on individual lives. In 1885, 60 per cent of the caseload concerned matters of real property; in 1910, divorce and family cases comprised 32 per cent of the caseload, and 7 per cent involved appoint-ment of fiduciaries to care for the insane, minors and other dependent persons, while contract and property cases together comprised about 40 per cent of the caseload.

The effects of industrialization were not limited to the lives of people of means. In addition to divorce cases, an unknown proportion of which were brought by members of the working class of Fayette, in 1910 13 per cent of all circuit court cases were workers' accident cases. In 1885, a very small number of these cases were brought in circuit court, primarily cases by employees of railroads. Few cases were brought by miners in any year prior to the passage of workers' compensation. Based on West Virginia Department of Mines statistics, at best fewer than 10 per cent, and for most of the period between 1885 and 1910, fewer than 5 per cent of all reported mine accidents led to litigation. Because accidents were self-reported by coal companies to the West Virginia Department of Mines, under-reporting was probable, and this estimate of the rate of litigation is likely to be inflated, particularly for the earlier years. Nevertheless, both the number of cases against coal companies and the rate of litigation rose gradually over time (see Munger 1987: 100). The number of accident cases brought against coal companies rose steadily in successive decades. Over the same period, actions against railroads reflected the construction of new lines, peaking in the 1880s when the C&O committed itself to coal shipments. In 1910, there were forty-five employee accident cases, forty-two against coal companies and three against railroads.

A significant change in the organization of law practice between 1885 and 1910 is apparent from Table 3. The four largest in-court practices in 1910 are partnerships. The largest of these, Osenton and McPeak, handled over one hundred cases in court, while some solo practitioners handled fewer than half a dozen. Firms and solo practices were not perfectly distinguishable in terms of size, the largest solo practice exceeding the size of the smallest firm, but they were distinct in other ways. While land disputes, contract and estate cases comprised a common denominator for law practices in 1885, there was no common denominator in 1910. Representation of businesses was highly concentrated in law firms, which handled about 70 per cent of the in-court representation of businesses. One partnership, Dillon and Nuckolls, handled 40 per cent of all the in-court representation of businesses, while half of the solo practitioners handled no cases in court for businesses and the other half handled at most two. Virtually all contract cases and most cases involving disputes over land for both individuals and businesses were handled by the law firms.[26] Although Charleston law firms had represented about 30 per cent of all businesses appearing in the circuit court in 1885, by 1910 their role was reduced to about 12 per cent. Businesses had increasing confidence in the competence of local law firms to handle at least some types of legal affairs in circuit court.

Solo practitioners represented almost exclusively individuals. Among the solo practitioners, a number specialized in divorce cases (e.g. Ryan, Anderson, Ellis, Essex, Sweeney), whereas others handled a variety of

Table 3 Lawyers' caseloads in Fayette County Circuit Court in 1910

Lawyers	Type of case											Total cases	Tort (ER)	Tort (EE)
	Business/organization clients						Individual clients							
	C	L	T	CHY	O	B/O (%)	C	L	T	CHY	O			
Partnerships														
Osenton and McPeak	15	3	2	1	2	22 (21)	17	8	40	11	5	103	2	38
Dillon and Nuckolls	14	0	42	1	5	62 (73)	6	9	1	7	0	85	42	2
Hubbard and Lee	12	1	1	1	1	16 (43)	6	6	0	9	0	37	0	1
Payne and Hamilton	8	0	0	0	2	10 (43)	2	10	0	0	1	23	0	0
Walker and Summerfield	0	1	1	1	1	4 (23)	2	7	0	3	1	17	0	0
Mahan, Bacon and White	0	1	0	0	0	1 (100)	0	0	0	0	0	1	0	0
Solo lawyers														
J.L. Ryan	1	0	0	0	1	2 (9)	1	1	3	12	3	21	0	3
A.L. Anderson	0	0	0	0	0	0 (0)	0	0	0	11	5	16	0	0
J.M. Ellis (Black)	0	0	0	0	0	0 (0)	0	0	1	11	0	12	0	0
J.T. Simms	3	0	1	0	0	4 (36)	0	1	4	2	0	11	0	2
T.L. Sweeney (Black)	0	0	0	0	0	0 (0)	0	0	0	9	1	10	0	0
B.D. Koontz	1	0	0	0	0	1 (10)	1	1	1	4	2	10	0	0
Other solo lawyers	5	0	0	0	4	9 (15)	3	8	4	30	5	59	0	2
Other lawyers														
Charleston lawyers	2	2	6	1	7	18 (46)	4	11	1	2	3	39	6	1
Others	2	3	0	0	0	5 (21)	4	13	1	1	0	24	0	1

Key: C, contract cases; L, land cases; T, tort cases; CHY, chancery other than land; O, other cases. B/O, total business/organizational cases; %, per cent business/organizational cases. Tort ER, employee accident cases in 1910, client = employer; Tort EE, employee accident cases in 1910, client = employee.

chancery and contract or debt cases (Champe, Koontz, Simms) (see Table 3). The largest firms and solo practices were all located in Fayetteville, but a number of the smaller, non-business practices were located in Montgomery, Glen Jean and Oak Hill, which were the population centres of the county, and included at least two black attorneys, T.L. Sweeney and J.M. Ellis, the latter practising at Glen Jean.

Unlike the 'hemispheres' of modern urban law practice, the differences between firm and solo practices in 1910 were blurred.[27] The law firms all represented many individual clients as well as business clients. Even Dillon and Nuckolls had a substantial number of clients who were individuals whom they represented in contract, land and family cases. Among the three firms which handled the largest number of cases for businesses – Dillon and Nuckolls, Osenton and McPeak, Hubbard and Lee – there were important differences that merit closer examination. The relative proportion of business clients varied from 75 per cent of Dillon and Nuckolls' cases to only 20 per cent of Osenton and McPeak's. These two firms handled about the same number of business clients, but Osenton and McPeak had a much larger number of clients who were individuals, including a large number of miners suing their employers. In 1910, both firms handled a substantial number of employee accident cases, but while Dillon and Nuckolls represented exclusively employer-defendants (with one exception), Osenton and McPeak represented exclusively plaintiffs (with two exceptions). Further, Osenton and McPeak had the most substantial criminal law practice of any Fayette law practice (not shown in Table 3), which though not numerically large, added to the predominance of clients who were individuals. Like Osenton and McPeak, the Hubbard and Lee firm also had a majority of clients who were individuals, though no miners' accident cases.

The differences among these firms show that the hemispheres of law practice for organizations and for individuals in industrial Fayette were not distinct. The fact that businesses were represented in court primarily by firms suggests a symbiotic relationship between firms and businesses, in which businesses received, or believed they received, superior service from the small group of law firms, and at the same time provided sufficient financial support to allow these practices to grow larger than others in the county. On the other hand, the very fact that businesses had legal adversaries created an additional market for services to individuals whose legal interests conflicted with those of businesses. A business was the adversary in many of the contract, land and tort cases in which firms represented individuals. Representing individuals in conflicts with business corporations not only called on the very expertise which made the law firms attractive to corporations, but used excess capacity of firms not employed in what may (or may not) have been more lucrative business practice. Thus, the increasing knowledge and capacity of law firms in the general area of business law may have created not only the capacity but an incentive to attract clients who opposed businesses. However, this argument does not explain the difference between the Osenton law firm, which seemed comfortable representing worker clients in legal conflicts with corporations, and the Dillon firm which represented no workers at all.

Unexpectedly, in 1910, miners were represented in actions against their employers by the largest county law firm. In 1885, the law practices of Fayette attorneys were, in size and types of clients, quite similar to one another, and between 1880 and 1900 almost all attorneys represented both miners and railroad employees in suits against employers. Even St Clair, friend of coal operators, brought as many actions against coal companies on behalf of employees as he defended for the companies. Prior to 1900, the relatively even distribution of employee accident cases among members of the profession might be attributed to the tradition of the general practitioner, who did not specialize in a particular type of case or client, or more concretely to an inability to depend on income from one type of case or client to make a living. By 1910, however, legal work for coal operators and other businesses was booming, and it was concentrated in law firms which had grown by means of the business brought to them by coal companies and other corporations. Under these conditions, it would make sense for the sharp differentiation between firm and solo practice that characterized lawyers' work in 1910 to reflect increasing commitment of legal resources to businesses and to be complemented by relatively infrequent representation of employees by the law firms that had become successful by representing coal companies. Instead, not only do we find representation of employees relatively widespread among solo practitioners, but we find representation of employees heavily concentrated in the county's largest law firm (in numbers of cases), while the second leading law firm represented exclusively employers.

One possible explanation of the difference between the Dillon and Nuckolls firm and the Osenton and McPeak firm, and also of the growing differentiation among law practices generally, is that law firms were willing to represent employees in inverse proportion to the number of coal companies or railroads represented by the firm, because attorneys cannot represent clients whose interests conflict. Dillon and Nuckolls had long-term relationships with a number of coal companies. There were, however, many coal companies who were not clients of Dillon and Nuckolls and the firm did not represent any of the major railroads in 1910. Yet, the firm represented no railroad employees or employees of non-client coal companies. Further, it might be argued that Dillon and Nuckolls hoped to attract to their practice more coal companies, since that would make the most efficient use of the experience and expertise of their firm. If so, they would have avoided representing the opponents of the clients they hoped to attract. But the same reasoning would have applied to their rivals, Osenton and McPeak, who also represented leading mine owners, including the industry leader Justus Collins.[28] Indeed, why would any law firm retain such a mixture of clients as Osenton and McPeak did in a community which seemed to permit expansion of the most lucrative client base at the expense of a poorer and less reliable one?

Osenton and McPeak's firm is not the whole story of legal representation of miners or members of the working class, because a number of solo practitioners were also willing to take occasional employee accident cases, but this firm's practice is particularly interesting. First, access by miners to the capacity and expertise of the most successful lawyers and largest law firm was a significant development assuming representation was more than perfunctory. Secondly, the firm's representation of miners, despite obvious disincentives – including potential financial and political pressures from other clients – presents a puzzle. Finally, and most intriguing, Osenton's firm was involved in other ways in legal representation of miners. In 1903, Osenton represented striking miners being evicted from company-owned housing. Legal representation of miners in individual litigations is one thing, but representing miners in bitter, contentious and public conflict arising from strikes may mean that the Osenton firm had quite a different identity altogether from the other partnerships. Whatever its source, this development had important implications for the working class and for conflicts between miners and mine owners in Fayette.

The evolution of Fayette's law firms

The first generation of Fayette attorneys had much in common, not the least of which was that they established practices at the same time and under the same conditions of great opportunity, giving them an advantage in attracting the most lucrative clients among Fayette's growing industries. Together with the younger attorneys who read law in their offices or who became associates in their law practices, many members of this group remained leading practitioners, in numbers of cases, reputation and representation of established business interests.

The earliest arrivals were alike in another way, namely their training consisted exclusively of reading law in a practitioner's office. Later arrivals reflected the slow change in legal education from reading law with a practitioner to enrolment in a law school (Auerbach 1976; Stevens 1983; Hobson 1984). We might speculate whether a law school education would affect the practices of lawyers, and in particular whether law school inclined lawyers to feel comfortable with labourers as clients or to have sympathy for those who were harmed by an industrializing economy. While law schools purported to provide broader, more thorough, more 'scientific' instruction in law, there is little basis for assuming that the content of law school instruction inclined attorneys to greater favour towards the causes of persons not already established as important clients of the profession or that it inculcated anything but the most conservative professional traditions.[29] The most important effect of law school may have been collegial. Law school graduates had greater freedom to choose how, when and where to establish a practice because, unlike would-be lawyers who had not graduated from a law school, they had no need to establish a relationship with an existing practitioner in order to enter the practice of law. Further, law schools may have provided a nucleus of networks that came into play when graduates established a law practice. Preferences in choosing partners, in referring business, in taking sides on professional and even public issues, may have been influenced by such ties.

Politics was an important factor in the environment of each new law practice that affected an attorney's relationship to the existing professional networks. Fayette attorneys practised in a highly politicized community, and West Virginia's political life was vigorous and complex. The political rise of supporters of industrialism in the last quarter of the century was opposed by other factions among West Virginia's elites: the 'redeemers' identified by loyalty to the antebellum south, the agrarians who represented anti-industrial economic interests in West Virginia and who thus were sometimes allied with Wheeling's labour Democrats, and the 'ring' of regional Democrats based in Charleston (Williams 1976).[30] Cross-cutting loyalties of Granger, Greenback, Free Soil, and fusion democratic parties slowed the growing hegemony of industrialists over state-level offices. State-level politics were only part of the picture. By the early twentieth century, industrialists dominated both the Democratic and Republican parties in West Virginia, but they never enjoyed exclusive control of state party politics. At the county level, politics were still more complex, often pitting idiosyncratic factions that defy easy summary.

Until 1880, Fayette's political loyalties were solidly Democratic. In 1884, reflecting a decisive state and national shift, the balance in Fayette County shifted to the Republican Party, which controlled county politics for the next two decades. Williams' (1976) analysis of county voting returns in presidential elections reveals a strong link at the county level between the establishment of mining, railroad, oil and manufacturing and the shift by voters to the Republican Party. Because mine operators had considerable influence over voting by the miners who lived in company towns, it is likely that the operators' power over miners helped produce the votes that put Republicans in office (cf. Gaventa 1980).[31]

Against this backdrop, an attorney seeking to build a law practice might not be directly influenced by factionalism, but he would certainly be aware of the concentration of economic and political power among the dominant mine operators. It is certainly not a coincidence that the leading business-dependent lawyer in each generation in Fayette reflected the dominant politics of the period; St Clair was an active Democrat and Dillon a prominent Republican. An attorney who sought political office, however, entered into highly factionalized conflict and assumed the burdens and benefits of intense loyalties. Many attorneys sought office, and a few were involved in bitter factional fights.[32]

Law firms represent the concentration of the most successful forms of cultural capital (Hagan *et al.* 1991). Not all attorneys can or choose to form firms, but the formation of a successful firm requires continuing success in the market for professional services, i.e. it requires qualities that continue to attract clients. The St Clair, Dillon and Osenton partnerships, judged by duration and numbers or attorneys and clients, were the most significant in Fayette County during the fifty-year period between 1870 and 1920. The contrasts between them will be explored further below by examining the client base of each group. But it should be recognized that they were not typical of practices of Fayette attorneys, most of whom were solo practitioners, or of Fayette law firms, many of which were small and short-lived. Of the seven attorneys who settled in Fayette County in the 1870s, four were in two-person partnerships. In 1885, of thirteen practising attorneys and sixteen attorneys in residence, six were in two-person partnerships. By 1910, between thirty and forty attorneys had resided in Fayette at some time (not all at the same time), and of these some seventeen had been in a two- or three-person partnership at some point, at least thirteen having been associated with St Clair, Osenton or Dillon.

Most Fayette law firms remained small and unstable. Alternative careers remained important, and migration to Charleston as practice matured became increasingly common as the members of the bar aged. The number of attorneys in practice in the county declined after 1910 (Peters and Carden 1926), and this says something about the shifting centre of action in law; Fayette was no longer where the profession was growing. By 1885, virtually all of the attorneys from Charleston who appeared in circuit court in Fayette were members of partnerships. Thus, the 'frontier' that attracted lawyers, and which produced more successful practices, lay in larger practices and in the representation of businesses. By no means all attorneys' careers lay in this direction, but the increasing concentration of practices in Charleston and the increasing size of those practices began to establish a new pattern. Ironically, as proportionately more attorneys settled in centres like Charleston, the practice of circuit-riding was re-instituted, made easier, of course, by new modes of transportation, and for the old reasons – lack of local expertise and the demand for the new corporate legal culture in the hinterland.

In the 1880s, St Clair's law practice emerged as first among equals. It may have been his own entrepreneurial behaviour and the qualities that made him a successful party leader which, in that environment, drew other men on the rise as clients or partners for his practice.[33] He read law in the mid-1870s with Theophilus Gaines, forming his first partnership with E.W. Wilson, who became governor in 1884. He was briefly a partner with Gaines' son, Joseph Gaines, who read law under his father's direction as St Clair had done a decade before. Joseph Gaines was another young man on the rise, soon leaving the county for Charleston and, ultimately, a place in McKinley's administration. St Clair was elected county prosecuting attorney in 1881 and state senator in 1891. In 1888, St Clair formed a lasting partnership with young attorneys S.L. Walker, a native of Fayette County, and C.R. Summerfield, a graduate of West Virginia University Law School, which continued until St Clair's death in 1906. Walker and Summerfield continued in practice together until 1912, when Summerfield was elected prosecuting attorney and Walker moved his practice to Charleston.

The continuation of St Clair's practice in the Walker and Summerfield partnership establishes a link between generations of Fayette attorneys, the first generation of attorneys laying a foundation for the success of law firms in the second generation. Of the five Fayette law firms in 1910, two may be traced directly back to leading practitioners in 1885. In addition to Walker and Summerfield's firm, in 1910, Payne and Hamilton continued the practice of Payne and Imboden. Curiously, the inter-generational link was most tenuous for the three largest law firms in Fayette in 1910. In 1887, Dillon read law in the office of Lud Gaines, who had the largest practice after St Clair, and who shared some of St Clair's connections to the coal industry. But Lud Gaines did not take Dillon into his practice, and Dillon made his own way to prominence through his political activity and formation of a highly successful alliance with a recent law school graduate, following St Clair's pattern in both respects. Osenton was a Georgetown Law School graduate who, as we shall see, drew on quite different county and party networks for his political and professional support. Hubbard and Lee were classmates at Virginia Law School. As law school graduates, Osenton, Hubbard and Lee could enter practice without establishing a close tie to a practising attorney. The still-growing coal industry outpaced the growth of the bar, providing sufficient legal work for new lawyers, but also for new associates if existing law firms had chosen to expand. While such factors as party preference (Osenton, Hubbard and Lee were Democrats) may have had some influence on firm foundation, it is more likely that their independence was in part a product of their law school training and in part a product of the fact that firms remained small because the reputations and social standing of individual attorneys and their personal relationships with clients continued to be the basis for a successful practice, qualities that are difficult to impart to a large group of associates in a trial practice (cf. Galanter and Paley 1991).

The career of C.W. Dillon, who built his practice from nothing to become lead partner in the leading business law firm in 1910, illustrates the continuing importance of personal success rather than connection to an existing practice. Dillon arrived from Virginia in 1884 at the age of twenty-one, taught in a school for two years while reading law with an established member of the 1870s bar, L.G. Gaines, and entered law practice in 1887. He formed a partnership with E.L. Nuckolls, who moved to Fayetteville shortly after earning a law degree at Washington and Lee School of Law in 1893. The partnership was immensely successful. Dillon was active in the Republican Party and, shortly after forming his partnership with Nuckolls, was elected county prosecutor for two terms between 1893 and 1901. In 1908, he was a delegate to the National Republican Convention, and in 1909 was appointed a member of the Commission on Uniform State Laws. In 1912, Dillon was the state Republican Party's candidate for governor. Nuckolls brought quite different strengths to the partnership, providing the technical skills that served the firm's continuing relationships with a number of the county's largest coal companies and other business firms. In 1900, Dillon and Nuckolls co-authored a widely used legal volume *The West Virginia Pocket Code*. The combination of a partner who was a public figure and one who was a legal technician may have provided a combination of publicity and legal expertise that could compete with the growing corporate bar of Charleston. While Dillon was a public figure, his career was different from that of lawyer/entrepreneur St Clair. Dillon was not an entrepreneur but a 'rainmaker', in association with Nuckolls, an office minder, reflecting what was perhaps a critical development in business law practice.

C.W. Osenton, whose firm had the largest practice in Fayette in 1910, owed even less than Dillon to the previous generation of lawyers. Osenton, born in Kentucky, moved to Montgomery, the largest town in Fayette County in 1886, working as a hotel clerk until 1893 while reading law. Before completing his legal training, Osenton's career took an upward turn through an appointment in the Treasury Department in Cleveland's administration. In Washington, D.C., he entered Georgetown Law School's night division, receiving an LL.B. in 1895 and an LL.M the next year. Returning to West Virginia in 1897, he began his practice in Fayetteville.[34] Osenton's first partnership was formed in 1897 with General C.C. Watts, an older Charleston practitioner and former circuit rider. Watts soon moved from Fayetteville to Charleston, and Osenton formed a new firm with two young practitioners, Vernon C. Champe and A.S. Smith, both from Montgomery where Osenton had worked before becoming a lawyer. By this time, Osenton was on a faster track than his two young associates and his election as county prosecutor soon led to the break-up of the partnership. While Osenton was prosecutor, he formed a brief association with established Charleston practitioner, Hon. W.L. Ashby.

By the end of his term as county prosecutor, Osenton had established his reputation as a criminal trial attorney and was known widely for his courtroom advocacy. He formed a stable partnership with E.M. McPeak and later included A.J. Horan, an attorney ten years older and more experienced that Osenton, who had recently arrived from Summersville, West Virginia. McPeak died in 1909, but Horan remained Osenton's partner until 1918, when Horan moved to Charleston and was replaced by W.L. Lee, a politically active attorney with a practice in Fayetteville. Osenton was a delegate to the National Democratic Convention in 1904 and 1908, and served on the Democratic National Committee in 1920. Like Dillon, Osenton mixed his practice with election to office early in his career and was politically well-connected at the state and national levels.[35] His many partnerships illustrate even more clearly than Dillon's career, the importance of the lead partner's reputation because, despite his firm's lack of stability, Osenton's practice prospered.[36]

In these histories, there are clues to the differences between the clients of the Dillon and Osenton partnerships. While Dillon read for the law, Osenton was a product of Georgetown Law School. Dillon was trained in the office of a leading local attorney, Lud Gaines, while Osenton was an outsider, having attended law school in Washington, D.C. Dillon's residence had always been the county seat, Fayetteville, while Osenton first established himself in Montgomery, and his choice of partners, Champe and Smith from Montgomery, reflected that earlier experience. Dillon's 'insider' career and Osenton's 'outsider' career might explain why Dillon was on an inside track with social and economic insiders, while Osenton's practice served clients on the social and economic margin. But Osenton's numerous partnerships, 'outside' training and connections did not prevent him and his partners from building a substantial clientele among the community's leading entrepreneurs and companies. The opportunities for both firms to build business-oriented practices seem to have been similar.

In the search for an explanation of the differences between their firms, the political party affiliations of Dillon and Osenton may provide an important clue to opportunities and choices not apparent from their training and professional associations. Dillon was active in the politically dominant Republican Party at both the county and state levels. Osenton was an active Democrat, but, more importantly, was tied to a network of lawyers associated with factions of the Democratic Party hostile to industrialists. Osenton's personal sympathies concerning his clients' causes cannot be documented directly, but his professional associations shed some light on the influence of political affiliations on his law practice.[37] The cluster of attorneys associated with Osenton at different points in his career – W.R. Bennett, C.C. Watts, A.J. Horan and, to extend the network one step further, Watts' close friends and associates in his circuit-riding days and later his Charleston law practice, James H. Ferguson and William A. MacCorkle – were all politically active Democrats. Watts and Ferguson were members of a faction in the Democratic Party that opposed the hegemony of the industrialists. Osenton's choice of professional associates displays a long-term preference for the party in opposition and included anti-industry democrats.

In summary, there are similar elements in the careers of Dillon and Osenton encompassing their public service and rise to prominence within their own political parties, their association with competent office-minders, and their lucrative business-based practices. The differences between their practices in 1910 are also striking, Osenton providing legal services to substantial numbers of miners and other members of the working class, while Dillon represented far fewer individual clients and did not represent miners. The fact that Dillon and Osenton belonged to different political parties may provide part of the explanation for these differences, but differences in opportunities to attract particular clients were also important. The interaction of values and opportunities underlying the growth of their practices is revealed more clearly by the changing proportions of cases in which the firms represented workers or employers in conflicts between them.

Representation of workers in accident litigation

There were many barriers to legal representation of miners in accident litigation. From an attorney's point of view, industrial accident litigation was unfamiliar legal terrain. Civil litigation by an employee to collect compensation from an employer was something new in Fayette County in the 1870s. Before the building of the Chesapeake and Ohio railroad, no case of this kind had been brought in Fayette. The absence of cases in Fayette County reflects the experience of lawyers throughout the state. The West Virginia Supreme Court did not issue its first decision interpreting the common law of West Virginia with respect to an employee's claim for compensation until the mid-1880s.[38] Thus, in the 1870s and 1880s, Fayette attorneys would have had no West Virginia precedents to work with. A handful of leading decisions in other states, if known to them, would have underscored the uncertainties of recovering damages for an employee and the grounds for an employer's appeal.[39]

In addition to the uncertainties of tort law, miners and railroad employees presented some unique problems as potential clients. Few employees came forward to sue their employers.[40] The expectation of recovering in court for employment-related injuries was not well established (Friedman 1987). Not only was the American system of tort compensation much less generous in 1890 than in 1990, but miners had some sympathy for the tort law principle that other employees were the main source of risk to miners (see Graebner 1978). Further, an employee who survived had debts to the employer to repay (Althey 1990) and his job to retain.[41] Employees who died no longer had to worry about displeasing an employer, but were likely to leave behind them an impoverished spouse and family with few resources and little stomach for litigation. Thus, an attorney was likely to have an ambivalent client, one prone to settlement pressure. Finally, not only was the expectation of compensation itself not well established, there were other barriers to seeking compensation in court, not the least of which was the fact that the client, either a labourer or his family, was also likely to be very poor and without the services of the principal wage earner as well. The client's poverty meant both that the attorney's fee would be small or non-existent, unless the attorney was successful, and that the attorney would be provided with few resources to draw on for litigation. These, among other factors, may have contributed to a settlement rate in employee accident cases of about 60 per cent (see Table 3),[42] and may explain the infrequency of employee accident cases against both coal companies and railroads relative to the number of injuries.

Despite the barriers to litigation, employee accident litigation increased not only in proportion to the miles of railroad constructed or the tons of coal mined, but increased at a faster rate in the early 1900s. The increasing employee accident litigation rate may have been caused by a number of factors, including active union organizing in Fayette, increasing sympathy from courts, or easier access to lawyers. With respect to the first, there is no evidence that safety was a union issue, though miners' behaviour might have been affected notwithstanding. There is some evidence that the circuit court was increasingly sympathetic to miners' accident cases after 1900 (see Table 4), but the growing favour was shown primarily in cases based on non-fatal injury, and no change in outcomes occurred in cases brought by a decedents estate.[43] Yet, most of the increasing numbers of accident cases in court were the result of fatalities, suggesting once

Table 4   Tort cases in Fayette County, West Virginia, 1872–1920

	1872– 1880	1881– 1890	1891– 1900	1901– 1910	1911– 1920[a]
Coal company defendants					
Cases filed	2	5	25	83	29
% Reaching court	100	60	36	14	55
% Won by plaintiff[b]	50	100	11	42	56
Railroad defendants					
Cases filed	10	25	28	32	44
% Reaching court	20	20	29	34	43
% Won by plaintiff[b]	50	60	37	64	84

Source: Fayette County Circuit Court case files and order books. Torts include all actions in trespass on the case.

[a] Workmen's Compensation statute enacted in 1913. [b] % of cases reaching court.

again that employees who lived were reluctant to sue an employer despite the mounting odds in favour of recovering damages. Changes in mining practices in the early twentieth century caused many mine explosions that caused the number of mining fatalities in Fayette County to skyrocket. Therefore, the most plausible reason for the rise in the number of accident cases has nothing to do with union support, or court decisions, but rather the rising death toll in the mines and, possibly, greater receptivity by lawyers.

Many attorneys represented miners or railroad workers in employee accident cases (see Tables 2 and 3). Between 1872 and 1900, virtually every lawyer handled a few. Between 1872 and 1920, sixteen attorneys, or more than half the active attorneys of the county, handled at least one accident case for an employee. By 1910, two important trends appeared. First, by 1910, most cases on behalf of employees were being brought by a law firm, though several solo practitioners had large numbers of these cases relative to the sizes of their practices and a number of other solo practitioners each had one. Secondly, there was an increasing tendency for particular law firms to represent either employee-plaintiffs or employer-defendants. The tendency is not only displayed by the differentiation among law firms in 1910, but by the *change* in clientele of each law firm over time. The practices of St Clair, and its continuation as Walker and Summerfield, Dillon and Nuckolls, Osenton *et al.*, may be compared over a considerable period of time (see Table 5). Considering all types of tort cases, all three firms represented more plaintiffs than defendants, both before 1900 and after 1900. Considering only litigation by employees against coal companies, however, the St Clair and Dillon partnerships

Table 5 Law firm clients in employee accident cases, 1872–1920

Time period/ Client	Cases by law firm[a]		
	St Clair	Dillon	Osenton
Before 1900			
Coal company	7	1	0
Mine worker	5	7	1
Railroad	2	2	0
Railroad worker	2	1	0
After 1900			
Coal company	7	21	3
Mine worker	0	2	21
Railroad	0	0	0
Railroad worker	0	2	0

[a] Based on a one-third sample of all tort cases filed in Fayette Circuit Court between 1872 and 1920.

represented both employees and employers before 1900, but after 1900 only defended coal companies in such cases. The pattern does not hold for litigation against railroads, where all three were plaintiff-oriented because none of the four clusters represented the most frequent target of railroad cases, the Chesapeake and Ohio Railway.

Increasing concentration of representation of miners in law firms between 1885 and 1910 may mean the cases were viewed as a risky investment of time and effort, and thus attorneys who could most easily absorb the risk would find the cases most attractive. A partnership had greater resources, and perhaps younger associates' time to invest, and, therefore, might well be more willing to take on such cases than a solo practitioner. Yet, solo practitioners were clearly quite willing to continue representing miners and railroad workers in suits against their employers, and continued to do so. The increasingly exclusive defence orientation of the St Clair and Dillon firms is equally puzzling, unless there was a magic point at which the commitment of the firms to coal companies made representation of employees in cases against coal companies uncomfortable, or more likely a point at which the low return in employee accident cases simply came to be viewed as wasting valuable resources that were needed as a reserve for more lucrative business.

The special characteristics of Osenton's practice, rather than the subtle politics of representing coal companies within St Clair's or Dillon's firm, might explain both why it was particularly efficient for Osenton to represent miners and at the same time explain the decline in numbers of cases accepted by other firms. Osenton established his practice as a criminal trial lawyer shortly before 1900. Soon after, he began representing miners in accident litigation, and immediately built the largest accident litigation practice in the county.[44] Not only might Osenton, the criminal lawyer, have possessed a superior network to these clients and a reputation as a prominent lawyer in some field other than corporate law, his skills were primarily those of a trial lawyer, which suited him well for tort claims work. The balance of his practice consisted of representing individuals, not corporations, though he and his partners represented many corporations, and his skills as an oral advocate may have had a strong influence over the continuing emphasis on the problems of individual clients. Finally, it is possible that the very volume of his practice may have drawn cases away from other attorneys, or may even have given an attorney such as Dillon an opportunity to decline cases and to refer them to Osenton.[45]

Legal representation of miners in labour conflicts

There were few instances of legal conflict in which workers and their employers were as directly opposed as in accident litigation. Most of the legal consequences of class conflict were displaced to legal structures for maintaining the individual economic or social actor's place in the community, typically involving laws maintaining market mechanisms of consumption or finance and laws maintaining public order in which the interests of an opposed class were only indirectly represented through the role of the market or the role of the government (Munger 1991).

Class interests were visibly and bitterly opposed in the rare instances in Fayette in which litigation grew out of collective action by miners. The most frequent form of representation in labour conflict was settlement of a strike in which miners had been evicted from their company-owned housing. MacCorkle (1928: 187) mentions having participated in negotiations on behalf of miners in the region on many occasions. Evictions sometimes reached court, and the miners were sometimes represented by an attorney. Prior to the establishment of Osenton's practice, there is no record of Fayette attorneys representing evicted miners. MacCorkle represented Fayette miners in 1882; Osenton and Bennett, Fayette attorneys, represented miners in 1902 and 1903. In 1918 and 1924, Fayette miners were again represented by an attorney from Charleston, this time H.W. Houston, lawyer for the United Mine Workers of America.

In labour conflicts, unlike accident litigation, miners were represented by a small and quite select group of lawyers. Bennett was an established solo practitioner and criminal court judge. Osenton, with whom we are already familiar, like Bennett, was a prominent attorney who represented miners in accident cases. No other Fayette attorneys are known to have represented striking miners in or out of court. What explains the fact that Osenton and Bennett represented striking miners while neither St Clair nor Dillon, the leading business firms, nor any of the other solo practitioners who did not depend on business clients, did not?

The pattern of legal representation of miners in strike litigation is distinct from the pattern in accident litigation. It is not difficult to see that the reasons for the differences lie in part in what was at stake for the conflicting parties and the more careful mutual selection by attorney and client. If there was any risk that the suspicions of the community generally about unions might be transferred to the lawyers who represented striking miners, it is easier to understand why prominent attorneys accepted the cases rather than younger or less prominent solo practitioners. But the selection of lawyers may ultimately have rested on the importance that miners themselves attributed to the outcomes of their conflicts with operators and on the care they exercised in choosing their attorneys. Both Bennett and Osenton were members of a network of lawyers in the Democratic Party, some members of which were actively opposed to the interests of industrialists. Above all, Osenton and Bennett had law practices that may have been more familiar to working-class clients and which seemed to welcome them. In return, the attorneys seem to have won the trust of the miners, even though neither attorney maintained a continuing relationship with the miners and their labour conflicts.

Class conflict and the reorganization of law practice

By 1910, Fayette attorneys practised in a society in which class was becoming an increasingly sharp dividing line. Class differences existed in American life on the frontier as in metropolitan life before industrialization, but these differences were brought to the centre of county life by the economic transformation that occurred. Industrialization made the growing power of capital much clearer because of its success in controlling people and resources. The legal issues of Fayette's rural proletariat, including divorce, crime and naturalization, as well as industrial accidents and control over the terms and conditions of work, were thrust upon them by the circumstances that industry had created. While the problems may have been uniquely those of the working class, they symbolized larger changes brought about by industrialization and the creation of a national market. Attorneys were necessarily sensitive to growing class differences, at the very least because class differences correlated with ability to pay for services. This did not mean that the working class went unrepresented, only that they were under-represented.

In Fayette, whatever the pattern may have been in larger metropolitan communities, the legal cases of the working class (as represented by accident cases) were widely distributed among members of the bar and not concentrated among marginal practitioners. Contrary to what we may have expected, even attorneys who represented many coal companies handled cases for employees seeking compensation from other coal companies. A prominent law firm's frequent appearance on behalf of miners and railroad employees in accident cases appears to have emerged as a by-product of the lead partner's emphasis on trial practice and his reputation as a trial attorney among the working class. The attorney's life-long associations within the Democratic Party may also indicate that his values supported a more diverse law practice than other prominent Fayette firms, but strong values do not seem to have been required in accepting accident cases. Miners' and railroad workers' accident cases seldom occasioned lengthy or bitter litigation that would have been costly for a losing lawyer or that would have focused attention on the problems of the working class, the conflict between workers and owners, or the lawyer's commitment to either group. Rather, accident cases quickly became routinized and assimilated to the rhythms of law practice. Between 1891 and 1910, over two-thirds of all miners' and railroad workers' accident cases never reached court; fewer than one in six was tried successfully. The success rate of miners at trial was one-third that of other litigants who tried cases against coal companies. There were almost no appeals.

By contrast with the episodic relationships between employees and attorneys, by 1910, coal mine operators and attorneys had begun to develop stable continuing relationships. Continuing relations with major businesses may explain the unique organization of Dillon's practice. His firm was characterized by a high degree of stability, in contrast to virtually every other legal practice in the county. Dillon's Republican affiliation is not surprising, because Fayette coal mine operators helped establish Republican hegemony in the county after 1884. Over time, Dillon's firm became increasingly loyal to his coal company clients, all but ending their representation of miners bringing any type of claim against coal operators.

The exclusion of miners' accident cases from some law firm practices occurred only after 1900, but prior to that date nearly every practice handled some cases for miners. In contrast, neither of the leading business-identified firms, the St Clair and Dillon partnerships, ever had any documented relationship to *organized* miners. Organized miners seemed to select legal representation only from among members of the bar who had earned the miners' trust. The lawyers who were selected to represent miners in labour conflicts were not marginal but rather prominent and had previously accepted miners' accident cases. The fact that they had also represented coal operators seemed not to matter.

Although miners' accident cases were handled by virtually all law firms in the early years of industrialization, after a certain point, some coal company-oriented firms stopped representing miners in these cases. Thus, the development of strong relationships between coal companies and a law practice resulted in 'capture' of some law practices in the sense that the lawyers no longer represented other clients who contested the rights of coal companies. Over time, it appears that the broader and more far-reaching the interests of the dominant clients and the more lucrative the relationship, the greater the range of other clients and interests which were excluded from simultaneous representation.

Miners faced the other side of this problem of capture, namely preemption from representation by the firms that were captured by coal operators. Because of the absence of any continuing organization that could recruit and pay for lawyers in Fayette County, miners had difficulty capturing lawyers of their own. The presence of the United Mine Workers of America in Fayette was largely a formality before the First World War, because it had been able to mount few strikes and its strength in Fayette faded after defeats in the strikes of 1902–1903. Periodically, local organizing for strikes resulted in recruiting attorneys to assist with strike-related issues, but the miners' inability to maintain a continuing and effective organization to represent them hurt the quality of the representation. Osenton represented a large number of striking miners in eviction cases in 1902. Yet, the miners for their part, were not able to provide Osenton with a continuing stream of legal business. Consequently, his investment in representing miners as a class interest does not seem to have extended beyond the brief period of union activity. None of the evictions was appealed; Osenton did not participate in resisting labour injunctions. The only practice in southern West Virginia that seems to have been sustained in significant part by unions was that of H.W. Houston, a Charleston attorney and a committed socialist, who represented the statewide United Mine Workers Union as well as other unions.[46]

Fayette County miners were not without their lawyer-allies, but these allies had independent bases of support and were not interested primarily in the miners' welfare. State legislator James Ferguson, a Charleston lawyer, introduced legislation that ended payment in scrip and required checkweighing in 1889. Both before and after passage of the laws, Ferguson and his partner C.C. Watts met with Fayette miners to discuss the law.[47] E. Willis Wilson, briefly in practice in Fayette in the 1880s before being elected governor as an agrarian Democrat, was also part of this loose network. In 1890, Governor Wilson appointed Daniel B. Lucas, a Jefferson County lawyer and state legislator with Granger leanings who supported the anti-scrip and checkweighman laws, to the position of chief judge of the state Supreme Court. While serving as chief judge, Lucas wrote an opinion sustaining both laws.[48] Yet, the support for labour by Ferguson, Watts and Lucas was derived from their own agrarian political ideology, and their consequent hostility to industrialists. In the long run, they were essential political allies in the state legislature and judiciary who helped obtain regulatory legislation that limited the industrialists' power over wages and working conditions, but they were allies who were not committed to winning greater political or economic control for labourers themselves in their collective conflicts with employers. In point of fact, few indictments were brought by the prosecuting attorney in Fayette County under the laws the anti-industrialists had helped to enact and to uphold, and after 1900 the laws were almost never enforced.[49] Attorneys helped very little in transferring power to the unorganized miners, and such a transfer of power would have to await the political organizing by labour of another era.

Conclusion

'Matewan''s tale of resistance romanticizes an American ideal, that law is ultimately about justice and the law's constitutive power does not inevitably reproduce class structure. In contrast, a tradition of historical research on the urban bar of the nineteenth century suggests a more pragmatic view of the impact of industrialization on the organization of legal practice and access to law. The rise to power of corporate lawyers and the marginalization of the lawyer for the individual middle- or working-class citizens flowed from the relative power of their clients in the wake of these changes in American society. However, research establishing the stratification of the urban legal profession has paid little attention to the process of change in particular communities and ordinary law practices, or to the role of the American legal order in social conflict suggested by 'Matewan' – its paradoxical role in supporting the authority of dominant social interests and simultaneously providing resources for resistance to them.

By examining social change and the reorganization of the legal profession in an Appalachian community, we have been able to observe more clearly how the industrialization of society led directly to the dependence of the legal profession on the class order of a community. At the same time, this closer look at change has revealed that the class domination of law is both less and greater than the picture of the stratified urban bar suggested. Class domination of the legal profession was less than that implied by the wealth differences among clients in urban communities because lawyers in rural Appalachia (and likely in New York or Chicago as well) were morally and pragmatically committed to opportunism, resulting in mobile careers and as broad a range of clients as the market encouraged. At the same time, class domination was more deeply embedded than the distribution of wealth among clients suggests, because class was maintained by other mechanisms as well as by the distribution of resources.

With respect to the first, lawyers must be seen as players in a larger frame of reference, not only as agents of a stratified professional culture, but as individuals with complete lives and careers. The law practices of Fayette practitioners typically had many temporal and spatial segments. Over time, the lawyers of Fayette County changed close associates and professional activities, as associates or partners came and went and as business, political and professional interests were pursued. Likewise, the careers of Fayette lawyers typically spanned a number of communities, the result of seeking training in one community and a location for law practice in another, the result of moving between courts and distant clients, or as a result of relocating a practice. Family, professional colleagues and political allies influenced these branching career paths. We might be seriously misled if we were to imagine typical professional lives in a growing American community as completely embedded in a single community, the organization of their practices influenced only by the immediate context of the current law practice, shaped only by choices among local clients, or driven by a desire to accumulate goodwill and capital in the immediate community. The diversity of lawyers' careers underscores the point that a career in law was an adaptable form of entrepreneurship as well as a profession.

Secondly, we must be cautious in attributing the choices made by potential clients seeking legal advice to the effects of wealth alone. Practices took on the character of clients, to be sure. The wealth of clients and the complexity of the remedies they could afford set some parameters for the location, size and organization of the practice. But clients were drawn in part by things other than the cost of the lawyer's services. A lawyer's initial clientele established networks into the community, capable of having an impact upon the future of a lawyer's practice independent of the lawyer's expectations. Who could have predicted that a prominent criminal attorney in Fayette would find that he was positioned to take advantage of employee accident claims when they appeared in large numbers? Further, a lawyer's political ideology may have had a more subtle influence on clients. While having a particular political ideology does not seem to have played a critical role in establishing a successful law firm, colleagues and activities in an attorney's life outside of law practice may have engendered trust (or lack of it) among prospective clients who considered themselves particularly vulnerable in that community. Thus, the choice made by striking union miners in Fayette to employ an attorney who had frequently represented miners in accident cases and who counted prominent pro-worker state legislators among his close friends seems anything but arbitrary.

Finally, the enlistment of legal support by the working classes for both individual and collective conflict was affected in important ways by constraints other than wealth – in tort litigation by the dependence of a miner on the goodwill of an employer who continued to employ him, and in labour litigation by trust and by the constraints on mobilization of resources for collective action, including the wealth and strategic planning needed to establish a continuing relationship with particular lawyers. Neither of these types of constraints alters the general picture of the unequal distribution of legal resources, but understanding them may greatly affect our view of the way law was linked to domination by class interests. Wealth was not the only critical issue, nor necessarily the key to change.

Epilogue: the personal and the professional in the evolution of law practice

Recognizing that the conflict between capital and labour had become an elemental force in West Virginia society, the president of the West Virginia Bar Association in 1903, George Price, devoted his annual address to the subject of labour's challenge to the rule of law. Price argued that the problem of labour conflict was legal rights:

> If the laborer's demands cannot be reduced to and expressed in the form of law, then they cannot be maintained in this country. Every man can get what the law gives him and no more. He must be willing

to bring his claim to the test of the law of the land. If it is such a claim as the law recognizes, the courts will enforce it for him. The bar will always be ready to lend its assistance to him in obtaining it, and the courts will see that his rights are established and protected. But if his claim is not recognized by the law, then he ought not to expect to enforce it. If it is such a claim as ought to be recognized and protected by law, then he must get the Legislature to amend the law so as to give his claim recognition and protection. But until this is done, he must not try to enforce it by force, by terrorism, by attacks upon a man's business, or his reputation, by boycotting or intimidation of the workmen employed by his employer.

(West Virginia Bar Association 1903: 65)

Defining the problem as one of rights, Price's vision of the role of law in class conflict had two elements. First, labour's problems with the division of profits or control of the workplace were matters of conventional politics and, therefore, conflict with capital must be confined to appropriate conventional political channels. Secondly, the legal profession and the courts are simply conduits for rights lacking any significant political role. Price appeared untroubled by the role that lawyers might play in distributing the benefits of rights, since he thought of rights as conventional, rather than political or ideological interpretations of rules, and conceived of advocacy as equally available to both labourers and capitalists.

Fundamentally, Price failed to recognize that the problem of conflict between capital and labour was one of class, rather than rights, and that, as a consequence of social class position, the choices of labourers in contending for power or rights were constrained. Lacking the resources to create the prerequisites for more conventional forms of contention for power – adequate and sustained support of a well-financed organization, public institutions or committed professionals – miners met sustained brutality by operators with episodic violence of their own. Moreover, Price's narrow view of the problem, as one that might be remedied through the addition of a few new rights in the workplace, meant that the manifestations of class conflict recognized by Price fell well short of the full range of life conditions that constituted social class and that determined the forms of conflict between capital and labour.

This brief examination of the careers and practices of Fayette's first lawyers has helped me understand the expectations that led to the establishment of their practices and the economic and social pressures that influenced both the availability of particular clients and lawyers' decisions to represent them. Price's address to the bar barely scratched the surface of the complexities of everyday practice, or of its routines. Yet, the beginnings of differentiation in the practice of law, which I observed in this rural county, explain why lawyers could not avoid confronting and rationalizing their position in class conflict. I have documented the differentiation of law practice along class lines, the concentration of business clients in larger practices, the focus of solo practices on individual matters such as domestic relations, the specialization of some practitioners in highly routinized representation of employees, and the tenuous, episodic commitment of lawyers to legal representation of workers engaged in collective conflict. The class-biased picture that emerges could not be ignored for long by attorneys.

The obviousness of the tilt may explain both the defensiveness of Price's declarations and their underpinnings in professional norms of political autonomy. Price's simultaneous acknowledgement that many contemporaries conceded the legitimacy of the extra-legal 'rights' claimed by labour, the defensiveness of his claims that courts have limited, apolitical powers while righteously defending the courts in upholding the rights of operators, together with the hypocrisy of sending the miners to a state legislature that had responded reluctantly and ineffectively, suggests that a change was in the making. Price's views tell us that mainstream lawyers were slowly being driven to consider class conflict as a central concern.

Further, Price's framing of the problem of class conflict may help us understand better why, in the final analysis, the representation of labourers by Fayette County lawyers had a profoundly political significance. Price reinforced one important value essential to the routines we have discovered in the representation of miners, namely the lawyer's autonomy in selecting clients. Price's arguments legitimate legal representation of all who command sufficient resources to hire an attorney, while deflecting consideration of the bar's role with respect to those who do not. Lawyers, by their own professional norms, are insulated from criticism of the effects of their work by professional colleagues or political partisans outside the profession, as long as representation of clients by lawyers is defined in legal rather than social terms. Thus, the distinction between specialization, or selection among clients to promote efficiency, and 'capture', that promotes the social interests defined by current clients, is of great political importance. The primary motivations for specialization by plaintiffs' attorneys in employee accident cases appeared to be economic, by virtue of the economies of scale of having large numbers of such cases, and the efficiency of using the same client mobilization networks for both accident cases and criminal cases. Exclusive representation of particular types of clients, such as businesses, or particular types of businesses, did not emerge in the first generation of Fayette law practices, but rather manifested itself at a later stage in firms heavily committed financially to particular types of clients. At this later stage, we might argue, the clients themselves made representation by lawyers a social rather than a legal issue. And, as Price illustrates, at the point of 'capture' by business clients, leading lawyers turned to strenuous justifications of their role.

Acknowledgements

My research on social change and litigation in three counties in southern West Virginia between 1872 and 1945 has been supported in part by an Appalachian Studies Fellowship from Berea College and by National Science Foundation grant SES-8121320. I would like to acknowledge the assistance of many helping hands. David Engel, Christine Harrington, Fred Konefsky and Jack Schlegel provided valuable comments on drafts of the manuscript. Kenneth Schagrin and Nicole Moss have supported my work with able research assistance. For many years, Steve Montgomery's patient and reliable examination of Fayette Circuit Court records has been invaluable, and I wish to thank Brenda Richardson and Keith Marine who assisted him on this project. My thanks to Joyce Farrell for help in preparing the manuscript.

Notes

1 This work is part of a larger study of law and change in three coal counties in late nineteenth-century West Virginia – Fayette, Raleigh and Summers. The study includes a detailed analysis of circuit court cases in the three counties between 1872 and 1945 (Munger 1988). In earlier phases of the research, I examined tort litigation in Fayette County, discovering a pattern of increasing litigation during strikes. Closer examination of the relationship between strikes and accident litigation suggested that the reorganization of law practices by local attorneys may have affected the litigation rate, in particular through the development of more specialized practices by attorneys willing to represent miners in more than one type of legal matter (Munger 1987). The present chapter examines this suggestion in greater detail.

2 A population of more than 2500 in 1870 was enough to classify a location as 'urban'. By 1900, about 65 per cent of Americans still lived in communities smaller than this (Bogue 1985: 109).

3 Although this story may have a contemporary appeal, it is also a story which distances and masks the contemporary problem. We think of labour history as belonging to a special period of the past – before the rise of the Welfare State and the disappearance of class conflict. Further, Appalachian exceptionalism is deeply rooted in our culture as a reflection of dominant culture images of improvement and change. Appalachia is viewed as a particularly troubled, particularly dependent social enclave (Shapiro 1978).

4 The substance of the work changed in other important ways. Lawyers not only invented corporation law that expressed and shaped the needs of business corporations (Gordon 1983), they organized litigation campaigns with long-range structural change in mind (McCurdy 1978). And they waged legislative campaigns to alter both law and courts to suit the market needs of clients (Freyer 1970).

5 The emerging stratification was not the effect of class divisions among clients alone, which, after all, existed prior to industrialization, but was strongly

influenced by the emergence of large institutions and organizations, the creation of specialized knowledge for corporate clients and, later, demands for specialized knowledge in the administrative law area (Hurst 1950; Halliday 1987).

6 Larson (1977) has argued that the ideological project of the professional elites was two-fold: first, control of market forces by creating a licensed monopoly; secondly, remaining a national political elite so that market control and status could be maintained. Part of the latter agenda was being able to speak broadly for society's interests, not a narrow class position, and this meant that the profession itself could not appear to be divided by class. Hence, differences within the profession were presented as differences in professionalization, not differences in the clients who were being served.

7 Research on law practice in large cities in our own time reveals a legal profession that is separated into distinct 'hemispheres' in which lawyers serve either clients who are organizations or clients who are individuals (Heinz and Laumann 1982). The implications of this transformation of the legal profession are profound, including class differences in access to lawyers (Carlin *et al.* 1966; Smigel 1969), commitment of far more legal resources to the representation of organizations than individuals (Miller and Sarat 1980–81; Heinz and Laumann 1982), and the disproportionate influence by lawyers acting on behalf of organizations over the evolution of competing interpretations of rights and even of fundamental ideas about responsibility in our society (Gordon 1984b).

8 There is little research on small town or rural lawyers. Landon (1990) offers the most comprehensive contemporary study comparing the attitudes, backgrounds and behaviour of small town and large city lawyers, concluding that the multiplex social relations in which small town practice is embedded yields a less differentiated profession. Landon's conclusion is ambiguous as to whether the lack of differentiation reflects the homogeneity of small towns or the dominance of a normative order that is resistent to conflict and difference created by divisions of class and culture that may be present. Research on changes in small town law practice in the nineteenth century is equally rare, notwithstanding the large number of retrospectives on circuit-riding written by contemporaries as the era passed. One on which I rely heavily is MacCorkle (1928). Calhoun (1965) is a classic study of the evolution of circuit-riding in Sumner County, Tennessee in the mid-nineteenth century. O'Brien's (1986) valuable study of rural North Carolina lawyers before and after the Civil War considers in far greater detail the impact of social change on the profession, but is less concerned with law practice or the influence of clients. In the latter respect, Konefsky and King (1982) is a valuable in-depth study of the antebellum rural law practice of Daniel Webster. Little work has been done on the impact of the growth of industry and population on typical law practices or on which lawyers, and how they represented particular clients.

9 The circuit included Greenbrier, Monroe and Fayette counties. Circuit riders in Fayette County came primarily from two locations – Lewisberg in Greenbrier County, and Charleston.

10 I have gathered information on the work of the circuit and on attorneys by employing, in part, quantitative methods. Three separate data sets are used in

this chapter. The first contains information about all circuit court civil cases appearing in the Fayette Circuit Court order books between 1872 and 1925. From this information, I have compiled statistical profiles of the cases in the circuit each year. For example, in 1872, 117 civil cases were initiated in the circuit court, seventy-five having to do generally with contractual obligations (including fifty-five actions in contract, debt, or 'notice' – a statutory action on a written instrument – and twenty suits in chancery arising from obligations secured by land), twenty private condemnation actions brought by the Chesapeake and Ohio Railway, three cases in tort, six appeals from decisions of petty justices and thirteen other miscellaneous cases. A second data set consists of a one-third sample of all of the tort cases in the first data set, about which I have gathered much more detailed information. The third data set consists of information about the lawyers who handled cases in two years, 1885 and 1910. The third data set was used extensively in this chapter and will be described in detail.

11 Calhoun mistakes the disappearance of circuit-riding as the population increased for a change in the nature of law practice. The functional equivalent of circuit-riding continues, of course, to this day, for many lawyers who specialize by type of court proceeding, by client or by cause of action maintain an inter-district practice.

12 I have assembled biographical material on Fayette lawyers from a number of sources. Several secondary works have been valuable in addition to MacCorkle (1928), including Peters and Carden (1926), Atkinson (1919) and Atkinson and Gibbons (1890). I have also used scattered archival sources and some newspapers. My chief primary source has been the circuit court records, which include not only orders and case files, but also reports of admissions to practice and memorial resolutions adopted by the bar on the death of an attorney that often contained a brief biography. Nevertheless, there remain many uncertainties. For many attorneys named in court records, there is little or no biographical material. Some of these attorneys resided in Fayette, but many may not have. Given the typical multi-county practice of circuit riders, attorneys appeared in many counties. In addition, there were a number of attorneys who never appeared in the records I examined. I learned of them through secondary sources, or because they held office in the county. A number of attorneys admitted to practice by the circuit court in Fayette are never mentioned again in the circuit court records, leaving questions about where they resided and if and where they practised law.

13 We know little about Gaines' practice. We know that his son, Joseph H. Gaines, became one of the first graduates of West Virginia University Law School and in 1887 began law practice in Fayetteville. The Gaines family retained its Washington connections, as evidenced by the fact that the son was appointed legal adviser to the US Shipping Board and later became US Attorney for the District of West Virginia. Imboden's father was one of the earliest promoters of investment in the New River area, journeying to London in the 1860s to interest English bankers in New River coal lands. In 1872, Imboden (the son) sold about 3000 acres of coal land in Fayette County to geologist David Ansted who had been commissioned by English investors to verify reports of coal and to act as their agent. Shortly afterwards, Ansted deeded this tract to the Gauley-

Kanawha Coal Company Ltd, which later became the Hawks Nest Coal Co., a company dissolved by the Federal District Court in the 1880s and reorganized as the Gauley Mtn. Coal Co. Imboden later established his law practice at Ansted, West Virginia, a village in Fayette County named after the English geologist. Brazie settled in Fayette County after a twenty-year career in the military, married and became an attorney. Of the three, he alone foreshadowed the career patterns of the next generation. Elected prosecuting attorney in 1871 and again in 1885, Brazie's practice was among the most successful in the county. More will be said about his practice presently.

14 The presence of substantial deposits of coal had been known since the eighteenth century, and two mines were established in the 1850s (Peters and Carden 1926: 250; Eavenson 1942). Although at mid-century coal was an increasingly vital commodity, as fuel for heating, for powering steam engines and later for the production of iron and steel, until 1873 a critical link between the southern West Virginia coalfields to a rapidly industrializing national economy was missing, namely transportation. In 1870, the owners of a small Virginia railroad determined to establish an alternative route west, through West Virginia, primarily for the purpose of creating a new trans-continental railroad. Speculation in coal lands began well before construction of the road. In the early 1870s, the railroad condemned land for its right of way, and soon after began construction, bringing the first wave of labourers to the region, most of them southern blacks. The line from Richmond to Huntington opened in 1873, and mines in Fayette began to produce and ship coal immediately (Peters and Carden 1926: 257–8; Bias 1979). Before 1880, the C&O did not emphasize coal transportation and production mounted slowly. The railroad's investors soon realized that the C&O's success could be ensured only by profits from the transportation of coal, and in the 1880s after the railroad was reorganized and redirected to transportation of coal, production in the county soared (Bias 1979: 173ff.).

15 Among the first attorneys to establish their practices, two partnerships were formed. W.D. Payne and A.W. Hamilton formed a partnership which was perhaps the first law partnership in the county, and one that survived until Payne left for Charleston. St Clair formed a partnership with E. Willis Wilson, another ambitious young attorney who left in 1884 to become governor. Partnerships are discussed at length below.

16 A year after his arrival, St Clair established a newspaper, the *Fayette Enterprise*. But, for St Clair, as well as for most of the other newly established Fayette attorneys, political office holding was the most important second component in his career. St Clair was elected prosecuting attorney for the county, held the office of state tax commissioner and, at the end of his career, chaired West Virginia's delegation to the Chicago Worlds Fair. Over the next two or three decades, the seven lawyers who arrived between 1870 and 1880 held an extraordinary number and range of public offices, including Mayor of Fayetteville, county prosecuting attorney, circuit court judge, criminal court judge, circuit clerk, state senator, state delegate, a number of appointed offices such as state penitentiary warden, state tax commissioner, and US District Attorney, and one was elected governor of the state. Of the seven attorneys who arrived before 1880, only two brothers, L.D. and J.H. Isbel held no offices at all that we know of.

17 Counting is a problem. In 1885, Fayette practices were still characterized by shifting co-counsel relationships typical of circuit-riding practitioners. Thus, the individual attorney was the basic unit around which practice was organized, but any count of cases handled by individual attorneys involves attributing many cases to more than one attorney's practice. Where partnerships were formed, counting is easy (e.g. St Clair and Wilson, St Clair and J. Gaines). Where regular patterns of co-counselling were established, with occasional exceptions, I have treated the cluster of attorneys as if they were partners (e.g. W.D. Payne and G. Imboden). Where an isolated co-counselship was involved, I have attributed the case to the practices of both attorneys, listing the attorneys separately (e.g. co-counsel by St. Clair and L.D. Isbel, or by H.W. Brazie and attorney from another county).

18 During the 1870s, the largest proportion of these cases, nearly 50 per cent, were contract or debt cases, while another 25 per cent involved title to land or debt secured by land. The third largest category of cases, about 15 per cent, involved appeals from cases heard by justices of the peace, usually debt cases or cases of minor property damage. This left about 10 per cent of the caseload of the circuit court comprised of a handful of matters involving torts, appointments of fiduciaries, special writs, citizenship petitions and other miscellaneous business.

19 Although representing the new enterprises in litigation and representing other litigants in actions against them constituted only a small proportion of the county's in-court legal business, it is likely that other legal work was done for these clients that never appeared in court. Some corporations, like the Chesapeake and Ohio Railway and the Gauley Mountain Coal Company Ltd, were incorporated outside of West Virginia, and for much of their corporate legal work they undoubtedly retained attorneys nearer their home offices, while employing local attorneys for in-court representation. Most of the coal companies that operated in the region were West Virginia corporations, as were the smaller railroads established to connect to trunk lines. For these corporations, and for most other businesses that were established as part of the growing county economy, Fayette or Charleston attorneys might perform such non-litigation activities as incorporation of the business, drafting by-laws or contracts, searching title to land, or negotiating settlements. How much office work and of which kinds was performed by Fayette attorneys may be indicated by the fact that there was only a small amount of litigation over corporate structures in the Fayette circuit court during the period of my study, 1872 to 1925. It may be that such work was performed increasingly by attorneys who specialized in corporate structure and management of corporate affairs who were located in Charleston or Wheeling, West Virginia. Even this inference does not rule out the possibility that Fayette attorneys performed many other types of non-litigation legal work.

20 Some have claimed this occurred in the last quarter of the nineteenth century as a result of representing corporations, entities which placed greater emphasis than other businesses on planning and on rational management (Hurst 1950). Others have claimed that in-office work was a later development specifically accompanying the growth of large manufacturing corporations and government regulation in the early twentieth century (Hobson 1984).

21 The Hawk's Nest coal company, established on the land purchased by English investors near Ansted (see note 13, above), was having hard times financially and was eventually dissolved in the federal district court. The debt actions in circuit courts are the only manifestation in local courts.

22 St Clair later owned other coal mines, indeed relatively successful ones.

23 Recall that the practices of Van Pelt and Isbel, who had the highest percentages of in-court business clients, did not survive into the second generation of attorneys, i.e. they were not among the most successful in the longer run.

24 Charleston lawyers appeared before the circuit court in Fayette primarily on behalf of businesses (see Table 2). One-third of all businesses in court in 1885 were represented by Charleston lawyers, and half of these Charleston lawyers were members of law firms.

25 In 1910, the county's industrial economy reached its peak growth rate, more than doubling the coal production in 1900, reaching a peak production of 9.4 million tons each year. The population had grown by 40 per cent in the same decade, the miners constituted over 70 per cent of the labour force. The largest town, Montgomery, still had fewer than 2000 residents, indicating little urbanization and virtually no development of a broader base for the county's economy. The previous two decades had witnessed a large number of mergers and buy-outs in the New River coalfield, corresponding to a period of widespread mergers in American business generally. A few giant coal companies emerged from this period, owning many mines, and controlled by investors or other corporate interests far from Fayette. The formation of large coal companies did not lead to the demise of small and middle-sized operators, however, and while the number of companies operating mines in Fayette County declined between 1900 and 1910, there remained many companies of all sizes.

26 Many of these transactions were associated with an on-going business but not conducted in a corporate or partnership name. A further reason for the predominance of firms in land cases was that land titles required highly specialized knowledge of West Virginia practice, and the senior members of the bar, those with the most experience in land titles, were in firms in 1910.

27 See note 7, above.

28 Similarly, in the 1880s and 1890s, St Clair was also heavily involved in representing coal companies and still represented mine and railroad employees and their employers in about equal proportions in accident litigation.

29 Stevens (1983) and others have provided a general picture based on a few east coast schools. But Fayette attorneys who attended law school graduated from places like West Virginia University School of Law and Washington and Lee Law School, about which we know far less. In general, the law school graduate probably received a broader education in law simply because of the availability of resources not available in a law office, and may have been less interested in the alternative careers in business or politics pursued by law office trained lawyers because of their investment in a formal professional education.

30 Williams (1972) describes the leading role of redeemer lawyers in drafting the 'lawyer's constitution' of 1872, which greatly complexified land title claims. This group of lawyers is described as having subsequently presided over the transfer of land titles to the representation of the new economic order.

31 But there is much evidence of a swing to the Republican Party in areas where owners did not have this form of influence and there were many ideological bases for the shift as well, including dissatisfaction with the economy during successive Democratic administrations and a belief that the Republican Party was the 'party of progress'. The close identification of the shift in the bases of political power with the changing base of the state economy produced a back-lash as well, in the form of hostility to blacks, and other immigrants who were said to vote Republican, and in the form of support for anti-industrial legisla-tion. The Democrats tried to exclude black voters (Williams 1976: ch. 1). More on the legislative alliance between agrarian and labour interests below.

32 For example, in 1903, a Fayette criminal court judge, W.R. Bennett, was forced to resign by impeachment proceedings. Recall campaigns were mounted from time to time against other lawyers serving in office.

33 It was not his technical skill or legal learning that won clients over, for, as MacCorkle (1928: 189) observed, 'as a young lawyer he had not given time to the study, nor had he time while he was in practice midst the turmoil of his life to study the principles of the law'. In this, St Clair was probably typical of his generation of lawyers.

34 It is likely that during his years in Montgomery, he became familiar with W.R. Bennett, the only attorney located in that town at the time, and may have read law under his supervision. Similarities between Osenton's and Bennett's prac-tices will be discussed below.

35 Office holding by attorneys in firms and attorneys who were solo practitioners followed different patterns. No fewer than seven solo practitioners were elec-ted to the office of state legislative delegate between 1870 and 1920, but no law firm lawyers held this position. Two law firm lawyers, St Clair and Osenton, held the position of state senator, but no solo practitioners were elected to this office. Other higher offices at the state and national level – governor, US Attorney, and member of a national or state commission – were held by law firm lawyers but contemporary sources do not report any solo practitioner in Fayette having held such an office. Both solo and law firm lawyers occupied county offices – prosecutor, circuit judge and county clerk.

36 In this pattern, we may be able to see an early illustration of the sharp differen-tiation between the organization of corporate practice and criminal trial prac-tice (Heinz and Laumann 1982; Galanter and Paley 1991).

37 It should be noted that partnership affiliations crossed party lines – Nuckolls was a Democrat and McPeak a Republican, though neither was particularly active in their respective parties. This may have been an asset in attracting clients. McPeak litigated a major case for Justus Collins in 1907.

38 *Cooper v. Pittsburgh Cent. & St.*, L.R.C., 24 W.Va 37 (1884).

39 A small number of early decisions by the Massachusetts Supreme Court had adopted common law legal principles that were uniquely applicable to cases brought by employees that could make winning such a suit particularly diffi-cult. With varying degrees of rigour, other state supreme courts were begin-ning to apply these principles (Schwartz 1981). Lower state courts were even more varied in their response (ibid.; Friedman and Ladinsky 1967).

40 As previously explained, only about 5 per cent, representing an overestimate, of all coal mining accidents were litigated.

41 Operators provided some medical care at minimal cost (Corbin 1981: 135), and it is possible that such care as was provided, together with the extreme loyalty of company doctors to their employers, dissuaded many miners who survived both the accident and the treatment from pursuing compensation for their losses in court.

42 This is to be compared with a far lower settlement rate of about 45 per cent for other kinds of cases brought against coal companies. However, the 60 per cent settlement rate is typical for *all* types of torts against all defendants, underscoring a general characteristic of the tort compensation system, namely the routinization of claims settlement to avoid the uncertainties of trial (cf. Friedman 1987).

43 It might be argued that the more favourable treatment of non-fatal cases was likely to have been attributable to the testimony and assistance in preparing a case that the eyewitness-client was able to offer.

44 In my 1987 article, I suggested that the establishment of this practice may have had an important effect, namely increasing significantly the rate of accident litigation.

45 Is it naive to assume that attorneys will turn away cases? The factors affecting a lawyer's decision to accept a client are many, even though the decision may become routinized with repetition, and include the pressures exerted by other clients, the availability of more lucrative business, and collegiality between attorneys. Here it is important that Osenton was a prominent and important member of the bar, not a marginal practitioner scratching for cases.

46 Significantly, the only extensive pro-labour litigation in West Virginia during this period was managed by this firm (Lunt 1979).

47 *Charleston Gazette*, 6 April 1896.

48 *State* v. *Peel Splint Coal Company*, 36 W.Va. 802 (1892).

49 While there were a number of indictments of Fayette coal companies for violations of safety laws between 1885 and 1896, I have found only twelve criminal indictments of coal companies between 1897 and the beginning of the First World War.

9 Feminist legal scholarship and women's gendered lives

Martha L.A. Fineman

Introduction

This chapter is about feminist legal scholarship and its relationship to practice in both academic and 'real' world contexts. It concerns the complex and difficult (perhaps impossible) goal of introducing feminist theory into legal discourses. In it I analyse existing and emerging themes that dominate contemporary feminist legal discourse which are of concern to me because of their limited usefulness in developing a theory of women's experience within law and legal institutions. On the broadest level, feminist legal thought seems unanchored, drifting between the extremes of 'grand theory', totalizing in its scope and ambitions,[1] and personal narratives, beginning and ending with the presentation of one individual's unique experience.[2] Both approaches, it seems to me, do little to further the discussion of feminist issues, typically obscuring more than they illuminate. Between these extremes, in that space between something so exclusively personal as to be beyond generalization or political content and something so general and abstract as to be removed from the everyday realities of women's lives, lies fertile ground for feminist methodology.

I should be clear that in my efforts to assess the future of feminist legal scholarship I am not concerned with merely including women in the legal profession, nor with ensuring that, once included, women in law share power and position equally with men. The presence of women in the profession, as teachers, practitioners, judges and so on, has not meant that feminist theory has followed. In fact, all too often in order to be successful, women have had to adopt assimilation as their intellectual strategy and equal treatment as their substantive principle.

Feminist theory (at least my version of it) is decidedly anti-assimilationist. It does not adopt the existing legal norms and merely assert equal entitlement for women to the benefits, with burdens distributed throughout our system of legal regulations. Rather, I believe feminist theory should question both the asserted universal 'ideal' of equality as it is espoused in dominant legal thought and the existing distributions of power and economic benefits that are held in place by the structure and nature of law. It should go beyond considerations of gender and address questions of value (what we deem worthwhile) and knowledge (how we construct truth).

I begin my consideration with a statement about the ideally antagonistic interaction of feminist theory with the law. While in my earlier work I have tried to locate my discussions between the extremes of grand theory and unique experience (Fineman 1991), here I have adopted a somewhat more abstract posture to assert that the central, pressing task of feminist theory is challenging existing law and legal doctrines through the articulation and establishment of a theory of difference. I hope the presentation has enough concrete examples so as to be assessable.

I have divided the theme of difference into two sections. The first section addresses the theoretical and political necessity of establishing the differences between men and women. Articulation of the extent and content of this manifestation of difference provides the basis for understanding that the law as it has developed has represented and reflected primarily male experiences and norms. In order to critique the law from a feminist perspective, it is essential to understand how women's perception and experiences may differ from men's and how such differences are relevant to the development and implementation of legal doctrines and theories.

The second theoretical consideration involved in developing the concept of difference is the realization that there are important differences among women. These differences are ones feminists must seek to overcome in both their practices and theorizing because the existence of these differences is, or can be, misused to divide women. The task of feminist theory in this regard must be to find ways of encouraging women to work together across differences so that the similar, shared gendered aspects of our lives do not continue to be invisible and unspoken in law.

In the final section of this chapter, I raise some questions about the notion of 'representation'. I am particularly interested in the conceptualization and articulation of the concept of representation as a legitimating criterion that affects our acceptance of an individual possessing an identified characteristic as 'typical' of a class or group possessing that same characteristic. Representation implies that an individual can typify a group or class merely because of a shared characteristic that serves the functions of both distinguishing him or her from the whole and unifying him or her with an identifiable sub-group. Representation in this regard is a totalizing concept, although it is initially premised on the recognition of difference. Representation is dependent upon the identification and priv-ileging of one characteristic from among the many any individual might possess. The identified characteristic is then representative of the individ-ual as well as of the group which the individual represents. So desig-nated, the characteristic publicly becomes the most politically, and perhaps socially, salient and significant of the features or traits that the individual possesses. The theme of representation as an ultimately total-izing concept, therefore, is integrally related to and an outgrowth of my earlier consideration of difference.

Feminist theory and law

Recently, there has been an increased interest in feminist scholarship. Law is an area relatively untouched by the post-modern currents that have washed through other disciplines, but now appears to be caught within tides of critical methodologies and conclusions that threaten its very roots. An examination of the concept of feminist legal theory reveals both a subject and a methodology that are still in the process of being born. There are no 'right' paths, clearly defined. The scholarship, how-ever, can be described as sharing the objective of raising questions about women's relationships to law and legal institutions.

Theory and practice

Given the newness of the inquiry, many 'practitioners' of feminist legal theory are more comfortable describing their work as an example of feminist 'methodology' rather than an exposition of 'theory'. This is cer-tainly true of my own work and I assert that method *is* theory in its most (and perhaps only) relevant form. In this chapter, therefore, I use the terms interchangeably, a concrete manifestation of my belief that method not only embodies, but transcends theory and is, for that reason, the more appropriate focus for critical examination. In this regard, my own ap-proach has been to reject the lure of abstraction and concentrate on diffi-cult, contextualized inquiry, trying to understand why there appears to be little relationship between women's social and material circumstances and the specific doctrinal representations of those circumstances (Fine-man 1983, 1991). My choice has been to 'do' feminist theory as an exercise in the concrete, both by focusing on specific areas of law and by using empirical information and stories of specific lives. This emphasis on spe-cifics is related to my understanding of the insights feminist methodology has produced for scholars.

The real distinction between feminist theory (legal and otherwise) and the more traditional varieties of legal theory is that feminist theory self-consciously focuses on method, adhering to a belief in the desirability of the concrete. Therefore, what makes any piece of work 'feminist', regardless of its location in a discipline and independent of the particular substantive issue it addresses, is a common methodology that mines the rich terrain of women's gendered lives. A belief in the emphasis on specifics and the focus on the concrete also has had rather honourable non-feminist adherents. For example, Robert Merton coined the term 'theory of the middle range' to describe work that mediated between 'stories' and 'grand' theory. He described such scholarship as being better than mere storytelling or mindless empiricism as well as superior to vague references to the relationships between ill-defined abstractions (Merton 1967: 68). Clifford Geertz (1973)[3] and James Boyd White (1985), among others, have noted that language or rhetoric itself is specific and tied to given material concerns. White has stated:

> Like law, rhetoric invents; and, like law, it invents out of something rather than out of nothing. It always starts in a particular culture and among particular people. There is always one speaker addressing others in a particular situation, about concerns that are real and important to somebody, and speaking a particular language. Rhetoric always takes place with given materials. One cannot idealize rhetoric and say, 'Here is how it should go on in general' . . . [R]hetoric is always specific to its material.
>
> (White 1985: 695)

Feminist scholarship, in non-law areas at least, has tended to focus on specifics.[4] Feminist legal scholarship, however, seems to be drifting towards abstract grand theory presentations. Carol Smart has recently warned that feminist legal theorists are in danger of creating in their writing the impression that it is possible to identify from among the various feminist legal theories that are in competition, one specific form of feminist jurisprudence that will represent the 'superior' (or true) version. She labels this totalizing tendency, evident in the work of many of the most well-known North American legal feminists, the construction of a 'scientific feminism', and she is explicitly critical of such grand theorizing (Smart 1989: 71; see also West 1988).[5]

While I agree with Smart's assertion, I am also aware that the tenure, hiring and promotion committees, in addition to the law reviews of elite American law schools, often reward grand rather than middle level theorists: the grander the feminist theory, the more it resembles and reflects mainstream scholarly format and content.[6] Grand theorizing represents the creation of a new form of positivism in a search for universal truths discoverable and ascertainable within the confines of the methodology of critical legal analysis. Middle range theory, by contrast, mediates between the material circumstances of women's lives and the grand realizations that law is gendered, that law is a manifestation of power, and that law works in ways that are often detrimental to women. These realizations have previously been hidden or ignored in considerations of those laws that regulate women's lives.[7] They are best exposed by referencing and emphasizing those lives.

Increasingly, I have become aware of the difficulty of trying to use middle range feminist methodology within the confines of legal theory. Not only is there the pull towards grand theory that operates to categorize less grand scholarship as 'non-theoretical', but I fear that feminist sensibilities become lost or absorbed into the morass of legal concepts and words. I have lost faith. Feminism, it seems, has not – and, perhaps, cannot – transform the law. Rather, the law, when it becomes the battleground, threatens to transform feminism. This is true I believe because of the obvious pull and power of the law as a 'dominant discourse' – one which is self-contained (though incomplete and imperfect), self-congratulatory (though not introspective nor self-reflective) and self-fulfilling (though not inevitable nor infallible).

The transformative potential of feminist thought is blunted because in order to even have a chance to be incorporated into and considered compatible with legal theory, feminist thought must adapt, even if it does not totally conform, to the words and concepts of legal discourse. Feminism may enter as the challenger, but the tools inevitably employed are those of the androphile master. And, the character of the tools determines to a large extent the shape and design of the resulting construction. It seems to me, therefore, that the task of feminists concerned with the law and legal institutions must be to create and explicate feminist methods and theories that explicitly challenge and compete with the existing totalizing nature of grand legal theory (Fineman and Thomadsen 1990). Such a feminist strategy would set its middle range theory in opposition to law – outside the formal legal categories.

Feminist methodologies

Because traditional legal scholarship has tended to ignore and seldom explicitly to recognize and address the existence of different 'realities' or perspectives, much of it proceeds upon the unstated assumption that the *status quo* is unbiased or neutral. This is the logical place for feminist analysis to begin – as presenting an explicit challenge to the notion of bias, as contrasted with the concepts of perspective and position. The insights based on the use of feminist methodology placed alongside existing legal theories, replete as they are with unstated assumptions based on incomplete information, can illustrate that what *is* is *not* neutral. What *is* is as 'biased' as that which challenges it, and what *is* is certainly no more 'correct' than that which challenges it, and there can be no refuge in the *status quo*.

Through the strategy of supplying information about women's lives, from the women who live those lives (information that has historically been missing from formal legal discourse), it is apparent that law has developed over time in the context of theories and institutions which are controlled by men and reflect their concerns.[8] Historically, law has been a 'public' arena and its focus has been on public concerns. Traditionally, women belonged to the 'private' recesses of society, in families, in relationships controlled and defined by men, in silence.

In my opinion, there are several characteristics that in various permutations and combinations provide the ingredients for feminist legal analyses that challenge existing legal theory and paradigms. First, feminist methodology should be critical. The critical stance should be gained from adopting an explicitly woman-focused perspective, a perspective informed by women's experiences. Feminist theory can *not* be 'gender-neutral' and will often be explicitly critical of that paradigm as having historically excluded women's perspectives from legal thought (Fineman 1983, 1986, 1988; Fineman and Opie 1987).

Recent changes in the family law context, for example, are illustrative of measures which deny the existence of women's gendered lives. In property reform, measures promoted in the late 1970s and early 1980s sought to impose 50:50 distribution schemes, consistent with the 'partnership' metaphor with which liberal legal feminists chose to characterize marriage. These legal feminists adopted this metaphor because of their uncritical acceptance of the necessity of establishing 'equality' through sameness of treatment (Fineman 1991). However, in light of the social and economic inequalities women experience in the market and in marriage and divorce, one-half of the accumulated marital assets is seldom sufficient to provide adequately for them and their children after divorce.[9] Similarly, within the context of child custody determinations, there has been a retreat from the historic preference accorded women under the 'tender years' doctrine – an evidentiary presumption under which women, unless 'unfit', received custody of their children – in favour of rule- and equality-based custody norms like joint custody (Fineman and Opie 1987; Fineman 1988). Such reforms reallocate power within marriage and at divorce, giving a non-primary caretaking parent the ability to bargain newly acquired equal custody rights for economic advantages in areas such as child support and property division.

'Gender-sensitive' feminism, however, should not be viewed as lacking legitimacy because of an inappropriate bias. Rather, it is premised on the need to expose and correct *existing* bias. 'Gender-sensitive' feminism seeks to correct the imbalance and unfairness in the legal system resulting from the implementation of perspectives excluding attention to the circumstances of women's gendered lives, even on issues that intimately affect those lives.

A second characteristic of feminist work is that it uses a methodology that critically evaluates not only outcomes but the fundamental concepts, values and assumptions embedded in legal thought (MacKinnon 1982: 239–40; see also Fineman and Opie 1987: 107). Results or outcomes in cases decided under existing legal doctrines are not irrelevant to this inquiry, but criticizing them is only a starting point. Too many legal scholars end their inquiry with a critique of results and recommendations for 'tinkering-type' reforms without considering how the very conceptual structure of legal thought condemns such reforms to merely replicating injustices (Fineman 1986). When, as is so often the case, the basic tenets of legal ideology are at odds with women's gendered lives, reforms based on those same tenets will do little more than the original rules to validate and accommodate women's experiences. The family law reforms noted above stand as harsh testimony to this phenomenon.

From this perspective, feminism is a political theory concerned with issues of power. It challenges the conceptual basis of the *status quo* by assessing the ways that power controls the production of values against which specific results and rules are measured. Law represents both a discourse and a process of power. Norms created by and enshrined in law are manifestations of power relationships. These norms are coercively applied and justified in part by the perception that they are 'neutral' and 'objective'. An appreciation of this fact has led many feminist scholars to focus on the legislative and political processes in the construction of law rather than just on what judges are doing (Fineman and Thomadsen 1990). It has also led many feminists to concentrate on social and cultural perceptions and manifestations of law and legality at least as much as on formal legal doctrinal developments.[10]

Implicit here is the belief that feminism must be grounded in a political, rather than a legal, method or theory. This, of course, is an implicit assertion about the interrelationship between law and social change that assumes the relative powerlessness of law to transform society. Those with a transformation agenda would do better to turn to other institutions, more directly and explicitly tied to the task of the social construction of ideology within our culture. Those of us who have seen the unpredictability of the law reform process and experienced the tentative and temporary nature of even the most hard fought changes, are left with the conclusion that law can reflect social change, even facilitate it, but can seldom if ever initiate or define and control it. No matter what the formal legal articulation, implementation of legal rules will track and reflect the dominant conceptualization and conclusions of the majority culture. Thus, while law can be used to highlight the social and political aspects it reflects, it is more a mirror than a catalyst when it comes to effecting enduring social change.[11]

An additional characteristic of feminist legal methodology is that it seeks to present alternatives to the existing order.[12] This may be, of course, a natural outgrowth of other characteristics of feminist legal thought, particularly when it is critical and political. I place it as separate, however, to highlight that an important goal of much of feminist work is to present oppositional values. Feminist scholarship is often at its core radically non-assimilationist, resistant to women's mere inclusion in dominant social institutions as the solution to the problems in women's gendered lives. In fact, the larger social value of feminist methodology may lie in its ability to make explicit oppositional stances *vis-à-vis* the existing culture. The task of the moment for feminism may be to transform society by challenging dominant values and defiantly not assimilating into the *status quo*. The point of making women's experiences and perspectives a central factor in developing social theory is to change 'things', not to merely change women's perspectives or positions *vis-à-vis* existing power relationships. To many feminist scholars, therefore, assimilation is failure, while opposition is essential for a feminist methodology applied to law.

It seems to me important to emphasize that feminist legal theory that effectively challenges existing paradigms will characteristically be *evolutionary* in nature. Feminist legal theory will not represent doctrine carved in stone, or even printed in statute books. Feminist methodology at its best generates contributions to what is recognized as a series of ongoing debates and discussions that take as a given that 'truth' changes over time as circumstances change and that gains and losses, along with wisdom recorded, are mutable parts of an evolving story. As feminist legal theory references women's lives, it must define and undertake the 'tasks of the moment'. The tasks of the future cannot yet be defined, and each piece of feminist legal scholarship is only one step in the long journey feminist legal scholars have begun.

Feminist legal thought contains explicit criticism as well as implicit disagreements about the wisdom of pragmatic uses of law, the effectiveness of law as an instrument of social change and, most broadly, the importance of law as a focus for feminist study. Some feminist scholarship reveals antagonism, even disagreement with other feminist works. Disagreements aside, however, it seems clear to me that feminist legal theory has lessons for all of society, not just for women or legal scholars. Ultimately, of course, it is the members of our audience that will judge the effectiveness and value of our individual and collective voices.

Feminist legal scholarship is critical, political and controversial; it is part of on-going debates and is concerned with methods and processes that comprise law. The very best feminist legal scholarship is about law in its broadest form, as a manifestation of power in society, and it recognizes there is no division between law and power. Law is not only found in courts and cases, and in legislatures and statutes, but in implementing institutions such as the professions of social work and law enforcement as well. Law is found in the discourses used in everyday life reflecting understandings about 'Law'. Law is evident in the beliefs and assumptions we hold about the world in which we live and in the norms and values we cherish.

Feminist methodology and issues of differences

Not surprisingly, much of feminist legal methodology considers the issue of 'differences'.[13] The examination of the questions concerning differences does not present an easy task and, in fact, much of the rather antagonistic interaction among legal feminists has been occasioned by disagreement about the very question of whether or not there are cognizable differences between men and women. The early, 'founding mother' members of a broadly defined legal feminist community would disagree with the exploration of such differences – the existence, or at least legal significance, of which they would typically deny (Williams 1982; see also McElroy 1982). More recently, there has been an emphasis on the recognition that there are differences *among* women, and the question arises as to how these differences should be considered and accommodated within feminist theory. While the types of questions and the political implications may change with the focus of inquiry, both areas of difference are important to explore and each will be addressed in this chapter.

Focusing on differences is particularly difficult for women trained in the law because any recognition of differences challenges dominant legal equality theory and accompanying paradigms, such as sameness of treatment.[14] The initial approach of early contemporary legal feminists trying to break the barriers of the profession was to develop the existing rhetoric of equality and seek laws that were gender-neutral. Equality in the market and in the home were their articulated goals and, as a strategy, early feminist theoreticians and lawyers minimized or denied the existence of significant differences between men and women (Williams 1982).

Recently, the representation of equality embodied in the 'gender neutrality' paradigm has undergone sustained attacks. Gender neutrality as a universal concept has been recognized as an objective that implicitly accepts the terms and structures of the *status quo*, the dominant culture. To argue that gender neutrality is or should be the goal of feminist reformist law is to further legitimate and validate the underlying institutions constructed and maintained in the context of patriarchy and dominance as neutral, objective and value-free. Such strategy assumes that existing institutions are themselves independent of the ideology which shaped them

– are not themselves embodiments of the values and norms from which they sprung. The problems with gender neutrality as the goal of feminist efforts is that all that is ultimately changed is the language used to describe untouched, unaltered structures which continue to function in and reflect the gendered culture and society in which they are located. Custody statutes may now refer to 'parent' rather than 'mother' or 'father', for example, but the gendered nature of caretaking within the institution of the family continues. All that is accomplished is that the still operative role divisions are obscured by lumping them together under the neutral term 'parenthood'.

It is the appreciation of such facts that led voices within the feminist legal community to articulate the liberating realization that anything we can legitimately call *feminist* legal theory must begin with a conceptual statement about differences because, by its very definition, *feminist* theory must be a gendered theory (Fineman 1983, 1991). In a world in which gender is more than semantics, feminist theory *cannot* be gender-neutral, nor can it have as its goal equality in the traditional, formal legal sense of that word. Feminist theory is woman-centred, gendered by its very nature because it takes as its raw building material women's experiences. Since women live gendered lives in our culture, any analysis that begins with their experiences *must* of necessity be gendered analysis.

Because differences between men and women have been the source of women's oppression, to recognize differences as the basis of feminist theory is to risk being dismissed as naive, advocating a position that will harm women.[15] Furthermore, advocates of differences have recently faced the possibility of being labelled 'essentialist' – advocating a belief in 'essential womanhood' that exists outside of language and society, insensitive to race, class and other differences among women (West 1988: 70).[16] The 'essentialist' label, in my opinion, is the more significant and, therefore, more difficult to address. I recognize that there are differences among women that may, in some instances, be more significant than the gendered life differences between men and women.[17] However, in the aggregate, I believe women's shared or collective gendered lives, both actual *and* potential, differ significantly from men's experiences in our society. These gendered experiences require adequate reflection and consideration in our legal system. These gendered experiences may be cultural and linguistic constructions, but they define the parameters of women's lives – even if only as constraints to resist and rail against. Incorporation of the gendered life experiences of women is not accomplished by rules conceived in and constrained by a system that refuses to recognize gender as a relevant perspective, imposing 'neutral' conclusions on women's circumstances. Furthermore, the recognition that there are differences among women should not defeat the attempt to 'gender' law.

The possibility that women's perspectives differ from men's is relevant because, given their perspectives and positions, women often make different observations, ask different questions, and consider different issues from similarly situated men. A difference in *perspective* is often reflected as a difference in *perception*. Women from different cultures, classes, races and economic circumstances might argue about conclusions, tactics and values, but they also understand a common gendered-life reference point that unites them in interest and urgency around certain shared cultural and social experiences. It follows, therefore, that legal theory uninformed or uninfluenced by these different perspectives and perceptions is incomplete, inequitable and indefensible.

The differences between women and men

The assertion of a gendered existence is contested in our legal culture (Kay 1985). Even when the premise is accepted, it generates issues concerning what significance should be attached to such a realization. My exploration of these issues has led me to reach some tentative (and perhaps totally idiosyncratic) conclusions about the types of gender differences that might be significant in legal theory.

I believe that many women experience society in significantly different ways from men and that there are certain real *or* potential experiences that can be described as constituting the basis for feminist development of a concept of a 'gendered life'. These experiences lead many women to develop a perspective that is qualitatively different from what is reflected in dominant legal ideology. This is *not* to assert that all women think alike or have identical experiences. My position is an experiential position not based on a belief in essential differences.[18]

Women's gendered existence is constituted by a variety of experiences – material, psychological, physical, social and cultural. Some of these experiences may be described as biologically based, while others seem more rooted in culture and custom. The actual *or* potential experiences of rape, sexual harassment, pornography and other sexualized violence women may suffer in our culture also shape individual experiences. So, too, the potential for reproductive events such as pregnancy, breast-feeding and abortion has an impact on women's constructions of their gendered lives. Further, some gendered experiences are events which are shared with men. For example, a life event such as ageing falls in this category. But, there is often a unique way in which these events are generally or typically lived or experienced by women as contrasted with men in our culture. Thus, while both men and women age, the implications of ageing from both a social and economic perspective for the genders are different (Zopf 1989: 109–111).

Human beings are products of their experiences. There is little or no independent 'essence' to an organism, distinct from its experiences. Of course, certain physical and chemical components or characteristics of human beings both provoke experiences and act as filters through which such experiences are processed. A person, therefore, is the sum of these physical attributes as acted upon, by and through his or her lived or social and cultural experiences. What we call knowledge, what we value and label virtuous, grows out of these experiences. The very questions we ask along with the answers we fashion express these experiences. It follows from this assertion of fundamental non-objectivity or non-essentialism that, if women collectively have different actual *and* potential experiences from men, they are likely to have different perspectives – different sets of values, beliefs and concerns as a group.

I am not asserting that *all* women react the same to, or draw identical conclusions about, issues in our society, nor do I suggest that all women inevitably experience any one or more of the gendered experiences. Uniformity in interpretation and experiences is not necessary to the concept of a gendered life. Individual experiences may differ from the socially constructed and defined nexus but they are still affected by them. Unadorned, uninterpreted events are not in and of themselves what one 'experiences'. Interpretation of events is an extremely significant aspect of this process of individual experiencing. Experiences do not take place in an interpretative vacuum, however, but are part of a social, interactive process. Culture and society provide the media through which experiences are understood.

Our twentieth-century society has universal, totalizing cultural representations of women and women's experiences.[19] Even those critical of such cultural constructions of essentialist images of women must recognize the force these images hold. None of us completely escapes the dominant images of the society within which we operate. Interpretation of events, the process whereby events are given meaning, is not an autonomistic, individualistic procedure. Social action and interaction as well as dominant cultural images, significantly contribute to individual interpretation of and reaction to events.

Further, I recognize that individual responses to similar experiences may differ as individual options (economic and otherwise) vary due to external circumstances such as race, social class and sexuality. In addition, previous experiences may filter new ones, having in some instances more significance than gender. To recognize that there may be differences *among* women does not, however, refute the observation that women's actual *and* potential shared experiences are female experiences, inescapably gendered within the larger culture and society.

Differences among women

A tendency has begun to emerge in feminist legal theory that calls into question the ability of any group of women to speak for others. Initially, this perspective developed in response to minority women's criticisms that feminism was a 'white middle-class, heterosexual movement'.[20] Such criticism has made many feminist theorists reluctant to speak unless they have first disclaimed the notion that they are representing anything other than their individual (and perhaps, their own class, race and sexual preference) perspective. Many feel they must rattle off a litany of differences among women at the beginning of any discussion about feminism, society and law – a distance placed between groups of women filled with assumptions about the nature of 'representation' and about the essential and determinative character of race, class and sexuality in defining an individual or group.

While few would (or could, legitimately) dispute that characteristics such as race, class and sexuality are significant to one's experiences, I think it is an error to proceed as though these markers of difference were the only relevant ones. Women may have other characteristics, or clusters of characteristics, that give them a basis for cooperation and empathy. Some of these characteristics may be even partially defined by our collective gendered experiences. For example, in addition to race, class and sexual preference, things like age, physical characteristics (including 'handicaps' *and* 'beauty' or lack thereof), religion, marital status, level of male identification (which is independent of both marital status and sexual preference – what Gerda Lerner refers to as 'the man in our head'),[21] birth order, motherhood, grandmotherhood, intelligence, rural or urban existence, responsiveness to change or ability to accept ambivalence in one's personal life or in society, sources of income (self, spouse and/or state), degree of poverty or wealth, substance dependency, among many others, shape how individual women experience the world.

Separating out a few differences and privileging them as conclusively and exclusively determinative, results in analyses that are impoverished reflections of the very complexity in women's gendered lives that feminists should seek to understand and address. Such separation also results in a privileging that fosters the creation of hierarchies of oppression and claims of exclusive or genuine oppression. This leads to a competition among oppressions that serves only the interests of the dominant social group. It is members of this group who benefit when the dominated groups fight among themselves at the margins of the powerful institutions in which room has condescendingly been made for only a few outsiders.

Privileging any one or two characteristics when there are so many that have the potential to inform and create women's gendered lives is simplistic and will impede an articulation of the problems women *share* in society. Hierarchies limit participation and exclude voices necessary for the creation of solutions relevant to a broad spectrum of women. It would be interesting to consider how some characteristics or clusters of characteristics may cancel out, compensate for or compete with others. For example, how do we place people with multiple sources of oppression in relation to others? If a white woman also is a welfare mother, can we consider her legitimately placed with the oppressors, the dominant groups in society, merely because she shares their skin colour? I would argue clearly not, but where, then, does she fit among the oppressed? Can she really be considered *always* more privileged merely because of her race in a ranking of oppressions? A hierarchy of oppression that always places race at the top would consider her so. I believe oppression to be much more complex. Exclusion leads to conflict and competition. This divisiveness and disunity impedes the aggregation of power necessary for women of all groups to push back the barriers that exclude most of us and our experiences.

The competition should not be with each other in the margins of society but with the powerful, dominant main structures whose visions and versions of 'reality' are reflected in society's institutions. The task, then, for feminists of all races, classes, characteristics and orientations, as well as for men who seek significant change in our social and cultural institutions, is to find common ground and work together. We must be aware of, learn about and be sensitive to the many differences among us, but they must not divide us to the point where we fight only among ourselves, each group urging its unifying source or sources of oppression as the only 'true' oppression and seeking to silence others. The task should be to bring the many manifestations of women's gendered lives into consideration, not to argue that only one version of gendered existence is entitled to be heard or addressed.

Questions of representation

The current obsession with differences among women has a negative impact in that it provides yet another means to decide who is given a voice and who is silenced. It also reveals a problem with the idea of 'representation'. It seems, at least initially, problematic that, by merely 'having' or embodying a characteristic or set of characteristics, an individual has the authority and legitimacy to represent definitively the positions of women sharing such characteristics. While characteristics may indicate experiences or potential experiences, they should not necessarily be considered in and of themselves sufficient or even necessary. It should not be the characteristics of the *speaker* which are most relevant, but the quality and nature of that which is *spoken*. We must focus on the discourse, the ideology. No groups, no persons, should be immune from a critical and political assessment of what they advocate.

I believe that in contemporary critical thought, there is a trend towards excessive reliance on the individual characteristics of the speaker to legitimate discourses. Such a focus erroneously furthers the idea that it is the individual who is the agent of social action and change and masks the manifold ways in which oppression takes place and is fostered within the structures and dominant ideologies of our society. It operates to place some discourse beyond criticism, accepted as authentic not because of the nature of the rhetoric but because of the nature of the individual speaker. In addition, from the most rudimentary political perspective, adhering to the notion that authority and authenticity are located exclusively in individuals who it is assumed are representative of the group with which they share a characteristic, risks conveying the impression that the token inclusions of such individuals are the 'solutions to the problems suffered by those groups'.

This version of representation was evident in the earlier, tokenistic moves to incorporate women into law. Social institutions and legal ideology remained unchanged in accommodating feminist concerns and criticisms by merely conceding a need for the presence of a woman or even several women. This manifestation of 'representation' equates one woman with another, making us fungible objectifications of the essential women. This type of representation in which an individual is deemed capable of acting for the whole, is totally insensitive to differences among women. It is also likely to act to eradicate the perception of differences between women and men because it is a characteristic-focused, not an experientially or ideologically focused, strategy.

Not surprisingly, a woman chosen to 'represent' her gender is often one whose interests and values coincide with those of the normalized male institutions that have deigned to include her. Furthermore, since ideology and structure are not relevant in the selection of the representative, the representative woman also often finds herself accommodating the behavioural norms and/or the professional standards of the institution, not challenging them, even if she initially had oppositional ideals.

This individualized concept of representation, initially adopted by feminists, has been refined and more finely tuned by adding other 'authenticating' characteristics to gender, such as sexuality or race. Perhaps these additions are concessions to the notion of experiences and ideology, but the basic tenet in this view of representation is still that an individual's possession of a characteristic or set of characteristics is both a necessary and a sufficient indication of 'authenticity'. The focus continues to be on the characteristics of the individual. The underlying assumption is circular: an individual having the designated characteristics can and does represent members of a community now defined by the characteristic.

This notion of representation is currently used simultaneously to legitimate and privilege some women's voices. The process of legitimation is accomplished within unchanged institutions which use the representative woman to deflect the radical potential of a discourse of gendered experience and ideology not capable of location within any individual woman. The notion of individual representation facilitates tokenism; furthermore, it can empower an individual woman at the same time that it renders her the most effective weapon to silence the interests and voices of the women she is supposed to represent. The individualized mode of representation operates to exclude discordant voices, to prompt the drawing of boundaries excluding potentially shared characteristics – placing barriers and dividing women on the basis of their difference. Individual-based representation minimizes or ignores the importance of characteristics that might operate in a more inclusive manner.

There are serious difficulties with a notion of representation that is dependent on the individual. It carries with it not only the potential for divisiveness but also the certainty of exclusion within the hypothetically available community of feminists. Moreover, individual-based representation allows tokenism to flourish and encourages continued resistance to radical potential for change through ideological and structural incorporation of feminism within institutions.

Conclusion

At this time, feminist concerns are, and probably will continue to be, the subject of discourses located outside of law. Law as a dominant rhetoric system has established concepts that limit and contain feminist criticisms. Feminist theory must develop free of the restraints imposed by legalized concepts of equality and neutrality or it will be defined by them. Law is too crude an instrument to be employed for the development of theory that is anchored in an appreciation of differences. Law can be and should be the *object* of feminist inquiry, but to position law and law reform as the *objective* of such theorizing is to risk having incompletely developed feminist innovations distorted and appropriated by the institutionalized and intractable dictates of the 'Law'.

In developing feminist legal theory outside of the formal and rhetorical constraints of Law, we will be free to confront the inevitable tensions that occur in undertaking any theoretical exploration, such as those that arise in any consideration of differences. Both as a political and theoretical endeavour, it makes sense for feminists to explore the differences between women and men so as to expose the exclusion of women's experience in law and to reveal the underlying power imbalance this represents. At the same time, focusing on the differences among women, while of theoretical significance, can and will be used politically to continue and justify exclusion. Feminism as a political, pragmatic methodology must be able to live with this type of tension which, given the current political arena, *cannot* be avoided at this time. There are different urgencies in considering differences that are dependent upon the contexts in which feminists must operate. Theory that arises from the circumstances in which women find themselves is destined to contain paradoxes.

Acknowledgement

An earlier version of this chapter appeared in 1990 as 'Challenging law, establishing differences: The future of feminist legal scholarship', *Florida Law Review*, 42:25.

Notes

1 Grand theory, for example, while valued in academic institutions, relies on abstractions not grounded in women's gendered life experience. Its application to women's lives, therefore, is usually irrelevant and occasionally detrimental.
2 The use of personal narratives is more difficult to critique and involves an intersection of two other themes in contemporary feminist legal discourse – the fetish about difference which impedes the development of viable theoretical underpinnings for strategies designed to advance the material circumstance of women and, what I term in this chapter, the 'ideal of representation' (see pp. 243–4).
3 In regard to grand anthropological concepts, Geertz states:

> If anthropological interpretation is constructing a reading of what happens, then to divorce it from what happens – from what, in this time or that place, specific people say, what they do, what is done to them, from the whole vast business of the world – is to divorce it from its applications and render it vacant. A good interpretation of anything – a poem, a person, a history, a ritual, an institution, a society – takes us into the heart of that of which it is the interpretation.
>
> (Geertz 1973: 18)

4 Grand theory represents a belief that there is a 'truth' to be discovered, a rejection of the idea that theory is constantly in process. Weedon (1987: 11) defines her feminist project as 'hold[ing] on to feminism as a politics' and 'mobiliz[ing] theory in order to develop strategies for change on behalf of feminist interests', rather than coming up with a 'definitive feminist theory – a totalizing theory of patriarchy'.
5 But see Olsen (1989) for a defence of grand theorizing in the context of reviewing the work of Catherine MacKinnon.
6 Academia has created a set of relatively well-defined scholarly norms which, to a certain extent, feminist theory seeks to expose and ultimately erode. For example, see Flax (1987).
7 For example, family law regulates intimacy, employment law regulates market activity and constitutional law regulates sexuality and reproduction.
8 Women were often excluded from the practice of Law. See *Bradwell* v. *Illinois*.
9 The content of the term 'gendered lives' is developed on pp. 234–5 (see Weitzman 1986). I have criticized these 'rule equality' reforms elsewhere (see Fineman 1983, 1986).

10 Two excellent illustrations of works that analyse the interplay between formal legal developments and their application in practice are Girdner (1986) and McCann (1985).

11 No-fault divorce reform is a good example of this phenomenon. Prior to the passage of these statutes, it was widely accepted practice for lawyers to coun-sel clients on how to 'create' grounds for divorce (see Friedman, 1973). Thus, rather than representing any legal 'change', no-fault reforms actually mirrored existing practice.

12 See West (1988) for a discussion of the construction of present goals in light of a feminist utopian vision.

13 For a collection of essays organized around the differences theme, see *Wiscon-sin Women's Law Journal*, 3, 1987, a compilation of the papers presented at the 1986 *Feminism and Legal Theory Conference* held in Madison, Wisconsin.

14 For a cogent discussion of the historic and contemporary conflict between strict or 'rule' equality and special treatment, or 'result equality', in British feminist thought, see Brophy and Smart (1985) and Fineman (1991: ch. IV).

15 It should be noted, briefly, that equal treatment has also contributed to the oppression of women, particularly poor, non-professional women.

16 For a critique of essentialism, see Harris (1990).

17 Rae (1981: 35) identifies three different types of equalities: 'simple', 'segmental' and 'bloc'. Simple equality is a comparison between individuals, while seg-mental equality is individual equality within a sub-class. By contrast, bloc equality is a comparison between groups or blocs and thus asks for something very different from simple or individual equality. Liberal feminist reform efforts tend to adopt a simple or individual model of equality. As a result, such efforts generally fail to assess seriously the implications of the total failure of women to achieve bloc equality with men in the economic sphere. Moreover, the differences between women present complicated segmental equality questions.

18 'Essentialist' also implies that the categories of gender, race or class are inher-ently meaningful and, therefore, universal. Even if one is 'sensitive' to race and class, one may still be essentialist by, for example, espousing a belief in an 'essence of woman' which cuts across all differences.

19 One example is that of motherhood. The construction of women as mothers affects all women's experiences in the culture whether they individually choose to be mothers or not. As women, they are at least partially identified and defined as mothers, potential mothers, or past mothers.

20 For recent critiques of mainstream feminist legal theory for its white middle-class, heterosexual bias, see Spelman (1988), Harris (1990) and Kline (1989).

21 This phrase comes from conversations between Gerda Lerner and the author. For a general discussion of male hegemony over that which is defined socially as 'universal truth', see Lerner (1986: 217–29).

10 Para-legals and prefiguration: working in black townships towards a post-apartheid South Africa

Wilfried Schärf

Introduction

South Africa is in a phase of rapid change. Despite continuous States of Emergency since June 1986, liberatory expectations are running high following the release of Nelson Mandela after twenty-seven years in prison. This chapter looks at the role para-legals play in prefiguring a post-apartheid order. Two competing visions are expressed in extra-parliamentary anti-apartheid politics as to how the transition to a post-apartheid society should occur. The one vision, a more populist approach which is encapsulated in slogans such as 'liberation now, education later', argues for all energies to be devoted to the overthrow of the racist regime, and once this has been achieved, work can begin on constructing the new order. The other approach, fostered by organizations that subscribe to the tenets of the Freedom Charter, argues that one cannot simply rely on people to act intuitively in terms of a new set of values after liberation. The new order, or elements of it, have to be carefully nurtured and sustained before transformation, so that the democratic culture can withstand pressures towards autocracy and militarism.

Some para-legals are paid para-professionals, working in advice offices in or near the black townships, but most of them are black political anti-apartheid activists living in the black townships. They have been mandated by their organizations to undergo short volunteer training courses. The role of para-legals to date has been largely one of assisting victims of apartheid in one way or another. In many instances, this help enables the victims to defend themselves against an autocratic state and simultaneously strengthens community cohesion. This process contains elements of prefiguration, but as the prospects of transition to a post-apartheid society become more of a short- to medium-term reality rather than a long-term one, so the phase of protest politics gradually has to shift into a phase of 'delivering the goods', for want of a better term. As the process of constitution-making draws nearer, the extra-parliamentary liberation movement is calling for broad-based discussion and consultation among the disenfranchised majority about the content of the new constitution. Para-legals are thus expected to broaden their knowledge, and no longer only to help township residents understand what their rights are and how to realize them through struggle – and one arena of struggle is the court – but they are also expected to begin asking residents what rights and structures they want in the future. Para-legals are encouraged to contribute towards the shaping of a rights culture, something that has been absent during the apartheid era.

One of the hallmarks of apartheid has been separate sets of courts for African and 'white' South Africans established as early as 1927 by means of the Native Administration Act. Native Commissioner's Courts were set up to hear intra-African cases in terms of an ossified version of African customary law (Bennett 1985: 47; Hund and van der Merwe 1986: 30–34). They were not under the authority of the Ministry of Justice but the ministry responsible for the administration of Africans (euphemistically called Cooperation and Development), and were perceived by the African population as corrupt, repressive and unjust (Hoexter Commission 1983: 29: Hund and Kotu-Rammopo 1983: 179; South African Institute of Race Relations 1984: 775). On the recommendation of the Hoexter Commission, Native Commissioner's Courts were abolished in 1986 (South African Institute of Race Relations 1986: 338).

The courts set up for Africans were so unpopular and so hostile that Africans throughout the country set up their own dispute-settling structures that have little or nothing to do with the state. There is a wide range of these structures existing in almost all African townships (Hund and Kotu-Rammopo 1983; Motshekga 1987; Burman and Schärf 1990; Schärf and Ngcokoto 1990; Seekings 1990). These informal structures have contributed to the shaping of particular notions of order. But they do not challenge the state formally with a view to pronouncements or enforcements of particular rights. Mostly, these informal structures only regulate the political economy of their area of jurisdiction on a micro scale. And whether the people who are elected to or volunteer for or impose themselves on these structures can be called 'para-legals' is also debatable. Although they play an active role in ordering the community in which they reside, they are not active in the formal legal arena. But their tribunals could possibly be 'elevated' into formal recognition as happened in Mozambique (Isaacman and Isaacman 1982) and in Zimbabwe (Ladley 1982, 1991).

The relationship of para-legals to these informal structures and to the formal legal profession is a complex one. Para-legals are either volunteers or paid workers who have little or no formal legal training. They help individuals and community groups understand the law and their rights, and they refer them to agencies or lawyers who will help people realize those rights. Particularly since the heightened challenge to apartheid from late 1984 onwards, many para-legals have also been political activists in the townships, serving as structures close to political organizations and setting up advice offices throughout the country. Most of these activists are familiar with the informal structures, and many were also at some stage members of people's courts during their brief appearance between early 1985 and June 1986 (Motshekga 1987; Schärf 1989b; Schärf and Ngcokoto, 1990; Seekings 1990).

Para-legals and access to justice

The South African legal system is a schizophrenic one. 'Whites' are by and large ruled in a way which lives up to the ideal of separation of powers and the independence of the judiciary. There is a legal aid system with limited funds, which is in theory available to all who qualify on a means test. Africans, on the other hand, have been ruled by a straitjacket of laws and regulations which, as the apartheid regime became more sophisticated in its mechanisms of control, shifted decision making away from the courts and towards administrators. Administrative discretion was largely kept out of reach of the courts except on limited grounds (Corder 1989). Any agitation for basic human rights was criminalized and the legal aid system excluded eligibility in cases of 'political' crimes and prior convictions.[1] Effectively, Africans had negligible access to legal representation (Slabbert 1981; McQuoid-Mason 1990). The state's attempt to criminalize the leadership of the African National Congress (ANC) in the early 1950s resulted in British anti-apartheid organizations setting up funds to finance their legal representation and support the families.

Legal representation for Africans came to be seen by the state as equivalent to supporting a banned organization and it has retained that stigma to date. The number of organizations abroad that fund legal support to victims of apartheid has grown considerably, and so has the range of groups that support such victims. All of them are funded from abroad and all are painted by the state as being somehow subversive. The state has made numerous attempts to discredit such organizations and prevent the funds from reaching their recipients, particularly the South African Council of Churches, the main channel of funding.[2]

A small network of non-state advice offices existed before the early 1980s dealing largely with influx control matters (Gross 1976). In terms of the Blacks (Urban Areas) Consolidation Act of 1945, the cornerstone of influx control laws, no African was allowed to be in a 'white' town or in the black township attached to the town for more than seventy-two hours unless he or she had the requisite stamp of authorization in his or her passport, which had to be carried on the person at all times. All other rights – the right to work, the right to occupy a house or hostel, the right to send children to school, the right to be treated in hospitals, receive disability or any other welfare benefit – depended on their entitlement to be in the black township adjacent to the white area. The Legal Resources Centre, a public interest group funded from abroad and set up in the mid-1970s to take on test cases, developed a para-legal training programme for advice office staff. The few advice offices that existed were usually set up by service organizations who had little or no township constituency – they were only user groups. Township individuals were usually taken on as interpreters or as low-echelon para-legals. The activists, if not in detention, were underground. There was very little para-legal activity in the townships, although service organizations in the 'white' areas gave what support they could under the circumstances. The advice offices were located mainly in the townships close to the cities, and frequently only in 'coloured' areas. There were very few advice offices in African townships.

It was really only after mid-1983 that advice offices mushroomed, after the United Democratic Front (UDF) was launched. This was an extra-parliamentary alliance of several hundred organizations comprising civic associations, youth groups, women's organizations, trade unions, sports bodies, service organizations and professional bodies of lawyers, teachers, social workers, psychologists and others. They all supported the principles of the Freedom Charter, which advocates a non-racial democratic unitary state. It was the largest internal opposition group to the apartheid regime. It had similar aims to the then banned and exiled ANC, but uses different methods of achieving those aims (Swilling 1988: 90–113). The ban on the ANC was lifted on 2 February 1990. Between 1983 and 1990, para-legals who worked at the township advice offices were usually also political activists and supporters of the UDF. UDF structures gradually also set up civic associations in opposition to the state, and from 1985 onwards formed street committees, block and area committees and people's courts (Bapela 1987). They launched rent and consumer boycotts to pressure capital to put pressure on the state and to highlight the unrepresentativeness of dummy black local authorities which 'owned' the vast majority of all township houses. These campaigns took place under the slogan of making the townships ungovernable by the state. The UDF tried to show the township residents that they could run their own lives. Several townships became no-go areas to the police (Swilling 1988). But until 1986, the advice offices in the African townships were by and large still not very widespread or prominent.

The 1986 emergency changes the need for para-legals

By June 1986, the first State of Emergency had not succeeded in diminishing protest activity to the degree desired by the state and it introduced a draconian new set of powers. All forms of 'alternative civic and adjudicative structures' were outlawed, as with people's courts, and the media were barred from reporting on certain aspects of these structures by a regulation introduced in December (Proc. R224, 1986 Reg. I (i), (vii), 11 December 1986). It became illegal to encourage people to participate in rent and consumer boycotts. A massive wave of detention put most of the remaining leadership behind bars. Official figures and human rights monitoring groups' statistics differ on the scale of detention, the latter estimating that just over 27 000 people were detained during 1986. Official figures cite 3857 detainees fewer (South African Institute of Race Relations 1986: 823–4).

'Security' force action in combating 'unrest' was also out of bounds to the media. The indemnity of the 'security' forces against prosecution or litigation arising out of any acts committed in good faith in combating 'unrest' was underlined. Their powers of entry, search and seizure were extended. The schools were put under virtual perpetual siege (Molobi 1988; Hyslop 1988). The security forces were given the power to deny people access to certain areas, which meant that no casual observer or researcher could gain access to townships if the 'security' forces wished to exclude him or her. The only 'news' that could be reported about the 'security' force actions in 'unrest' situations was 'news' that formed part of court cases (Emergency Regulations and Proclamation R109, 1986).

Although the streets still remained an arena of struggle, it served little purpose if that struggle could not be publicized by the media. The courts became the only medium through which abuses of power by the 'security' forces could still be publicized legally. Lawyers could still get access to townships if they were involved in a case, and there was some protection of the documents through attorney–client privilege (although this was frequently violated). There was also a growing realization in Cape Town that previous political protest had been focused on the cities where there is relatively easier access to support and service organizations. The townships outside rural 'white' towns had also been swept along in nationwide protest, yet there were very few support structures in place and residents were exceptionally vulnerable.

The Legal Education Action Project (LEAP)

As part of an initiative to research and document abuses of power, activist lawyers based at the University of Cape Town decided to launch a new project, which became LEAP. The aim was three-fold. The first aim was to train mandated members from organizations in the rural townships as para-legals so that they could in turn teach community members about their rights and, where appropriate, call on city-based progressive lawyers to use the appropriate means to defend communities against pervasive abuses by 'security' forces. The rural areas were chosen because residents in the townships outside the 'white' towns were particularly vulnerable. Residents by and large did not know that they had any rights, and if they did there was little hope of enforcing them, as they were indigent, the police were often obstructive to charges being laid against themselves, the only sources of help were through the telephone exchanges controlled by the 'white' town, frequently tapped by the security police, and the media seldom focused on them.

Secondly, LEAP workers wanted to connect the rural townships to the network of city-based service organizations that provide forms of assistance other than legal. These included detainee support networks, court monitors, sympathetic doctors and psychologists, pressure groups that monitor and publicize political causes, rape crisis organizations, organizations that specialize in assisting communities subjected to or threatened by forced removals or relocations, and sympathetic journalists. One of the distressing realities of the rural areas is that local lawyers are not usually prepared to take on 'political' cases (which is what abuse of power is considered to be) for fear of jeopardizing their paying clientele and because they usually believe that version of events as told by the 'security' forces.

The third aim was to gather research data that could not be collected by the use of conventional research methods. The first workshop for delegates from twenty-eight towns had to take place in the safety of the city, as the rural areas were ruled by an iron fist by this stage and all participants would have been detained under the Emergency Regulations (Regulation 2) as constituting a threat to public safety. The para-legals were only trained in matters that were considered most important at the time: protecting themselves and members of their communities against abuses of the 'security' forces. In keeping with the theory of counter-insurgency warfare adopted in May 1986 (Swilling 1988), and following examples set in Malaya and other counter-insurgency conflicts, the state recruited and trained several thousand Africans as special constables to enable the state to withdraw the army from the townships. These special constables, pejoratively called 'kitskonstabels' (instant constables), were recruited from a sector of the population that was barely literate, trained for six weeks, armed with shotguns, and let loose on the township populations. There are no clear patterns of deployment; where resistance to the state was relatively low, local residents were deployed locally as kitskonstabels (e.g. Aberdeen and Oudtshoorn). But where resistance was high (e.g. Hofmeyr), no locals came forward for recruitment, and outsiders were deployed. But in most cases, they had to be housed for their own protection apart from the residents they policed.

The first batch of kitskonstabels were deployed in October 1986 and successive new waves of recruits followed during 1987. Abuses soon became a very common occurrence in all townships in which they operated. Despite wide-ranging emergency powers and extensive indemnities against prosecutions, their actions were often so patently malicious that legal actions could be sustained against them. Most of these actions fit into a pattern of intimidating the residents into submissive fear. In the only serious analysis of the kitskonstabels, Fine summarized their activities as follows:

> From the first week of their deployment, serious abuses of power by kitskonstabels occurred in many areas, ranging from fatal shootings, arbitrary assaults and sexual abuse, to verbal abuse and harassment. What was notable about these abuses was that they were widespread and systematic, not confined to one or two areas or to a handful of 'bad eggs' or undisciplined policemen. The abuses took place both on and off duty, and the offenders were either in or out of uniform.
>
> (Fine 1989: 58)

Not long after the first wave of abuses, monitoring groups, city-based lawyers and the media began receiving calls for help by residents in some of the affected townships.

The first group of para-legals started reporting abuses and calling for help soon after they had returned to their respective townships. Two trainees returning from the workshops were detained and interrogated about the workshop, and all the pamphlets which explained citizen rights in accessible language were confiscated by the security police. They considered training African township residents to monitor the actions of the 'security' forces and to teach others to be aware of their rights as a new form of subversion and said so frequently to the para-legals and the lawyers who accompanied the LEAP team to assess and assist in cases.

Whenever a call for help was received from a rural township, some representatives of the LEAP team travelled to the affected township in a camper truck equipped with a portable word-processor, camera and all the paraphernalia necessary for taking statements, photographs and gathering evidence. Before they departed, the members obtained a brief from a firm of attorneys to act on their behalf. This made access to the township easier and provided some protection to the team. The camper truck was necessary first because the Cape Province is roughly 1200 by 800 km (larger than France) and many of the affected townships were in the Eastern Cape, where the long tradition of opposition to apartheid had provoked the harshest responses from the 'security' forces. Secondly, the LEAP team consists of African and 'white' men and women (in equal proportions) and most hotels and camping sites in the area were reserved for 'whites' only.

When the LEAP team arrived in any township, it had to be careful to park the truck in a spot that was considered 'neutral', because any association with one particular individual or family inevitably elicited recrimination and harassment from the police. Even parking outside the only African-owned shop in the township of Eluxolweni (outside Hofmeyr, 868 km from Cape Town) was not neutral enough in the eyes of the police, so they took out their displeasure on the owner. There were also occasions on which the security police tried to pry advance notice of LEAP visits out of members of township organizations. They would detain such activists (a term that commonly describes office-bearers of organizations involved in extra-parliamentary politics) and threaten them with some harm to themselves or their families were they not to become police informers and alert the police of the route the LEAP team was travelling and the estimated time of arrival. 'Accidents' and disappearances coupled with mysterious murders were still very fresh in the memory of everybody in that region following the murder of some of the most prominent anti-apartheid leaders, Matthew Goniwe and his colleagues (Bekker 1986). Another accident involving a car containing some civil rights campaigners, in which Brian Bishop and Molly Blackburn were killed, remains not above suspicion (South African Catholic Bishops' Conference 1987). Recent revelations about police death squads now confirm what everyone to the left of the government had suspected all along at the time (Pauw 1991).

Once the para-legal who had summoned the LEAP team was able to consult with the team, discussions were held about the most appropriate strategy. The LEAP team, composed of a lawyer, a community worker and four para-legal fieldworkers, are conscious of the benefits and shortcomings of legal remedies in the African township context. Its working principles do not accord primacy to legal interventions, but see the court as one of many tactical arenas to achieve the best results for a particular community. The emphasis is on choosing a strategy that benefits the largest number of affected people. South African law does not permit class actions and thus restraining interdicts protecting whole communities from abuse of power are fairly difficult to obtain.

In the climate of mid- to late 1987, communities usually first needed restraining interdicts against the police before they could even contemplate any other strategy. For if they succeeded in getting the interdict, they at least had a 'handle' on the police, for any violation of the interdict could result in contempt of court charges. But there were several difficulties in obtaining the interdicts. In order to succeed in getting an urgent interdict, communities had to prove that they had exhausted all other remedies first, such as laying charges against the police. Small towns like Hofmeyr, to use that example again – where there are an estimated 200–300 'whites' living in the town and *c*.3500 Africans living in the township 2 km outside the town – are not big enough for a full-time prosecutor. In this particular case, the officer commanding the twelve kitskonstabels was also the prosecutor who was supposed to charge them for abuses of power. Township residents experienced considerable difficulty having the police accept charges against themselves, and some anomalous situations developed, as appears from the affidavits, where the policeman at the charge-office desk was the very person against whom township youths wished to lay charges for torturing them (Fine 1989: 67).

But this was one area in which the help the community was receiving from 'outside' lawyers put the police on the defensive, and procedural irregularities like failing to note a charge diminished in time. It did not prevent the police from laying charges against township residents who came to lay a charge against them, but they soon discovered that such charges had to be well-founded.

Once the process of obtaining an interdict was in motion, the role of the township-based para-legals became vital. They had been trained to teach residents their rights, and they had received training in gathering the relevant evidence in the event of the inevitable further abuses. They were encouraged to pass on these skills to as many other members of the township as possible. This was a time when the Emergency Regulations forbade all meetings except bona fide church or sporting meetings (Swilling 1988). They could not get five or six people together to run a workshop without facing the danger of being raided by the kitskonstabels and detained without trial. Yet, despite these constraints, teaching did take place and it contributed substantially to the revival of morale in townships where residents felt crushed and vulnerable. The 1986 wave of detentions had been extremely severe. First, second- and third-tier leadership had been removed in most of the rural townships and the sense of hopelessness was counteracted only by the hope of some relief coming from the outside world.

Whenever the LEAP team returned to such townships on follow-up, the need to inform as many residents as possible and to spread skills as broadly as was practical was emphasized. In such a way, the cases became the focal concern around which organizational revival could commence. The para-legal activists, drawn from progressive organizations, were accountable to the communities in which they lived. When their cases reached the court and the judge ordered the police to desist from unlawful action, the lawyers arguing the case were encouraged to notify the media about it and so the struggles of small-town communites were put 'on the map' and a greater understanding of their circumstances was achieved through the media coverage.

The need for regular training of para-legals was recognized, and in August 1987 the Advice Office Training Committee – comprising representatives from the Legal Resources Centre, Cape Town, the Advice Office Forum (an alliance of Cape Town based advice offices), the Black SASH (a women's organization with predominantly 'white' middle-class members) and LEAP – was set up in Cape Town and began a regular programme of regionally located workshops in safe locations. Not only was the first group of para-legals given refresher courses and taught new skills, but more activists were drawn in from organizations in other towns. By the end of 1987, 160 para-legals from forty-three townships in the rural areas had been to at least one training course. But the political situation was such that it was still impossible to get advice offices running. Most para-legals remained volunteers who worked from within their organizations. Depending on the needs, new areas of the law were covered, and more booklets were devised. By October 1989, twenty-one booklets on a range of issues and skills had been compiled and sixty-two towns in the Cape Province had sent activists for training sessions as para-legals. The workshops varied in length from one to three days and two intensive residential month-long training programmes were held for fifty-five rural para-legals. The skills they learned extended to include issues such as how to combat forced removals of squatter communities, rape crisis type counselling, counselling of detainees and their families and, more recently, setting up detainee or hunger-striking support groups, doing basic monitoring of defiance campaign actions and marshalling peaceful marches, and advising how to liaise with the media. They were taught in a participatory style and encouraged in turn to use that style in transmitting those skills. So, for instance, when the police burst into a house, beat up the youths, search the women, confiscate or seize literature, etc., such scenes were role-played and the applicable legal position explained.

Throughout late 1987 and the whole of 1988, there was a spate of interdicts and civil claims against the various arms of the 'security' forces in many rural towns, the kitskonstabels being the main target of the cases as they were the most blatant abusers of power. That did not mean that the security police did not indulge in unlawful activities; they were merely more careful to ensure that there were too few witnesses to sustain a case. In the case of torture, a fairly common abuse (Foster *et al.* 1987), they became more astute in using methods that left fewer obvious traces of their actions (Hope 1989: 13–17; Vercammen 1989: 2–3).

Although the intervention of lawyers and para-legals by no means resulted in an immediate cessation of abuses of power, and in fact their intervention sometimes resulted in angry backlashes by the police against whom the interdicts were being sought, there was a gradual diminution of the more blatant abuses. Awareness spread in the affected townships that there were limits to police powers, and that there were agencies prepared to help when abuses did occur. The awareness in turn produced better evidence, which forced the police themselves to prosecute some exceptional cases. So, when three policemen arrested Andile Kobe, an activist, outside George (some 450 km from Cape Town), assaulted him and drove him to the police station where he was further assaulted, kicked and trampled to death, before being driven to the beach where his body was dumped in such a way as to make it look as if he had been robbed and murdered by civilians, the police version of events would have been sustained had the residents of that township not realized the need to gather as much evidence as possible immediately, and notify lawyers, the media and para-legal support groups the following day. The community in which Kobe lived had been the target of a long bitter battle to forcibly relocate it. A range of para-legal groups, each focusing on particular subjects (such as forced removals or court monitoring), had worked in that community prior to Kobe's killing. The media glare was too strong to allow the matter to be brushed over and the three policemen were tried while para-legals monitored the court proceedings and ensured regular media coverage. The policemen were convicted of murder.

Para-legals became extremely important links between community organizations and city-based progressive lawyers. This link was initially routed through the LEAP team, which consistently promoted the value and role of para-legals in the profession. But once a working relationship between the lawyers and certain community organizations had been established, there was no longer a need for LEAP to play the bridging role in every single case. It concentrated on finding new ways of helping para-legals and their organizations defend themselves. One such was the use of an attitudinal survey of particular townships in court proceedings. In Bhongolethu (outside Oudtshoorn, 500 km from Cape Town), the police alleged in their responding affidavits that an interdict sought against the kitskonstabels was an unfounded and malicious slur by communist-inspired organizations to discredit the police and was part of the total onslaught against the state. They alleged that the kitskonstabels were very popular in the community and that Bhongolethu Civic Association enjoyed negligible voluntary support in the community. When South African judges are faced with a choice between conflicting assertions of fact as uttered by senior 'white' police officers and poor African township residents, then there is little doubt which side will be favoured. Consultations between the Bhongolethu Civil Association, their para-legals, LEAP and the lawyers resulted in a decision to conduct an attitudinal survey. Researchers were recruited in Cape Town and trained for the survey. It

was conducted by using sound social science methods, as sound as possible under the circumstances, so that it would withstand the inevitable
challenge on methodological grounds were it to contradict the view of the
police. It revealed an overwhelming support for the Civic Association,
distrust and fear for the kitskonstabels, and minimal support for them
(Hofmeyr and Shefer 1987: 5–17). The survey strengthened support for
the Civic Association when the results were publicized extensively in the
township.

In another case, an attitudinal survey was requested by lawyers who
had heard of the Bhongolethu case. This was a desperate move on the
part of the lawyers because their 25 clients had already been found guilty
of murder on the basis of the controversial common purpose doctrine
(Davis 1990). In Paballelo, a township outside Upington (894 km from
Cape Town), there had been an incident in which a municipal policeman
had been killed, and although forensic evidence proved that only one
person killed him, 25 people were found guilty of murder on the basis of
common purpose. If no extenuating circumstances are found, the death
penalty is obligatory in South African law. Should extenuating circumstance be found to have existed, the judge has discretion in sentencing.
Judges usually say they take the feelings of the community into account
in sentencing. In our polarized society, judges seldom, however, have a
realistic idea of the feelings of black communities and usually impute
their own view. To provide this particular judge with some social scientific pointers on community opinion, a survey was commissioned. The
LEAP team, working with the staff at the Institute of Criminology at the
University of Cape Town, trained a number of additional volunteers in
interviewing skills. The survey was conducted and the findings were
submitted in court, but the judge rejected them as irrelevant and sentenced 14 of the 25 people to death (Institute of Criminology 1989).

Building advice office structures

From mid-1988 onwards, the political climate within South Africa was
influenced by the preparations for Namibian independence, the ending of
the war in Angola and the need for the South African government to be
perceived as an honest, trustworthy party in the process. By that stage,
international pressure and sanctions had made the apartheid regime a lot
more vulnerable to international opinion. On the domestic front, the
counter-insurgency warfare approach had quelled open conflict on the
streets and had silenced restricted organizations but had not been able to
deliver the improvement of township conditions that would supposedly
satisfy the aspirations of the majority of the population (Boraine 1988).

By this stage, there had been a year of legal and para-legal interventions since LEAP's founding and that had raised the awareness in rural

areas of how useful para-legal and other para-professional service groups can be. It had also brought home to city-based resource and service organizations the need for the possibility of working in rural areas. Even funding bodies, mostly from abroad, started channelling funds into rural structures. In that context, advice offices gradually began emerging, and the para-legal volunteers who had already been trained by the Advice Office Training Committee were often employed either full-time or part-time as workers in these offices. Their close links with civic organizations, which are mostly affiliates of the UDF, provided channels of account-ability to their communities. Advice offices were thus part of an ethos which stressed a democratic working style and a furtherance of broad community interests as well as dealing with particular individual problems. Thus when patterns of individual problems emerged, a collective response of those affected (with community support) was advocated. The amount of legal and other work that was generated by advice offices created the preconditions for LEAP-type structures to be set up in various regions, a process currently in progress. At the end of 1989, there were around 40 advice offices in the rural towns and townships of the Cape Province.

Not all of these offices are run by political organizations or civics. Some are run by service organizations that are part of the Mass Democratic Movement, and employ one or more Xhosa-speaking para-legals and have a number of para-legal volunteers who occasionally perform interpreting, organizing and other functions. Often, these volunteers are drawn into being part of the advice office initiative after receiving some legal or other assistance through the office. There are many peripheral roles that volunteers can perform, not least simply being alert to abuse.

An example of how such vigilance achieved a remarkable turn-around in morale comes from the classic influx-control village Lwandle (only 35 km from Cape Town). Designed as single-sex hostels for roughly 2000 migrant men in a horseshoe-shaped set of barracks with a beer hall as its only formal recreational outlet, the conditions are spartan to say the least, with 40 men to a double-bunked 'bungalow'. The absurdity of expecting 2000 men to remain unaccompanied in those circumstances was patent even before influx control was lifted in 1986 and wives, girlfriends and small children were brought in to live with their men and fathers. There are currently around 8000 Africans living there in appalling conditions. Police have customarily 'controlled' Lwandle through a process of targeted raids directed mainly at merchants of illegal goods – liquor (sold without a licence) and drugs (mainly marijuana). Some of the raids resulted in prosecutions, but others led to 'confiscation' of the merchandise only, and yet others ended in an informal 'fine' paid directly to the policeman without a receipt. Less frequently, there are raids during which suspected stolen property, such as bicycles, watches, transistor radios and the like, are 'confiscated'. The residents accepted this as part of the 'cost of living', a reality that they stoically suffered.

When an intensive research project into the power relations between the community and the police began documenting these raids, and assistance from the nearest advice office was summoned, the whole picture began to change. Four inhabitants were trained as co-researchers and interpreters. They were taught what the police are allowed to do and what procedures have to be followed during these 'raids'. They in turn taught other bungalow dwellers what to look out for during the raids. They accumulated all the necessary evidence immediately after the raids and contacted the advice office. Sympathetic lawyers launched spoliation orders and caught the police totally off guard. Before the matter reached court, the embarrassed police asked the residents to come and collect their 'confiscated' goods.

The co-researchers became volunteers at the advice office and started forming a youth organization. Soon the women attempted to organize collective day-care for their children, and their organizing efforts had the effect of diluting the extremely patriarchal monopoly of internal power which the men's committee wielded. The co-researchers have enrolled in a community-worker training course at a local university. The whole community is currently intensely involved in a case against a large employer. The flurry of activity around the case is resulting in support groups being formed by residents for the affected dismissed workers, and a sense of being able to take control over parts of their lives is becoming apparent, something which residents say has never existed before (Sloth-Nielsen *et al.* 1991). Members of Lwandle structures have become part of the steering committee of the advice office which is situated in the 'white' town. A strategic alliance is being formed which transcends class, race and language barriers in taking on the state.

Para-legals in the defiance campaign and working towards a new constitution

The Mass Democratic Movement (MDM), as it became known, took the place of the severely restricted UDF after February 1988 (Regulation 6A, Proclamation R96, 1987). But the MDM was a wider alliance of anti-apartheid organizations than the UDF had been. In 1989, the MDM launched an extensive defiance campaign against apartheid laws. Detainees went on hunger strike, 'whites'-only beaches were invaded, consumer boycotts targeted companies with union-bashing records, black people presented themselves for treatment at 'whites'-only hospitals and rode on 'whites'-only buses, the UDF and other organizations declared themselves unrestricted, mass marches were held and even some lawyers held illegal picket demonstrations.

The emphasis was on peaceful protest. It was essential to retain organizational discipline in order to retain the moral high ground. But in the face of brutal police intervention, that is not an easy task. Extensive preparations were made and all existing para-legals and hundreds of volunteers were recruited and trained in marshalling skills. The National Association of Democratic Lawyers (NADEL) took part in all these activities to provide credible witnesses should the need arise, to negotiate with the police if necessary, to handle any cases that arose from mass arrests, and to help ensure that the actions were non-violent. NADEL is a non-racial unofficial lawyers' organization which is an affiliate of the UDF. It came into being during the political upheavals in 1986 under the name of the Democratic Lawyers' Organization and changed to NADEL in early 1986. Under NADEL's co-ordination, law students and para-legals monitored literally hundreds of events throughout the country and contributed to their success.

The purpose of the defiance campaign was to pressure the government to commence negotiating with the organizations of the majority. The government had commissioned the Law Commission to explore the feasibility of a Bill of Rights and the ANC had begun circulating constitutional proposals for a non-racial democratic society. It requested the guidelines to be extensively and widely discussed. Para-legals were expected, as members of progressive organizations, to be part of and even co-ordinate some of the discussions at the grass-roots level. Under the auspices of NADEL, workshops were held throughout the country to hear from delegates of popular organizations their requests or demands for the future constitution.

Para-legals and the profession

The structure of the South African legal profession is modelled on the English system. Formal legal services only reach a miniscule proportion of the population as most cannot afford them. The legal aid system is hopelessly inadequate (Slabbert 1981; McQuoid-Mason 1990). Progressive lawyers are being faced with a challenge. If they are not only making money out of the struggle through foreign-funded political cases but want truly to be part of the democratizing process, then they will have to rethink the structure of the profession. It took on its current structure during or after the Industrial Revolution when lawyers became the articulators of the interests of the ruling classes and their representatives (van Zyl Smit 1983). If South African progressive lawyers want to become the representatives of the interests of the majority and be the articulators of their interests, then they should think of democratizing the profession. The Freedom Charter, the document on which the aspirations of the majority are based, asserts that 'the courts shall be representatives of all the people' (Suttner and Cronin 1986: 263). What that means at this stage is not too clear. But with the long history of informal courts in African townships (Burman 1983; Hund and Kotu-Rammopo 1983; Schärf 1989a) and the culture they have established for dispute settlement and problem solving, they may serve as a foundation on which post-apartheid models of democratization can be built. This history of informal adjudication and mediation may provide the groundswell for a de-professionalization in the post-apartheid society. It may well be that people's courts or elements of people's courts could become formalized and operated by lay people. Representation by practitioners may be barred in such structures, as is currently the case in the formal small claims courts. It is quite possible that today's para-legals, activists that they mostly are, could become the incumbents of these structures in the future.

And it is these para-legals who may in the future also begin pressuring the profession to loosen its definitions to allow them in. LEAP has developed a specialized training course for para-legals employed in conventional law firms. It has trained six to date and at the same time canvassed all progressive law firms in the Cape about the role that para-legals can perform. It has succeeded in placing some of them and in getting para-legals permitted to become members of NADEL. But, in general, the profession, notoriously slow to take on new ideas, has shown very little interest in changing its ways. There have been some rare exceptions where advice offices and law firms have developed a remarkable team approach to taking on the state. An example of this team approach is contained in the Lwandle case mentioned above. The attorneys that took this case have also represented cases emerging from the related advice offices in Stellenbosch and Grabouw (wine and fruit-growing areas), where labour abuses and manipulation of voter support in a black township by 'dad's army' was exposed and fought (Louw 1988: 15). What is special about this team effort is that the advice office staff, the client communities and the attorneys usually decide together what strategy to adopt to deal with any particular problem. They do not necessarily prioritize legal interventions, and if there is a danger that the community might relinquish power to the lawyers and mobilizing opportunities lost through the case, then other forms of maintaining community interest are devised in the form of parallel campaigns or the creation of support groups for those most affected by the case.

It may well be, however, that some pointers and pressures in the direction of democratizing the justice system could come from Namibia, which has recently moved from independence and adopted a new constitution and formed a new government. LEAP has been part of training para-legals of the Namibian Legal Assistance Centre at their invitation and has discovered a sympathy towards a system of justice in which informal structures will constitute the lower rungs of the adjudicative hierarchy. How these structures develop and how the para-legals relate to the professionals remains to be seen. It is a time for bold moves, and necessity may well press the new administration in that direction.

Conclusion

The patterns I have described do not characterize the *modus operandi* of all forms of para-legal activity in South Africa. A heterogeneous society such as this is likely to manifest a plurality of para-legal visions. The particular examples I have sketched are the products of an aspirant democratic culture. The Cape Province, in slight contrast to others in South Africa, is developing a political culture in which professionals and para-professionals do more than pay mere lip-service to the notion of account-ability to the client communities. This implies that decision making involves the affected communities, that campaigns, court cases or other forms of intervention exploit the potential for community participation and its consequent empowerment, and that the skilling process is spread as broadly as possible.

The drawbacks of this approach are that decision making, report-backs and discussions are slower and more cumbersome processes than if a group of professionals zapped in and out and performed all the impressive tricks. There is a tendency in some other regions for advice offices to reflect a little of this latter approach. The immediate media and other gains may be achieved in far more dramatic style but the processes of grassroots skills-shaping, building of political organizations, community empowerment and, indeed, prefiguring a democratic culture are passed by in the process. The praxis of para-legal intervention emerging from the Cape is that a beneficial dual role can be sustained by having political activists or, at the very least, politically versed para-legals, contributing simultaneously to selected and targeted legal interventions and to political empowerment and mobilization.

This particular vision of para-legals is closely related to the ongoing process of transition to a post-apartheid society. Only the idealists are able to sustain the expectation that liberation or 'freedom' will be achieved within a matter of months, and even should that happen, some miraculous consciousness gear-change will occur which rids this society of racism, sexism and the other many legacies of the past. The vision of transition taking hold in the Cape is one in which, whether one is defend-ing oneself against an interventionist state or involved in a defiance cam-paign, or shaping a new constitution and adjudicative infrastructure, one does so in terms of principles and processes that are already prefiguring the society one is hoping to build. In this process, para-legals, as one of many other categories of actors, have an important role to play. Not only because they help to take on the state, but they can also, if organized, take on the legal profession and who knows, perhaps even constitute the state in a democratic future.

Acknowledgements

This chapter was intended to be the product of a collective writing effort. Time pressures and the heady hurtle towards people's power meant that the key contributors, the members of the LEAP team, were in the field too often during the latter half of 1989 to make that possible. I have therefore undertaken to distil the contents of many discussions and experiences into this chapter. I would like also to thank my colleague Julia Sloth-Nielsen at Llwandle for stimulating the development of many new ideas.

Notes

1 That is the *de facto* position revealed by my interviews with several Cape Town attorneys in December 1989.
2 During 1988, the state attempted to introduce the Promotion of Orderly Internal Politics Bill (B50–88 (GA)), which evoked such an enormous local and international outcry that it was scrapped, and instead managed to pass the Disclosure of Foreign Funding Act 1989, which constituted a considerable stepdown.
3 See Proclamation R109 (1986) in terms of the Public Safety Act No. 3 of 1953, Regulations 3, 5, 7, 9–12 and 16.

11 The contradictions of radical law practice

Stuart Scheingold

Introduction

There is a grouping of British lawyers who, as legal professionals with socialist values, feel something of a common bond and are uneasy with the conventional professional culture. I refer to them as radical lawyers, although that somewhat controversial term[1] is less important than what these lawyers stand for: a commitment to the 'have-nots' in society; a tendency to think in terms of the class struggle; membership in, or sympathy with, the Haldane Society of Socialist Lawyers; and acceptance of a relatively modest level of income from a practice financed largely by legal aid – or through redistribution of the returns of lucrative commercial law to 'social conscience' work (Scheingold 1988: 123).

In this chapter, I explore efforts by these lawyers to develop a radical alternative to conventional professionalism. How do the conventional legal culture and the circumstances of legal practice constrain the emerging radical identity? I argue that the conventional professional culture poses three obstacles to the development of radical legal practice.[2] In the first place, lawyers are encouraged to think of the law as a vital and beneficent social institution. Secondly, they learn that their responsibility to the law is best served by their neutrality as legal advocates. Finally, lawyers are distanced from radical alternatives by the social organization and homogeneity of the legal profession. As we shall see, radical lawyers are both resistant to, and influenced by, these occlusive forces of conventional professionalism.

Conventional professionalism

There is something of a paradox at the positivist core of English professional ideology. Lawyers, by the very nature of the arguments that they develop on behalf of client interests, are fully aware of the socially constructed character of the law. None the less, it is part of the lawyers' credo to treat these constructions as social facts with lives of their own – including doctrines, principles, statutes and the rule of law itself. Lawyers, as Maureen Cain (1976: 230) puts it, 'face the endemic occupational tension of being sophisticated professional thing-makers required also to treat their constructs as self-existent'.

The law is seen as a timeless but evolving social institution that is the cornerstone of organized social life, particularly in complex and heterogeneous modern societies. At the heart of the matter is the law's procedural structure, which guarantees such cherished values as predictability, impartiality, fairness, justice and common sense. Part and parcel of the law's beneficence is its capacity for reform. British lawyers would, then, agree with Alexander Bickel, who argued that the law is not just another value but the 'irreducible value . . . the principle institution through which society can assert its values' (Bickel 1975: 5).

The standards of conventional advocacy that have been developed are rooted in ostensibly contradictory principles of conduct. Lawyers are called upon to combine neutrality with partisanship. On the one hand, the lawyer is to maintain a studied detachment from the client's broader circumstances; on the other, the lawyer is supposed to mount a highly partisan defence of the clients' legal interests – a defence which may include 'deception, obfuscation, or delay', and worse (Simon 1978: 36).

While appearing contradictory to the lay observer, this neutrality towards both the most odious and meritorious of clients is to the legal mind a precondition of effective partisan advocacy and is, therefore, essential to the law. These principles of conventional legal ethics run counter to everyday moral standards – amounting to 'an explicit refusal [by the lawyer] to be bound by personal and social norms which he considers binding on others' (Simon 1978: 30). Departures from lay morality serve the law, whose beneficent whole is greater than the sum of its suspect tactical parts. More specifically, the procedural standards which are at the heart of the legal enterprise have 'an inherent value or legitimacy . . . which makes it possible for a lawyer to justify specific actions without reference to the consequences they are likely to promote' (ibid.: 38).

The ideological structure of conventional professionalism is nurtured among *barristers* by a legal 'community in which thought processes and understandings about law can be shared transituationally in time and place, even between members who do not often come into contact with each other' (Cain 1976: 246). The starting point of this community, according to Cain, has been the 'relative *homogeneity* of background' found among members of the bar, which has become very much the province of the middle classes. Educational background in the public schools and at Oxbridge is particularly important, not because it leads to overt class favouritism, but because it nurtures 'an increasing identity of legal comprehension' (ibid.: 236).[3] Moreover, the small number of working-class barristers that have recently been called to the bar seem more likely to conform to, than to alter, this ethos (Abel 1988a: 76). This class bias is likely to continue given the substantial costs of legal training, including an unpaid period of apprenticeship and the likelihood of a very modest income in the early years of practice (Abel 1985a: 13–17).

The social and cognitive common ground is reinforced by the pressures of apprenticeship – securing pupillage and, subsequently, tenancy as a junior, in one of a relatively small and largely static pool of chambers (Gifford 1986: 67–9). Once established in chambers, one's career is dependent on reputation which is, in turn, dependent on both skill, as defined by the ideological community, and by the 'intimate conviviality' of the bar community, which is geographically and socially 'closed and close' (Cain 1976: 241). Clients are directed towards those who fit in – cognitively and socially – as, ultimately, are the rewards of 'taking silk' and ascending to the bench. The upshot of this is a bar community which is both coherent and 'necessarily out of touch' in so far as 'the unity of legal thought is contingent upon being impervious to the various day to day rationalities of other sections of the population' (ibid.).

Beyond the confines of the bar, radical lawyers are considerably less constrained. Although *solicitors* are also culturally homogeneous, they are spared the geographical and social community of the Inns of Court (Zander 1980: 23). And the costs of training and the rewards of the early years of practice tend to be more favourable to solicitors (Zander 1980: 27–37, 76–8; cf. Abel 1988a: 171–3). There is, also, more leeway for solicitors to strike out on their own. Should they join an established firm, radical solicitors seem to have a somewhat better chance of finding a practice dedicated to radical or progressive values. As for lawyers working outside conventional practice for publicly funded *law centres* and for *social action groups*, they are still more free of the constraints of conventional professionalism – although they are, of course, hemmed in by the organization's sense of identity and social purpose and, in some cases, by its scepticism about lawyers.

Radical advocacy

Radical practitioners have several grounds for resisting the traditional norms of legal practice. Their radical project is, however, inhibited by the residual force of conventional professionalism and by the contradictions of radical legal practice. The result is that British radical lawyers define themselves, at least in the first instance, primarily in a reactive way. They balk, in an *ad hoc* fashion, at some of the constraints imposed by conventional ideological and social structures, while accepting others. Accordingly, there has been little movement towards a radical alternative to conventional professionalism.

Radical lawyers in England are clearly uneasy with conventional restrictions on representation, because they distance lawyers from the broader interests of their clients. As a barrister well known for his criminal and public order work put it:

> [A] sense of commitment. Now that is something that when I started I was told I shouldn't have. I don't mean professional commitment – being good at your job – because obviously they would say: professionals are good at the job. But what they frowned upon, and I was told in very clear terms, is don't identify with the client. Don't get involved with the client, or more particularly, don't get involved with the client's cause if there is one (19 January 1987).

As he sees things, effective lawyering entails a close involvement with clients and with their causes:

> And I always found that extraordinary advice, because it seemed to me that the only way I personally was going to operate is if I could get inside the shell of the person I was representing, or the issue that he or she represented, and understood what was going on . . . In order to have an understanding, I had to have, not only a sense of justice, but a sense of experience . . . I had to get inside it (19 January 1987).

And a minority barrister said roughly the same thing:

> When the rules say you can't associate with your client: you don't feel; you are just there to defend. You are a barrister . . . That's the rules of etiquette – that you fight fearlessly but you don't get involved. Now that's wrong because if there's a riot in Bristol or in Brixton between black people and the police, now, if you don't get involved, you are a *straight* barrister . . . You can't effectively defend them, because you must appreciate the issues and you must be bold enough. As far as my profession will allow me, I associate with them (24 December 1986).

Accordingly, radical lawyers reject the cab rank rule 'whereby a barrister is expected to accept any brief regardless of his or her commitment to the client' (Cooper 1986: 175). They are equally uneasy with the prohibition against 'touting', which, among other things, has been interpreted to prohibit lawyers representing individual clients who are jointly charged from discussing common issues (ibid.). The former limitation is objectionable because it seeks to prevent lawyers from consistent identification with causes. The latter is problematic because it inhibits concerted activity, which is a step towards making a private grievance into a public issue – or, more generally, towards a proactive search for meaningful cases.

While virtually all radical lawyers are inclined to resist some of the constraints of conventional professionalism, the limits on overt politicization of legal grievances seem to be accepted as legitimate. Consider the position of an experienced solicitor working primarily on criminal and public order cases:

> Our objectives are legal; our clients' objectives are political and per-
> sonal. However, our legal objectives are informed by our political
> consciences, and our commitment to achieving those legal objectives
> is fired by our own political commitment and our own conscious-
> ness. But I never make the mistake myself of seeing the court as
> either a substitute for political debate, discussion and activity, or as a
> forum for political speech making. It isn't, and if you try to use it as
> such, in my experience your clients do themselves a disservice. We
> are about winning, we are about securing acquittals, and in the pro-
> cess we subject the prosecution's case to the most rigorous scrutiny
> . . . [while] seeking to draw lessons from the prosecution's failures
> and inadequacies and from the abuses of the process that have oc-
> curred – lessons that have a broader impact than simply the case at
> hand . . . But in terms of having any specific political objectives in
> taking on a case, no . . . What is our political objective in this case?
> That just doesn't arise (18 December 1986).

This effort to combine political sensitivity with a conventional sense of professional responsibility is typical of the radical lawyers whom I interviewed.

Given such a perspective, it follows that command of conventional legal skills would be a salient criterion for peer evaluation of effective radical lawyering. Of course, good legal training and political commitment are not necessarily mutually exclusive. But a preoccupation with the tools of the trade obviously makes it more difficult to transcend the standards of conventional advocacy.

Consider, for example, the substantial controversy over the law centres, some of which have been particularly politically active and self-conscious. On the surface, the controversy is over legal skills and client service. One dedicated solicitor, who had worked for a law centre in the past, put it this way:

> They have no hierarchy, and that has very serious consequences in
> professional terms, because there is nobody there to make sure the

work is being done properly. And in a firm like this I can now, having had many years of experience, go around and make sure junior staff are doing their work properly, look in their files. And if they are not doing it properly I will make damn sure that they are doing it properly. There is nobody playing that role in law centres, and the quality of the work they do is absolutely awful. It's amateurish (29 January 1987).

But this preoccupation with legal skills also conceals legitimate differences over the nature of radical practice. To what extent, in the first place, is a preoccupation with legal skills compatible with a view of legal process which acknowledges – indeed denounces – its structural biases? Why, in other words, would this politically compromised process be responsive to the skilled lawyer?

Beyond this theoretical point, there is a practical reason why law centres are less concerned with legal skills. Consider the following comment about affirmative action in the hiring of blacks by a law centre's solicitor.

There was a feeling of giving someone a sort of leg up – you know, an opportunity to do work in this kind of area. And I think we now see that really the issue is quite different. It's about whether it would ever be possible for a centre to meet the concerns of that section of the community without black staff (25 February 1987).

Because at least some law centres are concerned about the political dimensions of community legal work as well as traditional client service, their hiring priorities are bound to be different. In short, conflicts over skill levels should not be taken at face value, but should be seen as indicators of ideological tension among radical lawyers.

Thus British radical lawyers seem to adopt a moderately proactive conception of lawyering. This conception seems to share significant common ground with the ambivalent outreach which Simon characterizes as 'liberal advocacy'.[4] The responsibilities of conventional lawyering are supposed to begin when a manifest conflict develops within society *and* a client comes to the lawyer for assistance. The premise of liberal lawyering is that clients have interests as well as disputes, and that the lawyer's task is 'to determine whether a client's interests are best served by relatively individual and adversarial or by relatively collective and conciliatory practice' (Simon 1984: 474–5).

While liberal advocacy of the sort that British radicals seem to be embracing departs sharply from conventional premises, it is also a kind of unstable half-way house between conventional and radical conceptions of advocacy. The essential problem with liberal professionalism is that there is no entirely satisfactory way to determine when the client's interests are best served by collective or individual representation on the one hand,

and by adversarial or conciliatory representation on the other. So long as the client is perceived as the 'only authoritative judge of his interests' – and this is at the core of the liberal credo – lawyers must figure out ways to engage clients (Simon 1984: 482–3). As a result, the lawyers have tended to make controversial assumptions about client interests. While lawyers may be able to engender solidarity out of a variety of initially indeterminate issues, it must be acknowledged that the lawyers are in effect shaping rather than registering client interests.

Of course, the broader objective of radical advocacy is to promote an interactive relationship between political objectives and legal rights. Writing of the women's movement in the USA, and in particular the expansion of a woman's right to self-defence, Elizabeth Schneider claims:

> [T]he legal formulation grew out of political analysis, but it also pushed the political analysis forward. The particular legal focus on sex-bias in the law of self-defense, and on the absence of a women's perspective in the courtroom, clarified feminist analysis of the problems facing women who kill. It explained why both women defendants and lawyers representing them were more likely to claim insanity or impaired mental state rather than assert self-defense. The legal formulation thus moved the political work to a different level. It raised the political question of what a woman's perspective might be and what equal treatment would look like. It focused further legal work on the disparate hurdles that limited women defendants' choice . . . and laid the foundation for political and legal strategies to remedy the problems.
>
> (Schneider 1986: 609)

Such overt politicization of the lawyer–client relationship[5] is well beyond what virtually any British radical lawyer would be prepared to accept. Consider the response of a radical solicitor to the grass-roots defence committees that are ordinarily associated with police violence litigation:

> It is not our role to organize people to participate in the defence. Our role is to be there, to be available . . . but it is not to . . . be the community's leadership. We seek to identify that leadership, encourage it, work with it, but beyond that we don't go . . . We know what ought to go into the first leaflet after the disturbance . . . But we wouldn't write or distribute it . . . We never go before a call . . . It's never necessary to arrange a call, because the call invariably comes. And if it doesn't, one is best not down there (18 December 1986).

A well-known barrister makes roughly the same point.

> In the big cases there is nearly always a defence committee, but I do not participate in it . . . If they come to me and want advice I'll give

it. And if I want information I'll go to them. But again I am very clear about it. I don't get involved in what they are doing. They are doing a separate thing, though in collaboration and often in cooperation with us. But again the lawyers have got to be careful about that . . . So although there are these committees, I have never been on them, and I have never set them up (19 January 1987).

Radical lawyers are reluctant to make common cause with grass-roots political action, much less to take the leadership role that Simon recommends.

Organizing radical practice

Michael Tigar and Madeleine Levy have argued that radical organizing practices can make a direct contribution to political transformation. It is of fundamental importance that radical lawyers 'live out' alternative 'juridical principles' (Tigar and Levy 1977: 317). '[T]he way in which members of the resistance behave toward one another, and the alternative forms of social organization foreshadowed by their conduct – all these are different in principle from the operation of those voluntary organizations that acknowledge the supremacy of the brigands' rules' (ibid.).[6] Radical social organization can, in other words, provide a site for working through the dialectics of transformation.

Radical lawyers cannot ignore internal organizational issues that are part and parcel of their everyday professional lives, but they think about them in much less extravagant terms. Radical barristers and solicitors agree most fundamentally, that the provision of legal services to the disadvantaged should be 'decommodified' (i.e. respond to need rather than to the market). There is also agreement that race, gender and class bias should be eradicated from radical practice. More controversial is the commitment of at least one radical chambers, in many respects the prototypical radical chambers, to minimize their status and income differentials.[7] All of these organizational issues are, however, approached as problems of personal integrity rather than political action.

There is, however, an important middle ground between a personal and a transformative view of organizational reform. The test of organizational practices is whether radical lawyers can promote and sustain an effective radical presence. To be more specific, radical lawyers must be able to recruit dedicated practitioners; provide the kind of decent standard of living and satisfying work that will minimize attrition; and avoid internal conflicts that will sap radical energy. These organizational issues have a direct bearing on the coherence and staying power of radical lawyering.

While organizational issues are part and parcel of legal practice, only the prototypical radical chambers has been explicit, systematic and self-conscious about applying radical values to the management of radical practice. Other radical barristers and radical solicitors have approached organizational issues in a more *ad hoc* fashion. And while there is substantial agreement on two of the three organizational aspirations, the third generates a good deal of controversy. Yet whatever agreement there may be in principle, the contradictions of radical practice ensure imperfect realization of radical aspirations.

Decommodifying radical practice

While radical lawyers might like to decommodify the delivery of legal services, they are, in the final analysis, in business just like conventional practitioners. The exposure to the market inhibits efforts to decommodify radical practice and has a divisive and dispiriting impact on radical practitioners. As one dedicated but disillusioned partner in a firm of solicitors put it:

> It never crossed my mind to do the other kind of law. If I hadn't gone into this, I would have gone into a comparable caring profession of some other type: teaching or social work or whatever. I have toughened up a lot since then . . . I'm running a business now, and that's the difference. When I started [in a law centre] I wasn't running a business. So questions such as money and who earns it and how it's distributed were much less important . . . Originally I couldn't see any parallel between myself and people in the City. It never crossed my mind. Now I do see the parallel, because I don't see what they are doing as being fundamentally different from what I'm doing. Now I see we are both running businesses (29 January 1987).

Money matters are directly germane to the amount of time available for radical legal practice. The implications for radical elan and cohesion are less obvious but a constant concern – at least for solicitors.

A commitment to radical causes means in the first place that a great deal of radical practice is financed by legal aid, which does not pay particularly well. This puts radical lawyers in a significant bind:

> We have the constraints of running a commercial enterprise. Overheads are high and escalating, it's becoming more and more difficult to run an office on legal aid funding in central London. It's a constant worry; the pressure is now on. We don't cut corners, and we pay a price as a result of it, and the price is that without going into details, none of us makes much money (18 December 1986).

In the long run, will it be possible to recruit and retain quality lawyers and staff if a firm fails to provide its people with an income conducive to a decent and dependable standard of living and with challenging work?

Among solicitors, there seem to be half-empty/half-full kinds of disagreements about the adequacy of compensation for legal aid. One solicitor specializing in immigration and criminal work took a grudgingly positive view – much like his above quoted colleague, whose speciality is public order and criminal work:

> We tend to feel that if legal aid is handled efficiently, then there is no reason why it shouldn't provide a reasonable remuneration, even though obviously it's not as 'cream' as other types of work. It's not as well paid by the hour (20 February 1987).

But even the most optimistic practitioner would probably agree that it is at best 'very hard to make a living on legal aid' (29 January 1987). Certainly, they all seek to supplement their radical practice with more lucrative kinds of work.[8]

For some, these subsidies are only mildly problematic. Consider the views of a partner in a well-established firm with impeccable left-wing credentials. The miners' strike was the most noteworthy in a series of undertakings that involved trade-offs between financial stability and radical commitments.

> I was really at that time working 15 or 16, even one day 17 hours, just for the miners. I couldn't see my commercial clients. Some of them stayed on with me and others left. But now I am building up again. I've got a whole bunch of new ones . . . But I wouldn't have missed it for the world! It was my best time in the law so far, and I can't imagine there will ever be anything quite like it again in my lifetime. It was a struggle I was wholeheartedly in favour of and which really represented everything that was wrong with this government and everything that was right with workers (16 December 1986).

Of course, trade union work can be both politically correct and financially satisfactory, since the unions can afford to pay standard rates. Moreover, only a well-established firm can so easily turn its back, even temporarily, on well-heeled clients.

Among barristers such problems seem to be a good deal more attenuated. Because barristers do not practise in firms but are, so to speak, in business for themselves, they are in a good position to make their personal peace with distributional issues. But even in the one set of chambers which operates cooperatively, with 'a fee-sharing arrangement' in accordance with collective decisions 'which embrace both the legal personnel and the administrative personnel', there seem to be fewer tensions:

> We're the only people who offer a proper trainee wage to pupils, so that a pupil barrister who elsewhere would be lucky if she gets £1000 a year as a handout starts in these chambers at £6500, guaranteed,

plus all expenses . . . We also . . . provide . . . six months paid maternity leave for any woman in the group who has a child. We provide sabbaticals every five years, with three months pay. We provide full sick pay and insurance for any of us who go sick. And therefore we are in a sense model employers (15 January 1987).

Indeed, there is sufficient cushion in this cooperative structure to nurture principled choice:

If a particular barrister . . . wishes to become a specialist in the housing of lower-income families, public and private housing, for which legal aid pays low rates, that would be a sacrifice if he was in ordinary chambers, and he would ordinarily be seduced by financial pressures and by his clerk into more lucrative areas of work. We can make a commitment globally to that area of work and say we will be content . . . because we believe it is an important area to cover and the financial disbenefit is shared (15 January 1987).

Another barrister in that same chambers indicated that while they exist almost exclusively on legal aid, neither they nor other left-wing chambers had had to come to terms with the problems as had solicitors, 'because it's not biting on us yet – or not much' (19 November 1986). In short, radical barristers seem to be in more of a seller's market and/or better paid – with few, if any, chambers operating at the financial margins.

Rooting out race, class and gender bias

There is widespread agreement among radical lawyers that race, class and gender bias should not impinge on recruitment or on staffing practices. It is, however, one thing to reject such bias and quite another to neutralize it effectively. As a radical barrister working in the prototypical chambers put it:

We are particularly conscious when interviewing applicants that people who are working class, black, women, gay for example, may not have an opportunity to practise at the bar elsewhere. Women are and always have been in these chambers around 50 per cent and, unusually, our clerks have always been women. Our record on race has not been historically particularly impressive, although we do now have a number of black barristers. I think our record on sexual orientation has been reasonable so far as I can remember. Class? Well, I would say we are probably less solidly upper middle class than most chambers (19 November 1986).

Perhaps the recruitment problem is due, in part, to the staffing bias described by another member of the same chambers:

There is a very clear pecking order: there is the white middle-class male, then there's the white middle-class woman, or upper class, then there's the white working-class male and white working-class woman, and there's the blacks (18 February 1987).

If this is the basic picture in the chambers which has been most systematic and self-conscious about these issues, it should come as no surprise that bias is a fact of life within the radical bar and perhaps to a lesser extent among radical solicitors.

Race seems to be the most problematic of the barriers to radical solidarity. It has social as well as professional dimensions. 'I think the black members of chambers would say: "How many times have you been to my house? How many times have I been to your house? Compared to times you've done that with other white members of chambers?" ' (18 February 1987). As to the work problems:

In fact, that's something we are dealing with at the moment: the black members of chambers feel underused, and we're not sure whether it comes from clients, because they don't want to be represented by blacks or the solicitors who don't have confidence in blacks, or the clerks who don't push blacks hard enough, or what. Or whether it's just market forces. So we're actually dealing with that at the moment (18 February 1987).

The divisive impact of race extends beyond this one set of chambers. A well-established black barrister complained that while white barristers are regularly invited to participate in public order cases involving blacks, black barristers are excluded from trade union work:

They do the trade union things. We'd like to. We don't do it . . . Call it racism. Call it the way you like . . . Like the miners' union strike for example. All black cases, public order, have had a fair share of the radical bar in it. And, in fact, I have always said there should be a multi-racial team . . . But when it comes to miners they have the monopoly . . . [W]e are not part of the family – even the radical family, because they come from the universities together . . . We come from various places, from Pakistan, Zimbabwe (24 December 1986).

He also noted that the hiring of blacks in the radical chambers has progressed at a snail's pace and did not commence at all until 1980 or 1981 – and then, partly in response, he believed, to his constant prodding and his own example of a 50:50 hiring ratio.

As might be expected, given the distribution of blacks in conventional practice, there seem to be very few black solicitors in radical practice. In one of the leading radical firms, there is only one (an Asian) and, according to what he told me, he does only conveyancing and is not, therefore, really involved in the radical practice. I must acknowledge, however, that these issues arose a good deal less insistently in my discussions with solicitors and I am therefore hesitant about what conclusions can be drawn from my interviews and observations.

Women are certainly better represented than blacks in radical practice. There is at least one well-known firm that is, in effect, 'a women's firm' – albeit with men as junior partners:

> We try not to discriminate, really. We did end up by chance being three women partners at one point, and then we took on two men partners. They're junior to us. I think we would have felt differently about taking on two men who didn't come in as juniors, because I think that would have posed difficulties. There could have been strife and competition (29 January 1987).

Still, as a male senior partner in another radical firm acknowledges, women are subjected to a variety of subtle biases:

> Obviously, any racist is dismissed on the spot. Anyone making a racist remark or behaving in a racist way is dismissed and then we'll take whatever consequences in an industrial tribunal. Sexism is harder. I know some people say it should be treated as toughly as racism. We've found that very difficult because of the nature of some of the people who've worked here for years. But we're working on it and there's a bit of improvement about the way people talk at least (18 December 1986).

The contrast between race and gender bias is echoed by a woman in still another firm:

> Their discrimination in terms of blacks is considerable. And it operates on looking at who's got what jobs with the firm. In terms of a pecking order. There are obviously sort of male cliques and that. But people don't take so much notice (26 February 1987).

When women and blacks are compared, women seem better represented and are not really marginalized in radical practice.[9]

There are, however, gender-related tensions having to do with the cases and clients. Feminism and socialism combine to lead to distinctive priorities in cases involving abusive relationships. Not surprisingly, radical women lawyers are unwilling to represent 'violent men or men accused of rape' (26 February 1987). More generally in family abuse cases: 'We won't act for the local authority and we won't act for the battering husband or father. We do act for the battering mother' (26 February 1987).

As socialists, women are usually unwilling to act for the local authority against parents, because they believe that only lower-class families are subjected to these intrusions. As feminists, they distinguish between male and female violence:

> These rules grow historically and it's probably to do with the firm having feminist origins and the fact that men have a great deal more power in society and their acts of violence have historically been condoned and seen as normal in a way that women's violence hasn't been and isn't (26 February 1987).

In non-feminist radical firms, these priorities can create tensions. A senior partner in one such firm complained about the inclination of women to refuse to represent not just violent males, but 'even to act for a man in matrimonial proceedings . . . or even to do a piece of work on someone else's case, for example, to cover for them if they are ill or double booked' (20 February 1987).

> I think there has been an increasing view amongst the partners, where at first these views have always been respected, but they were also tolerated with a completely free heart, or even encouraged. There is less sympathy now, because when they are discussed . . . they don't seem to be inherently consistent, at least so far as the partners are concerned – like violence to children may not be a problem, or whatever (20 February 1987).

Women have been accepted among radical practitioners, but their feminist values remain suspect.

Finally, there are class tensions among radical lawyers – at least among barristers. As a senior woman in the prototypical chambers put it:

> Unlike many of my colleagues here, I am not a class traitor socialist although I know I sound like one. Because I am not to the manor born, I never had the kind of class arrogance which some of my colleagues have (19 November 1986).

Another working-class barrister in that same set elaborates:

> A working-class girl, why do I come to a job which is the ultimate upper-class grouping? In these chambers there are only about three or four of us who are working class, everyone else is upper class, landed gentry, people who've got private incomes – not everybody, but there are two or three people with private incomes. They've all been to private school, and they've all got ever such posh voices, and sometimes that's a real strain, just being with all those people all the time, suddenly your vowel sounds let you down. Oh God, back to Chelmsford . . . And then you think you're not getting along fine – and then you think, 'No, I'm not getting along so well as I should' (18 February 1987).

Class tensions, as such, did not surface in my interviews with radical solicitors, but there was a class-related issue in a well-known left-wing firm. A senior partner pointed out to me that the secretarial staff was unionized:

> We have a closed shop with the union, a post-entry closed shop, which means that you can get a job here if you're not a member of the union but you can join it the day you join the firm (16 December 1986).

According to another member of the firm, however, the post-entry closed shop was not accepted without a fight, which divided 'labour' from 'management': 'In this firm, there was a strike before the trade union was recognized – in the biggest left-wing firm in the country!' (26 February 1987). One can only presume that the interests and/or instincts of the small businessperson triumphed at least temporarily over those of the socialist lawyer.

More broadly, this persistence of race, gender and class bias among radical lawyers may have to do with consciousness. Or perhaps it is just unrealistic to believe that radical lawyers, regardless of their goodwill, can in their daily lives transcend the pervasive social presence of race, class and gender distinctions.

Equalizing status and income

A final, and decidedly controversial, radical aspiration among barristers is to minimize status and income differentials. I think this is because the ethos and forms of the conventional bar are so antithetical to egalitarian ideals of legal practice and because it is so difficult for radicals to break free of the bar community. Moreover, since barristers function as independent entrepreneurs whose clerks are compensated out of fees, competition, inequality and market values more generally intrude into conventional bar practice. Accordingly, the prototypical chambers felt compelled to move its premises outside the Inns of Court and organize in an egalitarian fashion:

> We are exceptional in terms of the English bar in that we work as a cooperative chambers. That is to say, instead of earning individual fees and paying individual rent, we operate a fee-sharing arrangement whereby we pool our fees and take an agreed salary from the collective fund. And our decisions are therefore also taken ultimately by a general meeting of all the members – that is to say the barristers and the clerks – so it is a collective which embraces both the legal personnel and the administrative personnel . . .

While one chambers has, therefore, embraced egalitarian aspirations, others have not followed suit. Perhaps, as one of my respondents suggested, hierarchical tendencies may be built into the barrister's traditional role irrespective of intent. There is an inherent tension between the barrister's professional need to 'know everything, be in control, and give orders' and a professed commitment to egalitarian and participatory social values (18 February 1987).[10]

Radical prospects

Progress towards a radical reconstruction of conventional professionalism has proceeded in a halting and contested fashion. Race, class and gender cleavages persist, as do the residual influences of conventional professionalism. The availability of legal services to the disadvantaged continues to be shaped by market forces and by the legal aid decisions of the state. More broadly, there is relatively little agreement among radical practitioners on the character of radical professionalism – even on the necessity or propriety of developing an alternative to the conventional model.

It could be argued that, given how much radical lawyers have achieved, it is gratuitous to call attention to the shortcomings of their activities. But these shortcomings may be indicative of fundamental flaws in the radical legal project – flaws which threaten its efficacy and staying power. Therefore, in order to assess the prospects for radical professionalism in this concluding section, it is important to determine in what measure the problematic aspects of the emerging radical legal professionalism are soluble and in what measure they are due to the inherent contradictions of radical practice.

There are a couple of different kinds of explanations for the failure of radicals to get beyond an *ad hoc* rethinking of their professional responsibilities – both of them rooted in the circumstances of radical practice. First, there is perhaps a valid scepticism about radical advocacy in advanced capitalist societies. Is it possible to create a viable and truly radical professional culture when the movement is so heavily dependent on the state which provides legal aid monies and finances the law centres? (Abel 1985b). And in so far as firms finance radical practice out of conveyancing and other forms of conventional practice, they are dependent on their commercial clients. The initial point is, then, that the contradictions of radical practice inhibit the realization of radical ideals (Greenberg 1986).

Secondly, British legal culture is likely to be extremely resistant to radical advocacy. Radical lawyers who are unwilling to accept politicization may simply be correct about its incompatibility with the British legal tradition. To the extent that politicization works in the USA, it is because the courts have been willing to broaden the legal arena and because of widely shared cultural understandings about the political significance of law (Scheingold 1974; Chayes 1976). In contrast, in the black letter world of British legal culture (Atiyah and Summers 1987), judges may simply be unresponsive to the politicization of litigation. In order to be effective, radicals cannot afford to take themselves outside the legal and professional systems that are both instruments and targets of reform.[11]

But to pose these obstacles to a neo-American radical professionalism is not to suggest that a British variant is necessarily out of reach, nor that thinking along these lines is bound to be unproductive. Indeed, I am inclined to believe that the fragmented character of radical lawyering in the UK has as much to do with a failure of imagination, will and energy as with material and perceptual barriers to radical advocacy.

Consider the recruitment of radical lawyers. There is widespread agreement among radical lawyers that they have different values and objectives from their conventional colleagues. None the less, only modest efforts are made to adapt recruitment procedures to needs of radical practice. To be sure, new recruits are ordinarily expected to demonstrate radical commitments and/or sensitivities. Still, while all of those whom I interviewed expressed contempt for the black letter emphasis of British legal education, no effort seems to have been made to reach out to students trained at institutions like Warwick, Kent and (until recently) Middlesex Polytechnic, where broader visions of the law are incorporated into the training of lawyers. Conventional professionalism, it seems, engenders a strong residuum of respect among radical lawyers for the black letter law which is taught in most law schools, or at least 'for academic excellence' as measured by the standards of the elite institutions of higher education in the UK.

More generally, there is little inclination to overcome divisions and inertia within radical ranks. There seems to be a divisive, perhaps destructive, competition among radical barristers for business and for status:

> It's always me, me, me. It's complete anathema, a complete contradiction of everything. As a feminist, very much one is trying to detract from the personality of oneself and is trying very much to just work with others, but it's all you on the front line, and I think that's a bit unhealthy. I think we're all prima donnas here, and that does get in the way actually of being radical (18 February 1987).

These problems seem less pervasive among solicitors who are generally speaking somewhat more down to earth. They practise in a less rarefied setting – closer to their clients both geographically and personally. As one radical solicitor put it to me:

Intellectual types tend to become barristers – or maybe self-proclaimed intellectuals or whatever – people who play around with, you know, juggle ideas about easily tend to be barristers. Solicitors tend to be more nitty-gritty. You've got to be fairly worldly to be a solicitor (16 December 1986).

These differences, in themselves, put some stress on radical solidarity. When these differences of circumstance and temperament are combined with the draining demands of radical practice, it is understandable that there is not much energy left for concerted reflection on the radical project.

Although radicals have not put much effort into developing an agenda – either for professional issues or for the socialist goals of radical lawyering – several lawyers I interviewed saw Tony Gifford's (1986) 'manifesto for law reform' as a promising step in that direction. Gifford offers a comprehensive critique of each portion of the justice system from the cabinet level to the magistrates' courts, including separate analyses of barristers, solicitors and law centres, as well as judges, juries and police officers.

With respect to professionalism, as such, Gifford proposes modest reforms exclusively focused on client service. He complains, for example, that entry to the bar is restricted by financial barriers and class bias and that barristers benefit unfairly from a variety of restrictive practices. Barristers are, moreover, poorly trained, according to Gifford, and are influenced by an ethos that often leads to slipshod and patronizing treatment of clients (Gifford 1986: 65–76). He is less critical of solicitors and, indeed, attributes their shortcomings primarily to legal aid. He recommends that reasonable rates be provided for legal aid work and that legal aid coverage be extended to pleadings before immigration, industrial and social security tribunals (ibid.: 82–4). Although sensible and progressive, these proposals are without political content or connotation.

Gifford's approval of the pro-active practices of the law centres (ibid.: 87) suggests support for radical professionalism. But his recommendation is not that other radical lawyers should take their cues from the law centres. Instead, he proposes that they be expanded and adequately and dependably funded. Gifford would confine rather than extend radical professionalism, and my guess is that most radicals would be reluctant to go even this far.

In my view, Gifford's radical agenda does not go far enough. There is, however, room for considerable disagreement on this matter. It is more important that the issue be addressed collectively by radical lawyers than that it be resolved in any particular way. What is required is some kind of organizational arena which will bring radical lawyers together around these issues and a sensible frame of reference for considering them.

The Haldane Society of Socialist Lawyers is the ostensible organization for bringing a reflective coherence to British radical lawyering – given the widespread identification with it among radical lawyers. As presently constituted, however, there is great scepticism about the Haldane Society, and it seems an unlikely vehicle for rethinking radical professionalism. It is underfinanced, the leadership has had considerable difficulty developing a substantial cadre of truly active members, and barristers are over-represented.

Nor has there been any serious effort to reach out to like-minded academics who would have the inclination, the time and the resources to provide the kind of reflective thinking necessary to work out a coherent vision of radical professionalism.[12] Given the dogmatic pragmatism of radical lawyers and the heavy demands of radical practice, it seems essential, if perhaps a sign of my own occlusive professionalism, that academics be incorporated into the radical colloquy. This is likely to be an uneasy, but a mutually enriching, partnership, which will be required in order to work out a realistic sense of the future of radical lawyering in the UK.[13]

Notes

1 The inclination to shy away from the radical label has to do with a tension between popular misconceptions of legal radicalism and the real thing. As a minority barrister put it to me: 'One assumes when one talks of the radical bar, it is a left-wing bar, but . . . this label . . . is being used and used consciously to get work. It's part of the sale. He can fight the police; he is radical' (24 December 1986). A solicitor made a similar point in questioning whether it was appropriate to think of her firm as radical: 'I think a radical or activist practice is seen as one that deals with political struggles and very often the most glamorous bits of them' (29 January 1987). In other words, the label has, to some extent, been misappropriated – providing false cachet to opportunists. Other terms that are used include socialist, left-wing, alternative and activist.

2 My primary data are interviews I conducted with twenty-five radical lawyers in London between September 1986 and March 1987. In addition to its London bias, my grapevine sampling under-represents lawyers working in law centres and in social action organizations like the Child Poverty Action Group and the Joint Council for the Welfare of Immigrants.

3 See also Abel (1988a: 75). Similarly, Zander (1980: 23) points out that in the late 1970s, about 83 per cent of students preparing for the bar examination were from professional/managerial and executive/administrative backgrounds. Not surprisingly, Abel discovers that blacks and women are under-represented among barristers. There have been substantial numbers of blacks called to the bar – but largely overseas blacks who were expected to practise in their home countries rather than in the UK. A large proportion of those who remain have been relegated to 'ghetto chambers'. Women are increasingly well represented among those called to the bar, but their progress into the upper

strata of the profession has been disappointing for a variety of reasons (Abel 1988a: 76–85).

4 Simon (1984: 474) argues that the 'liberal view insists that the legal system and lawyering are equally concerned with dispute resolution, with dispute-generating regulatory intervention, and with a third function – facilitation of transactions that are consensual but that would not take place without legal intervention'.

5 The American literature offers a variety of approaches to transformative styles of legal advocacy. See, for example, Tigar and Levy's (1977: 310–30) 'jurisprudence of insurgency' and Lynd's (1984) 'communal rights'.

6 These avenues were explored in the late 1960s by American radical lawyers who organized communal law firms (see Biderman 1971: 280–88; Lefcourt 1971: 310–26).

7 Virtually all London barristers work within the Inns of Court, a collection of buildings located on handsome well-kept grounds beside the Thames. Barristers are essentially independent entrepreneurs, but they organize themselves in chambers which are loose groupings of like-minded practitioners who share the same premises. On the English Bar, see Atiyah and Summers (1987: 360–69). The 'prototypical' radical chambers was the first to move their offices outside the Inns of Court and, due in large part to the Head of Chambers, Lord Tony Gifford, has been the most self-conscious about coming to terms with radical professionalism.

8 The Law Society and the bar have joined together in a struggle against the increasing inadequacy of legal aid payments. Some modest gains have been achieved by this concerted action, '[b]ut the present government's determination to cut costs seems certain', according to Abel, 'to triumph over the Law Society's efforts to increase the legal aid budget' (Abel 1988a: 230).

9 Among solicitors as a whole, the representation of women has been increasing at an imposing rate (Abel 1988a: 172–5). Their upward mobility has, however, been disappointing for a variety of reasons, which, according to Abel, 'are a product of both overt discrimination and passive acceptance of the traditional sexual division of labour' (ibid.: 175).

10 Among solicitors, these issues have not been directly confronted. There is more diversity and a greater willingness to live with it.

11 I am indebted to William Simon who called this point to my attention in personal correspondence: 'The dimension I have in mind repudiates any sharp distinction between working within the system and working to change it or between radical and reformist practice . . . I have tended not to see transformative practice as radically transcending the established system but more as revising it.' Simon, therefore, has mixed feelings about my findings that 'radical lawyers . . . have personal commitments that are in some sense bound up with their identities as lawyers, as well as their identities as radicals . . . I think that is a tough question whether this should be regarded as a failure of will or insight or as a plausible intuition that there is something genuinely satisfying or potentially redeemable about the traditions they are working with' (27 June 1988).

12 There are other organizations, like the Legal Action Group, that might serve this purpose, but to my knowledge only the Critical Legal Studies Conference has made an effort, so far unsuccessful, to bridge the gap between academics

and practitioners on these matters (personal correspondence with David Sugarman, 14 October 1988).

13 While there has not been much academic work on the professional dimensions of legal radicalism in the UK, on legal radicalism more broadly, see Dhavan (1986) and Dean (1985). As for partnership between academics and practitioners, see Cooper and Dhavan (1986).

Bibliography

Abbott, A. (1983) 'Sequences of social events: Concepts and methods for the analysis of order in social process', *Historical Methods*, 16: 129.

Abbott, A. (1986a) 'Jurisdictional conflicts: A new approach to the development of the legal professions', *American Bar Foundation Research Journal*, 2: 187–224.

Abbott, A. (1986b) 'Status and status strain in the professions', *American Journal of Sociology*, 86(4): 819–35.

Abbott, A. (1988) *The System of Professions*. Chicago, IL: University of Chicago Press.

Abel, R.L. (1979) 'Socializing the legal profession: Can redistributing the lawyers' services survive social justice?', *Law and Policy*, 1: 5.

Abel, R.L. (1981a) 'Towards a political economy of lawyers', *Wisconsin Law Review*, (6): 1117–87.

Abel, R. (1981b) 'Why does the ABA promulgate ethical rules', *Texas Law Review*, 57(4): 639–68.

Abel, R. (1982) *The Politics of Informal Justice*. New York: Academic Press.

Abel, R. (1985a) 'Comparative sociology of legal professions', *American Bar Foundation Research Journal*, 5.

Abel, R. (1985b) 'Law without politics: Legal aid under advanced capitalism', *UCLA Law Review*, 32: 474.

Abel, R. (ed.) (1985c) 'Lawyers and the power to change', Special Issue, *Law and Policy*, 7(1): 5–18.

Abel, R. (1985d) 'Les avocats, l'aide judiciaire et la reproduction du droit', *Annales de Vaucresson*, 23: 157–73.

Abel, R. (1986a) 'The decline of professionalism', *Modern Law Review*, 49: 1.

Abel, R. (1986b) 'The transformation of the American legal profession', *Law and Society Review*, 20: 7.

Abel, R. (ed.) (1988a) *The Legal Profession in England and Wales*. Oxford: Blackwell.

Abel, R. (1988b) *Lawyers in Society Vol. I: The Common Law World*. Oxford: Blackwell.

Abel, R. (1989) *American Lawyers*. New York: Oxford University Press.

Abel, R. and Lewis, P. (eds) (1989) *Lawyers in Society*, Vol. 3. Stanford, CA: University of California Press.

Abel-Smith, B. and Stevens, R. (1967) *Lawyers and the Courts*. London: Heinemann.

Adams, J.E. (1976) 'Licences made easy', *Conveyancer*, 40(1): 5.

Adler, S. (1987) *Rape on Trial*. London: Routledge.

Allen, H. (1987) *Justice Unbalanced*. Milton Keynes: Open University Press.

Althey, L. (1990) 'The company store in coal town culture', *Labour's Heritage*, 2: 4.

American Bar Association Commission on Professionalism (1986) *'In the Spirit of Public Service': A Blueprint for the Rekindling of Lawyer Professionalism*. Chicago, IL: American Bar Association.

Anderson, B. (1969) 'Provincial aspects of the financial revolution of the 18th century', *Business History*, ix: 12–30.

Arthurs, H. (1985) *'Without the Law': Administrative Justice and Legal Pluralism in Nineteenth-Century England*. Toronto: University of Toronto Press.

Association technique d'harmonisation des cabinets d'audit et de conseil (ATH) (1985) *L'Empire des chiffres: L'information financiere, l'audit et la comptabilite*. Paris: Fayard.

Atiyah, P. (1979) *The Rise and Fall of Freedom of Contract*. Oxford: Clarendon Press.

Atiyah, P. and Summers, R. (1987) *Form and Substance in Anglo-American Law: A Comparative Study of Legal Reasoning, Legal Theory, and Legal Institutions*. Oxford: Clarendon Press.

Atkins, G. (1919) *Bench and Bar of West Virginia*. Charleston, WV: Virginia Law Book Co.

Atkins, S. and Hoggett, B. (1984) *Women and the Law*. Oxford: Blackwell.

Atkinson, G. (1919) *Bench and Bar of West Virginia*. Charleston: Virginia Law Book Co.

Atkinson, G. and Gibbons, A. (1890) *Prominent Men of West Virginia*. Wheeling: WV.

Auchinloss, L. (1955) *Powers of Attorney*. Boston: Houghton Mifflin.

Auerbach, J. (1976) *Unequal Justice: Lawyers and Social Change in Modern America*. New York: Oxford University Press.

Auerbach, J. (1983) *Justice Without Law?* New York: Oxford University Press.

Bancaud, A. (1987) 'Le sociologue et le droit ou la tentation du sacrilege', paper presented to the *VIth European Conference on Critical Legal Studies*, Vaucresson, France, April.

Bancaud, A. and Dezalay, Y. (1984) 'La sociologie juridique comme enjeu social et professionel', *Revue interdisciplinaires d'etudes juridiques*, 12: 1–29.

Bancroft, G. (1939) *Stage and Bar*. London: Faber and Faber.

Bankowski, Z. and Mungham, G. (1976) *Images of Law*. London: Routledge and Kegan Paul.

Bapela, M. (1987) 'The people's courts in a customary law perspective'. Pretoria: University of South Africa.

Beale, H. and Dugdale, A. (1975) 'Contracts between businessmen: planning and the use of contractual remedies', *British Journal of Law and Society*, 2: 45.

Bekker, J. (1986) 'Die swaar skaduwee van Goniwe', *Die Suid Afrikaan*, Summer, pp. 36–40.

Belcher, V. (1985) *Boodle, Hatfield & Co.* London: Boodle, Hatfield and Co.

Bellow, G. and Moulton, B. (1981) *The Lawyering Process: Ethics and Professional Responsibility.* New York: The Foundation Press.

Bennett, T.W. (1985) *Application of Customary Law in Southern Africa.* Kenwyn: Juta and Co.

Bias, C.V. (1979) *A History of the Chesapeake and Ohio Railway Company and Its Predecessors, 1884–1977.* PhD dissertation, West Virginia University.

Bickel, A.M. (1975) *The Morality of Consent.* New Haven, CT: Yale University Press.

Biderman, P. (1971) 'The birth of communal law firms', in J. Black (ed.), *Radical Lawyers: Their Role in the Movement and in the Courts.* New York: Avon.

Billingsley, A. (1964) 'Bureaucratic and professional orientation patterns in social case work', *The Social Service Review*, 38(4): 400–407.

Birkett, N. (1961) *Six Great Advocates.* Harmondsworth: Penguin.

Birks, M. (1960) *Gentlemen of the Law.* London: Stevens.

Blaustein, A. and Porter, C. (1954) *The American Lawyer.* Chicago, IL: University of Chicago Press.

Blom Cooper, L. and Morris, T. (1964) *Calendar of Murder.* London: Michael Joseph.

Blumberg, A. (1967) *Criminal Justice.* New York: New Viewpoints.

Blumberg, A. (1977) 'The practice of law as confidence game: Organizational cooptation of a profession', *Law and Society Review*, 1: 15.

Bochnak, E. (1981) *Women's Self Defence Cases: Theory and Practice.* Sidney: The Mitchie Co.

Bogue, D. (1985) *The Population of the United States: Historical Trends and Future Projections.* New York: Free Press.

Boigeol, A. (1988) 'The French bar: The difficulties of unifying a divided profession', in R. Abel and P. Lewis (eds), *Lawyers in Society: The Civil Law World.* Oxford: Blackwell.

Boltanski, L. (1984) 'La denociation', *Actes de la recherche*, 51: 3–40.

Boraine, A. (1988) 'Wham, sham, or scam? – Security management upgrading and resistance in a South African township', paper presented at the *African Seminar*, Centre for African Studies, University of Cape Town, August.

Botein, S. (1983) 'What shall we meet afterwards in Heaven: Judgeship as a symbol for modern American lawyers', in G. Geiss (ed.), *Professions and Professional Ideologies in America*, pp. 49–69. Chapel Hill, NC: University of North Carolina Press.

Bourdieu, P. (1971) 'Genese et structure du champ religieux', *Revue Francaise de Sociologie*, 12(3): 295–334.

Bourdieu, P. (1972) *Esquisse d'une theorie de la pratique.* Geneve: Droz.

Bourdieu, P. (1976) 'Le champ scientifique', *Actes de la Recherche en Sciences Sociales*, 88: 88–104.

Bourdieu, P. (1979) *Le destinction.* Paris: Ed. de Minuit.

Bourdieu, P. (1980) *Questions de sociologie.* Paris: Ed. de Minuit.

Bourdieu, P. (1981) 'Décrire et prescrire', *Actes de la Recherche en Sciences Sociales*, 38.

Bourdieu, P. (1984a) *Distinction: A Social Critique of the Judgment of Taste.* Cambridge, MA: Harvard University Press.

Bourdieu, P. (1984b) *Homo academicus.* Paris: Ed. de Minuit.

Bourdieu, P. (1987) 'The force of law: Toward a sociology of the juridical field', *Hastings Law Journal*, 38: 805–54.

Bourdieu, P. and St Martin, M. (1978) 'Le patronat', *Actes de le recherche en sciences sociales*, Actes No. 20–21.

Bowker, A. (1961) *A Lifetime with The Law.* London: W.H. Allen.

Box, M. (1983) *Rebel Advocate: A Biography of Gerald Gardiner.* London: Victor Gollancz.

Boyer, R. (1986) *Capitalismes fin de siecle.* Paris: PUF.

Bradgate, J. (1987) 'Reservation of title – ten years on', *Conveyancer*, 51: 434.

Brathwaite, J. (1984) *Corporate Crime in the Pharmaceutical Industry.* London: Routledge and Kegan Paul.

Bresler, F. (1961) 'English law and lawyers', *Texas Quarterly* 3: 194–204.

Brigham, J. (1978) *Constitutional Language.* Westport, CT: Greenwood Press.

Brigham, J. (1987) *The Cult of the Court.* Philadelphia, PA: Temple University Press.

Brigham, J. and Harrington, C.B. (1989) 'Realism and its consequences: An inquiry into contemporary socio-legal research', *International Journal of the Sociology of Law*, 17: 41–62.

Brooks, C.W. (1981) 'The common lawyers in England *c.* 1558–1642', in W. Prest (ed.), *Lawyers in Early Modern Europe and America.* London: Croom Helm.

Brooks, C.W. (1986) *Pettyfoggers and Vipers of the Commonwealth: The Lower Branch of the Legal Profession in Early Modern England.* Cambridge: Cambridge University Press.

Brophy, J. and Smart, C. (1985) 'Locating the law: A discussion of the place of law in feminism', in J. Brophy and C. Smart (eds), *Women in Law: Explorations in Law, Family and Sexuality*, pp. 1–20. London: Routledge and Kegan Paul.

Brown, E. (1948) *Lawyers, Law Schools, and the Public Service.* New York: Russell Sage.

Browne, A. (1987) *When Battered Women Kill.* Glencoe, IL: Free Press.

Burck, G. (1957a) 'The bountiful world of Royal Dutch Shell', *Fortune*, September, pp. 15–181.

Burck, G. (1957b) 'Royal Dutch Shell and its new competition', *Fortune*, October, pp. 139–78.

Burman, S. (1983) 'Beyond apartheid's courts: Reaping the whirlwind', paper delivered at the *International Sociological Association's Conference of the Research Committee on the Sociology of Law.* Antwerp, Belgium.

Burman, S. and Schärf, W. (1990) 'Creating people's justice: Street committees and people's courts in a South African city', *Law and Society Review*, 24(3): 693–744.

Cain, M. (1976) 'Necessarily out of touch: Thoughts on the social organisation of the bar', in P. Carlen (ed.), *The Sociology of Law.* Sociological Review Monograph, No. 23. Keele: Keele University.

Cain, M. (1979) 'The general practice lawyer and the client: Towards a radical conception', *International Journal of the Sociology of Law*, 7(4): 331–54. Also in R. Dingwall and P. Lewis (eds) (1983) *The Sociology of the Professions.* London: Macmillan.

Cain, M. (1983) 'The general practice lawyer and the client: Towards a radical conception', in R. Dingwall and P.P. Lewis (eds), *The Sociology of the Professions.* London: Macmillan.

Cain, M. (1985) 'Beyond informal justice', *Contemporary Crises*, 9: 4. Also in R. Mathews (ed.) (1988) *Informal Justice.* London: Sage.

Cain, M. (1986) 'Who loses out on Paradise Island: The case of defendant debtors in County Court', in I. Ramsay (ed.), *Debtors and Creditors: Socio-Legal Perspectives*. London: Professional Books.

Cain, M. (1990) 'Realist philosophy and standpoint epistemologies, OR feminist criminology as a successor science', in L. Gelsthorpe and A. Morris (eds), *Feminist Perspectives in Criminology*. Milton Keynes: Open University Press.

Cain, M. (1992) 'For a comparative feminist criminology: A project for Europe in the 1990's'. Appearing in selected papers from the *British Society of Criminology Annual Conference*, York, July 1990.

Cain, M. (1993) 'Foucault, feminism, and feeling: What Foucault can and cannot contribute to feminist epistemology', in C. Ramazanoglu (ed.), *Foucault for Feminists*. London: Routledge.

Cain, M. and Kulcsar, K. (eds) (1983) *Disputes and the Law*. Budapest: Akademiai Kiado.

Calhoun, D. (1965) *Professional Lives in America: Structure and Aspiration, 1750–1850*. Cambridge, MA: Harvard University Press.

Cappell, C. (1982) *Professional Projects and the Private Production of Law*. PhD. thesis, University of Chicago.

Carlen, P. (1976) *Magistrates' Justice*. London: Routledge.

Carlen, P. (1983) *Women's Imprisonment*. London: Routledge.

Carlin, J.E. (1963) *Lawyers on Their Own: A Study of Individual Practitioners in Chicago*. New Brunswick, NJ: Rutgers University Press.

Carlin, J. (1966) *Lawyers' Ethics*. New York: Russell Sage.

Carlin, J., Howard, J. and Messenger, S. (1966) *Civil Justice and the Poor: Issues for Sociological Research*. New York: Russell Sage.

Carr, E.H. (1961) *What is History?* Harmondsworth: Penguin.

Carr Saunders, A. and Wilson, P. (1933/1964) *The Professions*. London: Frank Cass.

Cecil, H. (1958) *Brief to Counsel*. London: Michael Joseph.

Cecil, H. (1970) *The English Judge*. London: Stevens.

Chandler, A. (1977) *The Visible Hand: The Managerial Revolution in American Business*. Cambridge, MA: Harvard University Press.

Chayes, A. (1976) 'The role of the judge in public law litigation', *Harvard Law Review*, 89: 1281.

Clanchy, M.T. (1979) *From Memory to Written Record*. London: Edward Arnold.

Clancy, P. (1974) *Just a Country Lawyer: A Biography of Sam Erwin*. Bloomington, IN: Indiana University Press.

Clifford, C. (1991) *Counsel to the President: A Memoir*. New York: Random House.

Cohen, H. (1929) *History of the English Bar*. London: Sweet and Maxwell.

Cooper, J. (1986) 'Public interest lawyers in England and Wales', in J. Cooper and R. Dhavan (eds), *Public Interest Law*. Oxford: Blackwell.

Cooper, J. and Dhavan, R. (eds) (1986) *Public Interest Law*. Oxford: Blackwell.

Corbin, D. (1981) *Life, Work and Rebellion in the Coal Fields: The Southern West Virginia Miners, 1880–1922*. Urbana, IL: University of Illinois Press.

Corder, H. (1989) 'Crowbars and cobwebs: Executive autocracy and the law in South Africa', *South African Journal on Human Rights*, 5: 4–11.

Cork Committee Report (1984) Cmnd 8558. London: HMSO.

Cotterrell, R. (1983a) 'Legality and political legitimacy in the sociology of Max Weber', in D. Sugarman (ed.), *Legality, Ideology and the State*. London: Academic Press.

Cotterrell, R. (1983b) 'The sociological concept of law', *Journal of Law and Society*, 10: 241.

Dahrendorf, R. (1962) 'Ausbildung einer elite-die Deutsche oberschit und die Juristischen Facultaten', *Der Monat*, July, p. 15.

Daniel, T. (1976) *The Lawyers*. Chichester: John Wiley.

Darrow, C. (1957) *Attorney for the Damned* (edited by A. Weinberg). New York: Simon and Schuster.

Davidoff, L. and Hall, C. (1987) *Family Fortunes: Men and Women of the English Middle Class 1780–1850*. London: Hutchinson.

Davis, D. (1990) 'Capital punishment and the politics of the doctrine of common purpose', in D. Hansson and D. Van Zyl Smit (eds), *Towards Justice? Crime and State Control in South Africa*. Cape Town: Oxford University Press.

Dean, H. (1985) *Legal Dis-Service: A Critical Appraisal of Legal Service Provision and Proposals for an Alternative Approach*. Brunel Occasional Papers in Law, No. 2, Brunel University.

de Tocqueville, A. (1934) *De la democratie en Amerique*. Paris: Librarie de Charles Gosselin.

de Tocqueville, A. (1945) *Democracy in America* (edited and translated by H. Reeve, F. Brown and P. Bradley), Vol. 1. New York: Vintage Books.

Derge, D. (1959) 'The lawyer as decision maker in the American State legislature', *Journal of Politics*, 21: 408–433.

Dezalay, Y. (1985a) 'Vers une sociologie de la production du droit par et pour les professionnels de la mediation juridique', *Annales de Vaucresson*, 23: 5–14.

Dezalay, Y. (1985b) 'Des affaires disciplinaires au droit disciplinaire: La juridictionnalisation des affaires disciplinaries comme enjeu social et professionnel', *Annales de Vaucresson*, 23: 51–73.

Dezalay, Y. (1986a) 'From mediation to pure law: Practices and scholarly representations within the legal sphere', *International Journal of the Sociology of Law*, 14(2): 89–112.

Dezalay, Y. (1986b) 'Negotiation and legal rationality: Business arbitration as an illustration of the issues of mediation within the legal field', paper presented to the *Law and Society Association*. Chicago, June.

Dezalay, Y. (1989a) 'Le droit des Faillites: du notable a l'expert la restructuration du champ des professionnels de la restructuration des enterprises', *Actes de la Recherche*, Actes No. 76–77, pp. 2–30.

Dezalay, Y. (1989b) 'De nombreux clercs au service de l'Europe des affaires, Droit et justice sous la loi du marche', *Le Monde Diplomatique*, Septembre.

Dezalay, Y. (1989c) 'Putting justice "into play" on the global market: Law, lawyers accountants and the competition for financial services', *Tidskrift für Rattssociologi*, 6: 9–67.

Dezalay, Y. (1991) 'Negotiated justice within the field of law: the French example', in K. Platt and C. Meschievitz (eds), *Beyond Disputing*. Baden-Baden: Nomos.

Dezalay, Y. and Sugarman, D. (eds) (1994) *Professional Competition and Professional Power: Lawyers, Accountants and the Globalization of Markets*. London: Routledge.

Dhavan, R. (1986) 'Whose law? Whose interest?', in J. Cooper and R. Dhavan (eds), *Public Interest Law*. Oxford: Blackwell.

Di Federico, G. (1976) 'The Italian judicial profession and its bureaucratic setting', in D. McCormick (ed.), *Lawyers in Their Social Setting*. Edinburgh: W. Green.

Diamond, N. (1986) 'The Copernican revolution', in L. Levidow (ed.), *Science as Politics*. London: Free Association Books.

Dickens, C. (1971) *Bleak House*. Harmondsworth: Penguin.

Dillon, C.W. and Nicholls, E.L. (1990) *An Annotated Pocket Code of West Virginia*. Pulaski, VA: B.D. Smith and Bros.

Donner, A. (1968) *The Role of the Lawyer in the European Communities*. Edinburgh: The University Press.

Douzinas, C., Warrington, R. and McVeigh, S. (1992) *Postmodern Jurisprudence*. London: Routledge.

Downs, D. (1985) *Nazis in Skokie: Freedom, Community and the First Amendment*. Notre Dame: University of Notre Dame Press.

Dreyfus, J. and Rabinow, P. (1982) *Michel Foucault: Beyond Structuralism and Hermeneutics*. Brighton: Harvester.

Driscoll, M. (1990) 'Family of dead wife seek rights in court', *The Times*, 28 January.

Du Cann, R. (1964) *The Art of the Advocate*. Harmondsworth: Pelican.

Dulles, J.F. (1957) 'Foreword'. In A.H. Dean, *William Nelson Cromwell: An American Pioneer Corporation Comparative and International Law*. New York.

Duman, D. (1982) *The Judicial Bench in England 1727–1875*. London: Royal Historical Society.

Duman, D. (1983) *The English and Colonial Bars in the 19th Century*. London: Croom Helm.

Durkheim, E. (1957) *Professional Ethics and Civic Morals*. London: Routledge and Kegan Paul.

Eaton, M. (1983) 'Mitigating Circumstances: Familiar Rhetoric?', *International Journal of the Sociology of Law*, 2: 385–400.

Eaton, M. (1986) *Justice for Women? Family, Court and Social Control*. Milton Keynes: Open University Press.

Eavenson, H. (1942) *The First Century and a Quarter of the American Coal Industry*. Pittsburgh: Privately printed.

Edelman, M. (1988) *Constructing the Political Spectacle*. Chicago, IL: University of Chicago Press.

Edley, C. (1990) *Administrative Law: Rethinking Control of Bureaucracy*. New Haven, CT: Yale University Press.

Edwards, S. (1981) *Female Sexuality and the Law*. Oxford: Martin Robertson.

Edwards, S. (1986a) *Women on Trial*. Manchester: Manchester University Press.

Edwards, S. (1986b) *Gender, Sex & Law*. London: Croom Helm.

Eisenstein, J. and Herbert, J. (1977) *Felony Justice: An Organizational Analysis of Criminal Courts*. Boston, MA: Little, Brown and Co.

Epstein, C. (1970) *Women's Place: Options and Limits in Professional Careers*. Berkeley, CA: University of California Press.

Epstein, C. (1981) *Women in Law*. New York: Basic Books.

Erlanger, H. (1980) 'The allocation of status within occupations: The case of the legal profession', *Social Forces*, 58: 882.

Etzioni, A. (ed.) (1969) *The Semi-Professions*. New York: Free Press.

Eulau, H. and Sprague, J. (1964) *Lawyers in Politics: A Study in Professional Convergence*. Indianapolis, IN: Bobbs-Merrill.

Eymard-Duvernay, F. and Thevenot, L. (1983) *Les immobilisations de forme dans l'usage de la main d'oeuvre*. Paris: INSEE.

Farrand, J. (1978) 'Rent Act roundup', *Conveyancer*, 42: 397.

Farrand, J. and Arden, A. (1981) *Rent Acts and Regulation*, 2nd edn. London: Sweet and Maxwell.

Feeley, M. (1979) *The Process is the Punishment*. New York: Russell Sage.

Ferguson, R. (1980) 'The adjudication of commercial disputes and the legal system in modern England', *Journal of Law and Society*, 7 (2).

Ferguson, R. (1984) *Law and Letters in American Culture*. Cambridge, MA: Harvard University Press.

Feyerabend, P. (1975) *Against Method*. London: New Left Books.

ffyfe, D., Earl of Kilmuir (1964) *Political Adventure*. London: Weidenfeld and Nicolson.

Fifoot, C. (1936/1977) *Lord Mansfield*. Scientia Verlag Aalen.

Fine, D. (1989) 'Kitskonstabels: A Case Study in Black on Black Policing' in T.W. Bennett *et al.* (eds), *Acta Juridica 1989*. Wetton: Juta.

Fineman, M.L.A. (1983) 'Implementing equality, ideology, contradiction and social change: A study of rhetoric and results in the regulation of the consequences of divorce', *Wisconsin Law Review*, 4: 789.

Fineman, M.L.A. (1986) 'Illusive equality: On Wietzman's divorce revolution', *American Bar Foundation Research Journal*, p. 781.

Fineman, M.L.A. (1987) 'The impact of mediation in the development and application of legal norms: Child custody decision making', paper presented at the *Annual Law and Society Association Conference*, Washington, June.

Fineman, M.L.A. (1988) 'Dominant discourse, professional language, and legal change in child custody decision making', *Harvard Law Review*, 101: 727.

Fineman, M.L.A. (1991) *The Illusion of Equality: The Rhetoric and Reality of Divorce Reform*. Chicago, IL: University of Chicago Press.

Fineman, M.L.A. (1992) 'Feminist theory in law: The difference it makes', *Columbia Journal of Gender and Law*, 2(1).

Fineman, M.L.A. and Opie, A. (1987) 'The uses of social science data in legal policymaking: Custody determinations at divorce', *Wisconsin Law Review*, 1: 107.

Fineman, M.L.A. and Thomadsen, N. (eds) (1990) *At the Boundaries of Law: Feminism and Legal Theory*. New York: Routledge.

Fish, S. (1986) 'Anti-professionalism', *Cardozo Law Review*, 7: 645.

Fitzpatrick, P. (1983) 'Law, plurality and underdevelopment', in D. Sugarman (ed.), *Legality, Ideology and the State*. London: Academic Press.

Fitzpatrick, P. (1988) 'The rise and rise of informalism', in R. Mathews (ed.), *Practising Theory*. London: Sage.

Fitzpatrick, P. (1992) *Mythology of Modern Law*. London: Routledge.

Fitzpatrick, P. and Hunt, A. (eds) (1987) *Critical Legal Studies*. Oxford: Blackwell.

Flax, J. (1987) 'Postmodernism and gender relations in feminist theory', *Signs*, 12: 621.

Foster, D., Sandler, D. and Davis, D. (1987) 'Detention, torture, and the criminal justice process in South Africa', *International Journal of the Sociology of Law*, 15(2): 105–120.

Foucault, M. (1970) *The Order of Things*. London: Tavistock.

Foucault, M. (1972) *The Archaeology of Knowledge*. London: Tavistock.

Foucault, M. (1977) *Language, Counter Memory, Practice*. Oxford: Blackwell.

Foucault, M. (1978) *The History of Sexuality*, Vol. I. Harmondsworth: Penguin.

Foucault, M. (1985) *The Use of Pleasure: The History of Sexuality*, Vol. 2. New York: Pantheon.

Foucault, M. (1986) *The Care of the Self: The History of Sexuality*, Vol. 3. New York: Pantheon.

Freidson, E. (1970) *Profession of Medicine: A Study of the Sociology of Applied Knowledge*. New York: Dodd and Mead.

Freidson, E. (1983) 'The theory of the professions: the state of the art', in R. Dingwall and P. Lewis (eds), *The Sociology of the Professions*. New York: St Martin's Press.

Freidson, M. (1985) *A History of American Law*. New York, Simon and Schuster.

Freidson, E. (1986) *Professional Powers: A Study of the Institutionalization of Formal Knowledge*. Chicago, IL: University of Chicago Press.

Freud, S. (1925) 'Some psychical consequences of the anatomical distinction between the sexes', Vol. XXI Standard Edition of the *Complete Psychological Works of Sigmund Freud*. London: Hogarth Press.

Freyer, T. (1970) 'The Federal Courts, localism and national economy', *Business History Review*, 53: 343.

Friedan, B. (1963) *The Feminine Mystique*. New York: W.W. Norton.

Friedenthal, J. (1991) 'Too many lawyers', *George Washington University Magazine*, November, p. 2.

Friedman, L. (1970) *Profession of Medicine: A Study of the Sociology of Applied Knowledge*. New York: Dodd and Mead.

Friedman, L. (1973) *A History of American Law*. New York: Simon and Schuster.

Friedman, L. (1983) 'The theory of professions: State of the art', in R. Dingwall and P. Lewis (eds), *The Sociology of the Professions*. New York: St Martin's Press.

Friedman, L. (1987) 'Civil wrongs: Personal injury law in the nineteenth century', *American Bar Foundation Research Journal*, 12(2/3): 351–78.

Friedman, L. and Ladinsky, J. (1967) 'Social change and the law of industrial accidents', *Columbia Law Review*, 67: 50.

Frug, G. (1984) 'The ideology', *Harvard Law Review*, 97: 1276.

Fulbrook, M. and Skocpol, T. (1984) 'Destined pathways: The historical sociology of Perry Anderson', in T. Skocpol (ed.), *Vision and Method in Historical Sociology*. Cambridge: Cambridge University Press.

Gable, P. (1977) 'Intention and structure in contractual conditions: Outline of a method for critical legal theory', *Minnesota Law Review*, 61: 601.

Galanter, M. (1974) 'Why the haves come out ahead: Speculations on the limits of legal change', *Law and Society Review*, 9: 95–160.

Galanter, M. (1981) 'Justice in many rooms: Courts, private ordering and indigenous law', *Journal of Legal Pluralism*, 19: 1–47.

Galanter, M. (1983) 'Mega-law and mega-lawyering in the contemporary United States', in R. Dingwall and P. Lewis (eds), *The Sociology of the Professions: Lawyers, Doctors and Others*, pp. 152–75. London: Macmillan.

Galanter, M. (1984) 'Worlds of deals: Using negotiation to teach about legal process', *Journal of Legal Education*, 34: 268.

Galanter, M. (1984–5) 'The emergence of the judge as a mediator in civil cases', *Working Paper*, DPRP, Madison.

Galanter, M. (1985) 'A settlement judge, not a trial judge: Judicial mediation in the United States', *Journal of Law and Society*, 11(1): 1–17.

Galanter, M. and Paley, T. (1991) *Tournament of Lawyers: The Transformation of the Big Law Firm*. Chicago, IL: University of Illinois Press.

Garth, B. (1982) 'The movement towards procedural informalism in North America and Western Europe: A critical survey', in R. Abel (ed.), *The Politics of Informal Justice*, Vol. 2, pp. 183–213. New York: Academic Press.

Gaventa, J. (1980) *Power and Powerlessness: Quiescence and Rebellion in an Appalachian Valley*. Urbana, IL: University of Illinois Press.

Geertz, C. (1973) 'Thick descriptions: Toward an interpretive theory of culture', in *The Interpretation of Cultures*, pp. 3–32. New York: Basic Books.

Genn, H. (1988) *Hard Bargaining*. Oxford: Oxford University Press.

Gessner, V. and Plett, K. (1989) 'La justice informelle dans l'evolution du systeme juridique Allemand', *Annales de Vaucresson*, 29: 117–41.

Giddens, A. (1976) *New Rules of Sociological Method*. London: Macmillan.

Gifford, T. (1986) *Where's the Justice? A Manifesto for Law Reform*. Harmondsworth: Penguin.

Gilb, C. (1966) *Hidden Hierarchies: The Professions and Government*. New York: Harper and Row.

Gillespie, C. (1989) *Justifiable Homicide: Battered Women, Self Defence and the Law*. Ohio State University.

Girdner, L. (1986) 'Child custody determination: Ideological dimensions of a social problem', in E. Seidman and J. Rappaport (eds), *Redefining Social Problems*. New York: Plenum Press.

Goode, R. (1982) *Legal Problems of Credit and Security*. London: Sweet and Maxwell.

Goode, R. (1985) *Proprietary Rights and Insolvency in Sales Transactions*. London: Sweet and Maxwell.

Goodrich, P. (1986) *Reading the Law: A Critical Introduction to Legal Method and Techniques*. Oxford: Blackwell.

Goodrich, P. (1991) *Languages of the Law*. London: Weidenfeld and Nicolson.

Gordon, R. (1975) 'Introduction: J. Willard Hurst and the Common Law tradition in American legal historiography', *Law and Society Review* 10(9): 9–55.

Gordon, R. (1981) 'Historicism in legal scholarship', *Yale Law Review*, 90: 1017.

Gordon, R. (1983) 'Legal thought and legal practice in the age of American enterprise, 1870–1920', in G. Geison (ed.), *Professions and the Professional Ideologies in America*, pp. 70–110. Chapel Hill, NC: University of North Carolina Press.

Gordon, R. (1984a) 'Critical legal histories', *Stanford Law Review*, 36: 127.

Gordon, R. (1984b) 'The ideal and the actual in the law: Fantasies and practices of New York City lawyers, 1870–1910', in G.W. Gawalt (ed.), *The New High Priests: Lawyers in Post-Civil War America*. Westport, CT: Greenwood Press.

Gordon, R. (1988) 'The independence of lawyers', *Boston University Law Review*, 1–83.

Gordon, R. (1990) 'A perspective from the United States', in C. Wilton (ed.), *Beyond the Law: Lawyers and Business in Canada 1830–1930*. Toronto: Butterworths.

Gould, C. (ed.) (1984) *Beyond Domination: New Perspectives on Women and Philosophy*. Totowa, NJ: Rowman and Littlefield.

Gouldner, J. (1971) *The Super Lawyers*. New York: Weybright and Talley.

Gower, L. (1979) *Principles of Modern Company Law*, 4th edn. London: Stevens.

Graebner, W. (1978) *Coal Mining Safety in the Progressive Period: The Political Economy of Reform*. Lexington, KY: University of Kentucky Press.

Grahame, O. (1963) 'What is expected of a corporate law department?', *American Bar Association Journal*, 49: 159–61.

Gramsci, A. (1972) 'The intellectuals', in *Selections from the Prison Notebooks*. London: Lawrence and Wishart, pp. 5–23.

Green, M. (1976) 'The ABA as a trade association', in R. Nader and M. Green (eds), *Verdicts on Lawyers*. New York: Cromwell.

Greenberg, E.S. (1986) *Workplace Democracy: The Political Effects of Participation*. Itacha, New York: Cornell University Press.

Griffiths, J. (1985) 'Four laws of interaction in circumstances of legal pluralism', in A. Allott and G. Woodman (eds), *People's Law and State Law*, pp. 217–29. Dordrecht: Fores.

Griffiths, J. (1986) 'What do Dutch lawyers actually do in divorce cases?', *Law and Society Review*, 20: 135.

Grimshaw, E. and Jones, G. (1958) *Lord Goddard: His Career and Cases*. London: Allen Wingate.

Gross, P. (1976) *Legal Aid and its Management*. Cape Town: Juta.

Grossman, J. (1965) *Lawyers and Judges: The ABA and the Politics of Judicial Selection*. New York: John Wiley.

Hadden, T. (1983) *The Control of Corporate Groups*. London: Institute of Advanced Legal Studies.

Hadden, T. (1984) 'Inside corporate groups', *International Journal of the Sociology of Law*, 12(3): 271–86.

Hagan, J., Huxter, M. and Parker, P. (1988) 'Class structure and legal practice: Inequality and mobility among Toronto lawyers', *Law and Society Review*, 22: 9.

Hagan, J., Zatz, M. and Kay, A.F. (1991) 'Cultural capital, gender and the structural transformation of legal practice', *Law and Society Review*, 25: 239.

Haley, M. (1985) 'Avoiding the Rent Act: *Street* v. *Mountford* and beyond', *New Law Journal*, 135: 1053.

Hall, S., Critcher, C., Jefferson, T., Clarke, J. and Roberts, B. (1978) *Policing the Crisis: Mugging, the State, and Law and Order*. London: Macmillan.

Halliday, T. (1987) *Beyond Monopoly: Lawyers, State Crisis, and Professional Empowerment*. Chicago, IL: University of Chicago Press.

Handler, J. (1967) *The Lawyer and His Community*. Madison: University of Wisconsin Press.

Handler, J. (1978) *Social Movements and the Legal System*. New York: Academic Press.

Handler, J., Hollingsworth, E. and Erlanger, H. (1976) *Lawyers and the Pursuit of Legal Rights*. New York: Academic Press.

Harding, S. (1983) 'Is gender a variable in conceptions of rationality? A survey of issues', in C. Gould (ed.), *Beyond Domination, New Perspectives on Women and Philosophy*. New York: Rowman and Littlefield.

Harrington, C. (1982) 'Delegalization reform movements: A historical analysis', in R. Abel (ed.), *The Politics of Informal Justice*, Vol. I. New York: Academic Press.

Harrington, C. (1985) *Shadow Justice: The Ideology and Institutionalization of Alternatives to Court*. Westport, CT: Greenwood Press.

Harrington, C. and Merry, S. (1988) 'Ideological production: The making of community mediation', *Law and Society Review*, 22(4): 709–35.

Harrington, C. and Yngvesson, B. (1990) 'Interpretive sociological research', *Law and Social Inquiry*, 15: 135.

Harris, A. (1990) 'Race and essentialism in feminist legal theory', *Stanford Law Review*, 42: 581.

Hart, H. (1961) *The Concept of Law*. Oxford: Oxford University Press.

Hartog, H. (1983) *Public Property and Private Power: The Corporation of the City of New York in American Law, 1730–1870*. Chapel Hill, NC: University of North Carolina Press.

Hartsock, N. (1983) 'The feminist standpoint: Developing the ground for a specifically feminist historical materialism', in S. Harding and M. Hintikka (eds), *Discovering Reality*. Boston, MA: D. Reidl.

Hastings, Sir P. (1948) *Autobiography of Sir Patrick Hastings*. London: Heinemann.

Hawkins, K. (1984) *Environment and Enforcement*. Oxford: Clarendon Press.

Hays, S. (1973) *The Response to Industrialism: 1885–1914*. Chicago, IL: University of Chicago Press.

Hedley, S. (1987) 'Superior knowledge or revolution: An approach to modern legal history', *Anglo-American Law Review*, 18: 177.

Heinz, J. and Laumann, E. (1978) 'The legal profession: Client interests, professional roles, and social hierarchies', *Michigan Law Review*, 76: 1111.

Heinz, J. and Laumann, E. (1982) *Chicago Lawyers: The Social Structure of the Bar*. New York: Russell Sage.

Henry, S. (1983) *Private Justice*. Boston, MA: Routledge and Kegan Paul.

Heydebrand, W. (1977) 'Organizational contradictions in public bureaucracies: Toward a Marxian theory of organization', *Sociological Quarterly*, 18: 83.

Heydebrand, W. (1979) 'The technocratic administration of justice', *Research in Law and Sociology*, 2: 29.

Hickman, L. (1957) 'The emerging role of the corporate counsel', *The Business Lawyer*, April, pp. 216–28.

Hobson, W. (1984) 'Emergence of the large law firm, 1879–1915', in G. Gewalt (ed.), *The New High Priests: Lawyers in Post-Civil War America*. Westport, CT: Greenwood Press.

Hobson, W. (1986) *The American Legal Profession and the Organizational Society 1890–1930*. New York: Garland Publishing.

Hoexter Commission (1983) *Fifth and Final Report of the Commission of Inquiry into the Structure and Function of the Courts*, RP78/1983 (Part A). Pretoria: Government Printers.

Hoff, L. (1990) *Battered Women as Survivors*. London: Routledge.

Hoffman, P. (1973) *Lions in the Street: The Inside Story of the Great Wall Street Law Firms*. New York: Saturday Review Press.

Hofmeyr, P. and Shefer, T. (1987) *Bhongolethu Report*. University of Cape Town, Institute of Criminology, October.

Holderness, B.A. (1975) 'Credit in a rural community 1660–1800', *Midland History*, 5: 55–71.

Holmes, G. (1982) *Augustan England: Professions, State and Society 1680–1730*. London: Allen and Unwin.

Hope, P. (1989) 'Who are the terrorists – an account of security police operations in the Forbes and Yengeni Trials', Unpublished research paper, University of Cape Town.

Horowitz, M. (1977) *The Transformation of American Law 1780–1860*. Boston, MA: Harvard University Press.

Horsky, C. (1952) *The Washington Lawyer*. Boston, MA: Little, Brown and Co.

Howard, J. (1986) 'Advocacy in constitutional choices: The Cramer treason case, 1942–1945', *American Bar Foundation Research Journal*, p. 375.

Hund, J. and Kotu-Rammopo, M. (1983) 'Justice in a South African Township: The sociology of Makgotla', *The Comparative and International Law Journal of Southern Africa*, XVI: 179–208.

Hund, J. and Van der Merwe, H.W. (1986) *Legal Ideology and Politics in South Africa: A Social Science Approach*. Lanham: University Press of America.

Hunt, A. (1985) 'The ideology of law: Advances and problems in federal applications of the concept of ideology to the analysis of law', *Law and Society Review*, 19: 11.

Hurst, J.W. (1950) *The Growth of American Law: The Law Makers*. Boston, MA: Little, Brown and Co.

Hurst, J.W. (1970) *The Legitimacy of the Business Corporation in the Law of the United States, 1780–1970*. Richmond, VA: University Press of Virginia.

Hyde, M. (1964) *Norman Birkett: The Life of Lord Birkett of Ulverstone*. London: Hamish Hamilton.

Hyslop, J. (1988) 'School Student Movements and State Education Policy: 1972–87' in W. Cobbett and R. Cohen (eds), *Popular Struggles in South Africa*. London: in association with James Currey.

Institute of Criminology (1989) *A Survey of Community Attitudes to Sentencing: The Case of the State of Khumalo and Twenty-five Others*. Cape Town: University of Cape Town, Institute of Criminology.

Irons, P. (1982) *New Deal Lawyers*. Princeton, NJ: Princeton University Press.

Isaacman, D. and A. (1982) 'A socialist legal system in the making: Mozambique before and after independence', in R. Abel (ed.), *The Politics of Informal Justice, Vol. 2*. New York: Academic Press.

Israel, J. (ed.) (1972) *Building the Organizational Society: Essays on Associational Activities in Modern America*. New York: Free Press.

Jaffe, L. (1939) 'Invective and investigation in administrative law', *Harvard Law Review*, 52: 1201.

Jaffe, L. (1969) *English and American Judges as Law Makers*. Oxford: Oxford University Press.

Jagger, A. (1989) 'Love and knowledge: Emotion in feminist epistemology', in A. Garry and M. Pearsall (eds), *Women, Knowledge and Reality*. London: Unwin.

Jeammaud, A. and Lyon-Caen, A. (1982) 'Droit et direction du personnel', *Droit Social*, 2.

Jeantin, M. (1985) 'A propos de la reforme des procedures collectives', *Actes*, 48: 11–15.

Johnson, T. (1972) *Professions and Power*. London: Macmillan.

Johnstone, Q. and Hopson, D. (1967) *Lawyers and their Work*. Indianapolis, IN: Bobbs Merrill.

Jones, A. (1991) *Women Who Kill*. London: Victor Gollancz.

Jones, H. (1952) 'Bill drafting services in Congress and the State legislatures', *Harvard Law Review*, 65: 441–57.

Jones, R. (1971) *The Nineteenth Century Foreign Office*. London: Weidenfeld and Nicolson.

Kammen, M. (1986) *A Machine that Would Go of Itself: The Constitution in American Culture*. New York: Alfred A. Knopf, Inc.

Karpik, L. (1988) 'Lawyers and politics in France, 1814–1950: The state, the market, and the public', *Law and Social Inquiry*, 13: 4.

Katz, J. (1978) 'Lawyers for the poor in transition: Involvement, reform, and the turnover problem in the legal services program', *Law and Society Review*, 12: 275–300.

Katz, J. (1984) *Poverty Lawyers*. New Brunswick, NJ: Rutgers University Press.

Kay, H. (1985) 'Models of equality', *University of Illinois Law Review*, 1: 39.

Kemp, K. (1986) 'Lawyers, politics, and economic regulation', *Social Science Quarterly*, 67(2): 267-82.

Kennedy, D. (1980) 'Towards an historical understanding of legal consciousness: The case of classical legal thought in America, 1850–1940', in S. Spitzer (ed.), *Research in Law and Society*, Greenwich, CT: Jai Press.

Kennedy, D. (1985) 'L'enseignement du droit et la reproduction des hierarchies professionnelles', *Annales de Vaucresson*, 23: 189–99.

Kennedy, F. (1971) 'The whore house theory of law', in R. Lefcourt (ed.), *Law Against the People*. New York: Random House.

Kerruish, V. (1991) *Jurisprudence as Ideology*. London: Routledge.

Kessler, M. (1987) *Legal Service for the Poor*. Westport, CT: Greenwood Press.

Kirk, H. (1976) *Portrait of a Profession*. London: Oyez.

Klare, K. (1978) 'Judicial deradicalization of the Wagner Act and the origins of modern legal consciousness, 1937–1941', *Minnesota Law Review*, 62: 265.

Klaw, S. (1958) 'The Wall Street lawyers', *Fortune*, February, pp. 140–200.

Kline, M. (1989) 'Race, racism, and feminist legal theory', *Harvard Women's Law Journal*, 12: 115.

Klugar, R. (1975) *Simple Justice*. New York: Vintage Books.

Konefsky, A. and King, A. (eds) (1982) *The Papers of Daniel Webster, Vol. I: The New Hampshire Practice*. Hanover, NH: University Press of New England.

Kornhauser, W. (1963) *Scientists in Industry: Conflict and Accommodation*. Berkeley, CA: University of California Press.

Kostal, R.W. (1994) *Law and English Railway Capitalism, 1825–75*. Oxford: Oxford University Press.

Kraft, J. (1964) 'The Washington lawyers', *Harper's*, April, pp. 102–108.

Kritzer, H. (1984) 'The dimensions of lawyer–client relations: Notes toward a theory and a field study', *American Bar Foundation Research Journal*, p. 409.

Kritzer, H. (1988) 'Lawyers who litigate: Background, work setting, and attitudes', paper presented at the *Annual Law and Society Association Conference*, Vail, Colorado, June.

Ladinsky, J. (1963) 'Careers of lawyers, law practice, and legal institutions', *American Sociological Review*, 28: 47–54.

Ladley, A. (1982) 'Changing the courts in Zimbabwe: The Customary Law and Primary Courts Act', *Journal of African Law*, 26(2): 95–114.

Ladley, A. (1991) 'Just Spirits? In search of tradition in the customary law courts of Zimbabwe', *Proceedings of the VIth International Symposium, Ottawa, Canada, August 14–18, 1990*, Vol. 2.

Landon, D. (1990) *Country Lawyers: The Impact of Context in Professional Practice*. New York: Praeger.

Lane, W. (1924) *The Denial of Civil Liberties in the Coal Fields*. New York: Doran.

Larson, M.S. (1977) *The Rise of Professionalism: A Sociological Analysis*. Berkeley, CA: University of California Press.

300 *Bibliography*

Lascomes, P. (1985) 'Les commissions techniques', *Actes*, 85: 52–5.

Lascomes, P. (1986) *Des erreurs, pas des fautes*. Paris: CESDIP.

Laumann, E. and Heinz, J. (1977) 'Specialization and prestige in the legal profession: The structure of deference', *American Bar Foundation Research Journal*, 2(1): 155–216.

Law Society (1985) *Tax Law in the Melting Pot*. London: The Law Society.

Law Student's Helper (1902) 'Legal profession and its opportunities', *Law Student's Helper*, 10: 8.

Lees, S. (1992) 'Provocation as a defence in homicide trials', in D. Russell and J. Radford Twayne (eds), *Femicide: the Politics of Woman Killing*. Buckingham: Open University Press.

Lees, S. (1993) *Sugar and Spice: Sexuality and Adolescent Girls*. London: Penguin.

Lefcourt, R. (1971) 'The first law commune', in R. Lefcourt (ed.), *Law Against the People: Essays to Demystify Law, Order and the Court*. New York: Vintage Books.

Legal Education Action Project and BlackSash (n.d.) *Working for Justice: The Role of Paralegals in South Africa*. Cape Town: LEAP.

Lemmings, D. (1990) *Gentlemen and Barristers: The Inns of Court and the English Bar 1680–1730*. Oxford: Clarendon Press.

Lerner, G. (1986) *The Creation of Patriarchy*. New York: Oxford University Press.

Levi, M. (1984) 'Giving creditors the business: The criminal law in action', *International Journal of Sociology of Law*, 12: 321.

Lewis, J. (1982) *The Victorian Bar*. London: Robert Hale.

Lieberman, J. (1978) *Crisis at the Bar*. New York: W.W. Norton.

Llewellyn, K. (1930–31) 'Some realism about realism', *Harvard Law Review*, 44: 1222–59.

Llewellyn, K. (1933) 'The bar specialises – with what results?', *Annals of the American Academy of Political and Social Science*, CLXVII: 177–92.

Lloyd, G. (1984) *The Man of Reason: 'Male' and 'Female' in Western Philosophy*. Minneapolis, MN: University of Minnesota Press.

Lortie, D. (1959) 'Laymen and lawmen', *Harvard Educational Review*, 29(4): 352–69.

Louw, C. (1988) 'Gewere moet die boeke laat klop', *Die Suid-Afrikaan*, August/ September (16).

Luckhaus, L. (1986) 'A plea for PMT in the criminal law', in S. Edwards (ed.), *Gender, Sex and the Law*. London: Croom Helm.

Luhmann, N. (1979) *Trust and Power*. Chichester: John Wiley.

Luhmann, N. (1985) *The Sociology of Law*. London: Routledge.

Lunt, R. (1979) *Law and Order vs. the Miners: West Virginia, 1907–1933*. Hamden, CT: Anchor Press.

Lynd, S. (1984) 'Communal rights', *Texas Law Review*, 62: 1417.

Macaulay, S. (1963) 'Non-contractual relations in business', *American Sociological Review*, 28: 45.

Macaulay, S. (1966) *Law and the Balance of Power: The Automobile Manufacturers and their Dealers*. New York: Russell Sage.

Macaulay, S. (1979) 'Lawyers and consumer protection laws', *Law and Society Review*, 14: 115.

MacCorkie, W. (1928) *The Recollections of Fifty Years of West Virginia*. New York: G.P. Putnam.

MacKinnon, C. (1982) 'Feminism, Marxism, method and the State: An agenda for theory', *Signs*, 7(3): 227–56.

MacKinnon, C. (1983) 'Feminism, Marxism, method and the state: Toward feminist jurisprudence?', *Signs*, 8: 635.

MacKinnon, C. (1987) *Feminism Unmodified: Discourses on Life and Law*. Cambridge, MA: Harvard University Press.

Macmillan, Lord (1937) *Law and Other Things*. Cambridge: Cambridge University Press.

Maitland, F. (1901/1957) 'English law and the Renaissance', *Historical Essays*, pp. 135–151. Cambridge: Cambridge University Press.

Malcolm, J. (1966) *Let's Make It Legal*. Reading: Educational Explorers.

Mann, K. (1985) *Defending White Collar Crime*. New Haven: Yale University Press.

Mansfield, G. (1987) 'Techniques of tax avoidance', presented at the *Annual Law and Society Association Conference*, Washington, June.

Mansfield, G. (1989) 'The new approach to tax avoidance', *British Tax Review*, March (1).

Marbury, W.L. (1912) 'The lawyer of fifty years ago and the lawyer of today', *The Green Bag*, 24: 64.

Marx, K. (1905/1969) *Theories of Surplus Value*, Vol. I. London: Lawrence and Wishart.

Mathew, T. (1937) *For Lawyers and Others*. London: William Hedge.

Mathiesen, T. (1980) *Law, Society, and Political Action*. London: Academic Press.

Mathiesen, T. (1983) 'Civil disobedience at 70° North', *Contemporary Crises*, 7(1): 1–11.

Maugham, Viscount (1954) *At the End of the Day*. London: Heinemann.

Mayer, M. (1966) *The Lawyers*. New York: Harper and Row.

McBarnet, D. (1981) *Conviction: Law, the State and the Construction of Justice*. London: Macmillan.

McBarnet, D. (1984) 'Law and capital: The role of legal form and legal actors', *International Journal of the Sociology of Law*, 12(3): 231–8.

McBarnet, D. (1987) 'The construction of legal devices: Legal entrepreneurs and private law making', abstract presented at the *Law and Society Association Conference*, Washington, June.

McBarnet, D. (1988) 'Law, policy and legal avoidance: Can law effectively implement egalitarian policies', *Journal of Law and Society*, 15(1): 113–21.

McBarnet, D. (1991) 'Whiter than white-collar crime: Tax, fraud insurance and the management of stigma', *British Journal of Sociology*, 42(3): 323–43.

McBarnet, D. (1992) 'It's not what you do but the way that you do it', in D. Downes (ed.), *Unravelling Criminal Justice*. London: Macmillan.

McBarnet, D. and Whelan, C. (1987) 'The development of priority in insolvency', presented at the *Annual Law and Society Association Conference*, Washington, June.

McBarnet, D. and Whelan, C. (1988) 'Cooking the books: Creative accounting and the control of corporate finance', paper presented at the *Annual Law and Society Association Conference*, Vail, Colorado, June.

McBarnet, D. and Whelan, C. (1990) 'Regulating accounting: Limits in the law', in M. Bromwich and A. Hopwood (eds), *Accounting and the Law*. Englewood Cliffs, NJ: Prentice-Hall.

McBarnet, D. and Whelan, C. (1991) 'The elusive spirit of the law: Formalism and the struggle for legal control', *Modern Law Review*, 54(6): 848–73, November.

McBarnet, D. and Whelan, C. (forthcoming) *Law, Creativity and Control*.

McBarnet, D., Weston, C. and Whelan, C. (1993) 'Adversary accounting: Uses of financial information by capital and labour', *Accounting Organisations and Society*, 18(1): 81–100.

McCann, K. (1985) 'Battered women and the law: The limits of the legislation', in J. Brophy and C. Smart (eds), *Women in Law: Explorations in Law, Family and Sexuality*, pp. 71–96. London: Routledge and Kegan Paul.

McCann, M. (1986) *Taking Reform Seriously: Perspectives on Public Interest Liberalism.* Ithaca, NY: Cornell University Press.

McConville, M. and Mirsky, C. (1989) *Criminal Defense of the Poor in New York City.* Occasional Paper, Center for Research in Crime and Justice, New York University Law School.

McCurdy, C. (1978) 'American law and the marketing structure of the large corporation, 1875–1900', *Journal of Economic History*, 38(3): 631–49.

McElroy, W. (ed.) (1982) 'The roots of individualist feminism in 19th-century America', in *Freedom, Feminism, and the State*, 3–26.

McNeil, M. (1987) *Gender and Expertise.* London, Free Association Books.

McQuoid-Mason, D. (1990) 'Legal Representation and the Courts', in M. Robertson (ed.), *South African Human Rights and Labour Law Yearbook*, Vol. I. Cape Town: Oxford University Press, Durban: Centre for Socio-Legal Studies.

Medcalf, L. (1978) *Law and Identity: Lawyers, Native Americans, and Legal Practice.* Beverley Hills, CA: Sage.

Megarry, R. (1962) *Lawyer and Litigant in England.* London: Stevens.

Melone, A. (1979) *Lawyers, Public Policy and Interest Group Politics.* Washington: University Press of America.

Merry, S. (1988) 'Legal pluralism: Review essay', *Law and Society Review*, 22(5): 869–96.

Merton, R. (1967) 'On sociological theories of the middle range', in *On Theoretical Sociology: Five Essays, Old and New*, pp. 39–72. New York: Free Press.

Middler, C. (1986) 'Logique de la mode manageriale', *Annales des Mines*, June, pp. 74–85.

Miles, M. (1984) ' "Eminent practitioners": The New Visage of Country Attorneys', in G.R. Rubin and D. Sugarman (eds), *Law, Economy and Society: Essays in the History of English Law, 1750–1914.* Abingdon: Professional Books.

Miller, M. (1992) 'Lawyers and American politics: An interdisciplinary perspective', paper presented at the *Annual Law and Society Association Conference*, Philadelphia, May.

Miller, R. and Sarat, A. (1980–81) 'Grievances, claims and disputes: Assessing the adversary culture', *Law and Society Review*, 15: 525.

Mills, C.W. (1956) *The Power Elite.* New York: Oxford University Press.

Milman, D. (1984) 'More reservations about Romalpa', *Conveyancer*, 48: 139.

Mitra, C. (1987) 'Judicial discourse in father–daughter incest cases', *International Journal of the Sociology of Law*, 15(2): 121–48.

Molobi, E. (1988) 'From Bantu Education to People's Education', in W. Cobbett and R. Cohen (eds), *Popular Struggles in South Africa.* London: in association with James Currey.

Moon, W. (1988) *Mountain Voices – A Legacy of the Blue Ridge and Great Smokies.* Chester, CT: Globe Pequot Press.

Morris, Sir H. (1930) *The Barrister.* London: Jeffrey Bles.

Morrison, F. (1973) *Courts and the Political Process in England*. London: Sage.

Motshekga, M. (1987) 'Alternative legal institutions in Southern Africa', paper presented at a workshop on *New Approaches in Respect of the Administration of Justice*, Pretoria, University of South Africa, July.

Munger, F. (1987) 'Social change and tort litigation: Industrialization, accidents and trial courts in Southern West Virginia, 1922–1940', *Buffalo Law Review*, 36: 75.

Munger, F. (1988) 'Law, change and litigation: A critical examination of an empirical research tradition', *Law and Society Review*, 22: 57.

Munger, F. (1991) 'Legal resources of striking miners: Notes for a study of class conflict and law', *Social Science History*, 15: 1.

Murray, G. (1987) 'Women lawyers in New Zealand: Some questions about the politics of equality', *International Journal of the Sociology of Law*, 15(4), 439–57.

Napley, D. (1970) *The Technique of Persuasion*. London: Sweet and Maxwell.

Nelken, D. (1983) *The Limits of the Legal Process*. London: Academic Press.

Nelson, R. (1981) 'Practice and privilege: Social change and the structure of large law firms', *American Bar Foundation Research Journal*, p. 95.

Nelson, R. (1985) 'Ideology, practice, and professional autonomy: Social values and client relationships in the large law firm', *Stanford Law Review*, 37: 503–549.

Nelson, R. (1968) *Partners with Power*. Berkeley, CA: University of California Press.

Nelson, R. and Heinz, J. (1988) 'Lawyers and the structure of influence in Washington', *Law and Society Review*, 22: 237.

Nelson, R., Heinz, J., Laumann, E. and Salisbury, R. (1987) 'Private representation in Washington: Surveying the structure of influence', *American Bar Foundation Research Journal*, 12(1): 141–200.

Nelson, R., Trubek, D. and Solomon, R. (1992a) 'New problems and new paradigms in studies of the legal profession', in R. Nelson, D. Trubek and R. Solomon (eds), *Lawyers' Ideals, Lawyers' Practice*. Ithaca, NY: Cornell University Press.

Nelson, R., Trubek, D. and Solomon, R. (eds) (1992b) *Lawyers' Ideals and Lawyers' Practices: Professionalism and the Transformation of the American Legal Profession*. Chicago, IL: University of Chicago Press.

O'Brien, G. (1986) *The Legal Fraternity and the Making of a New South Community, 1848–1882*. London: University of Georgia Press.

Offer, A. (1981) *Property and Politics 1870–1914*. Cambridge: Cambridge University Press.

O'Gorman, H. (1963) *Lawyers and Matrimonial Cases*. Glencoe, IL: Free Press.

Olsen, F. (1989) 'Feminist theory in grand style', *Columbia Law Review*, 49: 1147.

Olsen, S. (1984) *Clients and Lawyers: Securing the Rights of Disabled Persons*. Westport, CT: Greenwood Press.

O'Meara, A. (1962) 'Organizational structure, operation, and administration of a large corporate law department (25 lawyers or more)', *The Business Lawyer*, 17: 584–94.

O'Neill, T. (1985) *Bakke & The Politics of Equality: Friends & Foes in The Classroom of Litigation*. Middletown, CT: Wesleyan University Press.

Osiel, M.J. (1989) 'Lawyers as monopolists, aristocrats and entrepreneurs', *Harvard Law Review*, 103: 2009.

Ost, F. (1983) *Juge pacificateur, juge-arbitre, juge-entraineur. Trois modeles de justice in Fonction de juger et pouvoir judiciaire: Transformations et deplacements*. Bruxelles: Fac. Univ. de St Louis.

Parrott, V. (1991) *A Difference of Opinion*. Occasional Paper in Politics and Contemporary History. Salford: University of Salford.

Parsons, T. (1954) 'A sociologist looks at the legal profession', *Essays in Sociological Theory*. Glencoe: The Free Press.

Parsons, T. (1962) 'The law and social control', in W.H. Evan (ed.), *Law and Sociology*. Chicago, IL: Free Press.

Parsons, T. (1968) 'Professions', in D. Sills (ed.), *International Encyclopedia of the Social Sciences*, Vol. 12. New York: Macmillan.

Pashukanis, E. (1980) 'The general theory of law and Marxism', in P. Beirne and R. Sharlet (eds), *Pashukanis: Selected Writings on Marxism and Law*. London: Academic Press.

Pauw, J. (1990) *In the Heart of the Whore – the Story of Apartheid's Death Squads*. Half Way House: Southern Book Publishers.

Pennington, R. (1960) 'The genesis of the floating change', *Modern Law Review*, 30: 630.

Peters, J. and Carden, H. (1926) *History of Fayette County West Virginia*. Charleston, WV: Jarrett.

Piore, M. and Berger, S. (1980) *Dualism and Discontinuity in Industrial Societies*. Cambridge: Cambridge University Press.

Piore, M. and Sabel, C. (1984) *The Second Industrial Divide: Possibilities for Prosperity*. New York: Basic Books.

Platt, A. (1969) *The Child Savers*. Chicago, IL: University of Chicago Press.

Podmore, D. and Spencer, A. (1982) 'The law as a sex typed profession', *Journal of Law and Society*, 9(1): 21–36.

Pollock, G. (1934) *Mr Justice McCardie*. London: Bodley Head.

Popper, K. (1965) *Conjectures and Refutations*, 2nd edn. London: Routledge and Kegan Paul.

Popper, K. (1968) *The Logic of Scientific Discovery*, 2nd edn. London: Hutchinson.

Powell, M. (1987) 'Professional innovation: Corporate lawyers and private lawmaking', paper presented at the *Annual Law and Society Association Conference*, Washington, June.

Powell, M. (1988) *From Patrician to Professional Elite*. New York: Russell Sage.

Prest, W. (1981a) 'Introduction', in W. Prest (ed.), *Lawyers in Early Modern Europe and America*. London: Croom Helm.

Prest, W. (1981b) 'The English Bar, 1550–1700', in W. Prest (ed.), *Lawyers in Early Modern Europe and America*. London: Croom Helm.

Prest, W.R. (1984) 'Why the history of the professions is not written', in G.R. Rubin and D. Sugarman (eds), *Law, Economy and Society: Essays in the History of English Law, 1750–1914*. Abingdon: Professional Books.

Prest, W.R. (1986) *The Rise of the Barristers: A Social History of the English Bar 1590–1640*. Oxford: Clarendon Press.

Prest, W. (1987) 'Introduction: The professions and society in early modern England', in W. Prest (ed.), *The Professions in Early Modern England*. London: Croom Helm.

Priest, T. and Krol, J. (1986) 'Lawyers in corporate chief executive positions: Career characteristics and "inner group" membership', *International Journal of the Sociology of Law*, 14(1): 33–46.

Priest, T. and Rothman, R. (1985) 'Lawyers in corporate chief executive positions: A historical analysis of careers', *Work and Occupations*, 12(2): 131–46.

Provine, D.M. (1986) *Judging Credentials: Nonlawyer Judges and the Politics of Professionalism*. Chicago, IL: University of Chicago Press.

Pue, W.W. (1987) 'Exorcising professional demons', *Law and History Review*, 5: 135.

Pue, W.W. (1989) 'Guild training *vs* professional education', *American Journal of Legal History*, 33: 241.

Pue, W.W. (1990) 'Moral panic at the English bar', *Law and Social Inquiry*, 15: 49.

Rabinow, P. and Sullivan, W. (eds) (1979) *Interpretive Social Science: A Reader*. Berkeley, CA: University of California Press.

Radford, J. (1987) 'Policing male violence – policing women', in J. Hammer and M. Maynard (eds), *Women, Violence and Social Control*. London: Macmillan.

Rae, D. (1981) *Equalities*. Cambridge, MA: Harvard University Press.

Reader, W. (1966) *Professional Men: The Rise of the Classes in Nineteenth Century England*. London: Weidenfeld and Nicolson.

Report of the Commission of Inquiry into the South African Council of Churches (the Eloff Commission) (1983) RP74/83.

Rights of Women (1992) *Submission to the Royal Commission: Proposed Amendments to the 1957 Homicide Act*.

Rippert, G. (1949) *Le declin du droit*. Paris: LGDJ.

Rodell, F. (1939) *Woe Unto You Lawyers*. New York, Pageant Press.

Rosenthal, D. (1974) *Lawyer and Client: Who's in Charge?* New York: Russell Sage.

Rostow (1949/1955) 'Review of "The Cravath Firm" ', in E. Cheatham (ed.), *Cases and Materials on the Legal Profession*, pp. 55–7. Brooklyn: The Foundation Press.

Rousseau, J. (1762/1974) *Emile: Book V*. Paris: Duchesne/London: Dutton.

Rowley, A.S. (1988) *Professions, Class and Society: Solicitors in 19th Century Birmingham*. PhD thesis, Aston University, Birmingham.

Rubin, D. and Sugarman, D. (1983) *Law, Economy and Society*. Abingdon: Professional Books.

Ruddick, S. (1990) *Material Thinking: Towards a Politics of Peace*. London: Women's Press.

Rueschemeyer, D. (1973) *Lawyers and their Society*. Cambridge, MA: Harvard University Press.

Rueschemeyer, D. (1978) 'The legal profession in comparative perspective', in H.M. Johnson (ed.), *Social System and Legal Process*. San Francisco, CA: Jossey-Bass.

Sachs, A. and Welch, G. (1987) 'The bride price, revolution, and the liberation of women', *International Journal of the Sociology of Law*, 15(4): 369–92.

Salais, R. and Thevenot, L. (1986) *Le Travail, Marches, Regles, Conventions*. Paris: Econimica.

Salokar, R. (1992) 'Lawyers for the legislature: The roles of the Senate legal counsel and the General Counsel for the House of Representatives', paper presented at the *Annual Law and Society Association Conference*, Philadelphia, May.

Sarat, A. (1988) 'The new formalism in disputing and dispute processing', *Law and Society Review*, 21: 695.

Sarat, A. (1992) 'Ideologies of professionalism: Conflict and change among small town lawyers', in R.L. Nelson, D.M. Trubek and R.L. Solomon (eds), *Lawyers' Ideals and Lawyers' Practices: Professionalism and the Transformation of the American Legal Profession*. Chicago, IL: University of Chicago Press.

Sarat, A. and Felstiner, W. (1986) 'Law and strategy in the divorce lawyer's office', *Law and Society Review*, 20: 93.

Sarat, A. and Silbey, S. (eds) (1992) *Trends and Opportunities in Disputing Research.* Amherst Studies in Law, Politics, and Society. Amherst, MA: Amherst University.

Savage, L. (1990) *Thunder in the Mountains: The West Virginia Mine War of 1920–21.* Pittsburgh, PA: University of Pittsburgh Press.

Schärf, W. (1989a) 'Community policing in South Africa', in T.W. Bennett *et al.* (eds), *Policing and the Law,* pp. 206–233. Cape Town: Juta.

Schärf, W. (1989b) 'The role of people's courts in transition', in H. Corder (ed.), *Democracy and the Judiciary.* Cape Town: IDASA.

Schärf, W. and Ngcokoto, B. (1990) 'Images of punishment in the people's courts of Cape Town 1985–7: From prefigurative justice to populist violence', in N.C. Manganyi and A. du Toit (eds), *Political Violence and the Struggle in South Africa.* London: Macmillan.

Scheingold, S. (1974) *The Politics of Rights.* New Haven, CT: Yale University Press.

Scheingold, S. (1988) 'Radical lawyers and socialist ideals', in R. Cotterrell and B. Bercusson (eds), *Law, Democracy and Social Justice: Journal of Law and Society,* 15: 122.

Schneider, E. (1986) 'The dialectic of rights and politics: Perspectives from the women's movement', *New York University Law Review,* 61: 589.

Scholz, J.T. (1984) 'Cooperation, deterrence and ecology of regulatory enforcement', *Law and Society Review,* 18.

Schwartz, G. (1981) 'Tort law and the economy in nineteenth century America: A reintegration', *Yale Law Journal,* 90: 1717.

Schwartz, M. (1987) 'Historical sociology in the history of American sociology', *Social Science History,* 2: 1–16.

Seeking, J. (1990) 'People's courts and popular politics', in G. Moss and I. Obery (eds), *South Africa Contemporary Analysis: South African Review 5,* pp. 119–35. London: Hans Zell.

Seron, C. (1992) 'Managing entrepreneurial legal services: The transformation of small firm practice', in R. Nelson, D. Trubek and R. Solomon (eds), *Lawyers' Ideals, Lawyers' Practices,* pp. 63–91. Ithaca, NY: Cornell University Press.

Sewell, W. (1985) 'Ideologies and social revolution: Reflections on the French Case', *Journal of Modern History,* p. 57.

Shanks, C. (1949) 'The lawyer in business: His opportunities and contributions', *The Record,* pp. 50–61.

Shapiro, H. (1978) *Appalachia on Our Minds: The Southern Mountains and Mountaineers in the American Consciousness, 1870–1920.* Chapel Hill, NC: University of North Carolina Press.

Shapiro, S. (1985) *Wayward Capitalists.* New Haven, CT: Yale University Press.

Shelter Housing Aid Centre (1975) *Annual Report 1974–75.* London: Shelter.

Sherwin, S. (1989) 'Philosophical Methodology and Feminist Methodology: Are They Compatible?', in A. Garry and M. Pearsall (eds), *Women, Knowledge and Reality.* London: Unwin Hyman.

Showronek, S. (1982) *Building A New American State: The Expansion of National Administrative Capacities, 1877–1920.* Cambridge: Cambridge University Press.

Simon, W. (1978) 'The ideology of advocacy: Procedural justice and professional ethics', *University of Wisconsin Law Review,* 29: 30.

Simon, W. (1984) 'Visions of practice in legal thought', *Stanford Law Review,* 36: 469.

Skocpol, T. (ed.) (1984) *Vision and Method in Historical Sociology*. Cambridge: Cambridge University Press.

Skocpol, T. (1985) 'Cultural idioms and political ideologies in the revolutionary reconstruction of state power: A rejoinder to Sewell', *Journal of Modern History*, 57: 86.

Skocpol, T. (1987) 'Social history and historical sociology: Contrasts and complementaries', *Social Science History*, 2: 17.

Skowronek, S. (1982) *Building a New American State: The Expansion of National Administrative Capacities, 1877–1920*. Cambridge: Cambridge University Press.

Slabbert, M. (1981) *The South African Legal System: Justice for All?* Cape Town: University of Cape Town Institute of Criminology.

Slinn, J. (1984) *A History of Freshfields*. London: Freshfields.

Slinn, J. (1987) *Linklaters & Paines*. London: Linklaters & Paines.

Slinn, J. (1989) 'The histories and records of firms of solicitors', *Business Archives*, 58: 22–9.

Sloth-Nielsen, J. Hansson, D. and Richardson, C. (1992) *'Chickens in a Box' – a progressive participatory study of Lwandle hostel residents' perceptions of personal safety*. Pretoria: Human Sciences Research Council.

Smart, C. (1986) 'Feminism and law: Some problems of analysis and strategy', *International Journal of the Sociology of Law*, 14(2): 109–123.

Smart, C. (1989) *Feminism and the Power of Law*. London: Routledge.

Smigel, E. (1969) *The Wall Street Lawyer*. New York: Midland Books.

Smith, D. (1988) *The Everyday World as Problematic*. Milton Keynes: Open University Press.

Smith, S. (1958) 'The business executive, corporate counsel, and general practitioner', *The Business Lawyer*, January, pp. 220–29.

Snyder, L. (1985) 'Legal reform and social control: The dangers of abolishing rape', *International Journal of the Sociology of Law*, 13(4): 337–56.

South African Institute of Race Relations (1984) *Survey of Race Relations*. Johannesburg: South African Institute of Race Relations.

South African Institute of Race Relations (1986) *Survey of Race Relations*. Johannesburg: South African Institute of Race Relations.

Southern African Catholic Bishop's Conference (1987) *The Last Affidavits*. Randburg: SACBC.

Spelman, E. (1988) *Inessential Women: Problems of Exclusion in Feminist Thought*. Boston, MA: Beacon Press.

Sperber, H. (1989) 'Rationality and relativism in beliefs', in A. Garry and M. Pearsall (eds), *Women, Knowledge and Reality*. London: Unwin.

Stanley, L. (1987) 'Biography as microscope or kaleidoscope: The question of power in Hannah Cullwick's diaries', *Women's Studies International Forum*, 10(1): 19–31.

Starr, P. (1982) *The Social Transformation of the American Medical Profession*. New York: Basic Books.

Stevens, R. (1983) *Law School: Legal Education in America from the 1850s to the 1980s*. Chapel Hill, NC: University of North Carolina Press.

Stewart, A. (1981) 'Jurisprudence as an object of knowledge', in B. Fryer (ed.), *Law, State and Society*. London: Croom Helm.

Stewart, J. (1983) *The Partners: Inside America's Most Powerful Law Firms*. New York: Simon and Schuster.

Stumpf, H. (1975) *Community Politics and Legal Services: The Other Side of the Law*. Beverly Hills, CA: Sage.

Sugarman, D. (1987) *In the Spirit of Weber: Law, Modernity and 'the Peculiarities of the English'*. Madison, WI: University of Wisconsin Institute for Legal studies.

Sugarman, D. (1991) 'Lawyers and business in England, 1750–1950', in C. Wilton (ed.), *Beyond the Law: Lawyers and Business in Canada, 1830–1930*.

Sugarman, D. (1992a) ' "A hatred of disorder": Legal science, liberalism and imperialism', in P. Fitzpatrick (ed.), *Dangerous Supplements: Resistance and Renewal in Jurisprudence*. London: Pluto Press.

Sugarman, D. (1992b) 'Writing "law and society" histories', *Modern Law Review*, 55: 292.

Sugarman, D. (1994) ' "The best organised and most intelligent trade union in the country": The private and public life of the Law Society, 1825–1914', in E. Skordaki (ed.), *Social Change and the Solicitors' Profession*. Oxford: Oxford University Press.

Sugarman, D. (forthcoming) *Company Law and the Rise of Capitalism*.

Sugarman, D. and Rubin, G.R. (1984) 'Towards a new history of law and material society in England, 1750–1914', in G.R. Rubin and D. Sugarman (eds), *Law, Economy and Society: Essays in the Histories of English Law, 1750–1914*. Abingdon: Professional Books.

Suttner, R. and Cronin, J. (1986) *Thirty Years of the Freedom Charter*. Johannesburg: Ravan.

Swaine, R. (1948) *The Cravath Firm and Its Predecessors 1819–1948*, New York: Privately printed, Ad. Press Ltd.

Swilling, M. (1988) 'Reform, security, and white power: Rethinking State strategies in the 1980's', paper presented at the *African Seminar* of the Centre for African Studies, University of Cape Town, June.

Szelenyi, I. and Martin, B. (1989) 'The legal profession and the rise and fall of the new class', in R.L. Abel and P.S.C. Lewis (eds), *Lawyers in Society: Comparative Theories*. Berkeley, CA: University of California Press.

Temkin, J. (1987) *Rape and the Legal Process*. London: Sweet and Maxwell.

Teubner, G. (1984) 'After legal instrumentalism: Strategic models of post-regulatory law', *International Journal of the Sociology of Law*, 12(4): 375–400.

Therborn, G. (1980) *The Ideology of Power and the Power of Ideology*. London: Verso.

Thompson, E.P. (1975) *Whigs and Hunters*. New York: Allen Lane.

Thomson, B. (1857) *The Choice of a Profession*. London: Chapman and Hall.

Tigar, M. and Levy, M. (1977) *Law and the Rise of Capitalism*. New York: Monthly Review Press.

Tilly, C. (1980) 'Historical sociology', in S.G. McNall and G.N. Howe (eds), *Current Perspectives in Social Theory*. Greenwich, CT: JAI Press.

Treiber, H. (1987) 'Lawyers' lives – in Germany', *Contemporary Crises*, 11(2): 159–91.

Treitel, G. (1981) *Doctrine and Discretion in the Law of Contract*. Oxford: Clarendon Press.

Twiss, B. (1942) *Lawyers and the Constitution: How Laissez Faire Came to the Supreme Court*. Princeton, NJ: Princeton University Press.

Van Zyl Smit, D. (1983) 'Professionalism and the access to legal services', in N. Olmesdahl and N. Steytler (eds), *Criminal Justice in South Africa*. Cape Town: Juta.

Vercammen, C. (1989) 'On policing the police – a study of how the South African Police Force is made accountable, with specific reference to the use of abuse by police in the exercise of their powers, duty, and function', unpublished research paper, University of Cape Town.

Ward, A. (n.d.) *Stuff and Silk.* Ramsey: Gansey Publications.

Wasik, M. (1982) 'Cumulative provocation and domestic killing', *Criminal Law Review*, 30(1): 29–37.

Weber, M. (1954) *On Law in Economy and Society* (edited by M. Rheinstein). Cambridge, MA: Harvard University Press

Weber, M. (1964) *On Bureaucracy.* London: Routledge and Kegan Paul.

Weber, M. (1966) *On Law in Economy and Society.* London: Routledge.

Weber, M. (1978) *Economy and Society* (tome 2). Berkeley, CA: University of California Press.

Weedon, C. (1987) *Feminist Practice & Poststructuralist Theory.* Oxford: Blackwell.

Weitzman, L. (1986) *The Divorce Revolution: The Unintended Social and Economic Consequences of Divorce Reform for Women and Children in America.* New York: Free Press/London: Collier Macmillan.

West, R. (1988) 'Jurisprudence and gender', *University of Chicago Law Review*, 55: 1.

West Virginia Bar Association (1903) *Proceedings of the Eighteenth Annual Meeting of the West Virginia Bar Association.* Wheeling, WV: West Virginia Printing Company.

Weyraugh, W. (1964) *The Personality of Lawyers.* New Haven, CT: Yale University Press.

Wheeler, S. (1991a) 'Lawyer involvement in commercial disputes', *Journal of Law and Society*, 18: 241.

Wheeler, S. (1991b) *Reservation of Title Clauses.* Oxford: Clarendon Press.

White, J. (1985) 'Law as rhetoric, rhetoric as law: The arts of cultural and communal life', *University of Chicago Review*, 52: 684.

Wickenden, O.D. (1975) *The Modern Family Solicitor.* London: Stevens.

Wiebe, R. (1967) *The Search for Order, 1872–1920.* New York: Hill and Wang.

Williams, J. (1972) 'The Old Dominion and the new: Ante-Bellum and statehood politics as the background of West Virginia's "Bourdon" Democracy', *West Virginia History*, 32: 317.

Williams, J. (1976) *West Virginia and the Captains of Industry.* Morgantown, WV: West Virginia University Library.

Williams, P.H. (1970) *A Gentleman's Calling: The Liverpool Attorney-at-law.* Liverpool: Incorporated Law Society of Liverpool.

Williams, W. (1982) 'The equality crisis: Some reflections on culture, courts, and feminism', *Women's Rights Law Reporter*, 7: 175.

Wilson, A. (1978) *Finding a Voice.* London: Virago.

Wilson, C. de Kay (1984) 'Marty Lipton's poison pill', *International Financial Law Review*, May, pp. 10–13.

Wilson, W. (1910) 'The lawyer and the community', *The North American Review*, 152: 604–22.

Winter, G. (1985) 'Bartering rationality in negotiation', *Law and Society Review*, 19.

Wolfe, A. (1977) *Limits of Legitimacy: The Political Contradictions of Contemporary Capitalism.* New York: Free Press.

Wood, A. (1976) *Criminal Lawyer.* Connecticut: College and University Press.

Yates, D. and Hawkins, A.J. (1986) *Landlord and Tenant Law*, 2nd end. London: Sweet and Maxwell.

Zander, M. (1980) *The State of Knowledge About the English Legal Profession.* Chichester: Barry Rose.

Zopf, P. (1989) *American Women in Poverty.* New York: Greenwood Press.

Zunz, O. (1987) 'Towards a dialogue with historical sociology', *Social Science History*, 2: 31.

Index